SEAHENGE

SEAHENGE

New Discoveries
in Prehistoric Britain

FRANCIS PRYOR

HarperCollins*Publishers*

HarperCollins*Publishers*
77–85 Fulham Palace Road,
Hammersmith, London W6 8JB

The HarperCollins website address is:
www.**fire**and**water**.com

Published by HarperCollins*Publishers* 2001
3 5 7 9 8 6 4 2

A catalogue record for this book
is available from the British Library

ISBN 0 00 710191 0

Maps and diagrams
by Leslie Robinson and Rex Nicholls

Set in PostScript Linotype Minion with Photina display
Typeset by Rowland Phototypesetting Ltd,
Bury St Edmunds, Suffolk

Printed and bound in Great Britain by
Clays Ltd, St Ives plc

To the memory
of my father-in-law,
DAVID SMITH

CONTENTS

PLATES

The immediate effects of de-watering on waterlogged Neolithic
wood (3800 BC) at Etton.

The base of a Bronze Age notched log ladder (1000 BC) found
at the bottom of a large quarry pit at Fengate.

The notched log ladder from the Fengate quarry pit.

A notched log ladder in the courtyard of a disused Tibetan
Buddhist temple in the Himalayas north of Kathmandu,
Nepal. (Photo: Felix Pryor)

Reconstruction of the first Bronze Age roundhouse (c.1500 BC)
to be found at Fengate.

Skeleton of a young woman found at Fengate and radiocarbon
dated to 3030–2500 BC.

Bronze Age weapons (1300–900 BC) from Flag Fen.

Bronze Age wheel found at Flag Fen, dating to about 1300 BC.

Middle Bronze Age stone roadway (1200–1300 BC) at Yarnton,
Oxfordshire.

Clothes of a young Middle Bronze Age woman (1400–1200 BC)
found in a barrow at Egtved Farm in southern Jutland,
Denmark. (Danish National Museum)

John Lorimer holds the bronze axe that started the Seahenge saga.

A view along the Holme-next-the-Sea peat beds at low tide,
autumn 1998, showing the timber circle.

The team from the Norfolk Archaeological Unit start working
on the ground-plan of the Seahenge timbers.

A close-up of the post circle, showing the eroded and damaged
state of the timbers.

The initial exploratory trench within the circle of timbers,
autumn 1988.

Part of the inverted oak tree exposed by the excavation.

A post being prepared for removal.

The team's soil scientist, Dr Fran Green, records the precise
position of sample tins placed in the section on either side
of a post.

A group of Druids occupy the central tree in an attempt to
prevent its removal.

Sheets of foam being attached to the central tree to cushion the
straps which would be used to lift it.

The lifting of the central oak tree.

The tree trunk was carefully checked when clear of the ground,

in case any votive offering or other unexpected find might
still be adhering to it.

Members of the Norfolk Archaeological Unit preparing to lift
the final two timbers of the Seahenge circle.

The central tree in a shallow water bath at Flag Fen.

The flat underside of the central oak tree was found to be
covered with axe-marks, believed to be the earliest left by a
metal tool yet found in Britain. One of the towing loops,
still with honeysuckle rope in place, is also visible. (Photo:
F. Pryor. Courtesy of English Heritage)

One of the Seahenge timbers being carried to the washing
tanks at Flag Fen.

Wide axe-marks, similar to those on the central oak tree, were
also found on the lower, chopped ends of the oak posts of
the timber circle. (Photo: F. Pryor. Courtesy of English
Heritage)

The freshly de-barked oak-tree stump with one of the two
towing loops and a length of twisted honeysuckle rope
ready for the reconstruction of a full-size replica of
Seahenge by Channel 4's *Time Team*.

The *Time Team* reconstruction reaches a critical stage, with the
oak tree poised above the hole dug to receive it.

The roots of the central oak are levered upwards, and the
two-ton tree drops into position.

The tree is manhandled upright.

Aerial view taken during the final stages of the reconstruction.

The interior during the reconstruction.

Excavators working on the Bronze Age religious site at Flag
Fen.

An archaeologist reveals part of a wooden axle which had been
jammed between two large posts at Flag Fen.

The oak axle from Flag Fen (1200–1300 BC), the oldest known
axle found in Britain.

Objects thrown into the waters around the Flag Fen posts as
offerings to the gods and ancestors.

A later Iron Age village at Cat's Water, Fengate, dating to the
final three centuries BC.

MAPS AND DIAGRAMS

DATES AND PERIODS

Date	Period	Approximate period	Events and innovations
AD 650	Early (or Pagan) Saxon		
AD 410			Roman troops out
	Roman		
AD 43			Roman conquest
	Late Iron Age		Wheel-made pottery
200 BC		Later Iron Age	Celtic art flourishes
	Middle Iron Age		
400 BC		Earlier Iron Age	Population grows
	Early Iron Age		
600 BC			
	Bronze/Iron Age transition		Emergence of 'Celtic' society
700 BC			Introduction of iron
	Late Bronze Age		
1000 BC		Later Bronze Age	First hill forts
	Middle Bronze Age		
1500 BC		Earlier Bronze Age	
	Early Bronze Age		Beaker pottery flourishes
2500 BC			Earliest British fields
	Neolithic/Bronze Age transition		Copper and bronze tools in use
2700 BC			
	Late Neolithic		Henges and round barrows
3000 BC		Later Neolithic	
	Middle Neolithic		Causewayed enclosures
3500 BC		Earlier Neolithic	Long barrows (Britain)
	Early Neolithic		Passage graves (Brittany)
5000 BC			Introduction of farming
	Mesolithic		Hunting and gathering food
			Gradual return of people to Britain
9000 BC			Ice Age ends; woodlands re-established

ACKNOWLEDGEMENTS

First I must thank my agent Bill Hamilton, who helped me shape the initial idea; also Richard Johnson and Robert Lacey at HarperCollins, who encouraged me throughout the writing and subsequent editing. I would particularly like to thank John Lorimer for being so open with me about his discoveries. I also owe a debt of gratitude to Mark Brennand and Bill Boismier of the Norfolk Archaeological Unit, and to Chris Evans of the Cambridge University Archaeological Unit for information on Whittlesey. As always, Malcolm Gibb and Toby Fox at Flag Fen made everything run smoothly.

The Quest

I DECIDED to write a book on prehistoric religion about two years before the discovery in spring 1998 of the site which has since become widely known as 'Seahenge'. My original aim was to demystify the subject, to blow away the fog of romance which so often appears when it is raised. I wanted to show how ancient shrines such as Avebury and Stonehenge were made and used by people who were like ourselves. Although they constructed places of worship that seem remote, alien and strange to us, they themselves were none of those things.

I was fascinated by the outward form – the appearance – of their religion. Why, for example, did circles play such an important role? Why were offerings placed in the ground? And why were many sites placed within the fields and lanes of the working countryside, while others were hidden away in inaccessible and remote places? We can only attempt to answer these questions if we try to understand the social context of these ancient beliefs; and to do that, we must examine the evidence provided by archaeology.

I also wanted to write about the way in which modern archaeologists can study discarded prehistoric rubbish, long-lost objects and the fragmentary remains of ancient places to recreate the way people thought and behaved. Like fictional detectives, we make deductions from the slightest of clues; but today, increasingly, we go further than that: we try to understand the motives that drove people in the past to construct great monuments like Stonehenge, or small shrines like Seahenge. Almost daily, new scientific techniques are removing the ties that once restricted our imaginations. But these new freedoms carry with them new responsibilities. It's becoming easier to sound authoritative, simply by quoting evidence uncovered by science. To reveal a precise date through some new wonder-technique is one thing, but it is quite another to understand *why* something happened in the past. In this book I want to make a start at answering some of those *why* questions.

The practice of religion has always happened in the here and now, and I wanted my book to be set in a real prehistoric world, in which children were born and educated, families farmed the land, and law and order prevailed – a world which has been rapidly revealed by excavation in the 1970s and subsequent decades. I decided to use the discoveries made on my own particular excavations to colour the picture I wanted to paint.

My research into British prehistory has been a long quest. It began in 1971 when I directed an eight-year excavation at Fengate, near Peterborough. Fengate is one of the best-known sites in British prehistory. It was continuously occupied for four thousand years, from Neolithic to Roman times, and possesses an extraordinarily diverse succession of settlements, field systems, barrows and burials. After Fengate I turned my attention to two major religious centres: the Bronze Age henges and other shrines at Maxey in Cambridgeshire and the partially waterlogged Neolithic ritual enclosure at nearby Etton. Etton was one of the earliest sites of its type yet found in Britain, and is certainly the best preserved. Then, in 1982, I discovered the waterlogged timbers of what is probably the largest Bronze Age religious site in Europe, at Flag Fen, on the outskirts of Peterborough. I have been working there ever since.

These are major excavations and they have produced a wealth of material, not to mention eight volumes of scholarly research. It is, however, hard to extract the essential narrative thread from this sea of published detail. Moreover, the story emerged only slowly as the research progressed – and this was necessarily at a measured, academic pace. My intention in this book is to tell that tale in a way which reflects, I hope, some of the excitement of the quest itself.

I had scarcely begun putting pen to paper when I learned about the timber circle which had been discovered on the beach at Holme-next-the-Sea on the Norfolk coast, just over half an hour's drive from where I live. It was an extraordinary coincidence, and one I couldn't possibly ignore. The discovery created enormous public interest, excitement and indeed controversy. It was certainly remarkable, but to those of us who have been working in the area, it was not unexpected. Large parts of the coastline of eastern England are constantly being eroded by the waves, and significant prehistoric finds are regularly exposed there.

Although Seahenge's near-perfect state of preservation made it unique, as a small wooden shrine it was not out of the ordinary. Indeed, I myself have seen and dug several like it. This was one of the things that made it supremely important, as it meant that it could be placed within a known sequence of development. We knew approximately where it fitted both chronologically and in the lives of Early Bronze Age communities. We also knew what it may have signified to them. Or rather, we thought we did. But when we started to excavate and study the timbers, we were wholly unprepared for what we actually encountered.

FRANCIS PRYOR
Flag Fen
Peterborough
Cambridgeshire

July 2000

John Lorimer's Discovery

IT WAS EARLY SPRING, 1998, on the south side of the Wash in north-west Norfolk. John Lorimer and his brother-in-law Gary took the path through the pine woods, climbed up the dunes and stood at the top to catch their breath. The tide was now well on its way out, and the peat beds, which ran along the beach midway between high and low tide, were just beginning to be exposed. Between them John and Gary held a brand-new shrimping net, and today was to be its first outing. It was home-made, but sturdy and built to last. They knew it would be futile to test the net until the tide had retreated beyond the peat beds, as only then would the seabed be smooth enough to allow them to drag it through the water, so they decided instead to go crabbing and to test the net in an hour or so. At least that way they'd have something to take home for tea.

Just beyond the beach, behind a coastal barrier of dunes, was Holme-next-the-Sea Nature Reserve. It was a land of birds and dunes, of thin wiry grasses, orchids and Scots pines. And then of course there was the wind. It was always with you at Holme. Sometimes you thought it had dropped entirely, and that the air was truly still. Then you looked at the ground and saw that the blades of grass had never stopped nodding. It was as if someone had just left the room and had shut the door firmly behind them. There were little swirling drafts – not wind, not even a light breeze. Other times, when the weather came from off the Wash, the gales tore at the dunes with a destructive force that even a modern army couldn't match. Coastal defences were ripped up. I have seen the aftermath of a fierce storm, when wire, fencing, young trees and posts had been hurled inland. In just two hours, a whole summer's patient dunes-conservation programme could be reduced to a useless, tangled mess.

The Nature Reserve Warden, Gary Hibberd, and his wife Alison lived in The Firs, a large, late-Victorian house that had been built as part of a speculative venture which never got off the ground sometime around the turn of the century. One of the ground-floor rooms had been converted into a small shop and Visitor Centre, and Gary would chalk up a list of rare birds that could currently be seen in the reserve.

The pine trees that were presumably planted when The Firs was built covered the dunes between the house and the beach. They were mainly Corsican pines, a more vigorous species than our native Scots pine and better able to cope with the fierce conditions of this coast. They grew particularly well along the Holme dunes.

John and Gary knew that the best crabs were to be found lurking in dark nooks and crannies below the shelves of peat. John was walking in the shallow water along the edge of the peat. Before he'd even bent down to feel for a crab, his eye was suddenly taken by something green and metallic in the mud. Without thinking, he picked it up and turned it over in his hands. It wasn't iron, he knew that. Was it brass? Probably. In which case it could have been a fitting – perhaps part of a porthole, or something from off the bridge – from the old wreck behind him, which he could see was just beginning to emerge from the waves. Still, he thought, it doesn't exactly look *brassy*. He had seen pieces off wrecks before, and somehow this wasn't right: it was more coppery, and with a strange, red-gold surface sheen.

Gary saw John standing slightly bent forward, with furrowed brows, turning the thing over and over in his hands, and wandered across to see what he'd found. John was always collecting things from off the beach. He was a regular jackdaw. His house a few miles away at North Creek was stuffed full of treasures: shells, blanched bones, driftwood, weird-shaped stones, pieces from wrecks. If he found anything attractive, John would want to take it home.

Gary looked at the piece of metal, shook his head and agreed it was probably something from the wreck. But they had work to do, so they thought no more about it. True to his jackdaw instincts, John slipped it into his back pocket. By now the tide had retreated well beyond the peat, and the timbers of the wreck were fully visible,

surrounded by huge expanses of smooth, damp sand. Together John
and Gary carried the net out into the shallow water, just above knee-
depth. Then they tested it. It worked. In fact it worked well, and is
in regular use to this day.

John and his wife Jacqui are special-needs workers, who look after
children with particular problems. John has found that taking his
charges out in the mini-bus for a trip to the beach can do wonders
for them. But they must have something useful to do when they get
there, or they soon get bored, and mischief is never far behind. Towing
a shrimping net and then sorting through the catch is ideal. And once
the work's over, the small brown shrimps are delicious for tea.

During the next four weeks, John visited Holme beach regularly,
seeking crabs and shrimp. He would often return to the spot where
he had found the metal object, which he was becoming increasingly
convinced had nothing to do with the wreck. The more he looked at
it, the more certain he was that it was an axe. With its crescent-shaped
blade, he reasoned, it couldn't be anything else.

It was a week or two after finding the object that he first noticed
a large tree-trunk, with two strange-looking branches, like the stumps
of amputated arms. It was close to the spot where he'd made his
discovery, and was the same colour as the peat beds around it. But it
looked odd. As he told me later, he couldn't put his finger on why it
looked so strange, but it did. Just like the metal object, there was a
simple explanation, but it didn't seem to apply. Holme beach was the
site of a prehistoric 'forest bed' of tree stumps. And that's what every-
body said: his odd-looking stump was just part of the old forest. But
John wasn't happy with that explanation.

The peat didn't actually touch or cover the strange stump, but
stopped three or four paces short of it. John noticed that as the tide
swirled around it, the water wore the sand and mud from around the
trunk. Soon a natural trench began to form, and he was able to feel
well down into the grey mud that lay directly below the beach sand
into which the tree was embedded. He knew that not even the deepest
roots of the forest trees went down this far.

The weeks passed, and John couldn't stop thinking about that
peculiar metal object that now sat on the mantelpiece at home. The
more he looked at it, the more he became convinced that it had

nothing to do with the wreck, which was less than a century old – the remains of a freighter that used to ply a regular route from Norway to King's Lynn, carrying ice. Besides, he knew what a ship's fire-fighting axes looked like, and this bore no resemblance to them.

One evening he took it down from the shelf and examined it, long and closely. Various things struck him as odd: the clear casting line where two moulds had once joined together; signs of hammering at one end, and at the other the smoothly crescentic cutting edge. It was certainly an axe, but it wasn't like any axe he had ever used. For a start, there was no hole for a shaft. And besides, it was made from bronze or brass, not from steel. Then he had a bright idea. A friend of his in Fakenham was a keen metal-detectorist, and took all the magazines. Maybe he'd know what it was.

The next day found John in Fakenham with a cup of tea and surrounded by dozens of magazines. He leafed through them. There were stories about horse brasses, about Roman coins, about merchants' tokens, about buckles, about everything under the sun – except axes. Then he struck lucky: in an article about Bronze Age metalwork he found a picture of a three-thousand-year-old bronze axe that looked *fairly* similar to his. It was by no means identical, but it was certainly close enough to set his mind racing.

In the days that followed he couldn't let the matter rest. Again and again he thought, if it *was* a Bronze Age axe, then how on earth did it get there? Was it from an ancient wreck, or what? The more he pondered, the more curious he became. Eventually he phoned the Castle Museum at Norwich and described the object. The voice at the other end sounded interested. Could he bring it round to them?

The axe was at the Castle Museum for about four weeks. They were in no doubt that it was Bronze Age, and had been made around 1200 BC. They couldn't find a local axe in their collections that was anything like it. Their best guess was that it may have been made in Ireland.

While he waited to hear from the museum, John returned to Holme beach several times. He noticed that the tide was slowly wearing away the surface around the strange stump. Then one day, a few feet away, he spotted the top of another stump. The next day he found another one. And then another. By the end of the week he could clearly discern a circle of stumps around the much larger central tree. The stumps had been hidden below the sand and mud, and as the tides swirled around the central tree they were gradually being exposed to the air.

John studied the smaller stumps closely. The circle was positioned on the seaward side of the peat beds; close to them, but not beneath them. Were they *all* tree stumps from a drowned forest? He knew that was the explanation for most of the wood found on the beach. But a circle? How could that be natural? Surely that *had* to be man-made?

By now John knew he had found something important. But how could he get somebody 'out there' interested? He lost no opportunity to talk about his discovery, but nobody seemed to take him seriously. John and his axe and his stumps. He began to feel that people were starting to laugh about him behind his back. Eventually someone came out from the museum to have a look at John's circle. The expert pronounced that it was probably a fish trap or a salt pan, then walked over to the old wreck and spent the rest of the afternoon photographing *that*. John told me later he could have exploded with frustration.

In August, two weeks after the visit from the museum official, John received a letter from him in which he was told that, far from being unimportant, his find was causing great interest in the museum world. Next, he was contacted by Mark Brennand and Dr Bill Boismier, two members of the Norfolk Archaeological Unit, the team of archaeologists whose job was to investigate new discoveries in the county. They came to Holme beach to have a look, and John showed them the circle of stumps and the strange-looking tree at their centre. Mark and Bill took one look and stood back in silence, thunderstruck. Words seemed superfluous.

John was desperate to know more, but Bill wasn't willing to commit himself. A man of few words at the best of times, he was not going to raise any false hopes at this stage. His field of expertise was the effects of tillage processes on artefact distributions in the ploughzone. Tillage processes had nothing to do with prehistoric religion, but in their hearts Bill and Mark knew what that circle of 'stumps' was. And it certainly wasn't something as mundane as a fish trap or salt pan. As they drove back to the Unit, they could talk of nothing else. Was it *really* what they both thought? *Could* it be? They *must* get some further opinions. That evening, the phone lines from the Norfolk Archaeological Unit hummed.

CHAPTER ONE

Setting the Scene

ARCHAEOLOGY IS ABOUT human life in the past, but in my experience it isn't as simple as that. Very often it's about the life one is living in the present, too. I've no idea how it happens – and I know from talking to friends and colleagues that others have experienced this as well – but in some strange way archaeological discoveries happen that are appropriate to the way one is thinking at a given time. When, for example, I started my professional life in 1971, I excavated a well-known site at Fengate, on the eastern side of Peterborough. Here I began to discover details of the way prehistoric people organised their daily lives. This suited me fine, as I was then concerned with practical things too, such as how to organise a large excavation, how to assemble coherent published reports, and so on.

About ten years later, I became more interested in the way people thought, and how they ordered their religious and social lives. And what happened? I found myself working in a prehistoric landscape strewn with religious sites, near a small village in Cambridgeshire called Maxey. This more than whetted my appetite for ideology and the afterlife. I was treated to both in ample measure when I then excavated a large Neolithic ceremonial centre at another small village called Etton, near Maxey. But still I wanted more. And it was then, in 1982, that I had the good fortune to discover the extraordinary Bronze Age religious site at Flag Fen, near Peterborough.

Flag Fen is a wonderfully rich and complex site, and understanding it – or rather, trying to understand it – has stretched my imagination to the limits, and has been an invigorating and rigorous (although sometimes very frustrating) challenge. It was while I was deeply immersed in Flag Fen in 1998 that John Lorimer reported his remarkable discovery on Holme beach. And then things began to fall into place, and I realised I had to step back from Flag Fen. I was forced to appreciate that prehistory is best understood as an unfolding, continuing story. It is not about individual sites, however fascinating they might be, but is a saga of human beings, and the different ways they chose to cope with their own particular challenges.

The process of archaeological discovery has been deeply enmeshed with my professional life, and I don't see how the two can be disentangled. So I won't attempt the impossible, but will tell the tale as it unfolded around me, blow by blow. My own life and my research life will be part of the same story. But first I must turn the clock back to the final years of my childhood, when the wonders of archaeology were first revealed to me. It was an afternoon that will live with me forever. The time was autumn, the year 1959, and the place Eton College.

There was a warm, dusty smell to the wood-panelled room. A smell I have grown to love: of old books and maps, field notes, brown paper bags, Indian ink, pottery and flint tools. It's a musty, peaceful sort of smell. A smell that says the world is in proportion. Perhaps it is the atmosphere of antiquity – I don't know. But whatever it was, it pervaded the Eton College Myers Museum of Egyptology through and through.

George Tait was a senior master, and in the late fifties he was also Curator of the Myers Museum, which was housed in a purpose-built wing at the rear of School Hall. One day I found him working on several heaps of papers, which lay across the big central table and cascaded down to the floor by way of three chairs, an old orange crate and something that had once resembled a foot-stool. He could see I was at a loose end. My head was bandaged from a football injury I had received the day before, and the prospect of a tedious afternoon stretched before me.

'Wait,' he said. 'I'll find you something to sit on.' He cleared away the papers from one of the chairs, then said, 'I've got something over here that may interest you.' After a moment or two, he reappeared holding two huge volumes, which he placed on top of the papers already on the table in front of me. I was amazed. The two enormous tomes were for *me*?

George Tait returned to his side of the table and lit his formidable pipe. It was a vast smoking machine with a long, straight stalk and a furnace-like bowl, doubtless hewn from timbers drawn from a mummy's tomb. Into this he stuffed leaves picked from plants grown in his own garden. The dense clouds of smoke smelled just like an autumn bonfire, and bore no resemblance whatsoever to the distinctive aroma of tobacco. Soon my eyes were running freely. But George puffed on regardless, poring over his papers. He was miles away.

I started to read. I had been given Howard Carter's account of the discovery and excavation of Tutankhamun's tomb in 1922. It was an inspired choice, and I soon found myself completely gripped by the story of the discovery of the boy king's mummified body and the fabulous treasures which surrounded him. As I read, I was there, amidst the sands of the Nile and the eerie, cool, dry darkness of the tomb.

After that day I made many visits to the Myers Museum and its larger-than-life curator. But although George Tait had a huge, commanding and at times stern presence, he was a gentle teacher, and was particularly good at helping his pupils grasp difficult concepts. Thanks to him, I grasped the basic principles of the subject that would soon form the centre of my life.

Tait's archaeology was about people and the way they had lived. It was *not* about treasures and valuable finds, unless they could shed light on the way ancient communities behaved. Above all else, he explained that archaeology is a methodical discipline: that although Howard Carter made all those extraordinary discoveries in the tomb, he also spent days and days preparing a minute catalogue of his discoveries. He pointed out that Carter was at pains to draw meticulous plans of where everything was found. It took me some time to realise why such care was so crucially important. With hindsight, Tait's improvised explanation worked well.

'Just suppose,' he said, 'that you're an archaeologist working two thousand years from now. You discover a room, and in it are two armchairs and a mysterious polished wooden box with a thick glass sheet on one side of it. You have absolutely no idea what this box was used for. Maybe it was worshipped? Maybe it was used to cook with? Who knows? So you decide to seek the help of other archaeologists. Now what do you do?'

'I send them a list of what I've found,' I suggested, 'and I describe the chairs and the shiny wooden box as closely as I can.' It was feeble, but I couldn't think of a more sensible answer.

'I doubt if they'd be any the wiser. Would you be?'

I had to admit I wouldn't.

'But if you included a sketched plan of the way the armchairs were arranged, how they faced the glassy side of the polished wooden box, then they might work out that the box was a television set.'

He had taught me an important archaeological lesson. Things only make sense in terms of the way they relate to other things. Later I was to learn that archaeologists refer to these inter-relationships as *context*. To an archaeologist nothing matters so much as context. Context is all. Without context, a find is just a find, a dead object; but with context it comes alive.

My 'gap' year out of school in 1963, on what was then known as the Digging Circuit, taught me a great deal about life. Some of the Circuit diggers were perfectly happy to stay as they were. They moved from one dig to another, living in winter squats, tents in summer, or ramshackle caravans. One or two had drink or drug problems, and I soon realised that a high proportion of them were using the Circuit as a retreat from the rat-race. Some of these people were quite sad, but they nearly all shared a belief in what they were doing. I suppose, in the final analysis, that vocation had taken the place of self-esteem, which for many of them had reached a low ebb.

Today, things have changed for the better. For a start, most diggers have a professional qualification, or are in the process of earning one. All are vastly better paid than they were in the early sixties. Site conditions have improved enormously, too: there are self-contained mobile toilets, safety clothing and warm site accommodation. Better pay also means that tents are only used in summer, and then by choice, not of necessity. But despite all these improvements, the life of a professional field archaeologist is still hard. Job security is poor, and most people spend large parts of their lives moving from dig to dig all over the country, and abroad. And then there's the British climate.

As a result of my afternoons with George Tait at the Myers

Museum, I had decided to study archaeology at Cambridge. If you can't think about broad issues at university, then you'll never think about them. In our lectures, my fellow students and I learned what George Tait had drummed into me: that archaeology is the study of the past, based on material evidence – pottery, flints and scientific information – rather than on written documents alone (the province of history). We also learned that archaeology is an effective way of studying broad changes through time – topics like, for example, the decline and fall of the Roman Empire, or the origins of farming. It's less good at examining historical events, such as the Norman Conquest – a topic like that is best handled by historians, or by historians and archaeologists working closely together.

In my first year at Cambridge, the Professor of Archaeology was a great man: Grahame, later Sir Grahame, Clark. Grahame was a pioneer of what is today called environmental archaeology. As we shall see, it will play a major role in our quest. With his friend the botanist Sir Harry Godwin, Grahame was able to paint an extraordinarily vivid picture of life just after the last great Ice Age, about seven thousand years ago. He relied to a great extent on Sir Harry's work on the pollen grains and seeds preserved within the peats found at various sites in southern Britain. This botanical research, together with work on preserved bones, insects and shells, provided the evidence they needed to reconstruct what the ancient countryside would have looked like. It showed that nine thousand years ago the East Anglian country-side consisted of stands of birch trees and pools of open water, and that the fauna included fish, herons and other birds, eels and beavers. On the drier land were large oak forests in which deer, wild boar and bear roamed freely.

I would never pretend to be a scientist, or even a scientific archae-ologist, but I can understand what scientists are saying, and I know enough to ask them questions in their own language. It was not difficult for me to decide, in my first year at university, that this broadly environmental approach would be my own style of work. All my subsequent research has been carried out in a closely-knit team; it's the only way to do good environmental archaeology. Nowadays my role would be described as 'Team Leader'. My job is to make sense of the team's results when we come to write the final report; it is up to me to achieve compromise when there are strong differences between individuals, and to see that the team runs smoothly and happily. It's a great job, and I love doing it. In my opinion it's far and away the most successful and satisfying sort of archaeology.

Grahame Clark retired from teaching while I was a student, and he was succeeded by Professor Glyn Daniel. They were as unlike as any two archaeologists could possibly be. It used to be fashionable in certain circles to patronise Glyn Daniel. He was an archaeologist, but he was also a supremely successful populariser of the subject. No other archaeologist has ever been voted 'TV Personality of the Year', an accolade he earned by chairing the hugely successful BBC quiz show *Animal, Vegetable, Mineral?* At his best, Glyn was a superb lecturer, and he managed to inspire me with a love of his own favourite period, the Neolithic (or New Stone Age), which I have never lost.

Everything that ever mattered seems to have originated in the Neolithic Age. All of life and death is there. I know Neolithic folk have been dead for nearly five thousand years, but as far as I'm concerned they could have died yesterday. My passion for the Neolithic and the Early Bronze Age (which in social and cultural terms is much the same thing) is directly due to Glyn's inspiration.

Glyn taught a course on the Neolithic, Bronze and Iron Ages at Cambridge. The dates of the various periods tend to wander somewhat, as research progresses, but the Neolithic comes first, and in Britain lasted from about 5000 to 2700 BC. It was followed by the Bronze Age (roughly 2700 to 700 BC). The Iron Age was the final prehistoric period, which extended from the close of the Bronze Age to the Roman Conquest of Britain in AD 43. Glyn's course was known to the university authorities as NBI. Perhaps predictably to the students, it was of 'No Bloody Interest'. I chose not to study the other option of Iron Age, Roman and Anglo-Saxon, or IRA – which for some reason never seemed to acquire a student name.

I remember being puzzled by archaeologists' periods. Were Neolithic people aware when they woke up on the first morning of 2700 BC that they were entering the Bronze Age? Of course not. The Ages were invented by some inspired Danish archaeologists, working on museum collections in the last century. They came up with the Three-Age System (Stone followed by Bronze and then Iron) in the first instance simply as a way of ordering their collections. Only later did it gradually acquire a wider significance.

At university we were taught that the Three-Age System would soon be a thing of the past, to be replaced by the flood of radiocarbon dates that were then just beginning to arrive. They have indeed had a profound effect on our understanding of the past, but I can see no consistent evidence that the old Three-Age labels are actually being replaced. I think they'll be with us for a long time yet.

At Cambridge, British archaeology was taught in a rather rigid framework, or straitjacket, of 'cultures'. In theory, 'cultures' were meant to be synonymous with actual communities of people – tribes or confederations of tribes. But in reality 'cultures' were no more and no less than types of pottery. So we were taught about the Beaker Culture or the Grooved Ware Culture, and I have to say I found it extremely difficult to imagine the actual people lurking behind these arcane concepts.

The various 'cultures' were accompanied by long lists of sites, where the particular types of pottery which were believed to be characteristic of them were found. The lists were, in turn, accompanied by maps, covered with dots and arrows which purported to show how these people/pots moved around Europe. It was all extremely mystifying, and I remember wondering why on earth these people *wanted* to move around all the time. It seemed, and indeed it still seems, an odd way to behave.

There was a third lecturer at Cambridge who was to have a very profound influence on my subsequent career, partly because, like me, he is a practical, down-to-earth person. He comes from Canada, where I spent much time during my formative years as a field archaeologist. John Coles is remarkable because he has turned his hand to numerous types and styles of archaeology. His doctoral research was on Scottish Bronze Age metalwork, but he is also, or has been, an authority on experimental archaeology, Scandinavian Bronze Age rock carvings, the Palaeolithic (or Old Stone Age) and wetland archaeology, for which he is perhaps best known.

In the mid and later sixties John was doing far more than his fair share of lectures in the Archaeology Department, and he supervised me in a variety of topics. I don't think I was a very good pupil towards the end of my time at university, because I couldn't see that there was a future for me in the subject. Archaeological jobs were extremely scarce, and were invariably snapped up by people with good first-class degrees. I knew I stood little chance against that sort of competition. But John persisted, and somehow he managed to cram sufficient knowledge into my skull to earn me a decent enough honours degree.

I don't want to be unfair to other lecturers in the department, but John seemed unusual in that his head was not stuck in the clouds for most of the time. He was then working in the peatland of the Somerset Levels, and his lecture slides were not just of disembodied artefacts and distribution maps. Instead, he showed us photographs of people with muddy hands, digging trackways in wet peat, or felling trees with flint axes, or wrestling with hazel wattles while reconstructing prehistoric hurdles. Frankly, his lectures were almost the only thing that kept my flickering flame of interest in the subject alive.

Archaeology in the mid-sixties was superficially calm. Old ideas, such as the pottery-based 'cultures', still just managed to hold on, but a tide of new thinking and new scientific techniques was about to rip through the old order. The subject would never be the same again. As has been mentioned, one of the most profound instruments of change was radiocarbon dating. Although I'm now older and wiser, I still find it almost magical that one can take a piece of bone or charcoal, pop it into a machine for a few days and then be told how old it is – to within, say, fifty years. And if you're lucky enough to have a decent-sized sample (a teacupful of charcoal, say) it will only cost about £200.

Before Willard F. Libby, a chemist at Chicago University, invented radiocarbon dating in 1949, archaeologists researching in remote places (such as Britain) had to work almost blind. If they wanted to date something – let us say a Neolithic stone-built tomb – they had to find similar tombs elsewhere across Europe, until eventually they reached the well-dated world of the eastern Mediterranean. In areas such as the Aegean it was believed that the dates were more secure, because actual written records – such as the famous Linear B script of Crete and Greece – extended back as far as 1400 BC. These dates may well have been more secure, but the problem didn't lie there. It lay in the chain of false – or perhaps more truly *forced* – reasoning that linked the eastern Mediterranean to more peripheral areas. Radiocarbon was to expose this ruthlessly.

The idea behind radiocarbon dating is quite straightforward. Libby was researching into cosmic radiation – the process whereby the earth's outer atmosphere is constantly bombarded by sub-atomic particles. This produces radioactive carbon, known as carbon-14. Carbon-14 is unstable and is constantly breaking down, but at a known and uniform rate: a gramme of carbon-14 will be half broken-down after 5,730 years, three-quarters broken down in twice that time (11,460 years), and so on. Libby's breakthrough was to link this process to living things, and thence to time itself.

Carbon-14 is present in the earth's atmosphere – in the air we all breathe – in the form of the gas carbon dioxide. Plants take in carbon dioxide through their leaves, plant-eating animals eat the leaves, and carnivores, in turn, eat the plant-eating animals. So all plants and animals – even vegetarians – absorb carbon-14 while they are alive. As soon as they die they stop taking it in; and, far more importantly for archaeology, the carbon-14 in their bodies – in their bones, their wood or whatever – starts to break down. So by measuring the amounts of carbon-14 in a bone, or piece of charcoal, fragment of cloth or peat, it is possible to estimate its age very accurately.

But there are problems. First of all, cosmic radiation has not been at a uniform rate, as Libby at first believed. Sunspots and solar flares are known to cause sudden upsurges of radiation. Nuclear testing has also filled the atmosphere with unwanted and unquantifiable radiation. As if these problems weren't enough, the quantities of radiation being measured in radiocarbon laboratories around the world are truly minute, especially in older samples. All this uncertainty means that radiocarbon dates are usually expressed in the form of a *range* of years, say 1700 to 2000 BC, rather than a single central spot-date like 1850 BC.

There was a period of about ten years after the publication of Libby's initial idea before any reliable datings became available. Then the pace began to hot up. By the time I was sitting my final exams, in May 1967, the early trickle had already become a flood. Today, radiocarbon dating is a completely routine process, carried out in various parts of the world hundreds of times every day.

Those early radiocarbon dates got me thinking about the prehistoric past in a new way. Perhaps it was the scientific certainty they implied, the fact that radiocarbon doesn't lie. They seemed to connect us directly to the past, and in a way removed a part of the curtain of mystery which hung between us and them – those shadowy figures of the Neolithic twilight.

The new tide of radiocarbon dates produced some extraordinary results. At first, some of the dates were much earlier than archaeologists had expected. But, being human, they were loath to throw out their old ways of doing things just because some scientists told them their dates were wrong. So they pressed on regardless. Then, as the evidence accumulated around them, some conceded that they had underestimated the true age of the Neolithic and Bronze Ages, and that both periods seemed to have lasted roughly twice as long as was previously believed. All of this they could take: their scheme was basically right, just a bit too young and a bit compressed. They were shortly to be proved wrong.

By the time I was doing the revision and research for my final degree exams, it was becoming increasingly apparent that the radiocarbon revolution was not about dates alone. Prehistory was being reassembled in a new order that would have profound effects not just on *what* we researched – i.e. the subject-matter of our enquiries – but on our thought-processes themselves. In Britain, America and elsewhere in the mid-1960s, archaeologists were questioning the very way they thought about archaeology. How could the processes of archaeological reasoning be improved? Most important of all, how could they be made more explicit, more open to scrutiny and review? Some felt that the new wind blowing through the subject was cold and cheerless. Myself, I found it invigorating. It was good to see the cobwebs being blown away.

As a British archaeologist, working on British material, I had always felt something of a poor cousin compared with those who studied the Classical world, Egypt and the Near East. But all of that was about to change. As I realised what was happening around me, I began to feel – and it was a *feeling*, not a consciously worked-out idea – that British prehistory really did matter. It had its own identity and integrity. It was not a devolved by-product of someone else's creativity, a feeble copy of something magnificent in the Aegean. No, it was well worth studying for its own sake. That was enough for me: somewhere deep inside I could detect the distant sound of a huntsman's horn. Without knowing it, I was about to start the quest of a lifetime.

CHAPTER TWO

The Hunt is On

THE GREAT MEGALITHIC STRUCTURES of Neolithic and Bronze Age Europe demand explanation. They simply cannot be ignored. For a start, the word itself (derived from the Greek *large stones*) has a semi-mystical resonance. And the sites themselves are wholly captivating. It's impossible to pass the 'hanging stones' of Stonehenge, or to enter the spectacular circle of Avebury, or to walk along the mysterious stone alignments of Carnac, without wondering who built them – and why? And when? One cannot call oneself an archaeologist without having at least some knowledge of these extraordinary sites: they cry out for, and demand, explanation. And that's what Glyn Daniel's lectures at Cambridge provided.

I've mentioned three of the best-known megalithic monuments, but there are thousands of others, in the Mediterranean basin, in western Spain and Portugal, right across France, all over Ireland, in north and western Scotland, in Wales and parts of England and in Holland, northern Germany and southern Scandinavia. Far and away the majority of these sites are tombs of one sort or another. Often the tombs are communal and hold (or held, as most have been robbed) the remains, or partial remains, of dozens, even hundreds of individuals.

Glyn's explanation of megalithic tombs arose naturally from the prevailing archaeological theories of his time. It was his bad luck that the mass of new radiocarbon dates showed those theories to be mostly worthless. It was my bad luck, too: the course I had opted for was now something of a non-event. Hence the great man's uncharacteristically lacklustre lectures. It was clear to all of us – lecturer and students – that the whole point of the course had been destroyed.

Glyn's explanation of the monuments was based on the notion that the megalithic builders were initially a distinct community of people, a culture that had its origins in the eastern Mediterranean. This culture – these people – and their ideas spread westwards by two routes, through the Mediterranean via Spain to Ireland and the north, or across France to Scandinavia. England was influenced by both streams. The spread (or 'diffusion', to use the jargon word of the time) of megalithic culture was by no means unique. The concept of farming was also thought to have spread across Europe from the eastern Mediterranean, and there were successive waves of diffusion from central and eastern Europe involving Beaker pottery and metal-working in the Early Bronze Age, and Celts in the Early Iron Age. If all this to-ing and fro-ing really did take place, then prehistoric Europe must have been in a permanent state of turmoil – for which there is no archaeological evidence whatsoever. Today, with the possible exception of farming, most of these 'diffusions' are seen as at best the spread of a set of ideas, rather than the wholesale movement of people or populations.

With hindsight, Glyn's explanation could not have been otherwise. Like all European prehistorians he relied on the well-documented areas of the Aegean and eastern Mediterranean to provide him with the dates he needed for his far-flung monuments. This method of dating held within it the seeds of its own fallibility. By looking east for a date, it was also natural to look east for an *origin*. And that was the fatal flaw which led to the theory's eventual collapse: when the first radiocarbon dates arrived for megalithic tombs in Ireland and Brittany, they were found to be thousands of years earlier than their supposed progenitors in the eastern Mediterranean. It must have been a bitter pill indeed that Glyn, and many other archaeologists, had to swallow.

I finished at Cambridge in 1967, and spent two years out of archaeology. At the time I had no intention of returning to it, but events conspired to draw me back. My time out of archaeology had been very frustrating, and in an attempt to break free from the life I was then leading, I followed the advice of an old friend of the family and made my way to Toronto, where I registered as a landed immigrant in 1969.

After a few weeks of unemployment spent among the huge population of US draft dodgers in Canada I eventually got my first 'real' archaeological job, as a technician in the Royal Ontario Museum. The ROM was the largest museum in Canada and has magnificent collections, particularly of Chinese antiquities. The Chief Archaeologist, Dr Doug Tushingham, was an anglophile and was proud of the museum's collections of prehistoric European material, which included a fine assemblage of Bronze Age metalwork that had been dredged from the Thames in the early years of the century.

I worked directly for Doug Tushingham, as his technician, for about a year. At the time he was writing up a site he had excavated in Jordan, at a place called Dhiban. My job was to prepare maps and plans for publication, draw and repair pottery and glass, and work through the various sections he had drawn in the field. Sections are a vitally important part of archaeology, and can be difficult to understand. But the principles behind them are straightforward enough.

Because the Near East is so dry, people have tended to live in the same places, usually those with good access to water. Over the millennia the houses, which were usually built from unfired mud bricks, collapsed and new ones were built; rubbish accumulated; new roads were constructed; and slowly the ground surface began to rise, in some cases forming huge man-made hills, known as tells. Early in the history of modern archaeology it was realised that if one cut a deep trench into these hills it would expose all the layers that had accumulated over the years. The wall or side of the trench would tell the story. These vertical faces were known as sections.

The situation in northern Europe was completely different. Here, if tells occur, as they do in parts of Holland, they were deliberately built up to keep people clear of rising water. The damp climate and the widespread availability of water meant that people could settle down and live almost anywhere, so it's unusual to find deep sections on excavations out in the countryside. In towns and cities, like London or York, where people have been living on the same spot for two thousand years or more, the sections can be fairly substantial – but even so, they're shallow by Near Eastern standards.

Sections are important, even on shallow rural sites, because they show how the deposits within a particular feature accumulated. Let's suppose that someone once dug a hole to receive a post. These post-holes are the commonest of archaeological features, and are the bare bones of vanished buildings, or timber circles – or whatever. The hole is dug and a post is dropped in. Earth and stones are then back-filled and rammed home around the post to keep it firm. The post forms part of a house, which is then used for a generation. Thirty years later, the occupants die or move away, and eventually the roof falls in. The post then rots, usually at ground level first, and finally collapses. Within a few years it has entirely rotted away, above and below ground. As it rots below ground level, topsoil slowly accumulates where the wood had once been. This topsoil is darker and finer than the stones and soil that had been rammed into the hole all those years ago. Quite often the dark soil accurately preserves the shape of the original post; this is known as a post-pipe. If excavated carefully, the outline of the post-pipe can be recorded in plan view, from above, or as section cut down through the centre of the original post.

The variety of buried archaeological features reflects the variety of ancient life: as well as post-holes, there are ditches that may once have run around fields, or alongside roads; there are shallow gullies which took rain from house roofs; there are wells, hearths, kilns and rubbish pits. Above-ground features may occasionally survive, such as road surfaces, stone walls, huge standing stones like those at Stonehenge, or the humble earthen banks that once ran alongside field hedges.

The sections at Dhiban were extremely complicated. There were vast numbers of different layers: early house floors were cut through by later house walls, which were in turn cut by even later drainage ditches. And so it went on, for hundreds and hundreds of different, separate deposits. It took Doug and me weeks to work out how it all fitted together, but in the end it made sense. This was superb experience for me: a combination of detective work and jigsaw puzzle – but much better fun than either. Eventually, after almost a year, we finished the technical phase of the Dhiban writing-up, and my services were no longer required. The job had been completed, more or less on time, and Doug seemed well pleased. It was now up to him to write the main report narrative, which took another six months.

I had effectively been out of British archaeology for two years, and in that time a lot had been published, which of course I'd missed. As I read my way through this backlog of literature, I was struck by the fact that medieval archaeologists had a great deal to teach we prehistorians. There is so much medieval archaeology in Britain that it is necessary to work on a grand sale. As I read I could discern a shift away from minutiae towards a bigger picture. Many medievalists were excavating entire villages; having done that, they turned their attention to the countryside round about. To put it another way, they worked with entire landscapes, rather than on single, one-off sites. That was precisely what I wanted to do for prehistoric archaeology.

While we were completing our work on Dhiban, Doug and I had discussed what I should do next. Doug had long cherished the idea of launching an ROM expedition to Britain, alongside the museum's existing projects in Central America, Peru, Iran, Egypt and of course in Ontario. He had set aside the then princely sum of £1,500 for me to use as 'seed corn' – in effect to buy my way back into British archaeology. Given my growing predilection for medieval archaeology, I made contact with Peter Wade-Martins, one of its leading exponents. Peter was directing the excavation of an Anglo-Saxon village in deepest rural Norfolk, at a place called North Elmham. I made him my offer, and just as Doug had predicted, he welcomed the money and myself with open arms.

I owe an enormous debt to Peter and his team. From them I learned the benefits of opening up huge areas, rather than small trenches. With an open area you can appreciate how everything fits together. You do not need to worry whether a ditch exposed in Trench 1 is the same as another exposed in Trench 15, a hundred metres away, because it's there for all to see. You can even walk along it. But open-area excavation also demanded a whole battery of new skills, which I had to learn in double-quick time.

In order to open huge areas of ground, you have to use earth-moving machines. It's important to know how to use the various diggers and dumpers to shift the topsoil quickly, but without causing damage to the archaeological layers below. The power of the machines has to be controlled and harnessed, or else they are capable of doing immense harm. Open-area excavation also requires planning (i.e. map drawing) if it is to be fast and accurate. Nowadays one would use laser technology to survey rapid plans, but in those days that hadn't been invented. So we fell back on ingenuity.

While I worked with Peter's team, I also had my ear closely to the ground. Back in Toronto I had read that the small English city of Peterborough, about eighty miles north of London, was going to be expanded into a huge New Town. The New Towns – there were several of them – were arranged in an inner and an outer ring around London, and were intended to take the capital's 'surplus' population, housing, entertaining and, most important of all, employing them. It was a major piece of social engineering: Peterborough's population in 1968 was 80,000; today it is closer to 200,000.

I knew from my university courses that Peterborough was famous for its prehistoric archaeology. Indeed, one of those horrible pottery 'cultures' was even named after the place. We had been taught that Peterborough pottery and the Peterborough Culture played an important part in Later Neolithic Britain, around 2500 BC. I am still not at all sure what the Peterborough 'Culture' means or meant, but the term did at least suggest that sites in or near Peterborough had yielded important prehistoric finds. That was good enough for me. I determined to visit the place and see for myself. I didn't know it then, but my quest was about to start in earnest. For the next quarter of a century I would barely have the time to draw breath.

Early autumn has a particular charm in England. Country gardens are at their best. Old-fashioned roses – the kind with loose flowers, kind colours and strong scents – are in their second flush, and even the midday sun lacks the strength to fade them. The true season of mists and mellow fruitfulness has yet to begin, and one is in a never-never world, where summer still lingers and the stillness of evening retains its warmth. It's my favourite time of year: a little wistful perhaps, but not yet so much as a whisper of melancholy.

It was September 1970, and I was looking forward to the drive ahead of me. Norfolk is one of the most attractive counties in England. Noël Coward's over-quoted 'Very flat, Norfolk' simply isn't true: it's a county of gently undulating hills, with little villages nestling in the valleys. By and large it's an unspoiled county that has been spared the gentrification that has blighted many of the once-beautiful villages of the Cotswolds.

I decided not to take the direct route along the main road, but to let my car have its head, while I used the sun as a guide to ensure that I went in roughly the right direction. After half an hour, the rolling countryside gave way to the flat coastal plain of north Norfolk, and before I knew it I found myself driving through the beautiful ancient port of King's Lynn.

Today the town is by-passed, and few people bother to divert from the traffic jams that are now an unavoidable part of summer weekends. The roads around King's Lynn seize solid as the wealthy of the East Midlands migrate towards their seaside holiday homes in shiny four-wheel drives. Lynn is one of the most gorgeous towns of England. In medieval times it was prosperous, and the citizens built magnificent churches and whole streets of splendid timber-framed houses. The prosperity lasted into the seventeenth and eighteenth centuries, but then there were harder times, and the town was spared the wholesale redevelopment that afflicted more prosperous places during the Industrial Revolution. Sadly, the worst damage to this jewel of the North Sea coast took place in the second half of the twentieth century – in the name of 'improvement'.

King's Lynn is the port on the river Great Ouse, at the point where it enters the Wash. East of the town is the higher ground of Norfolk, including the sandy countryside in which stands Edward VII's grand country seat, Sandringham House. I once heard Prince Charles say that he always regarded himself as a Norfolk boy, thanks to the happy days he had spent in and around Sandringham.

To the west of Lynn, the landscape is altogether different. This is a less yielding, sterner country. The land is flat, and transected by deep drainage ditches. The roads run dead straight, and I soon found my car was travelling far faster than the police might have wished. I didn't slow down, but roared onwards. This was the life!

I was back in the land of the Fens, a part of the world I have grown to love. I like its bleakness. I like its clear, luminous daylight. Above all, I feel free in the Fens: free to breathe deeply and be myself. I also like Fen people. True, they are reserved and rarely press their attentions on one; but I like that, too. There's warmth aplenty when you need it, but only when you need it. They live in a landscape of space, and they give other people space too.

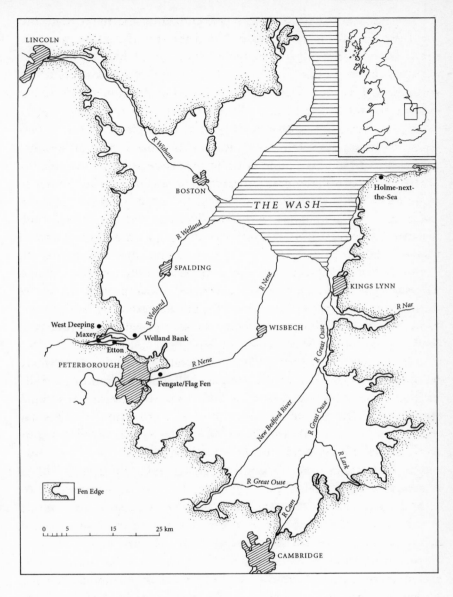

FIG 1 *The Fens*

The next town I came to was Wisbech (pronounced Wis-beach). Like Lynn, it had once seen prosperous times, but then the river Nene which was the source of the town's wealth silted up, and the cargo ships which had brought loads of timber from the Baltic ports could no longer sail up the river from the Wash. As a result, Wisbech too was spared the depredations of our Victorian forebears. I wasn't familiar with the town, and as I drove through its centre I was stunned by the fine Georgian houses which fringed the river along North Brink. I know now that this is possibly the finest Georgian streetscape in Britain.

Once I was out of Wisbech and heading west, the signs told me I was thirty-four miles from Peterborough. Again the landscape changed. Between Lynn and Wisbech the Fens are more accurately known as Marshland. The landscape I had sped through on leaving Lynn had been formed by the sea. Storms and tides from the Wash have laid down thick layers of sandy-coloured silts, which are now among the most fertile arable soils in Europe. It's a countryside of orchards, rose and garden-plant nurseries, and vegetables. More vegetables are grown in Marshland than anywhere else in Britain. Sometimes the stench of frosted cauliflowers on the air can be overpowering.

West of Wisbech the Fens become different, and much darker. Spiritually darker too, I sometimes think. Before the widespread land drainage of the last three centuries, this was the haunt of Fen Tygers, those wild young men who wore their long hair in a pigtail and cherished their freedom to hunt and fish the common land and streams within their watery world. Out in the open fen there were huge expanses of water. Whittlesey Mere was the largest lake in Britain, before its drainage in 1852. Closer to the edge were sprawling woods of alder and willow. Here decomposing vegetation gave off methane gas, which spontaneously ignited to form the dreaded 'corpse candles' – which on drier land only formed in churchyards, above freshly filled graves. To outsiders it was a dark country in more ways than one.

The Black Fens acquired their name because of their rich peat soils, which formed in pre-drainage times in a wide natural basin between the silts of Marshland to the east, and the higher ground of the fen edge to the west. For thousands of years peat grew and accumulated in this complex network of ponds, lakes, meres and creeks. Before their drainage, which took place mainly in the seventeenth century, the Black Fens were Britain's largest natural wetland. It was a drowned landscape, but it was also a rich land. There was peat for fuel, reeds for thatch and huge numbers of duck, geese, eels and fish to eat. Elsewhere, in upland Britain, folk went hungry in winter, when protein was always in short supply. But never in the Fens.

You can see a long way in a flat landscape. Perhaps the finest building in Britain, Ely Cathedral, high on its 'island' hill, can be seen from twenty miles away. Hence its local name, 'the Ship of the Fens'. Peterborough Cathedral was built on lower-lying, less spectacular land, but it is still extremely impressive. These buildings were undoubtedly built to the glory of God, but the way they dominated – and still dominate – their landscapes leaves me in no doubt that they were also symbols of real political power down here on earth.

I first caught sight of Peterborough Cathedral from ten miles away, as I drove out of the little village of Thorney. By now I was back on the main road, as I had no idea how to navigate my way through the narrow Fen lanes. I knew from past experience that it's easy to get *almost* there in the Fens. You follow your nose, and arrive close to your destination, except that there's a huge drainage ditch (or dyke, as they're known in the Fens) blocking the way. And then you discover that the nearest bridge is ten miles away.

Peterborough looked familiar as I drove towards the city centre. It was late afternoon and the sun was sinking behind the cathedral tower. Crows were calling to one another in the large trees of the Bishop's Palace garden, as if they were getting ready for tea. Which would not be a bad idea, I thought, as I pulled into the car park outside the museum.

Peterborough Museum is a fine stone building in Priestgate, the only street left which gives a feeling of what the old city would have been like. The rest was swept away – today we would say 'redeveloped', because it sounds nicer – when the main railway line arrived around 1850. The resulting prosperity carried all before it, including nearly every old building, except of course the churches. They couldn't pull them down. As Bob Dylan once sang: 'Money doesn't talk, it swears.'

Inside the museum I was shown into the library, a tall, dark room lined from floor to ceiling with bookshelves. There was that wonderful booky, musty smell I had first encountered in the Myers Museum at school, and for a too-short moment I was transported back to my youth. The librarian showed me the shelves that held their archaeological titles. In amongst the dusty volumes I noticed a clean paperbound book with a green spine and the letters 'RCHM' in bold black type at top and bottom. Far from being a museum piece, this book, *Peterborough New Town: A Survey of the Antiquities in the Areas of Development*, had only been published the previous year. It was a survey by the Royal Commission on Historical Monuments, and I had been trying to get my hands on a copy for several weeks, but every bookshop I tried had sold out. I ignored the wisdom of the ages on the shelves all around me, and opened the book eagerly. The site I was interested in lay on the eastern fringes of the city, at the point where the dryland stopped and the once-wet fen started. It was known as Fengate (from two Norse words meaning 'road to the fen'), and I wanted to know to what extent it would be affected by the New Town.

It was immediately clear that most of Fengate would be destroyed by factories when work on the New Town started in earnest, in 1971 and 1972. Although I was sad for the people and buildings of Fengate, this threat of development meant that I stood a good chance of raising money from the British government, as well as from the ROM. Nowadays developers have to pay for any archaeological excavation their proposals might require, but in the early seventies it was up to government, local government or sometimes archaeological societies to fund such work. With dual sources of funding I might be able to carry out a large-scale open-area excavation. Maybe I'd get the chance to do a proper, wide-ranging project on a landscape which the Royal Commission report suggested would mainly be of pre-Roman date. My mind was racing. Could this be the site I had been looking for?

I knew a bit about Fengate – every archaeology student in England knows a bit about Fengate, as it's one of the key sites of British prehistory. It was Fengate that produced those Late Neolithic Peterborough pots. The sherds of pottery that gave the Peterborough Culture its name were found in hand-dug gravel pits that had been worked in the first three decades of the century. What I had to know now was simple: was anything left? Had the gravel pits destroyed everything? I was itching to find out.

The librarian told me that the museum was about to close, and the car park would be locked up in fifteen minutes. I still hadn't answered those key questions, and was almost exploding with frustration; but at least I now had the book safely secured in my briefcase. This time I drove across the Fens to King's Lynn and my lodgings in North Elmham using the most direct route possible. I don't think I have ever driven so fast, or with such abandon, before or since.

I took the stairs three at a time and leapt onto the bed, as there was nowhere else to sit. I started to read, and rapidly the truth began to dawn. What a site! It was extraordinary. I couldn't believe it. The meticulous survey showed that the hand-dug gravel quarry pits were confined to about a quarter of the area of Fengate, and the rest of the prehistoric landscape lay out there, untouched. Intact. And what a landscape it was. I had never seen anything like it before. I was aware that I must be looking at one of the richest archaeological areas in the country. Even the Royal Commission, never noted for extravagant hyperbole, enthused: 'This area shows *massive* evidence for occupation from the Neolithic period onwards . . .' I lay back and stared at the ceiling. I couldn't believe it. I had hit the jackpot.

======

CHAPTER THREE

A Trans-Atlantic Commuter

I NOW FOUND MYSELF in a strange situation: I was an Englishman working in England for a foreign institution. I was resident – and indeed taxed – abroad, but most of my team were British. After the initial exploratory expedition of 1970 I returned to Canada for the winter, and drew up proposals for a five-year project which would examine all the land threatened by the expansion of the New Town. Although our main funding was from Canada and the British government, the local authority (in this instance the New Town Development Corporation) also provided us with essential help in kind, which included accommodation, storage facilities and the like.

From 1971 to 1978 I would work in Britain for the four or five months from spring to autumn. I had to be careful not to stay for more than six months, or I'd find myself paying both British and Canadian taxes – and my salary wasn't big enough to take such a knock. The digging season usually started in May, when North American students became available. From June onwards we employed more British students, and the excavations would close after the first frosts and rains of autumn, which were usually in October.

Most of the digs I had worked on previously had been either small and amateur or large and professional, and to be honest I found neither very satisfactory. The small, amateur affairs were relaxed and friendly, but the pace was too slow, there was an enormous amount of talk and not much action. The big digs were less to my liking – that is, as gatherings of human beings (they even had cooks and field kitchens) – but as a way of getting large quantities of archaeology done, they were superb.

Even if I did manage to squeeze big sums of money from my

sponsors, I knew that funds wouldn't be limitless. I also knew that it would take me some time to come to grips with the local geology, and until I had mastered that, it would be impossible to find useful work for a large team. Familiarising yourself with the geology is something that every dig director has to do. Unless you know in detail how the natural subsoil formed and how it was altered after its formation, you cannot hope to identify the slight marks left on it by the hand of man.

At Fengate the subsoil was gravel that had formed during a warm period in the Ice Age, over ten thousand years ago. The gravels were laid down by rivers, and when they froze and ceased to flow during the next cold spell in the Ice Age, the gravels were torn apart by ice and glaciers. The results of this tearing apart sometimes resembled man-made features, such as ditches, which was to prove a major source of confusion during my first season of excavation.

I suppose I was looking for reasons not to have a big team, because that's what I eventually chose to do. I decided I would organise a small group – perhaps six or eight students – with two or three experienced professional site supervisors to keep a controlling eye on things. That way, we could combine the best of the amateur and professional ways of digging. In the event it worked well; in fact I still dig with a small, select team. I made a flying visit to England over Christmas 1970 and recruited two supervisors and a field assistant, all of whom were about to start post-graduate research at Manchester University. I also found somewhere local to live the following summer. As dig houses went, it wasn't a palace, but it would have to do. And it was free – offered as a contribution to the project by the local authority.

The contrast between mid-winter England and Canada was extraordinary. In Toronto the snow had been lying for three weeks, but in England, five hundred miles closer to the North Pole, the roses were still out. As I drove back to Heathrow in early January a few suburban lawns were being given a light trim.

I returned to England for my first full season as an excavation director in April 1971. I was twenty-six years old, and although I did my best to appear supremely confident, I was quaking in my boots. Walking out onto my own site for the first time was a strange experience. There they were: my team of three senior staff and five newly recruited students. Eight pairs of eyes looked to me to make the first move. I knew instinctively that to appear indecisive would be fatal. But we were alone in a field, our tools hadn't yet arrived, nor had the site huts or the digger. We couldn't so much as brew a cup of tea. And I certainly couldn't ask them to scratch at the ground with their bare hands.

I had begun to experience a tide of rising panic when there was a shout from the road. It was the truck delivering the hut sections. With a huge sigh of relief I sent everyone across to help unload. I had learned the first lesson of any dig director – ensure that you have work for people to do, no matter how futile the tasks might seem. It's always better to do something – anything – than nothing. A team's morale is crucially important, and as soon as it starts to slip, everything else will rapidly follow.

I have always believed in leading from the front, and this is particularly important when everyone on the team is of roughly the same age. A team leader's job is not just about co-ordination and morale; it's also about inspiration and motivation. In time, our team began to believe that we were the best in Britain. And we may have been, for all I know. This growing sense of pride showed itself in a number of ways. We always made visitors welcome, and I was at pains to see that nobody rammed our growing reputation down other people's throats; but I was also at pains to see that no visitor left without being seriously impressed by what we were doing. What was happening was no more than the growth of a close-knit, motivated team. Many of us have since moved elsewhere – back to Canada, to continental Europe, even to Hawaii – but we still keep in touch, nearly thirty years later.

The first few days of a dig can affect the way the entire season runs. The biggest influence is undoubtedly the weather, and there's nothing one can do about that. A rainy start is the worst. The huts go up wet; they seldom sit square on the ground, and never seem to lose their dampness. The various delivery trucks stick in the mud, and someone always manages to fall over – but they never hit grass; invariably it's a broken bottle or a rusty iron spike. Nowadays wooden huts have been replaced by stackable, portable cabins which come ready equipped with electricity, water and well insulated walls. These have made an enormous difference to the quality of life on site.

The arrangement of the huts would reflect the way the dig was organised, and I always made a point of agreeing the layout of the compound with my two senior supervisors well in advance. That first season I came across the pair of them, entirely by chance, in a student pub, and together we sketched something incomprehensible on the back of a beer-soaked envelope – which I promptly lost. Anyhow, the compound more or less matched what we had agreed.

The huts were arranged around a small, open-sided 'yard' which faced onto the areas we were digging, and was surfaced with gravel taken from the dig. The largest hut, which sat at the centre of the yard, was the domain of Anne, our finds assistant. The finds assistant is possibly the most important member of a team. His or her job is to supervise the washing, marking, cataloguing and storing of the finds. They have to be rigorously methodical, and know where anything is at any time. The numbers of finds will vary depending on the type of site one is digging, but I suppose a typical day at Fengate would have yielded perhaps two or three hundred finds; of these, about 30 per cent would be man-made artefacts of one sort or another and the remaining 70 per cent would be animal bones.

Sometimes the artefacts were complete objects – brooches, pins, needles or small pots – but more often they were fragments of pottery or sharp flint flakes, the by-products of chipping flint to make tools. Like the artefacts, the animal bones were either found whole or, more usually, broken. They had to be treated with the same care as artefacts, because they could yield just as much information – about the cuts of meat that were eaten, the type of animals kept and the way they were farmed. If, for example, we found a high proportion of bones from older beasts, that might suggest that the younger ones were regularly transported to market.

Next to the Finds Shed was a small hut for tools, and a larger Tea Hut in which wheelbarrows were kept overnight. There was a hut given over to the storage of plans and records, and another in which I did my accounts and administration work – which took me about an hour every morning. People soon learned that doing the accounts made me grumpy, and if they were wise they'd stay well clear of my hut between ten and eleven o'clock. The sanitary arrangements were primitive in the extreme, and involved the liberal application of pungent blue liquid.

This was our self-contained world for the summer. We baked in the sun, froze in the cold, and soon grew extraordinarily weather-beaten. Most of us wore heavy boots, tattered shorts made from cut-off jeans, and old T-shirts that might once have been coloured. Nowadays, when I look at photos of the team, I'm surprised by how little our appearance has dated, when compared with the images in the glossy magazines of the time, which invariably appear extreme and ridiculous. A 1970s field archaeologist could readily slip unnoticed into a twenty-first-century team.

As soon as the panels of the huts were erected, Anne took a small party to town to buy essential supplies, while the rest of the crew started to nail down roofing felt. Rain was forecast overnight, so we had to make everything waterproof by the end of the day. While this was going on, our on-site foreman Sandy and I sat in the Land-Rover with a large aerial photograph and scratched our heads as we tried to decide where to start digging. We had a lot of land and potential archaeological features to choose from.

Aerial photography has had a profound effect on archaeology, since its first widespread use during the Great War. In lowland England years and years of ploughing have removed most of the humps and bumps from the actual surface of the ground, but in aerial photographs long-vanished features such as trackways, field ditches, even house foundations, can be seen as dark marks in growing crops. In a dry year, and only in a dry year, the roots of crops such as wheat and barley need to dive deep to find moisture. Above buried and long-filled-in ditches, wells or rubbish pits, the roots find dampness and the crops grow thick, lush and luxuriant. This darker growth shows up clearly from the air.

The cropmarks on the photos that Sandy and I were examining looked like a painting by Jackson Pollock: there were lines everywhere. Some were straight, one was a perfectly circular ring, others were squiggly, and there were seemingly random dots and irregular dark splodges. The splodges and squiggly lines were caused by water freezing and thawing during the last great Ice Age, so they could safely be ignored. But the other marks were interesting. The dots might or might not be ancient wells, while the circular ring was almost certainly the quarry ditch around the outside of a Bronze Age barrow, or burial mound. Unfortunately, it was in a neighbouring field, and we were unlikely to get a chance to dig it until at least 1973, when it was scheduled by the New Town authorities to become available for commercial development.

One of the frustrating aspects of so-called rescue archaeology, undertaken ahead of specific commercial developments such as factory building or quarrying, is that you cannot carry out a logical pattern of research. Ideally, I like to work my way back in time, starting with the recent material and finishing with the most ancient. But it doesn't work like that in rescue archaeology. You excavate the land which is under the most urgent commercial threat, whatever the age of the archaeological deposits it contains. In effect this means that the archaeologist has to maintain a number of distinct, but often interweaving, threads or themes in his head. Many times I have found myself looking at an Iron Age grave or house foundation of 300 BC, while my brain is thinking about Neolithic problems of 3000 BC.

We decided to place our first trench across two long, straight, dark marks of parallel ditches. By this time I had bought several copies of that RCHM survey which I had first seen the previous year in Peterborough Museum. The survey reckoned that the two parallel crop-marks were probably the drainage ditches on either side of a Roman trackway. Roman features in the Peterborough area were often crammed full of pottery, because from the late second century AD to the end of the Roman period (AD 410) there were highly productive potteries in the lower Nene valley, immediately west of the modern city. Large potteries like those in the Nene valley were among the first true factories, and they produced cooking and tableware for the prosperous homes of the later Roman Empire on a truly industrial scale.

The pottery itself looks remarkably modern, and were it not for the fact that it's unglazed, you would not be surprised to see it holding salt or sugar on a modern-day kitchen table. Most of the Nene valley production sites are known, and to walk across one is a strange experience, especially when the land has recently been ploughed. You walk into what seems like a perfectly ordinary flat field, and suddenly have a strange feeling, as if you were walking on thousands of broken ostrich eggs. The 'eggs' are sherds of pottery, and they're crunchy underfoot.

Exactly how these huge quantities of pottery found their way from the industrial suburbs of a Roman town to the field boundary ditches of Fenland farms ten miles away is still a mystery to me. But that's what happened. Maybe the local peasants were employed by the wealthy pot-factory owners to smash the stuff, in order to keep prices up? Or maybe they were mad? Or just careless? Or perhaps, like farmers today, they simply took their animals to market and bought the pottery, cheap, while they had money in their pockets.

Sandy was sure that a trench across the two parallel ditches would establish their date. Once that was done we could start investigating the possible wells, which were potentially far more interesting. I agreed, and we sent the digger off to remove the topsoil, closely watched by one of our supervisors.

Later that afternoon I walked across to the trench. I looked in, and saw the two ditches, just as they appeared on the air photo. Then I glanced in the finds trays by each ditch, and was slightly puzzled. There were a few scraps of bone, probably of cattle; a small flint flake, of no particular date, but certainly pre-Roman; and two tiny scraps of soft hand-made pottery, again probably prehistoric. Only one find was of any interest, and it could have been Roman or earlier. It was a small piece of baked clay 'daub'.

Although the Romans introduced mortar and plaster to Britain, the ordinary country people still usually lived in roundhouses built in the traditional pre-Roman, or Iron Age, manner. The walls were made from woven hazel 'wattles', which resembled coarse basketwork. This wattlework core was then smeared with a thick layer of clay, usually mixed with straw and cow dung to give it flexibility and strength. The mix of clay and straw was known as 'daub'. When a house burnt down, which happened quite often, the clay became fired, rather like crude pottery. This firing meant it could survive in the soil indefinitely – ultimately for archaeologists to discover. The piece of daub in my hand was like others I had excavated. I could clearly see the impression left by one of the woven wattles of the wall core. That was encouraging. At least we now had evidence of a house, or houses, somewhere in the vicinity of the two ditches.

The single flint and the tiny piece of pottery could have been in the topsoil for several centuries before the Roman British farmer dug out his trackway ditches. To use the technical word, they were probably 'residual' from an earlier period. The fragments of animal bone couldn't be dated. So we were no further forward. Still, we were digging real archaeology on our first day; the sheds were up and water-tight, and the crew hadn't tried to lynch me. All in all, it had been a good start.

The next day it rained as it can only rain in a green and pleasant land. By the end of the afternoon our two ditches were filled to the brim, so when I got back to the house I had rented in town that evening I ordered the digger to return the next day. The driver, Chris Clapham, arrived bright and early, and I decided we should simply extend the trench we had started on the first day and cut another section through the ditches. We could always return to the two flooded sections when they had dried out. Failing that, we could hire pumps, but that was expensive. Then, at the end of the day I had a thought. What on earth was I doing clearing little trenches and fiddling around in this small-minded fashion? Surely my aim was to think big – to think in terms of whole landscapes? So I retained the digger, and did not send it back to the depot. Chris, who soon became very interested in the project and who worked with us for several years, was delighted. It was clear that he was always sad to have to return to normal construction work at the end of each season.

By the time I had finished with Chris and the digger, about five days later, we had exposed the two ditches, and the trackway between them, for a distance of some forty metres. The rain held off, and then the weather began to improve. The sun shone, birds sang, and all was suddenly well with the world. We removed the loose earth left by the digger with shovels, and then used onion-hoes to scrape the surface clean. When we had done this, the dark soil which filled the two ditches showed up quite distinctly as two rich brown parallel lines.

My suspicions were first aroused while we were still scraping the machine-cleared ground surface with the onion-hoes. I had deliberately positioned myself in such a way that I was scraping down the centre of the most southerly of the two ditches. Normally I would

have expected to find small, worn sherds of Roman pottery at the top
of a filled Roman ditch. But there weren't any. Not so much as a
scrap. It was peculiar.

About a month into the dig, I had to return briefly to Toronto
to make the final arrangements for an exhibition of finds from North
Elmham that Peter Wade-Martins had kindly loaned to the Royal
Ontario Museum. I was away for three weeks, and on my return I
learned, to my utter amazement, that we had *still* not found anything
in either of the two ditches that could be reliably dated. There was
certainly nothing even remotely Roman. Poor Anne was getting fed
up with the trickle of scrappy finds. To vent her frustrations – and I
couldn't blame her – she decided to lay everything we had found to
date on a table in the Finds Shed, for me to see on my first day back
on site.

Through hollow, jet-lagged eyes I viewed Anne's tabletop exhibition. I was already feeling a bit low, but this display of scrappy
potsherds, like so many crumbs of wet digestive biscuit, together with
mis-shaped pieces of clay 'daub' and nondescript splinters of bone
was, quite frankly, pathetic. It was almost more than I could bear.
'What on earth,' I thought, 'will Doug make of this? I'll arrive in his
office at the end of my first season of excavation for the ROM proudly
bearing a shoe-box of finds before me. "There," I'll announce, "that's
what you paid thousands of dollars to discover."' No, I couldn't bear
it – it was too depressing for words.

I think my misery must have communicated itself to Anne, whose
eyes had gone moist. She was starting to bite her lip. I put an arm
around her shoulder and was about to make some pathetic excuse
along the lines of 'Honestly Anne, it's not the finds, it's just the jet-lag,'
when the door was noisily kicked open. We almost jumped out of
our skins. It was Sandy holding a finds tray which contained something
which looked like – I rushed across to have a closer look – which
looked like . . . a large lump of mud.

Somehow I concealed my extreme disappointment (not to mention irritation) and picked the thing up. I turned it over carefully in
both hands, in case it fell to bits – and it was just as well that I did,
because on the underside I saw that what looked like earth was not
earth, but grey-coloured baked clay. A sharp-eyed student digging in

one of the trackway ditches had spotted this too, and had put the entire lump in the tray.

Although the clay had been quite lightly fired, possibly by being dropped into a bonfire for an hour or so, it held together well and I was able to remove the earth that clung to its surface. As I gently lifted off the soil, piece by piece, the object began to take on a familiar shape. By now I was getting excited, and was having trouble preventing my hands from trembling. Three or four students who were working in the Finds Shed sensed this excitement and drew close around me, partially obscuring the light. But I didn't care.

I turned the object gingerly on its end, and suddenly recognised it for what it was. So did everyone else. As if on a command, every head rose, and the frowns of a few minutes ago were replaced by the broadest of smiles. The object in my hand resembled a large, short length of giant macaroni, and weighed as much as a bag of sugar. It was the hole through the centre that had made us all look up. It was round and neat, and just big enough to fit one's thumb. We all knew it could only be one thing. I was ecstatic. I could have hugged everyone. Instead, being British, I patted Sandy on the shoulder in a manly sort of fashion.

To give it its technical name, the object was an axially-perforated cylindrical clay loomweight. (I love the precision and rhythm of that academic description. It says it all, in a wonderfully rich way – like thick, brown, beefy gravy.) I knew from my textbooks that loomweights of this sort were made and used in the Later Bronze Age, in the two or three centuries before and after 1000 BC.

Most axially-perforated cylindrical clay weights weigh about the same, and they are nearly always found near settlements. On the Continent weights of this type have been found in the ground close together and lying in neat rows, as if an upright loom had been abandoned, and the weights which hung from bunches of warp threads below it had simply fallen to the ground. In wet areas some apparent 'loomweights' may also have been used as fish-trap or net sinkers. After about 500 BC, in the Early Iron Age, cylindrical loomweights were replaced by triangular weights with holes at the corners. Clearly loom technology had changed, and the requirement was now for an altogether different, more sophisticated style of weight.

I had never actually handled a cylindrical loomweight before, and I looked at it closely. It had been quite carefully made, and the outer surfaces had been smoothed by hand – it was even possible to make out the faintest traces of fingerprints. It may well have been made indoors, because a small flint scraping tool, probably from off the floor, had stuck to the clay, only to be mixed into the weight when the clay was kneaded. Two points struck me forcibly. First, although fired, the clay was by no means hard. If I were to tap it quite lightly it would break into pieces. Second, it was 80 per cent complete, and what little damage there was (it was confined to the ends) could well have happened while it was in use, because it would have hung along-side, and sometimes bashed against, the other weights below the loom. That slight damage apart, it was in remarkably fresh condition.

Now, something as fragile as a clay loomweight that had been made in the Middle or Late Bronze Age could not possibly have survived on the ground surface for over a millennium, and it certainly wouldn't have come through the process of Roman ditch-digging without so much as a scratch. I was forced to conclude that the weight had been placed, or had rolled into, the bottom of the ditch, a short time after it was cut from the loom, perhaps as long ago as 1400 BC. That meant that the ditch couldn't possibly be Roman. It had to be Bronze Age. And that, of course, would explain the absence of any Roman pottery from all the trenches we had dug.

Suddenly, now that the immediate excitement was over, those unimpressive finds on the table made sense to me. I rushed over and picked up the supposed piece of burnt clay 'daub' we had found before I left for my quick visit to Canada. I looked at it again, more closely this time. Armed with our new discovery I could see at once that the 'wattle impression' was nothing of the sort: it was straight, not curved, and it was neat and circular – *and* thumb-sized, just like the hole in the loomweight which Anne was beginning to clean with a fine watercolour paintbrush.

So, I reflected, for the best part of two months we had been digging the side-ditches of a Bronze Age road or trackway. At the time, such things were almost unheard of, except in the wetlands of Somerset, where special wooden trackways were built across boggy ground. But to find one in Peterborough . . . And it was big – at least five metres wide, far bigger than the Somerset tracks, which were more like large footpaths than roads capable of taking two-way traffic. But what did it all mean? My preconceptions about the site had been turned upside-down.

We continued work for several weeks, and still all we found were scraps of soft handmade pottery, a few dozen more flint tools and another nearly complete cylindrical loomweight. But now I was far more calm, even though I wasn't at all sure what it signified, in terms of the archaeology of the ancient landscape, that is. I had phoned Canada late in the afternoon of the day after we found the first loomweight, and told Doug about it. At the end of my breathless account I started to apologise for the scrappiness of what we'd unearthed so far, but he didn't seem to mind. He told me not to worry about finds; they'd come soon enough. He also advised me to relax and enjoy running the dig. I suspect he had an intuitive feel that the pace of my life would shortly quicken. He told me that in two weeks he'd be in England, for a conference in Oxford. He'd come and see me then. And with that he rang off.

Doug had been friendly and reassuring on the phone, but I was aware that he was no fool, and that although Britain was a long way from his main research interest in the Near East, he would require a coherent story from me. Like many archaeologists of the previous generation, he liked to hear narrative. A dig should tell a story. It was not good enough merely to list the various finds and features one had found. They had to *mean* something. And if you couldn't explain why they were there and what they meant, then you had no business to be excavating at all.

Given what I knew at this stage, I didn't feel at all confident that I could fabricate a convincing narrative around my two Bronze Age ditches. And I only had two weeks in which to think. 'That's a ditch a week,' I thought grimly. My previous confidence was slowly being replaced by nagging anxiety. I was learning that discoveries only become significant when one can attach a convincing explanation to them. Without a good narrative they remain curiosities – no more, no less. Unless I was careful, I might be remembered as the man who found two Bronze Age ditches near Peterborough. I tried thinking around the periphery of the problem. What if the two ditches had nothing to do with a track or roadway at all? What if they happened to run parallel purely by coincidence? There was a simple way to test this.

The field next to the one where we were working had been growing a crop of potatoes the year the air photos were taken. For various reasons, potato plants do not produce cropmarks when they grow, so the photos of that particular field were blank. I wondered whether, if we were to ask the farmer nicely, he would let us dig a couple of trenches in this field, about two hundred metres away from our present dig. If the two ditches were still running parallel, and five metres apart, at this distance away, it would strongly support the road or trackway theory. If, on the other hand, they diverged or came together, I'd have to come up with another idea.

The farmer agreed, we dug two quick trenches by hand, and lo and behold, there were the ditches, five metres apart, parallel, and running as straight as a die. So it simply had to be a road. And a straight one, at that. No wonder the RCHM survey had it listed as 'probably Roman'. Every school child is taught that Roman roads are straight (very often they're not, in fact).

It just so happened that a few days later I was driving my ancient Land-Rover along King Street, the Roman trunk road that runs north of the small Roman town of Durobrivae, near the modern village of Water Newton. The buildings of Durobrivae have long since vanished, and it only survives as a series of large banks and smaller humps and bumps, about five miles west of Peterborough. As the Land-Rover, with its rock-solid suspension, bounced slowly along, my mind wandered off to a known Roman road that runs diagonally across the landscape at Fengate. That road is known as the Fen Causeway, and scholars of the Roman period reckoned it was constructed in the years AD 60 and 61 by military engineers who had been ordered to force a route from the garrisons around Durobrivae, and then straight across the Fens. Once they had crossed the Fens, the legions would march into Norfolk, where the Briton Queen Boadicea (Boudica to archaeologists) was leading a successful rebellion against the Roman occupation. Sadly, however, the revolt failed, quite probably because of the reinforcements that came along the Fen Causeway.

As I ground slowly along in four-wheel drive, it struck me that

LEFT The prehistoric landscape at Fengate, Peterborough, was located on the nearest flood-free land to the Fens, Britain's largest wetland until their drainage in the seventeenth century. The Bronze Age fields were used by livestock farmers between 2500 and 1000 BC and were laid out in a ladder-like pattern subdivided by a series of major double-ditched droveways, tracks mainly for the use of animals. In the background is the peaty basin of Flag Fen.

BELOW When ancient ditches were abandoned, they naturally filled up with soil darker than the ground into which they were originally dug. Here, unexcavated Bronze Age droveway ditches at Fengate show on the stripped gravel surface as dark marks, beyond the excavators working in the foreground.

BELOW Very often the traces of prehistoric above-ground features, such as walls and banks, are destroyed by modern farming. At Fengate the bank that ran alongside a Bronze Age ditch (in which the figure is standing) was preserved beneath upcast from a modern drainage dyke. In this view, the bank has been partially sectioned and the layers within it have been labelled.

LEFT A minor Bronze Age double-ditched droveway being excavated at Fengate. The smaller droveways were the prehistoric equivalent of farm tracks, and were often more sinuous than the major droves that parcelled up the landscape. Here, the banks that would have accompanied the two ditches have been destroyed by modern ploughing.

BELOW The body of a young man buried at Fengate sometime between 3500 and 3000 BC, in the Neolithic period. In the same grave were the bones of two children and a young woman. The young man had been killed by a flint arrowhead (circled) which was found lodged between his eighth and ninth ribs. Its tip had broken off, probably on impact with the bones.

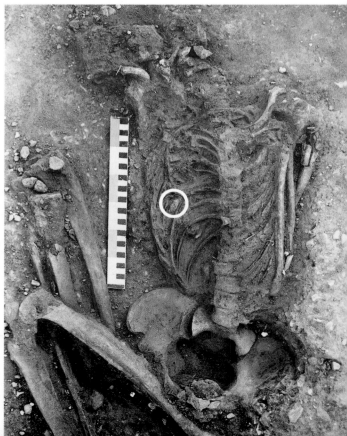

LEFT The people of Early Bronze Age Wessex were probably ruled by a powerful elite class. The rich burials of the so-called Wessex Culture are found shortly after the last building of Stonehenge. These gold objects are from Barrow G.8 at Wilsford, Wiltshire (2000–1800 BC): a large conical button (top centre); two pendants, perhaps worn on a ribbon or as part of a necklace (lower left); and two gold-covered amber discs (right).

RIGHT Powerful people in communities outside Wessex copied the richness of Wessex Culture burials. These gold grave-goods (a decorated plate, probably worn on the chest, and pieces of a miniature drum-like box) are from a barrow at Little Cressingham, Norfolk (2000–1800 BC). Although superficially fine, close examination of the workmanship shows it to be inferior to that of the true Wessex master-craftsman.

BELOW Fine goldwork was carried out in other parts of Britain. The extraordinary sheet-gold cape from Mold, Flintshire, Wales, was found in 1833. It covered a body which lay under a stone mound, or cairn, in a gravel pit (2000–1800 BC).

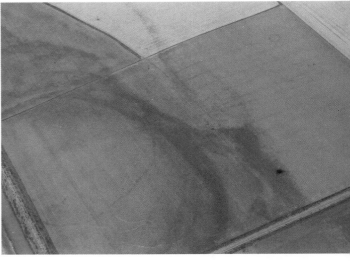

ABOVE Massive standing stones were not confined to Neolithic and Bronze Age religious sites in Britain alone. The Carnac alignments were erected near the coast of Brittany during the Late Neolithic period, around 3500 to 2500 BC.

RIGHT The aerial photograph which first revealed the faint cropmarks of the Etton causewayed enclosure (3800 BC). The dark swirl is the mark left by an old course of the river Welland. The ditch of the causewayed enclosure is a curving broken line to its right. On the other side of the river are the parallel furrows of the medieval field system and two ring ditches of Bronze Age barrows.

BELOW RIGHT The Neolithic causewayed enclosure at Etton was a sacred place, and ordinary objects were treated in special ways. Corn-grinding stones, or querns, were symbols of domestic life, and this large example (it is half a metre long) was buried in a pit, on edge – a position suggesting that the stone cannot be used.

the Fen Causeway might just clip the corner of the field where we were working. I knew a Roman road would be right up Doug's street, so to speak, and it might draw his attention away from the two narrative-free Bronze Age ditches, which were giving me prolonged anxious moments. Besides, the Boudica link was well worth examining, and Roman roads are always an interesting topic. I could see the subject would certainly appeal to the ROM's membership, and would make a good piece for the museum's house journal *Rotunda*. All in all, it had a lot going for it.

I headed home to have a closer look at the air photos, reasoning that if the road did indeed enter the field where we were working, it ought to show up quite clearly as a pale parch-mark. Roman roads were usually made from rammed-down gravel, and there was precious little moisture in them. As a result, in dry years, crops planted over them would grow pale and parched. Sometimes these pale cropmarks are known as negative cropmarks. As negative cropmarks went, the Fen Causeway was remarkably striking.

I got home at about six o'clock and found an air photo that clearly showed the Roman Fen Causeway as a sharply distinct negative cropmark which headed straight towards our field. On the photo it seemed to pass under the modern road that ran along our northern boundary, but strangely it didn't appear on the other side, where we were working. I looked at the photograph through the small folding magnifying glass I usually carry in my pocket. No, there could be no doubt at all. So where had it gone? It had either stopped, which seemed most unlikely, or else it turned west and ran directly below the modern road, where it would lie hidden. On the whole I still think that is the most likely explanation. Often modern and medieval roads made use of the hard foundations left behind by Roman engineers.

I was staring at the photo in a blank sort of fashion, pondering these problems, when my eye was caught by three parallel dark crop-marks, doubtless ditches, which quite clearly ran beneath the Roman road. At this point my subconscious clicked in. The ditches ran precisely parallel to the two ditches we were currently digging. That was odd. My pulse quickened immediately.

The first thing I had to do was to check that the three ditches were indeed parallel with the two we were digging. That wasn't quite as simple as it seemed, because the air photo that showed them best was taken at an oblique angle (i.e. the plane was not directly overhead), so I had to play around with some elementary geometry and a large-scale map before I could be certain. That done, I was convinced. They were indeed parallel.

By now I was getting excited. Whatever these Bronze Age ditches were, they weren't tracks or roads in the normal sense of the word. There were simply too many of them. Then I looked at the photos lying on the carpet around me. I remember frantically scrabbling though my desk drawer trying to locate my largest and best magnifying glass. When I had found it I stared long, close and hard at each photo in turn. It was an eerie feeling. Everywhere I looked I saw the crop-marks of parallel ditches, either singly or in pairs. I rubbed my eyes. Was I imagining them? Was I going mad? I took a quick stroll outside, then came back and took another look. No, I wasn't – they were definitely there.

I spent the next day plotting the cropmarks onto a map as accurately as I could. As I worked methodically through each photo, I found ditches that ran at right angles to the main ones. Some of these also had smaller ditches that branched off them, but always at right angles. When I had plotted every ditch I could find, it was absolutely clear that these were not roads, but the ditches that had been dug around a large and carefully-set-out system of Bronze Age fields.

As I dropped off to sleep that night, I reflected that I had always wanted to work on a prehistoric landscape, and now I had discovered it – and it could well prove to be one of the earliest in England. I think I sensed, with just a hint of wistfulness, that I was passing through possibly the most important moment of my archaeological life.

When I look back on my years digging the successive prehistoric landscapes at Fengate, it always makes me smile to recall that the big discovery, the one that set the ball rolling, wasn't made beneath a blazing sun. There was no trowel in my hand, no native workmen staring wide-eyed into the dark recesses of the long-lost tomb. Just a weary archaeologist surrounded by a scatter of well-thumbed photos on the carpet.

To date we have spent twenty-eight years excavating those Bronze

Age field ditches, and I shall be digging some more in the coming years. It's a huge system, and it's important because these particular fields did not appear by accident, fully formed, as it were. They were never placed in the middle of nowhere. Farmers only lay out and maintain fields if there's a good reason for spending so much time and effort on them.

The Fengate Bronze Age fields were carefully laid out to lie at the core of a working landscape. It was a landscape in which countless generations of human beings lived, died and were buried. I knew that it would provide an ideal setting to study *people* and their histories. If you know how to go about the task, the landscape can reveal an immense amount. But it takes time, some luck, and an enormous amount of patience. As the months turned to years, I became increasingly aware that I was bearing a huge responsibility – to the shades of the people who had lived in this place.

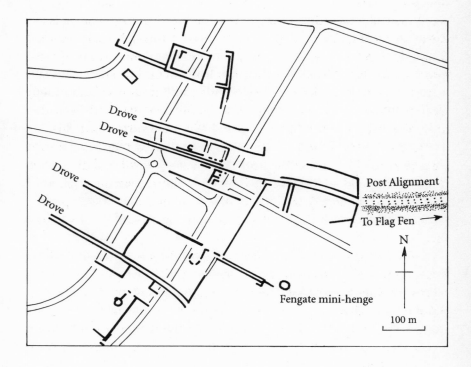

FIG 2   *The Fengate Bronze Age fields*

Modern development was ripping the old landscape apart. Fields were vanishing, to be replaced by factories and warehouses. Farm tracks, ancient and modern, were being upgraded to roads. Trees were being felled, hedges grubbed up and the rough wayside verges, rich in wildflowers and diverse grasses, were being carefully sculpted into yet another characterless 'landscaped', mown suburban streetscape. While these unsympathetic 'improvements' were taking place, while old Fengate was being transformed into Peterborough New Town's Eastern Industrial Area, I could almost hear the screams of protest coming from the inhabitants of the Bronze Age landscape. It was as if the people of my quest were looking over my shoulder. I *had* to do their story justice, while there was still something left to tell. I could not sell them short. It's a thought that still haunts me.

After that first season of 1971, Doug must have been impressed with what we were doing, because he set about raising large sums of money in Canada. While he worked on one side of the Atlantic, I worked on the other, and together we accumulated sufficient cash to carry out the large-scale open-area excavations that this complex landscape demanded. My main sources of funding were the British government and the New Town authorities, but I also raised a fair amount from private individuals, local landowners and industry. I now had the financial freedom to do the job properly, and there could be no excuses.

I won't describe how we excavated every Bronze Age field boundary ditch, because many of them were extremely unexciting. Like the two ditches at the start of the project, they produced few and scrappy finds; but as time progressed the few finds slowly accumulated, until we had quite a sizeable collection. We were also able to assemble a number of radiocarbon dates, and we now have solid evidence that the system of fields was first laid out around 2500 BC, at the start of the Early Bronze Age, and went out of use in the first half of the first millennium BC – probably between 1000 and 500 BC. So, in broad terms, these long-vanished fields were in use for two millennia. That's something to think about. Put another way, the Fengate fields had been in use for a thousand years when the young King Tutankhamun was laid in his fabulous tomb in ancient Egypt. Not only were these fields old, but they must also have worked well, for why else would they have been maintained in use for such a long time? I believe they worked well because they suited the landscape and the climate.

The eastern half of Britain is the side of the country with the driest climate and the flattest landscape. Today these conditions allow the farmers of East Anglia and Lincolnshire to grow arable crops, often on a vast scale more akin to the North American prairies than Europe. But it was not always like this. In medieval times, for example, the rich grasslands of eastern England supported huge flocks of sheep. The once-flooded Fens around the Wash have changed perhaps more than any other landscape in Britain. Today they grow huge arable crops, including more daffodils than anywhere else on earth; but again, in the remote past things were different.

In effect, the Fens are an inland extension of that huge shallow bay the Wash, which forms such a distinctive feature of the English east coast. Before their drainage in the seventeenth century, the Fens covered about a million acres of Cambridgeshire and Lincolnshire, and parts of Norfolk and Suffolk, too. Within them, particularly around the edges, were areas of higher ground that formed dry 'islands' amidst the reeds and waterways. The Isle of Ely is the best-known and largest of these.

The edges of the Fens slope gradually, and when you drive through the modern, drained Fen landscape it can often be difficult to decide whether you are on once-wet fen or on dry ground. If the road suddenly becomes uneven it's a sign that it was built on unstable peaty ground, and when that happens you can be sure you're driving through drained wetland.

The gently sloping plain of drier ground around the edges of the regularly flooded Fens was where prehistoric people liked best to live. By 2500 BC the forest cover here had largely gone. The ground was naturally well-drained, light and fertile, ideal for farming. That is most probably why the various prehistoric field systems at Fengate were laid out on this plain, right on the edge of the regularly flooded fenland. At Fengate the regularly flooded land is known as Flag Fen.

Like the medieval Fenland landscapes three thousand years later, the Early Bronze Age landscape at Fengate was laid out at right angles to the regularly flooded fenland. This expanse of wetter land was by no means a watery wilderness. Far from it. To us it may seem flat and featureless, but that's because we and our immediate predecessors have drained the heart, soul and guts out of it. Now it's little more than a vast growing-bag. Before drainage it was otherwise. It was a complex world, or series of worlds, each one of which was subtly different and could yield to the discerning hunter, fisherman or farmer abundance in a variety of forms. All it required to exploit these landscapes was a wealth of experience handed down from previous generations, and the acknowledgement that human beings were just a single, small element in a far larger Creation. To become arrogant and too self-assured in a landscape as potentially dangerous as the low-lying Fens is to court disaster. I fear we will soon learn that lesson the hard way ourselves.

My thoughts were first turned to the neighbouring fen when we had a visit from the late David Clarke, one of the key figures in twentieth-century archaeology. He had just completed his doctoral research into Beaker pottery and was then a junior lecturer at Cambridge. I regarded him then, and indeed I do now, as something of a hero. In his best-known book, *Analytical Archaeology* (1968), he set down the principles of a new and explicitly scientific approach to the subject. This approach, which has since been superseded several times, was known as the New Archaeology, and was of course vigorously opposed by most of the established authorities of the day. But there was another side to David. He wasn't entirely cerebral, but enjoyed handling real objects, and loved to visit field projects (although he admitted he wasn't much of a field archaeologist himself).

When I first started to research the prehistory of Fengate I assumed that the fen nearby was just wet, wet, wet and of no importance, but David was not so sure. At the time he had just finished work on a reinterpretation of the Glastonbury Iron Age Lake Village in Somerset. This had made him think about the way people on the fringes of wet areas lived and how they used the neighbouring fens or bogs. He turned my attention to books on medieval history, and I soon found myself reading about the farmers of the great monastic Fenland estates, at places like Ramsey, Crowland and Thorney Abbeys. The monastic system of farming made use of the fact that the Fens were rarely entirely flooded – inundated – and certainly not all year round. In the drier months of summer there were huge areas of grass and reeds. Sheep and cattle love reeds, so this lush grazing was ideal for the young lambs and calves, and of course for their mothers, who required vastly more food and water when they were in milk. So the farmers of the Middle Ages would take their herds of cattle and flocks of sheep out into the Fens when water levels fell in the springtime, then return to their 'island' or dryland base in the late autumn, when the weather broke.

It struck me that the Bronze Age fields at Fengate must have been on the winter, or home base, part of this cycle. They were laid out in a closely similar way to their medieval counterparts, with double-ditched droveways running down to the wetter ground, at right angles. Droveways are still a common feature of the Fenland landscape. In effect, they are green roads, built to be used by animals. They tend to be quite straight and are bounded by deep ditches and impenetrable hedges. Often the ground between the two ditches was built up with soil from the ditches on either side. This helped to keep the grass surface of the droveway dry.

The ditched droves at Fengate were laid out at regular intervals, of approximately two hundred metres, and the fields and paddocks between each drove seemed to have been laid out in different shapes and styles – rather as if the blocks of land defined by the droves belonged to different farmers or farming families.

At this early stage in the project we had yet to discover where the people of Fengate lived, where they were buried and how they had organised their lives. We just had the barest of bare bones. But it was a start. It was a framework, a grand design, and I could sometimes imagine fragments of the picture that was eventually to emerge.

CHAPTER FOUR

Direction and Disorientation

THE FIRST THREE SEASONS of research at Fengate were wholly
absorbing. I wasn't aware of it at the time, but I was actually becoming
too heavily involved. I was so immersed in what I was doing that I
was in danger of losing sight of the wood – so extraordinary were its
many trees. To be *so* absorbed is bad if the final objective of one's
research is the reconstruction of life 'in the round'. An obsessed
archaeologist will find it hard to stand back and see his work in
perspective. This was a lesson I was about to learn from some of my
newly-acquired friends in British academia.

As our team worked, we found that we were slowly piecing
together a picture of Bronze Age life on the Fengate site. We unearthed
the foundations of our first Bronze Age roundhouse in 1974, and
several others in subsequent seasons, and were also able to excavate
their yards and outbuildings. The roundhouses themselves were very
substantial buildings, with a floor area about the size of a Victorian
two-up, two-down cottage. They had stout walls and thick roofs (made
from thatch or turf, or a combination of the two); these roofs were
well insulated and kept the buildings warm in winter and cool in
summer. We worked on a very large scale and were able to place these
small farmsteads within their own fields and droveways. Gradually the
components of a long-lost landscape were starting to emerge.

Bronze Age life-spans may have been short – most modern estimates suggest that you were old by your mid-thirties – but your three
or four decades on earth were pleasant enough; provided, that is, you
survived the trials of birth. The roundhouses where people lived were
substantial, the fields were carefully laid out and the ditches around
them were properly maintained. The discarded meat bones we had

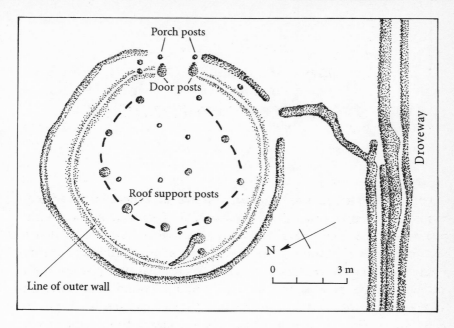

FIG 3   *Excavated ground plan of a Bronze Age roundhouse at Fengate*

found suggested that domestic animals were well-fed. It all appeared efficient and well regulated.

At the end of the second season in 1972 I gave a paper at a conference in Newcastle, in which I described the emerging picture of well-regulated life in the Bronze Age. No sooner had I stepped down from the stage than half a dozen academics declared that such order and organisation could only be due to the presence of a powerful political elite, who controlled those otherwise unruly prehistoric Fen folk. I don't know why, but this assumption irritated me. Why couldn't they control the way they behaved themselves? Why do some people always have to look for a ruling class, just because ordinary people seem to be running their lives efficiently and well? But despite my strong gut-feelings to the contrary, I couldn't counter these arguments with facts of my own. So I held my tongue – which is not something I have ever found easy.

One of the academics at the conference was Professor Richard

Bradley. Richard was then a lecturer at Reading University, and he had taken a special interest in our work at Fengate. The previous year he had sent me some of his best and brightest students, and it was an arrangement that was to continue for many years. It was good to have close contact with students – they never let any of us rest on our laurels. If we had a bright idea, we had to test it and then see what could be made of it. This was stimulating, and gave rise to some creative archaeology. I remember thinking that sometimes the chat in our Tea Hut had more in common with a university common room than a draughty field in the Fens.

On the train home from the conference, I reflected that it had indeed been useful, as it had given my quest a new impetus and a new direction. The resulting shift in emphasis, away from straight landscape reconstruction and towards patterns of prehistoric social organisation, was to have far-reaching consequences. I did not know it then, but I would soon find my quest moving from the world of the living to the lands of the dead.

The train sped through the huge, open plain-like fields of Lincolnshire, and I was struck by the fact that even the relentless advance of modern, intensively farmed arable agriculture had not managed to destroy everything – yet. As we flashed through tunnels and cuttings I could just spot, through the flying trackside trees and scrubby hedges, that the open countryside still included isolated fragments of earlier landscapes: pockets of woodland, ploughed-out hollow ways, small villages nestling within shrunken remnants of meadows and paddocks. I knew that it was these earlier fragments which will allow future historians to place the modern changes in context. Their survival could tell them much about the type of land that was not needed for modern farming – and by implication the sort of land that *was* needed. The enlargements and modifications to farmhouses, and the conversion of old livestock buildings such as stables to farm offices, would reveal much about the size and organisation of the estates that made these changes. In other words, to understand the process of change, you need both a 'before' and an 'after'. And it's good news indeed if you can find a 'during'. Unfortunately, they are rare.

I sat back in my seat, closed my eyes and tried to assemble my thoughts. It was difficult: I was tired, the conference had been good fun and I hadn't slept much. My brain refused stubbornly to work. So I dozed off. When I awoke we were approaching Peterborough. The sun was low and caught the magnificent Early English west front of the great cathedral. Then light dawned inside me. I had successfully used medieval analogy to illuminate the workings of the Bronze Age Fens. Surely, I reasoned, I could also turn the process on its head. To understand how social organisation worked in the Bronze Age, I should try to see how it differed from the previous period, the Neolithic.

Hitherto I had tended to concentrate on the 'after' rather than the 'before'. This approach had worked well, but I knew there were limits to what it could reveal. Essentially I was using a historical approach, whereas what I really needed was one that was much more radical. To understand the remote past I would have to examine the even more remote past; a daunting but exciting prospect. It was time to think in time-depth – to see how the lives of people and the landscapes in which they lived gradually changed. I had spent too long contemplating a single millennium. It had been rewarding and exciting, but it was now time to turn the clock back a long way indeed.

I was aware that I had already made a start on this way of thinking the previous season, when we had discovered the slight foundation trenches of a small rectangular building, measuring about seven by eight and a half metres. It was one of those completely unexpected discoveries that happen from time to time, and which make archaeology such a delight. As it was later to prove so important to my quest, I shall describe how we found it in some detail. I won't deny that it was a piece of luck, but I also like to think it was rather more than that – let's call it structured luck.

Sometimes the work at Fengate could be frustrating. 1972 had been a hot summer, and while sunshine is far better for team morale than continuous rain, it does make for practical problems in the dig. When the machines have removed the topsoil, we clear away all loose earth and scrape the freshly exposed surface clean with hoes or trowels. Usually there is enough moisture left in the ground for its natural colours to show up clearly, so ancient field ditches, post-holes or wall foundation slots that have been filled in for thousands of years will appear as dark marks on the surface of the subsoil. This darker colour is partly because they contain soil that slipped into them when they were abandoned, but partly too because they are damper – which, of course, is why they cause cropmarks to form. After a dry summer, the marks are much fainter and more difficult to detect.

In time a really good field archaeologist will develop almost a sixth sense. He or she (I think women, possibly because they usually have better colour vision than men, are often better at this) will be able to look at a patch of freshly cleaned subsoil and spot any number of post-holes and ditches, most of which would have been missed by a novice. This skill in 'reading' the ground is tested to the full with Neolithic and Bronze Age features. For some reason, possibly to do with the 'washing effect' of the seasonal rise and fall of water in the ground, Iron Age, Roman and later features are much easier to spot: they seem to have sharper, more distinctive edges and good dark earth within them.

It was high summer, and the machine had finished clearing the topsoil. Now it was time to clean the exposed surface by hand. There was nothing on the air photo of the area where we were working, but I had a hunch (and a few slender clues) that we might find evidence for a Bronze Age building, so I told Chris and the machine to go ahead. The sun burned down relentlessly and the sweat poured off us as we hoed the ground as fast as we could. But we couldn't go fast enough: the earth was drying out about a metre behind us as we hoed. After two hours we had finished, and although I stared at the ground for about a quarter of an hour I could see nothing. Nothing at all. It was a dejected team that sat exhausted and fed up in the Tea Hut that afternoon.

Although we couldn't see anything, miracles can sometimes happen, so I let it be known that until further notice, nobody was to walk across the trench we had just hoed clean. Everyone knew that footprints blotted out soil colours, and nobody wanted to rehoe the surface, so the instruction was scrupulously obeyed.

About a week later we had the rain we so urgently needed. I remember noting that the sky to the east, over Whittlesey, was completely black. As we watched, we could see lightning flash and a few seconds later came the rumble of thunder. I reckoned the storm would hit Peterborough in about fifteen minutes, and prayed it wouldn't be too severe. A torrential downpour would undo all our patient work, and we'd have to reclean the surface yet again.

The first drops of rain began to fall, but mercifully the main body of the storm passed by, further east, and we only caught a fringing shower. But it was enough to dampen the ground. I immediately walked across to the trench, and there, right in the middle, were the just-detectably darker stains of four slight ditches, arranged in a rough square. The sun came out, and almost at once the marks began to fade. I pulled a trowel from my back pocket, jumped down into the trench and scored a deep line around the edges of the darker soil. As I worked I noticed that the ditches did not sit in isolation: there were several pits or post-holes with them. It took about fifteen minutes to mark the ground, and when I climbed back out of the trench I could see no colour differences whatsoever. They had completely vanished.

Our first task was to make an accurate plan of the features I'd outlined on the ground. When that was done I could have shouted for joy. There, on the paper before me was a plan of a small building, similar to one excavated at Haldon in Devon before the last war by my old professor, Grahame Clark. It took us several weeks, and a lot of fine misted water from watering cans and hand-held sprayers, to excavate the four ditches. But it was well worth the effort. The ditches and the small pits and post-holes near them produced an astonishingly rich and diverse collection of finds: lots of flint, big pieces of pottery, but no animal bones. Like those from Haldon, our finds dated to the Earlier Neolithic period, and a radiocarbon date taken from a burnt corner-post gave a date range of 3310 to 2910 BC. There was no doubt about it: our newly discovered house predated the Bronze Age landscape by up to half a millennium.

I had thought little more about our Neolithic house until the train journey back from the Newcastle conference, and even then it was difficult to deconstruct and reinvent something we had discovered so recently. It's much easier to revise one's views when they've had a little time to 'settle in' and mature. As part of my newly-made resolution to examine the 'before' landscape of the Bronze Age fields I laid the plans of the Neolithic house on the kitchen table and stared at them long and hard. But I had no moment of revelation, no blinding flash of

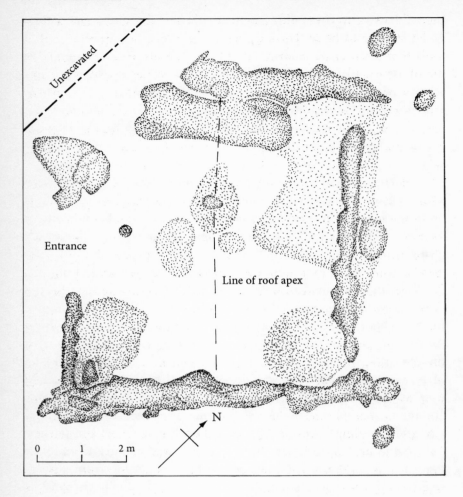

FIG 4   *Ground plan of the Fengate Neolithic 'house', or mortuary structure*

insight. They looked much as I remembered them. I knew that somewhere on those plans was something trying to catch my attention,
some key that would unlock the secrets that lay within, but I couldn't
spot it.

Most years we dug from April to October. Towards the end of
the season I would carefully pack up our finds and send them to
Canada by sea. It normally took them about six weeks to arrive, and

then I'd work my way through them during the Canadian winter. It felt strange to be in Toronto, handling pieces of pottery and flint tools that often came in dried muddy bags, each of which reminded me of a particular wet day on the other side of the Atlantic. But this pattern of work was effective, and allowed me to stay on top of my report-writing as the project progressed. It also meant that I was able to reflect on the previous year's results before the next season began, and to work out the questions we had to address the following year.

A few days after the conference we returned to Canada for the winter. By now I was getting better at coping with jet-lag, but my brain was never at its most active in the three or four days immediately after the flight. So you can imagine my feelings when I discovered, on returning to my office in Toronto, a pile of proofs sitting on my desk, accompanied by a note from the Museum Academic Editor to the effect that they had to be read through and corrected by the end of the week – which was in three days' time.

The proofs consisted of the unbound pages of my first report on the Fengate project, which was to be published on 28 February 1974. Proof-reading requires a great deal of concentration. Every letter of every word has to be checked and rechecked. I began the task, and soon found my jet-lagged concentration was lapsing. It was hopeless, but I knew that if I missed the deadline, the printer would start another job, and the publication of the report would be delayed for months. So I had to deal with those proofs *somehow*. Rather than do nothing, I decided to check the artwork first, because I find illustrations some-times require less close attention. As I was checking through the line drawings I came to the main plan of the Neolithic house. I checked the two scales – one metric and one imperial – and was about to turn the page when I spotted an important omission. For some reason – it's quite easily done – I had left out the arrow indicating north.

Normally the north arrow points upwards, but in this case I had jiggled the drawing slightly, so that the rectangular building sat square on the page. I knew I wasn't meant to alter the picture proofs them-selves, so I took the original artwork across to my drawing board. I suppose I ought to have moved the artwork that was already there, a plan of the paired Bronze Age droveway ditches, but I couldn't be bothered, and simply taped the plan of the house on top of it and added the north arrow. When I had finished, I stood back to admire my handiwork and let the ink dry. And then something odd caught my eye.

One would normally expect a square or rectangular building to follow the alignment of the landscape; it looks odd if a new building is positioned without any regard to the features of the land around it. Thus, houses are usually positioned parallel to roads or at right angles to them. There is plenty of evidence to suggest that that rule also applied in Neolithic times, but it was immediately apparent from the two superimposed plans on the drawing board in front of me that the alignment of the two landscapes was significantly different.

If something as profoundly important as the orientation of a landscape can change, then that implies an equally profound change in the way the landscape was used, and indeed in the way people organised themselves to use it. My point is that we don't realign landscapes willy-nilly. Even stark modern agri-desert landscapes tend to follow the 'grain' of the pre-existing countryside. Nowadays, nobody would contemplate setting out the existing landscape afresh, from scratch. It would be pointless and horrendously expensive. But that is what appears to have happened in the period between the construction of our Neolithic house and the laying out of the Bronze Age ditched fields in 2500 BC.

Now for a word of caution. As archaeologists, we have to work with the bits and pieces that time bequeaths us. We're adept at reconstructing entire Roman inscriptions, such as gravestones, from fragments of just two letters. Or we can imaginatively reconstruct a house on the basis of four post-holes. Unfortunately, sometimes we get things wrong – as, for example, when I mistook a loomweight for a bit of daub. This business of landscape orientation was a case in point. Was it really wise to suggest something as radical as the wholesale reorganisation of a landscape on the basis of just one house? Was I seriously prepared to stand up at a conference and make the case before three hundred highly sceptical colleagues? I decided to wait for further proof. I had had the insight, but unfortunately modern archaeology expects more by way of evidence for such bright ideas.

The following season was spent excavating huge tracts of Bronze Age fields, together with their farms and droveways. It was exciting and rewarding work, but I was conscious that I had ceased to break new ground. But then, in archaeology, as in life, one cannot always be exploring virgin territory. Sometimes one has to pause and consolidate. When I returned to Canada for the winter I was rushed off my feet sorting through finds and preparing illustrations for the Second Fengate Report. I hadn't worked so hard for a long time. Consolidation can often be labour-intensive and time-consuming.

I returned to England for our fifth season of excavation in April 1975. It was to be one of the busiest I have ever experienced. By now, much pressure was being brought on me to clear land which the New Town authorities wanted to use for building factories. Fengate was starting to live up to its new name, the Eastern Industrial Area, and factories in this part of Peterborough would soon provide most of the employment for the city's rapidly expanding population. It was a case of dig or bust.

Early in the summer we exposed several more acres of Bronze Age fields, and then started work on a substantial Iron Age village, which was occupied between about 350 BC and into the early Roman period – say AD 150. The inhabitants had placed their hamlet on the edge of the regularly flooded land, close to a small stream known as the Cat's Water. Like many Iron Age sites in eastern England, the Cat's Water settlement was producing huge quantities of material, and we were all kept extremely busy.

The story of the next discovery in our quest begins towards the end of the excavation, when we were running out of time and energy. To make matters worse, money was also in short supply. Summer was rapidly turning to autumn, and quite soon the rain would start in earnest. For these and other reasons I was extremely keen to finish.

One morning, while doing the rounds through the various trenches, I came across our new principal site supervisor, David Cranstone, on his hands and knees trowelling away at a patch of pale silt. After several years I had learned a great deal about the natural subsoil at Fengate, and I prided myself on being able to distinguish man-made from natural features. It struck me at once that the patch Dave was trowelling was *not* a man-made feature. It looked very ordinary indeed:

maybe it was the filled-in hole left by the roots of an ancient tree that had blown over a few thousand years ago – who knows? Such things (we call them tree-throw pits) are not uncommon, and given the rush to finish the season's dig, I couldn't understand why David wanted to spend time digging one. I could think of many more urgent things that needed doing, but I managed to keep my irritation under wraps, consoling myself with the thought that he was bound to be doing something more constructive in a few hours' time.

That afternoon I passed through the trench for a second time, and Dave was still at it, trowelling steadily down through the silt patch. This was too much.

'Dave,' I said as calmly as I could manage, 'it's just another tree-throw pit. For Heaven's sake, man, you must have more important things to finish, haven't you?'

He seemed quite impervious to my exasperation. He didn't even look up when he spoke. He was completely wrapped up in his work.

'Calm down, Francis. It won't take long.'

I had been dismissed. More than a little surprised at Dave's off-hand reply, I continued on my way. I was not in the most sunny of tempers.

The following morning I was detained with the project's accountants in town, and did not arrive back on site until the afternoon. I almost exploded when I saw that Dave was still on his hands and knees in the same spot. I stormed across to his trench.

'For Christ's sake, Dave!'

He smiled up at me, holding a small flint blade on the palm of his hand. It glistened in the damp sunlight against his silt-stained skin.

I was staggered at his nerve. Small flint blades and other scraps of ancient flint-working debris frequently find their way into tree-throw pits through the action of earthworms, moles or other animals, so to find a flake on its own meant absolutely nothing. After a few minutes I was again dismissed, and this time I left with ill-concealed irritation. Out of the corner of my eye I could see other members of the team beginning to take an interest in what Dave was up to. I'm not noted for a quick temper, but I knew I was approaching the end of my fuse.

Throughout the whole of the next day, Thursday, I studiously avoided Dave's trench. By now it was quite deep, and I could only see the top of his head when he straightened up to empty a bucket of soil into his wheelbarrow.

By Friday we only had a week to finish the dig. In seven days' time the workmen would be arriving on site to start building factories. There would be a ghastly public row if we held them up, so I assembled the crew together in the Tea Hut and suggested we should work through the weekend to get things finished. Everyone nobly agreed, although a few bad-tempered looks went Dave's way. It was clear that I was not the only person who considered him to have taken temporary leave of his senses. That night Dave and his 'bloody great hole' featured prominently in our talk at the pub.

On my way to the site the next day I made up my mind that 'Dave's hole' had now become a major issue. Something had to be done about it, or else I'd look stupid in the eyes of the others. As is the way of these things, I had learned in the pub the previous evening that some of the younger members of the team thought I was losing control over my Principal Supervisor. It was ridiculous to fall out with a good friend like Dave over such a minor matter, but the crunch could not be avoided. It was him or me: site morale – something my mental antennae have always been quite well attuned to – was beginning to creak.

I was about to leave my shed to have the nose-to-nose confrontation I was dreading when there was a rap at the door. It opened, and Dave stood there, grinning hugely. I knew that look: it said 'I told you so!' in letters a yard high.

I have always tried to discourage the team from gathering around the scene of a new discovery – but so far, I have to admit, without much success. As Dave and I walked rapidly across the site, we saw that half a dozen folk had already congregated around his pit, and that others were coming to join them.

When we got there, I was amazed at the size 'Dave's hole' had grown to – he had certainly been hard at work. The bottom of the hole was flat, where Dave had been scraping off silt with his trowel. This smoothed, flat base gave the impression of still water with just the lightest of ripples – the marks left by the trowel. Towards one end of the pit, as if freed from an underwater necropolis, a human skull could be seen emerging. Parts of another, perhaps smaller, one were next to it. Several limb bones and a few vertebrae lay round about the two skulls, like grisly flotsam on the water's surface.

I have seen many burials, but it was hard not to be moved by the sight of this one. A question immediately came into my mind: what on earth had these poor people done that had led to such an ignomini- ous end, in an unmarked pit on the edge of the Fens? My archaeolo- gist's eye noted that the grave-pit was a large one, and it was soon apparent that it had been dug to contain more than just two skulls and a few loose bones. There had to be more bones or bodies.

After I had seen the skulls, Dave, with characteristic grace, tried to spare me the large slice of humble pie that was now my rightful lot; I ate it nonetheless, and in public. But how on earth had he known that that apparently unpromising patch of silt would turn out to be so exciting? When I ask him, as I still do whenever our paths cross, he simply shrugs his shoulders and smiles enigmatically. Whatever it was, something made him persist against the full force of my growing fury and the unconcealed scepticism of everyone around him. More- over, it was not as if he had a record of eccentric behaviour. Frankly, I can't explain it; nor, I suspect, can Dave.

We now confronted the practical problem that faced us. In theory there were just six and a bit days of excavation to go; but I knew that the discovery of what was probably a complex multiple burial had strengthened our hand enormously. Nobody, not even in those days, could simply have taken a bulldozer to human remains. I took the problem to the powers-that-be, and was eventually able to negotiate a three-week stay of execution that allowed us to excavate the contents of 'Dave's pit' properly. In the event, this required extraordinary care.

The two skulls that were first revealed belonged to a young woman, aged twenty-five to thirty, and a child (hers?), aged eight to twelve, whose bones had been placed higgledy-piggledy in a pile at one end of the pit. At the centre of the pit were the small bones of a younger child, aged three to four. The only complete skeleton was that of a young man, of about the same age as the woman. He had been buried on his side, with his legs drawn up to his stomach, as if crouching.

Like many burials, it was difficult to be certain of its age. We did know that the upper filling of the pit had been cut through by a farm ditch of the much later Cat's Water Iron Age settlement. That meant that the digging of the pit had to predate the ditch, which we knew was dug sometime around 200 BC. That was some help, but not a lot. The silt that had been thrown into the grave was a whitish pale-brown colour, and we knew that pale soils were often old. My guess was that the grave pit had been dug sometime in the Neolithic period. For all anyone knew, it could have been at the time the house we had found in 1972 was in use, around 3000 BC, or even earlier.

Our guessed date was proved triumphantly correct when Dave's meticulous excavation revealed how the unfortunate young man had died. Between his eighth and ninth ribs Dave revealed a beautifully made leaf-shaped flint arrowhead with its tip snapped off. Similar damage had been noted in Scandinavia on arrowheads that had been fired into hunted animals, so I reckoned that ours had probably lost its tip when it struck the rib bones. There could be little doubt: the young man had been shot with an arrow.

The discovery of what was then one of the earliest deliberate killings in Britain caused enormous public interest. Breaking with tradition, we decided not to remove the bones one by one and reassemble them for a museum display. Instead, we lifted the entire burial intact in two large blocks of gravel, which we consolidated in a type of liquid plastic (Polyvinyl acetate) and then transported to Peterborough Museum, where it now forms a central part of the prehistoric display. The arrowhead is still in place, undisturbed, exactly where we found it.

That year I returned to Toronto somewhat later than normal, because I was unable to arrange for over 20,000 pieces of pottery and probably half a tonne of animal bone to be transported across the Atlantic. Instead, we made arrangements with Peterborough Museum for space to store and study the finds. I took some key maps and plans with me, and several boxes of flints – tools and chippings – which I would study during the long, cold Canadian winter.

Back in my office at the Royal Ontario Museum, I started work on the complex plans of the Cat's Water Iron Age village. We had discovered over fifty round houses and huge numbers of pits, wells and other features, including several Iron Age graves. I had been

working through the plans for about a week when I found myself
looking at the sketches and plans of 'Dave's hole'. At the time these
looked far more inviting than the complexities of the later settlement,
so I decided to work on them first.

My initial concern was simple: did the burial pit have any connection with the rectangular house we'd dug in that hot summer, back
in 1972? There was only one way to find out for sure. I went to the
shelves and pulled down the large-scale map of Fengate on which I
had drawn the parallel droveway ditches of the fields that afternoon
when lying on the sitting-room carpet surrounded by aerial photos.
Subsequently I had added the rectangular house and anything else
important. I suppose you could call it my Master Plan.

It took me a few minutes to measure everything in, but when I
had finished I was rather disappointed: nothing seemed to line up. I
rolled the Master Plan up and was about to throw it back on the shelf
in frustration when I remembered two parallel ditches we had also
found in 1972. By rights, these should also be included on the Master
Plan. They were different from the 'main', Bronze Age parallel
droveway ditches, being altogether smaller and shallower, and we
found them over a kilometre 'inland' from the edge of the fen. Most
importantly, they had produced no finds other than a fragment of a
rare Neolithic polished axe made from Langdale stone.

I suppose I should have remembered to examine the alignment
of these smaller ditches when I was proof-reading the First Fengate
Report, but my jet-lagged brain failed me. This time I determined to
do better, and rolled the Master Plan out on my drawing board for
a second time. It took me a few minutes to plot the two shallow
ditches accurately, but when I had finished it was quite apparent that
their alignment was significantly different from that of the main
Bronze Age system. I was pleased that this shift in orientation showed
up so well, but for some reason I wasn't exactly surprised.

Then something clicked. The two shallow ditches were pointing
directly at both the Neolithic house and the multiple burial in 'Dave's
hole'. It was so obvious, I could hardly believe it. We now had three
quite separate sites on approximately the same general alignment, and
this alignment was significantly different from that of the Bronze
Age fields. My theory – that the pre-Bronze Age landscape was set

out on a significantly different alignment – was beginning to gain support. But could I be certain that the two shallow ditches were in fact Neolithic?

Happily for me, the site notes and archive for 1972 were still in Toronto. I went down into the museum basement, and when I had got all the papers and finds bags before me I began to sort through them. In 1972 we had opened several trenches, and the one in question was at Vicarage Farm. It sounds a peaceful rural idyll, but in reality it lay next to a Gas Board storage depot and the largest diesel-engine factory in Europe. Peaceful it was not.

The air photos of Vicarage Farm showed cropmarks of several large pits which had been cut into an unusual outcrop of limestone. After removing the topsoil we found, as is usually the case, that the aerial photos only revealed a small proportion of the features that were actually present below the ground. When we dug them we found that the pits were wells, and around them were all sorts of other features belonging to a small Iron Age village of about 500 to 100 BC. Like most such settlements, the features at Vicarage Farm yielded large quantities of pottery, bone and other debris.

Now, the two shallow ditches ran across part of the Iron Age settlement, yet they did not produce so much as a scrap of pottery. I'm certain that this could not possibly have been the case if they had been open when the Iron Age settlement was occupied. There would simply have been too much debris lying around the place, and some of it was bound to have been kicked into an open ditch by someone. By the same token, the ditches were unlikely to have been later than the settlement, otherwise debris would have found its way into them as residual finds lying around in the topsoil. Even the modern drainage ditches around the edges of the factory had residual Iron Age pottery in them. It was everywhere, and hard to avoid.

As if to clinch the matter, the only find from either of the two ditches was the fragment of a Neolithic polished stone Langdale axe. In the New Stone Age (which is what 'Neolithic' means) stone was the most important material for making edge-tools, such as axes. Some stone was much better for this purpose than others, and became much prized. Like many things we humans touch and cherish, there was a fine balance between beauty and utility. And the most beautiful stone of all was quarried high in the mountains of the Lake District, at a place called Great Langdale.

Langdale stone is hard, fine-grained and a subtle greyish-green in colour. It looks even better when polished to a silky sheen – and Neolithic axes were almost always patiently polished to a fine, smooth finish. As well as Langdale there were other so-called 'axe factory' sites in Britain, in Wales, Cornwall and elsewhere, and they all exported their products to distant parts of the country. A large number of Langdale axes were sent to communities on the other side of the country. Fengate, for example, is 175 miles south-east of Langdale. There seemed little doubt that the two shallow ditches were Neolithic – and probably Earlier Neolithic, too. I would guess they were dug well before 3000 BC.

As I've already mentioned, the rectangular house had produced many finds, including some rather unusual pieces. One of these was a large flake that had been deliberately removed – with a sharp blow – from a polished Langdale axe. Another was a beautifully-made and highly-polished jet bead. This wasn't a little bead – it was large enough to have just covered, say, the top joint of one's thumb. Jet is a shiny, coal-like material whose nearest source is the beautiful Yorkshire seaside town of Whitby, some 130 miles to the north of Fengate. In addition to these rare finds there was a lot of fine pottery and a remarkable collection of flint implements, including a most unusual and beautifully-made sickle blade in lustrous blue-black flint.

I returned upstairs from the basement and spread some of the finds from the rectangular house on my desk. They really were beautiful. Could they, in all truthfulness, have been cast aside as debris – mere rubbish, the sweepings off the kitchen floor? As I handled the large flake of Langdale stone, my doubts vanished. I was now certain that the rectangular building was not merely a house. It had to be a special place.

I must now take the story temporarily forward a few years. I completed the Fengate project in 1978, and spent the next two years writing the final two reports, which were published in 1980 and 1984. Part of my background research included a detailed survey of all previous excavations in or near Fengate. The last excavation to have happened before our campaign began was in 1968, at a place called Site 11.

The site was first spotted on an air photo, as a cropmark, and it looked a bit strange. It consisted of a straight-sided rectangular enclosure, defined by a continuous single ditch, with sharp corners. It measured about fifty by thirty metres, but there was no sign on the air photos of an entrance of any sort. This made me sit up and take notice. The excavations produced decorated pottery and flint tools in the distinctive style of the Early Bronze Age Beaker 'Culture'. In the brief report that appeared shortly after the dig, it was suggested that the enclosure and the pottery belonged together, and that the whole site was a small farmstead or settlement of some sort. This seemed a quite reasonable conclusion at the time, but when I came to re-examine the Site 11 report at the end of the Fengate project, I couldn't reconcile it with what we had found. It simply didn't fit in.

By now alignment and orientation were becoming something of an obsession with me. I checked the orientation of the Site 11 enclosure, and it bore no relationship at all to the Bronze Age fields in which it was supposed to sit. If the dating of either the fields or the enclosure was correct, they *had* to have been in use in the first few centuries of the second millennium BC. So how could they fail to share a common alignment? It didn't make sense.

This was something of a side-issue to my main work, the writing of two large reports, and I resolved to go back to the original site notes and records from 1968 to see if they would clear matters up for me. They did, but in a completely unexpected fashion. In one of the notebooks I came across an unpublished pre-excavation pencil sketch-plan. It was a good sketch-plan, and was annotated in an elegant italic hand. Subsequently it had been scratched out by, possibly, a different hand. The features shown in the initial sketch bore an uncanny resemblance to the first Bronze Age roundhouse we had excavated back in 1974. Everything was there: the front-door posts, the ring-gully eaves-drip gutter; even the alignment of the doorway was right. It was simply too good to have been invented.

When I examined the records further, it became clear that the Early Bronze Age Beaker pottery came from this house and from features, such as fireplaces, that may have been part of it. There was

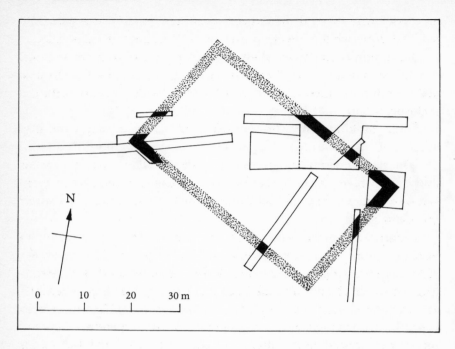

FIG 5   *Ground plan of Fengate Site 11, showing the position of*
archaeological trenches

no reason to suppose that the rectangular enclosure had anything to
do with the house at all. They could have been constructed centuries,
even millennia apart.

It felt good to have sorted this little problem out. But why didn't
I pursue the matter further? What about the rectangular enclosure,
for Heaven's sake? I suppose I was too keen to get back to the writing
of those two great volumes. But I had missed a trick. It was to be
another five years before the next piece in the jigsaw fell into place.

I was spending the weekend with the eminent authority on the
Neolithic period, Dr Ian Kinnes, at his house in Guildford. On the
dinner table before us were drawings of Neolithic pottery from Etton,
the site I was then digging and which I'll discuss later. The drawings
were annotated in Ian's elegant italic hand, and suddenly I
remembered the handwriting in the Site 11 notebook. Was Ian the

supervisor who made those notes, I asked. He was. It was a part-time job he'd done while he was a post-graduate student at Cambridge.

He couldn't remember why his sketch-plan had been crossed out, and he shared my view that if the structure was indeed a Bronze Age roundhouse, then it went with the later fields, and not with the enclosure.

I was thinking aloud. 'So that leaves the enclosure high and dry, I suppose?'

'Oh, no it doesn't,' he said. 'Quite the opposite. That house was always a problem. Take the house away, and you're left with a mortuary enclosure – like the ones that turned up the other day on air photos in Essex.'

An article about the Essex enclosures had recently appeared in an academic journal, so I was familiar with what he was talking about. Mortuary enclosures and structures were special places that were constructed in the Neolithic and Early Bronze Age to receive recently deceased corpses. By and large, they do not seem to have been used as permanent resting places, although burials are often found in them. Sometimes, indeed quite often, the enclosure takes the form of a surrounding wooden wall, or even a roofed building. More often than not, the original enclosure may become incorporated within a later burial mound, or barrow. In short, they are complicated sites and are probably best considered one at a time, as individuals.

As soon as I returned home, I unrolled my well-used Master Plan, which was now rather grubby and dog-eared. I had not added the Site 11 enclosure to it, as my team hadn't dug it. As I was drawing it in in its rightful place, I was immediately aware that its alignment precisely followed that of the 'house' and the pair of shallow ditches at Vicarage Farm. All four Neolithic sites appeared to process across the Fengate landscape in an orderly row, from north-east to south-west. It was quite extraordinary.

By this time I had come to the conclusion that the 'house' we had dug in 1972 was a mortuary structure, but without a body. Some mortuary structures, indeed most barrows as well, are thought deliberately to echo the houses of the living – as Houses of the Dead. Certainly the rich finds from the 'house' would be appropriate for a mortuary house.

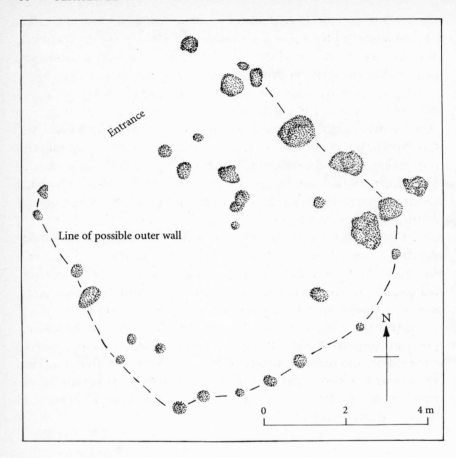

Entrance

Line of possible outer wall

N

0   2   4 m

FIG 6   *Ground plan of the Neolithic mortuary structure at Fengate discovered in 1997 by the Cambridge University archaeological team*

The latest piece of this jigsaw, which so far has taken over a quarter of a century to assemble, fell into place in July 1997. By this time the old way of doing research, in which a local team tried to grapple with the particular problems of a given region, had been replaced by the modern system of competitive tendering, where the lowest price wins. All too often this system produces half-digested results that are not adequately tied into the regional story. The work is done for money – and it shows. But in this case the project, at the edge of my earlier

Cat's Water excavation, was won by a team from Cambridge University, with which I have always been friendly. They did an excellent job, and kept me closely informed. However, this was a truly independent excavation – independent of me and my pet theories, that is.

The Cambridge team were digging at the extreme edge of the wet ground on a low gravel knoll, which reached out a short distance into the shallow waters where peat had begun to form around 2000 BC. On this knoll they found a rectangular arrangement of small pits and post-holes and a collection of finds which included big pieces of Neolithic pottery, but no animal bones. As with the 'house' I had dug twenty-four years previously, it would appear that the objects found in the ground were not a random selection of household debris, but gave every appearance of having been carefully selected. Quite independently, the Cambridge team interpreted their site as a mortuary structure. And when they came to plot its position on the map, lo and behold, it was orientated north-east to south-west; what is more, it lined up beautifully with the other four Neolithic sites.

It had taken nearly twenty-five years to uncover evidence to support my original theory. It was now clear that the landscape had changed its orientation sometime between four and five thousand years ago. But why? And what did it mean? Most important of all, why was there this emphasis on death, with a multiple burial and three mortuary structures?

CHAPTER FIVE

Gardens of Creation

MY QUEST INTO the lives of prehistoric people was taking me in unexpected directions – such as, for example, Death itself. I knew that I wanted to bring their world forward, into our time, but I was finding myself being drawn back further and further into theirs. It was as if I was the centre of a ghostly tug-o'-war. I felt they were leading my footsteps, holding my hand, like wise grandparents with a young child. Where, I wondered, were they going to take me next? The quest was now about to enter a philosophical, almost a mystical, stage.

I was facing some of the Big Questions of human existence. I knew full well that I could never do these Big Questions justice, because – like most of my colleagues – I simply don't possess the necessary philosophical background. Having said that, I feel it is arrogant in the extreme to dig up religious and mortuary sites without making at least some effort to understand what those places might have meant to the people who built them.

I should have realised that one cannot hope to understand the lives and deaths of ancient people – *any* people – if one chooses to ignore their history. By history I don't mean a dry account of a succession of archaeological 'cultures', or indeed of presidents, prime ministers, kings or queens. I mean history in the sense that we all understand it, as a series of stories about the past that provides us with an all-enveloping explanation of why and how we are here. The Battle of Britain affirms my reluctant feeling of patriotism, and tales of my grandmother – such as the time she was supposed to have wrestled a crocodile to its death somewhere in India – make me feel part of my family. We each have all sorts of histories: individual, family, local and national. All of these different stories comprise history as it affects our daily lives. Prehistoric people also had histories of this sort, and they were probably equally old, odd, at times jingoistic and improbable. But the huge time-span of archaeology has taught me that the individual events of history don't matter. It's the broad pattern and purpose behind them that tells a human story.

It began to be apparent to me that my interest in landscape development was fine as far as it went, but it was too impersonal. To see things from the perspective of once-living people, I had somehow to take myself back; and in such a way that I could imagine what their histories might have included. What, for example, might Bronze Age folk have seen as The Beginning? All societies need Creation myths. Today, if we are unbelievers we have the Big Bang, if we are Christian we have Adam and Eve in the Garden of Eden, and there are hundreds of others. Creation myths justify our place in the world and give us a sense of belonging.

The story of human beings is essentially one of continuous change and gradual development. There are few times when the whole world is suddenly turned on its head. One such occasion was undoubtedly the Industrial Revolution. In archaeological terms it was remarkably swift – a mere two to three hundred years at the outside – and nowadays there is hardly anywhere on the globe that has not felt its effects. Hidden within the Industrial Revolution were other revolutions, which could not have taken hold without the new context created by the industrial world – revolutions such as the Agricultural Revolution or the Medical Revolution. Currently we all have to grapple with a great-grandchild of the Industrial Revolution, the Information Revolution, which some of us have attempted to master with greater or lesser success.

There is something rather attractive about the idea of revolutions. They imply phenomena bigger than mere human beings. A revolution is something that happens despite our wishes; it has a momentum all of its own. There is more than a hint of the hand of God. So when in the 1930s someone suggested the notion of the wonderfully portentous-sounding Neolithic Revolution, the archaeological community greeted it with acclamation.

The Neolithic Revolution was quite simply the invention or beginnings of farming. From this came settled life, the production of pottery and a number of other typically Neolithic traits, such as the use of polishing, instead of chipping or flaking alone, to make stone axes. Communal tombs and villages also came with the Revolution. It was an attractive idea, and in certain parts of central and southern Europe the spread of the new Neolithic way of life must have seemed like a revolution.

I was taught about the Neolithic Revolution at university; then the first radiocarbon dates, those ultimate spoilsports of our subject, came along and showed that, as revolutions went, this one was slow (in Europe it lasted for about three millennia). Further dates then demonstrated that it happened at various times in different parts of the world, which makes the use of the singular word 'revolution' problematical.

The core of the original Neolithic Revolution concept was the invention of farming. This too was sometimes given a portentous-sounding definition – like, for example, the shift from hunter-gatherer to food producer. Unfortunately the basis of the 'Neolithic Revolution' was flawed. It assumed that a clear, distinct and rapidly-formed fault-line separated food producers from those who hunted and gathered. But it was not as simple as that.

Research into modern hunting-and-gathering communities has shown that they don't simply breeze through the woods plucking ripe mulberries when the mood takes them. Their way of life is far more rich and complex. For a start, they conserve and husband their resources. And it's not a big step from husbanded resources to animal husbandry – which of course is an important form of farming.

Another precept behind the Neolithic Revolution was the idea that hunter-gatherers spent most of their time and energies gathering nuts and berries or stalking elusive deer. Farmers, on the other hand, were thought to have the time to sit around the family hearth, recite myths and legends, and generally develop a rich and complex ideological world. I remember attending a lecture in Canada by the University of Toronto anthropologist Richard B. Lee, in which he turned this idea on its head. He showed that the Bushmen of the Kalahari Desert of southern Africa were so efficient at procuring their food that they had plenty of time to weave the richest of ideologies; the same can be said for the Aboriginal peoples of Australia. Meanwhile farmers had to spend wearisome hours guarding their crops and flocks, while in constant pain, unable to focus their thoughts, as dental caries ate into their teeth – a condition rare amongst hunting societies.

Research into the lives of hunting people has also shown that they conserve prey with great care. They encourage beasts to congregate in the same places, such as clearings made around watering-holes, so that the hunters are not forced to take part in long-distance stalking. The idea is to hunt efficiently and not to expend energy unnecessarily. The difference between encouraging wild animals regularly to enter a clearing, and actually farming your own domestic flocks, seems pretty minimal.

Large parts of lowland Britain were covered with forest after the retreat of the last Ice Age some twelve thousand years ago. We know this from the patient work of archaeological scientists over the past sixty or seventy years. In the 1930s and forties Sir Harry Godwin and other pioneers of pollen analysis were able to reconstruct past environments by identifying and counting prehistoric pollen grains preserved in lake beds and peat bogs. Their work was to inspire contemporary archaeologists and other environmental scientists, who then turned their attention to our subject.

One might reasonably ask how hard science can possibly help us investigate something as deeply rooted in the world of the imagination as a myth of creation. The answer is that archaeological science has become far more than a mere 'add-on' to conventional archaeology. Science, and most particularly environmental science, allows us to recreate the surroundings in which people lived. We have learned that past communities did not merely react to changes in their natural environment; they helped to cause changes, then modified the landscape and the way they lived within it once the changes had happened. We now know that this relationship between people and their landscapes was both subtle and complex. And we owe many of these insights to science.

Some archaeologists have acquired a full scientific training; they still see themselves first and foremost as archaeologists, but with specific scientific skills. Like any non-scientific archaeologist, such as myself, their main interest is in past *people*. Science is just a technique that allows them to approach this ultimate goal.

One of my oldest friends and closest colleagues, Charly French, is Canadian. He was a key member of the various teams I led from 1975 until 1989, and he wrote his doctoral thesis, for the Institute of Archaeology, London University, on the ancient environment of Fengate and the Peterborough region. In those days his main techniques were sediment and molluscan analysis, which perhaps need a few words of explanation.

Sir Harry Godwin showed how the analysis of preserved pollen grains could help recreate the numbers and types of plants that were growing in the past at any particular time. This general approach works well for other things too. The shells of molluscs, of which snails are the most commonly found, resist decay quite well and are often preserved in the ground. We're all familiar with large garden snails, a common species of which was introduced to Britain by the Romans as an edible snail. But there are also hundreds of other, much smaller snails which lurk in shady spots, in water, in ditches or even underground. Snails are fussy about the conditions they require.

The technique of molluscan analysis takes all snails, great and small, from a sample of ancient soil and uses the 'fussiness' of the individual species to draw a picture of conditions in the past. So if you find species of snails that like it wet alongside those that like it dry, you can reasonably assume that the local environment was regularly flooded, but dried out in hot seasons. Unlike pollen analysis, which receives pollen grains from miles away, molluscan analysis paints on a smaller canvas; but sometimes the pictures can be remarkably accurate.

Charly's other skill in our early days together was sediment analysis. This is a geological technique which examines the physical composition of a soil or sediment. The size range of particles within a sample can tell how it was formed: whether, for example, it was laid down by flooding water, or whether it washed down the side of a hill. In the Fens hill-wash is rare, but thick layers of water-borne clay, known as alluvium, are crucially important. They blanket the ground surface, enriching and building up the topsoil beneath. After many years, alluvial deposits can accumulate to massive thickness, and their presence on the surface protects archaeological features buried beneath them from damage by modern intensive farming. Although it is sticky, horrid stuff to walk over, Fenland archaeologists have grown to love alluvium.

Charly's most recently acquired technique bids fair to be the most important. It has a daunting name: soil micromorphology (known as 'micromorph' for short). It takes time to prepare micromorph samples, and it takes both time and knowledge to interpret them. But the results are well worth the effort. Let's say we discover a layer of Bronze Age garden soil buried below a thick layer of clay alluvium. We are curious about this soil, and we want to know how it formed and was used. Was it ploughed or dug? Or did it carry pasture? Or perhaps it formed in the deep shade of the forest? To find answers to such questions, Charly takes a block of this soil about the size of half a brick, and carefully labels the top and bottom. In the laboratory he lets the block dry and then soaks it in a clear, varnish-like, Polyvinyl acetate (PVA) liquid. Once the PVA has penetrated to the centre of the block, he removes it and sets it aside to dry. He then cuts the block into slices, rather like a loaf of bread. Next he selects a good slice and starts to grind it down, and down, and down, until eventually it is thinner than paper, so thin that light can readily pass through it. He then transfers this thin section, as it is termed, to the microscope.

The structure of soil is complex, and holds within it the story of its origins, growth and development. In some respects, it's like a living thing. Soil scientists, such as Charly, who specialise in micromorph have examined a variety of modern soils from known sources, such as ploughed fields or woodland. By comparing the microscopic structure of the ancient soil with that of its modern counterpart, it's possible to reconstruct its history with a great deal of accuracy.

The evidence provided by Charly and his soil micromorph will play an important role in our story. Not only can he tell how soils (or other archaeological deposits such as trampled earth floors) formed, he can also spot when ditches, for example, have been deliberately filled in. On Fenland sites, stone is hard to come by and often turf cut from grass fields was used as a substitute in walls and buildings. Charly's technique can spot cut turves, recognise ground from which turf has been cut, and even spot when a turf has been stacked in the ground upside down.

One final point about Charly: he is also a first-rate excavation director in his own right. This powerful combination of science and good old-fashioned archaeological expertise has enabled him to make major insights into ancient life, particularly when it comes to the reconstruction of detail in the ceremonial use of sites like barrows (burial mounds). Or indeed timber mortuary structures.

One of the big issues in European prehistory is, and probably always will be, the clearance of the primeval post-Ice Age forests for farming. How did it happen, and when did it happen? In the case of Britain and Atlantic Europe, the most likely answer is that it happened at different times, in different places. In other words, it was a piecemeal process.

We have noted that hunting groups make clearings in the forest, around water holes. As well as encouraging their prey to use these areas regularly, they allow access to the water, encourage grass growth and provide a clearer field of fire for arrows or spears. These clearings are, in effect, fields within the forest. But few hunting-and-gathering people remain static. By and large the available sources of food tend to shift with the changing seasons. So hunting may be better in hilly country during the summer, but in winter it's time to return to the river valley for fish. The movement of modern hunter-gatherers is never random. So far as we know there have never been true nomads, who wander the surface of this globe unfettered. Everyone, it would seem, follows a route of some sort. In other words, communities have their own territories; humans, like birds, dogs and most other animals, are territorial beasts. As I write, I can see two male blackbirds trying to settle a territorial dispute. They both want to control the path leading to my front door. The two birds perform their little leaps and dances – and to my astonishment I'm suddenly aware that I'm supporting the bird who is defending the territory nearest my office window, against the intruder from outside. I've no reason whatsoever to support one particular bird over another; but I do, instinctively and irrationally – because, of course, I'm a territorial animal too.

Human territories are 'nested' in a hierarchy of holdings. In modern England, which is based on the Anglo-Saxon world, the political map is divided into parishes, districts, counties etc. This is reflected in the settlement pattern, where we find farms, villages, towns, cities and so on. Other countries have broadly similar systems, but with different names. Pre-industrial societies could be much more flexible. Thus the hilly district of a particular region might have been the territory of a hunting group in the summer, but was taken over by reindeer herders in the winter. Both groups regarded it as their territory, but only at the mutually agreed time of year.

Like most archaeologists, I was happy to accept the idea that the gradual felling of the primeval forest for farming happened as a series of widely separated isolated clearances that simply grew and grew. But there are problems with such a view. At what point in the seasonal round did the system stop? How did all movement suddenly freeze? To explain a complete change of this sort one *has* to suggest a wholesale movement of new people into any given area. This may possibly apply to the great plains of central Europe, but I'm convinced it doesn't apply to Britain, Scandinavia and Atlantic Europe. So what was going on?

Let's take Britain, and most probably large areas of north-western Europe too. The British Isles have a wet, oceanic climate, with warm winters and cool summers. These are ideal conditions for growing grass – hence William Blake's 'green and pleasant land'. The more I look at the archaeological evidence, the more convinced I become that the first farming in Britain was livestock farming. Pigs would help clear trees and scrub as they snuffled their way through the woods; cattle would graze the taller, coarser grass; and sheep would clip the remaining grass to a fine lawn-like texture.

We have already seen that it would have been a relatively small step to move from the managed hunting of, say, red or roe deer to the keeping of farm animals, so I see no reason to suppose that new populations arrived in Britain around 5000 BC, bringing with them the Neolithic Revolution. New animals certainly had to be introduced: domestic cattle, sheep, goats and perhaps pigs (although wild boar were native), but these few new arrivals hardly constitute an invasion. A Dutch colleague, Professor Leendert Louwe-Kooijmans, has shown that there must have been continuing contact between the east of England and Holland in the third millennium BC, and I can think of no practical reason why animals could not have been shipped across the Channel around 5000 BC. Back in 1969 the archaeologist Humphrey Case considered the types of boats that might have been available to make such a crossing, and concluded that it would have been perfectly feasible. Whether it was feasible or not, the fact remains that they did it.

If we accept this idea of the gradual adoption of farming by a population of hunter-gatherers, we must also accept that farming was taken up by a population that was mobile. If one could somehow take an aerial time-lapse film of the British Isles in the centuries after 5000 BC it would resemble the swirling water seen through the window of a washing machine: cycles within cycles, groups of people flowing round and round the landscape in a complex but pre-ordained fashion. But there's a snag: this vision of Early Neolithic Britain is difficult to prove archaeologically.

Some human activities become more archaeologically 'visible' than others. Anything that involves, for example, the repeated use or dis-carding of pottery or flint – materials that are almost indestructible – will leave some archaeological trace. But the size and clarity of the trace will depend greatly on whether the activity happens in the same place, or at many spots across the landscape. It's much easier to identify flint or pottery at one concentrated spot on the ground surface than the same quantity of material spread across a parish. Another factor affecting visibility is sheer quantity: a large population produces a proportionately larger amount of waste than a small one. It also helps if the pottery being discarded is hard, well fired, and resistant to attack by the natural humic acids that are present in the topsoil.

The earliest pottery in Britain, and in most of Europe too, was introduced in the Neolithic. It was a time when people had only just mastered the complex technology lying behind the control of fire, so the pottery they produced was often unevenly, or under-, fired. Frequently, material such as ground-up shell was added to the clay to make it fire better; and also, it has recently been suggested, to make it more water-tight. Shell, being calcareous, is susceptible to acid attack.

So if we add the three complications of a small population, a mobile population and soft, shell-gritted pottery together, it is not at all surprising that there is little direct archaeological evidence for the earliest Neolithic in Britain.

Quite recently it occurred to me that I already possessed a clue as to how the earliest Neolithic landscape in Britain was formed. I had just finished reading Julian Thomas's brilliant book *Rethinking the Neolithic*, which was published in 1991. He had bemoaned the invisibility of the fifth millennium B C, and he attributed it, as I do, to the three 'visibility' factors I've just mentioned. So far so good. But then I thought: 'This is mad. I've been digging one of the earliest landscapes in Britain. It's groaning with Neolithic archaeology, and although none of it belongs in the "invisible" fifth millennium B C, surely some trace of earlier times must survive there somewhere.'

Suddenly, for some reason my attention was arrested by the reflection, in a framed picture on the wall, of something outside – maybe it was a passing white van or car. Anyhow, it left me looking at the picture, which was a coloured reprint of an early nineteenth-century, pre-drainage map of Whittlesey Mere, the largest body of freshwater in England, prior to its drainage in 1852. It's decorative, it didn't cost more than a few pennies, and I'm fond of it.

After looking at the map on the wall, I opened a modern map of the area, and started to compare the fields of today with the situation before the mere was drained. I still don't know why I did it – just out of idle curiosity, I suppose. The modern map had lost the exact outline of the mere's edge, but its shape was nonetheless perfectly clear from the layout of modern ditches, roads and dykes. So it was still there, but at the same time it was not there – like a ghostly presence in the landscape, a kind of negative image. No sooner had this thought struck me than I realised that the same 'ghost' principle applied to that strange line of three Neolithic mortuary structures at Fengate, the multiple burial and the two shallow ditches at Vicarage Farm. Surely they too were the ghosts of something? But what?

The clue lay in those two shallow ditches at Vicarage Farm, which up to now I have neglected somewhat. They looked like some of the later, Bronze Age, droveway ditches, which we had been able to prove were indeed droveways by using a technique known as phosphate analysis. The principle is simple: animal dung is rich in phosphate, and if the ground conditions are right, the phosphate locks itself into the chemical structure of the soil. Years, centuries, even millennia later, one can chemically measure the background level of soil phosphate and compare it with areas where animals have been housed or penned.

The results will show greatly enhanced phosphate levels anywhere animals were kept.

We did phosphate tests along the Bronze Age droveways, and to our delight the levels were well above the background level of the fields round about. This suggested that there were sufficient animals present to break through the grass cover and stir the soil into a good, rich, smelly pudding – to use an old word, a 'piss-mire'.

'Could it be,' I thought, 'that the line of separate sites was actually a "ghost" left from the origins of the Neolithic landscape? Could it be that this long line of early sites reflected the way the earliest farmed landscape on the site was formed?' Maybe the primeval forest wasn't removed by enlarging isolated clearings, as the conventional wisdom has it. This would make sense if the population of people and animals was mobile, and not static – as the 'isolated clearing' theory of forest clearance would have us believe.

Maybe the trees were cleared along seasonal migration routes through the forest? To mark those trails, and to claim them for a particular community, it would be perfectly natural to construct way-side shrines at key points along the route. And one of the key points simply had to be where the trail met the edge of the wetter ground. Maybe, as the travellers and their animals paused before they embarked on the hazardous journey into the huge pastures of the open Fen, they sought blessings from the spirits of the ancestors, who resided in the stillness within the mortuary houses.

It seemed to me that a dynamic pattern of land clearance and landscape development fitted the available evidence better than a static model. So instead of clearings enlarging, eventually to meet up with other clearings, it might be more accurate to think of narrow passages becoming broad corridors and then, after perhaps one or two millennia, these corridors growing into self-contained landscapes. This view of the clearance of the forest also acknowledges the fact that even as long ago as 5000 BC people had populated the landscape with a rich set of myths and legends. And many of these would have had roots in previous millennia, when people gained their livelihood from hunting and gathering.

The more I thought about it, the more the idea appealed to me. The notion that sites to do with death, such as barrows and mortuary structures, must also play a crucial role in the world of the living was important. These sites existed to serve the living in a wealth of complex ways that tell us an enormous amount about the people who used them – and the way they viewed the parallel worlds around, above and below. They served the living by way of their ancestors, who moved in the parallel world where the mysteries of life were ordered. How else could representations be made to the beings who controlled such key issues as disease, childbirth, weather and the recurrence of the seasons? Prehistoric barrows and mortuary structures were far more than mere memorials. They were not in the least like modern gravestones, which are mute testimonies to a departed soul. They were a means of communicating with the higher forces that played a key role in the management of the landscape and people's daily lives.

The clearance of large tracts of countryside in the Neolithic and Bronze Ages was an extraordinary achievement, with far-reaching consequences for European society. The onset of the Neolithic was not a revolution, but the period did alter the look and feel of the landscape beyond all recognition. Modern archaeologists such as Julian Thomas have pointed out that many of the items found on Neolithic sites express in a symbolic way that mankind had acquired a new control of his surroundings. Pits and ditches were dug and then filled with a selection of animal bones. On many Neolithic sites the bones of wild animals, which we know were abundant at the time, were deliberately excluded from these pits in favour of those of farm animals. This may have been a statement of intention: perhaps Neolithic folk *wanted* to control the landscape, but were having trouble doing so.

Human beings are good at sidestepping the reality of their own situation in this way. In the Christian Church, for example, bodies are buried without grave-goods of any sort, because we are taught that all men and women are equal in the eyes of God. That's fine; but if you want to see a really potent symbol of the English class system in action, visit a country parish church at Christmas. The expensive four-wheel drives in the car park tell a different story. The lonely corpse in the coffin expresses our view of the world as we would wish it to be, not as it actually is. It's important to remember this when one is trying to understand burial rites in the past. What we are seeing in a Bronze Age grave is what people wanted others (and thereby us) to see. It is not necessarily what one would have witnessed, had one been a time-travelling anthropologist, five thousand years ago. It's easy to be hopelessly naïve in archaeology. Nothing is ever what it seems.

Having spent many years digging Neolithic religious and ceremonial sites, I find it hard to avoid the conclusion that Neolithic people seemed to delight in their 'Neolithic-ness'. Everywhere are the expressions of the new farming way of life: domestic animal bones, corn-grinding stones, pottery, polished stone axes. In a few generations the first farmers had changed the landscape, and in effect they had created their own world. It seems to me natural indeed for their Creation myth to be about just that: the creation of the Neolithic era.

There's one final point to make, and it concerns those two landscapes at Fengate: first, the long line of Neolithic sites, and second, the fields and droveways of the later, Bronze Age, system. They are indeed different landscapes, not just similar ones that happened to have been set out on different alignments. The earlier landscape was formed when the neighbouring Fens were themselves beginning to form. It is a landscape that expresses movement, not static settlement. In Earlier Neolithic times there was abundant land, and little pressure on grazing or other natural resources. I see this landscape as a product of a simpler age, when there was less to do and fewer mouths to feed.

The later landscape is different. It is highly organised, even regimented. There was pressure on winter grazing and the nearby Fens were beginning to flood with worrying frequency. We will see in future chapters how the powers of the ancestors were called upon to prevent disputes over access to ever-scarcer grazing and, more important still, to combat the relentless natural rise of the waters. Sadly, it was to prove a hopeless task.

CHAPTER SIX

Ritual Landscapes

I'M AFRAID I do not believe in a comfortable prehistoric Britain, where long-haired maidens plucked Celtic harps and bards intoned sagas rooted in the wisdom of the Earth and the Ages. I leave that sort of stuff to writers of fantasy. Life in the past, like life in the present, was built around oneself and one's relationships with other people. Viewed from a non-personal standpoint it revolved around families and the need to eat and travel, around competition for power or authority, and the rule of law. The worlds of myth and ideology existed within that mundane social context, and they formed an integral part of it. Indeed, the two were inseparable. But it was a hard world, and I can see no place there for the romantic visions of the Celtic Twilight – which owe much to our own time, and nothing to prehistory. The more we learn, the more apparent it is that the prehistoric concept of the next world was rooted in the realities of this one. The two must have reflected each other in some way. I do not believe that they could have incorporated alien concepts whose origins lie in Western culture – in, for example, the writings of Rousseau and the early Romantics. Whatever else prehistoric life was, it was no rural idyll. Nor were the people of prehistory Noble Savages.

Prehistoric religious sites are indeed strange and mysterious. Nobody could walk past the Stones of Stenness, in Orkney, or the Rudston Monolith, in a rural churchyard in Yorkshire, or the great chambered tombs of the Boyne Valley in Ireland, without experiencing a feeling of awe. There has always been a magic to these places; but I believe strongly that knowledge enhances a sense of wonder; it does not detract from it. Ignorance – and worse, deliberate ignorance – fosters superstition and narrow-mindedness. As archaeologists we can make one major contribution towards understanding sites like these better. We can set them in context.

I must now briefly depart from the personal exploration of prehistoric religion to place our quest within a broader setting. To do this I have chosen perhaps the three best-known religious monuments of prehistoric western Europe: Stonehenge, Avebury and Carnac. They all share one thing in common: the movement and erection of massive stones. But we will not just ponder the great stones, most of which were erected in the latter stages of each site's development. Instead, I want to take a wider perspective and examine the history of each place in its landscape setting. Only in that way do we stand any chance of unravelling some of the mysteries that surround them.

The first point to make is that none of these great constructions of the past sits in isolation. All are surrounded by dozens – hundreds even – of smaller monuments, including barrows of all sorts, henges and the like. These areas, packed full of Neolithic and Bronze Age religious shrines, have been termed 'ritual landscapes' by archaeologists. The second point is that ritual landscapes are found in many other places in Britain and mainland Europe. In some of these, such as the Orkney Islands or the Boyne valley in Ireland, there are stone-built sites that rival the three I have chosen in magnificence. In others, such as the Welland valley, a few miles north of Fengate, there is no suitable local source of stone, so the sites were built from earth and timber. These latter landscapes look spectacular from the air, but on the ground there is little to see – until, that is, you start to excavate. That, however, will be the topic of the next chapter.

I have always found Avebury the most magical of places. To my mind it is far more spectacular than Stonehenge, and it is constructed on an altogether grander scale. The best-known part of the ritual landscape around Avebury is the great henge itself. It's surrounded by trees and is set in the rolling countryside of the Marlborough Downs, not far from Devizes, in Wiltshire. To me, Avebury is at its stark best in the winter, in low light, with the trees bare.

The great henge consists of a huge, roughly circular ditch with a high grassy bank around the outside. This encloses an area of 28.5 acres (11.5 hectares). The ditch is broached by four entranceways, aligned very approximately on the cardinal points of the compass.

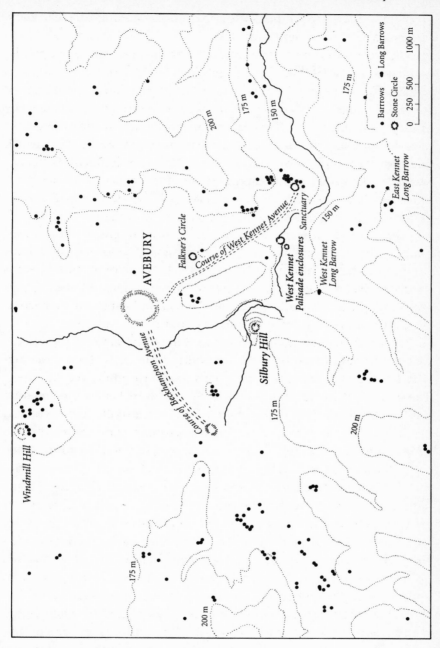

FIG 7   *The main features of the Avebury ritual landscape*

Near the inner edge of the ditch is a great circle of massive upright sarsen stones. At the centre were two smaller circles of stones, one of which is known as the Cove. Today, right at the centre is a small hamlet, complete with its own pub.

Recently there have been some major developments in our understanding of this ritual landscape's development. These have happened as a result of meticulous excavation, and go to show how important it is that research should continue. Whenever it stops, the site in question 'fossilises' and its importance seems to diminish. Of course research does not necessarily require large-scale open-area excavation. Often very small trenches, or close study of air photos, will reveal exciting new discoveries.

The origins of the Avebury ritual landscape lie outside the great henge itself, on a neighbouring hill known as Windmill Hill. Windmill Hill is extremely well-known to students of archaeology, and gave its name to one of those Earlier Neolithic 'cultures' that I learned about at university. It also gave its name to a style of rather plain and unexciting Earlier Neolithic pottery.

The site was first excavated between 1925 and 1939 by Alexander Keiller, of Dundee Marmalade fame. In August 1923 it was decided that the hill was going to have a Marconi radio mast erected on it. The archaeological world was outraged, and Keiller and his millions bought Windmill Hill for the nation; but by then the mast idea had been cancelled. This left Keiller in possession of one of the key sites of British prehistory. Slightly later, he purchased Avebury as well, and the estate now belongs to the National Trust. Keiller was a remarkable man: an archaeological philanthropist. Although he was himself an 'amateur', he could afford to buy the services of some of the best archaeologists of his time.

Windmill Hill is perhaps the best-known site of its type in Europe. In plan, it consists of a triple ditched enclosure which was placed slightly off-centre at the top of the hill. When viewed from the air it appears round. Its diameter averages four hundred metres, and its three concentric ditches are broached by over seventy gaps. The number of these gaps, or causeways, have given this class of site the name 'causewayed enclosures'. From the air these strange discontinuous, interrupted ditches resemble giant strings of sausages.

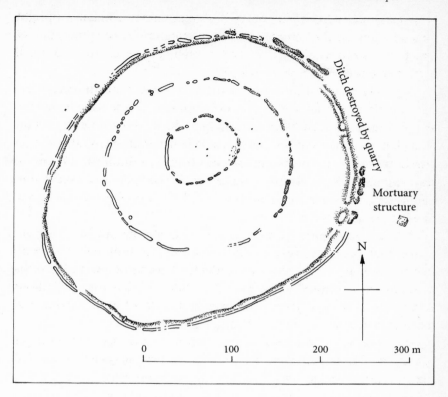

Ditch destroyed by quarry

Mortuary structure

N

| 0 | 100 | 200 | 300 m |

FIG 8   *Ground plan of the causewayed ditches at Windmill Hill, Avebury*

Alexander Keiller's excavations were published in 1965 by Isobel Smith, a distinguished Neolithic scholar and the curator of Keiller's museum in Avebury, in a superb report which pulled together all that was then known about the Avebury ritual landscape. Like all important research it stimulated new work, and the Avebury area has recently been the scene of much excavation and new survey projects. Recently Windmill Hill was re-examined by a team from University College, Cardiff, directed by Alasdair Whittle. Alasdair's work is thorough, but it is also imaginative, and he makes much use of anthropology and the study of modern tribal societies. I first met him in the 1970s, when his team were working on a famous Neolithic site in the Fens. Then he transferred his attentions further west, and his discoveries in the Avebury area have been extraordinary.

Alasdair has re-examined Keiller's original results, and he also carried out a small excavation in 1988. He showed that Windmill Hill, which was wooded in Earlier Neolithic times, was probably a special place before construction of the causewayed enclosure began in 3500 BC – although it is difficult to pin down the pre-Neolithic evidence. As we will see in the case of Etton, hunter-gatherer communities did not generally dig holes in their religious sites – which makes life for archaeologists very difficult. But Alasdair was able to show that the area enclosed by the three ditches was used in a carefully structured way: different spaces would have had different meanings to different people, and these meanings seem to have changed or perhaps 'drifted' through time.

We will examine many of these issues when we consider the causewayed enclosure at Etton. For the time being, it's enough to note that the two sites, although widely separated, have an extraordinary number of points in common; when I read Alasdair's report I had the eerie feeling that I was reading about my own work at Etton, although we had excavated the two sites at different times and entirely independently. The two causewayed enclosures had far more in common than did the later sites and monuments – the henges, barrows and processional avenues – which subsequently appeared in their respective ritual landscapes. A process of regional divergence seems to gave gathered pace in Britain from about 3500 BC.

This was quite fascinating. I can only explain it as the emergence and development of separate and distinctive local identities, which by the end of the Iron Age – nearly three and a half millennia later – emerged in the form of regional kingdoms and rulers. The best-known of these regional royals was the Icenian Queen Boudica. Cunobelin, king of the large tribal kingdom the Catuvellauni, ruled over most of southern East Anglia. He is best-known as Old King Cole, in the nursery rhyme. These, and their various feuding relations, were the rulers with whom Julius Caesar and other Roman generals negotiated (and battled) in the centuries before and after the birth of Christ. The process whereby regions acquired their own distinctive identity was of fundamental importance, and led to the nebulous archaeological sub-groups or cultures of the Neolithic becoming the coherent southern British kingdoms encountered by Caesar in his expeditions to Britain in 55 and 54 B C. Inevitably attention is concentrated on the last two millennia of our history, whereas we tend to forget that changes of comparable importance also took place in the last three thousand years B C.

One might suppose that these processes of change were gradual and progressive. But when you examine the origin and evolution of ritual landscapes, you gain quite the contrary impression. The component religious sites and monuments around Stonehenge and Avebury arrived, evolved and were abandoned with extraordinary rapidity. The same can be said of the timber-built barrows, henges and shrines of eastern England.

A new series of radiocarbon dates have shown that the landscape around Avebury was a major religious centre for a full millennium and a half, starting at Windmill Hill before 3500 B C and ending after 2000 B C with the erection of the standing stones. There is also evidence to suggest that the primeval woodland began to be cleared of trees at around 4000 B C. The great central henge was approached by two processional avenues, marked out with standing stones and side-ditches. One, the Beckhampton Avenue, which approaches Avebury from the west, was rediscovered recently. The West Kennet Avenue approaches from the south-east and was first traced by Alexander Keiller in the 1930s.

There is something about Avebury which fosters archaeological loyalty, and Mike Pitts is a case in point. For many years he ran Stones, a superb vegetarian restaurant at the heart of the village, but he is also a professional archaeologist and writer with a special interest in the people who dug at both Avebury and Stonehenge. He came across a fascinating story of personal and professional jealousy when he examined the notes and diaries of excavators in the Avebury area in the 1930s (he gives an account of these goings-on in his excellent book *Hengeworld*).

Mike directed an excavation at the Sanctuary as part of his research for *Hengeworld*. The Sanctuary today is a rather bleak spot, on a hill beside a busy road, but in prehistory it formed the terminus of the eastern, West Kennet Avenue leading to Avebury. So it was a site of some importance back in 3000 B C. I remember learning as a student that the Sanctuary consisted of a succession of three post-built round timber buildings, which were finally replaced at the beginning of the Bronze Age by a circle of standing stones. But this simple interpretation wasn't borne out by the diaries and records of the archaeologists who actually did the work. Mike and his team excavated to learn what really *had* gone on.

What they found has astonished the archaeological world. Instead of three buildings, they found a forest of posts and pits. Posts were first erected and then pulled out of the ground. Pits were dug and filled. It was as if the repeated erecting, digging and filling were important in their own right. So the timber phase of the Sanctuary was never completed in the way that, say, a Christian church is completed, consecrated, and then used for worship. In the case of the Sanctuary, like Windmill Hill before it, its protracted construction *was* its use.

As I said, this discovery amazed the archaeological world; but, in fairness, not all of it. Some of us were surprised that this pattern of continuous, seemingly pointless digging, filling and renewal had not been found previously in or around the great sites of Wessex, as it had been known about for many years in the non-stone-using areas of eastern England and the Thames valley. So although the outward form of prehistoric religious sites on either side of the country may have been different, many of the rites that took place within them must have been fundamentally the same.

The westerly avenue into Avebury was recorded in some detail by early antiquarians, and this early work was rediscovered and reassessed as late as 1991 by a team of archaeologists and historians led by Professor Ucko, of London University. Their reassessment stressed the longevity and complexity of the various components of the Avebury ritual landscape, and most particularly highlighted the documentary evidence for the Beckhampton Avenue. As part of their project they carried out a geophysical survey to find the Avenue, but sadly this proved inconclusive.

Archaeological geophysics is a field which has recently grown in importance, with the introduction of miniaturised electronics and portable computers; these are able to process data rapidly and produce instant accurate printouts, which are very useful when you are trying to decide precisely where to place your trenches. There are various techniques of geophysical survey, but all involve the detection of different textures of archaeological layers below the ground. Some techniques involve the use of ground-penetrating radar, others are based on magnetometry, or the measurement of below-ground resistance to the passage of an electrical charge. Normally they involve one or two people who walk across the surface of the ancient site with hand-held scanners, or a series of lightweight probes. So far as is known, none of these techniques has any effect on buried archaeological remains.

There are drawbacks to geophysics, as there are to any other technique of survey. Small features may sometimes be missed, and I have known very convincing, but sadly non-existent, 'ghost' features appear. Happily such things are rare, because mistakes can prove expensive. However, the main obstacles to geophysics are high levels of water in the ground and thick surface accumulations of river-borne clay alluvium. In my experience, if an archaeological feature is too deeply buried to show up as a cropmark on an aerial photograph, it probably won't be revealed by geophysics either. It should go without saying that these two drawbacks are particularly significant to those of us who work in and around the Fens.

In 1997 a cropmark appeared in a field about a kilometre west of Avebury. This field – Longstones field – is remarkable for two large standing stones, known locally as Adam and Eve. The cropmark was of an oval ditched enclosure, measuring about 100 by 140 metres, one side of which had been straightened. A team of archaeologists from the universities of Newport, Southampton and Leicester was called in to investigate, and they confirmed that the straightened side of the enclosure lined up well with the possible course of the Beckhampton Avenue. They then carried out another geophysical survey and discovered the remains of six huge standing stones that had been buried or destroyed in the Middle Ages and as late as the eighteenth century. These stone sockets were arranged in pairs and were spaced at precisely the same distance apart as the known stones that lined the West Kennet Avenue, to the east.

When the oval enclosure was excavated it was found that the stone sockets entered it by way of an unusually wide entrance, and that the enclosure ditch was dug in short segments which hadn't been joined together very tidily. It resembled a causewayed enclosure ditch, but was not as large and didn't have neatly defined causeways between the different segments. But it produced Early Neolithic pottery, similar to that found at Windmill Hill nearby, which indicated that the stones of the Avenue were actually later than the enclosure at its end. So the enclosure had been abandoned, and its ditch had become largely filled with soil. But the memory of its former importance must have lingered on. And what about Adam and Eve? Eve fits well with the alignment of the Avenue, but Adam is set at a distance from it. William Stukely, the great eighteenth-century antiquarian (who was born in the Fens at Holbeach), mapped the position of the Beckhampton Avenue stones with remarkable precision, and he shows a large stone standing in Adam's position. Around it, on his plan, is a group of stones forming a small cove. I would guess that cove will be the next thing the team looks for.

Silbury Hill is almost as famous as Avebury itself. It is the largest man-made mound in ancient Europe and is located just over a kilometre south of the great henge. It has intrigued people for centuries, and a shaft was dug into it from the top in 1776–77, but it failed to reveal anything exciting. The last major effort to get to the heart of Silbury Hill was made in 1968 by BBC Television, who organised a tunnel at the foot of the mound through to its centre. The work was supervised by archaeologists and the tunnel was dug by a team of Welsh miners. Again, nothing exciting – in television terms – was found: no grinning skulls, gold sarcophagus or evidence of even a humble cremation. So they made the most of what they had, which wasn't much. A great deal of fuss was made about the discovery of the remains of a winged ant (*Myrmica rubra*); these insects only fly in July and August, and a rapt audience was told that there was now good evidence of the time of year the huge mound was built. But sadly, winged ants' nests are often surrounded by dead ants, and the fragments from the mound could just as readily have been dumped there from an old nest on the surface of the ground that was quarried for chalk.

The construction of the immense mound took many centuries, starting from before 2800 to 2500 BC and most probably ending before 2000 BC. At the centre of the mound was a core, mainly of turves cut from open, grazed grassland. The main bulk of the hill was built up from chalk which was quarried from the ditch at the base of the mound. Both mound and ditch were fashioned to give the impression that the hill was rather bigger than it actually was. This impression was cleverly heightened by positioning the mound on a low natural spur, then cutting the quarry ditch around it.

There does not appear to have been a central burial. So what was the purpose of this immense mound? Again, we are witnessing long-term and uninterrupted work, as Mike Pitts observed at the Sanctuary. So the building of the hill may also have served its own purpose, of bringing people together in a structured, organised fashion. I have long held the view that Silbury Hill was perhaps a symbolic tamed, or controlled, Windmill Hill (I mean the hill, not the causewayed enclosure on it), which was, after all, the start of the religious explosion around Avebury. Unfortunately that's just an idea, and probably not something that could ever be proven.

It might be supposed that after more than two hundred years of archaeological and antiquarian activity, no large significant site remained to be discovered in the environs of Avebury. But in 1950 the greatest aerial archaeologist of them all, J.K. St Joseph, photographed two large timber-walled enclosures near the river Kennet, just 1.5 kilometres south of Avebury. The walls were mainly made from oak. The enclosures were partitioned by radial wood walls and enclosed several smaller circles of posts. Again the excavator Alasdair Whittle found evidence for repeated episodes of construction and destruction. Alasdair and I agree that the West Kennet enclosures mark a new departure in religious monuments. Maybe we are witnessing here evidence of the rise of powerful leaders, capable of exercising their authority to make entirely new sites – the enclosures are very similar, and were probably built in single episodes involving large numbers of people and much timber; it would be hard to marshal such a workforce without strong leadership. The sites were placed away from the long-revered centres, but still nonetheless within the larger ritual landscape. At all events, the enclosures were constructed towards the end of the long Neolithic succession, and they foreshadow the construction of that most individual of monuments at Silbury Hill – which most probably took place shortly after the West Kennet enclosures.

I have concentrated on the grand sites at the centre of the Avebury ritual landscape, but they are in many ways just a small component of it. The landscape around is peppered with barrows and burial sites of all shapes, sizes and descriptions, ranging from the massive stone-built long barrow at West Kennet to smaller, humbler Bronze Age round barrows. The sheer number of these sites never ceases to amaze: over twenty Neolithic long barrows are known within a radius of ten kilometres from Windmill Hill. By the Bronze Age I would estimate that the number of barrows has increased five- or six-fold. In effect, a quantum leap – a shift from dozens to hundreds.

The best-known ritual landscape in Europe is undoubtedly that around Stonehenge. Like the Avebury landscape, that part of Salisbury Plain around Stonehenge had been cleared of trees, and was open grazed grassland, by the time the first Neolithic ceremonial sites were being constructed. Unlike Avebury, where Neolithic activity began at Windmill Hill, the Stonehenge landscape does not, at first glance, appear to have a causewayed enclosure lying at its heart. Robin Hood's Ball, the nearest true causewayed enclosure, lies over four kilometres north-west of the stones. But there is a possible contender.

Around the outside of the famous stones is a rather uneven circular ditch with two accompanying banks: a large one on the inside, and a slight one on the outside. The ditch has two entranceways through it: a main one facing north-east, towards the midsummer sunrise, and a much smaller double one, facing south. There was also a probable second main entranceway, to the south-west, opposite the main one, but it was blocked a few centuries later.

Roughly half of the interior and the enclosing ditch around Stonehenge was excavated by a remarkably little-known archaeologist, Lieutenant-Colonel William Hawley, between 1919 and 1926. The half-ditch that Hawley excavated was found to have been dug in a series of twenty-eight segments. The rather peculiar double southern entrance was probably a remnant of the original segment and causeway pattern which had become obscured over time. As has been noted, at Windmill Hill and Etton, from the air the segment-and-causeway pattern of the interrupted ditch resembles a string of sausages; at Stonehenge the outer ditch as exposed by Hawley looks more like a string of large, rounded beads. But the general similarity of the two types of ditches cannot be denied, and of course recently a second Stonehenge-type ditch has been found at the end of the Beckhampton Avenue at Avebury. The main north-easterly entrance at Stonehenge was undoubtedly always an entrance, and was marked by special offerings of animal bone (including cattle jawbones and an ox skull), which were placed on the bottom of the ditch.

Now we come to one of the least-known and most extraordinary aspects of Stonehenge. When the modern car park on the opposite side of the A344 road to the stones was being constructed in 1966, archaeological excavations revealed a straight row of four large pits, running east to west, and about ten to twelve metres apart. Three of these pits were actually large post-holes of about 1.5 metres diameter and depth. Each contained clear evidence for a post-pipe of a large post (0.75 metres diameter). There was evidence that the posts were of pine, which caused surprise at the time, as pollen analyses had shown pine to be rare in southern England in the Neolithic.

Another large pit, similar to the three found in 1966, was discovered when the Visitor Centre at the end of the car park was enlarged in 1989. This time the post had been removed, so no post-pipe was found, but there were quantities of charcoal – again from pine. The pine wood from the pits was radiocarbon dated and the results showed that the pits were dug in the Early Mesolithic period, at some time between 8500 and 7650 BC. That's at least four and a half thousand years earlier than the outer ditch, the 'earliest' feature of Stonehenge.

Environmental samples from within the pits showed them to have been dug in an open pine and hazel woodland. Then, sometime between 2550 and 1600 BC, there was a dramatic change in the local environment, from pine woodland to grazed grassland. This change coincided with the construction of Stonehenge, some five thousand years after the original Mesolithic use of the site. But what did that 'use' involve? Of course we cannot be certain, but there is absolutely no evidence that Mesolithic hunter-gatherers in England lived in structures built from massive posts. In fact quite the contrary: so far as we know their way of life was mobile and their dwellings were appropriate to a roving lifestyle. In any case, a single row of posts is not the same as two parallel rows, which could in theory support a roof.

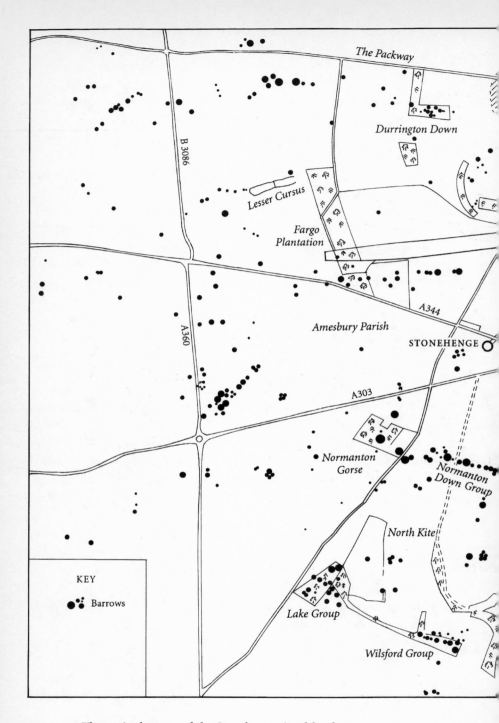

The Packway

Durrington Down

Lesser Cursus

Fargo
Plantation

A344

Amesbury Parish

STONEHENGE

A303

Normanton
Gorse

Normanton
Down Group

North Kite

KEY

Barrows

Lake Group

Wilsford Group

B 3086

A360

FIG 9   *The main features of the Stonehenge ritual landscape*

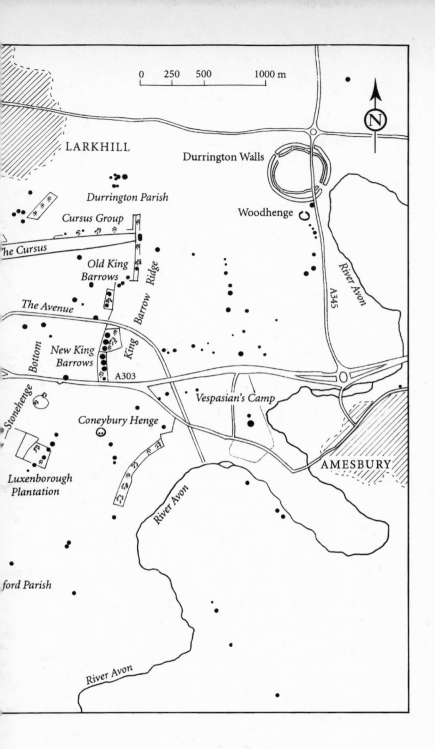

0   250   500   1000 m

LARKHILL

Durrington Walls

Durrington Parish

Cursus Group

Woodhenge

The Cursus

Old King
Barrows

The Avenue

King Barrow Ridge

River Avon

A345

New King
Barrows

A303

Stonehenge Bottom

Vespasian's Camp

Coneybury Henge

AMESBURY

Luxenborough
Plantation

River Avon

ford Parish

River Avon

N

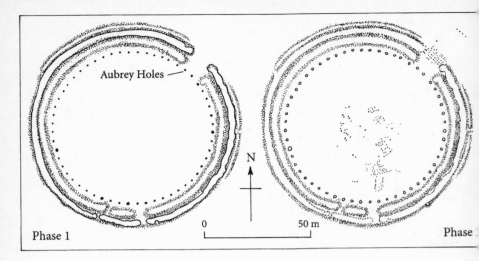

Aubrey Holes

N

0   50 m

Phase 1   Phase

The only plausible explanation for these great posts is that they formed part of a religious or ceremonial structure of some sort. But for some reason many archaeologists seem reluctant to take this view. Is it that the primacy of the stones is somehow being subverted? I don't know, but the extraordinary longevity of the place as a religious and ideological centre might well help to explain the absence of a causewayed enclosure.

There is a large chronological gap between the car-park posts and the outer ditch around the stones; but then, little of the area outside Stonehenge has been excavated – or indeed is ever likely to be excavated. So it is quite probable that yet another religious site, or sites, belonging to the intervening four or five millennia, might well be lurking under the well-trampled turf outside the stones.

It was said in medieval times that Stonehenge was the work of giants. Clearly that is fanciful, but the fact remains that the people who built these extraordinary monuments carried out feats appropriate to giants – and that suggests the existence of a sophisticated command structure and a motivated workforce.

The great stones are only a part of the Stonehenge story, which has recently been painstakingly reassembled from the original field notes of Lieutenant-Colonel Hawley and the many others who over

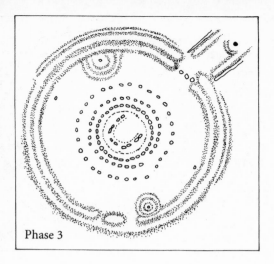

Phase 3

FIG 10 *Simplified plan of Stonehenge, Phases 1–3*

the years had been unable to resist excavating there. A very full account of the various excavations at Stonehenge has recently been made available in one huge volume.* As at the Sanctuary, Silbury Hill and elsewhere at Avebury, it's the persistence of activity and the almost obsessive attention to detail which strike one most forcibly. Between the original segmented ditch and the contemporary circle of Aubrey Holes (regularly spaced along the ditch's inner edge), the second phase sees the positioning of dozens of cremations and the digging of dozens of post-holes, which block the main entrance and cover the ground in the area where the stones were later to be erected.

The great stones themselves were erected, dismantled and then erected again during no fewer than six episodes or sub-phases of the third phase of development. They were laid out in a horseshoe shape and an internal oval setting. There were also three circles of stones, including the great sarsen circle, with the continuous overhead lintel. Initially bluestones were set in two circles (the so-called Q and R holes), but these were then dismantled. Two circles of stone-holes were dug, but were never used to hold stones (the Y and Z holes).

---

* R.M.J. Cleal, K.E. Walker and R. Montague, *Stonehenge in its Landscape: Twentieth Century Excavations* (English Heritage Archaeological Report no. 10, London, 1995).

Other arrangements of huge stones were erected, dismantled or modified, until we were left with the familiar stone setting that survives to this day. Again, one cannot escape an impression of almost frenzied, obsessional activity: build, modify, tear down, then build again. It appears to be very much activity for its own sake – but bear in mind what this activity involved. We're not dealing here with erecting wooden posts, but with toppling and moving massive stones, weighing tons. It was hard work, and also very dangerous work. This third phase in the overall development of Stonehenge lasted between 2550 and 1600 BC.

Two sorts of stone were used at Stonehenge. One was comparatively local, the other came from much further afield. The largest stones are sarsen, which was most probably obtained from the Marlborough Downs, about thirty kilometres away. Some of the upright sarsens are truly massive (weighing about forty-five tons), and this journey (which must have involved moving these colossal weights uphill) was every bit as remarkable as the better-known long-distance journeys of the more exotic, but very much smaller, bluestones. Controversy still surrounds the source of the bluestones. Aubrey Burl, the widely acknowledged authority on prehistoric stone circles, is adamant that they were moved to the Stonehenge area by natural means – most probably by a glacier. Others, including glaciologists, disagree equally adamantly.

My own mind was made up when I stayed with the recently retired Chief Archaeologist of English Heritage, Dr Geoffrey Wainwright, in his home in south-west Wales. As is so often the case in archaeology, it was emotion and aesthetics – not intellect – that actually tipped the balance. Geoff *believed* – almost as an act of faith – in the Welsh origin of the Stonehenge bluestones, and by the end of a very special afternoon I was as convinced as him. He took us to a spot in the Preseli Hills, where bluestone occurs naturally. The wind howled around us, and I remember struggling with a map of south-west Britain. Eventually we smoothed it open on a sheltered rock face. We were 210 kilometres north-west of Stonehenge.

It was an extraordinary place, high in the hills, atop a steep cliff. But the way the stone itself outcropped was most remarkable. It had a natural vertical pattern of cleavage which echoed Stonehenge itself, but on a larger scale. Even if you did not know about the bluestones at Stonehenge, you could not avoid a strong feeling that the place was connected in some way with the lost Megalithic world. It was high, windy and lonely. The huge mass of seemingly upright, bare rock dominated everything around it – just like the distant stones themselves. After that windy visit my scepticism died, and I now fully support the view that the bluestones were transported to Salisbury Plain by the efforts of prehistoric people.* The actual process of transporting the bluestones and the sarsens was just as important as the construction of Stonehenge – and indeed Avebury. Again, we are looking here at a religious *process*. Transport and construction were an integral part of the constant cycle of building, demolition and rebuilding that we saw at the Sanctuary. It's not impossible that some of the stones were removed from Stonehenge and ceremonially broken up elsewhere. We just don't know. It has also been suggested that the bluestones could have come from a stone circle demolished in or near the Preseli Hills. Again, we don't know. But I would not be at all surprised if either, or both, of these theories were one day to be proved correct.

The Avenue was constructed during this phase. It consists of two parallel ditches some twenty-one to thirty-four metres apart. Like the ditch encircling the stones, the banks quarried from the Avenue ditches were placed on the inside. The course of the Avenue is unusual. One would expect it, like a processional way such as The Mall, to run dead straight towards the stones. But it doesn't. It leaves the main, north-easterly entrance in the stones, and heads north-east. Then, after just over half a kilometre, it abruptly turns eastwards, at a point known as the Elbow. It then runs straight and slightly south of east for three quarters of a kilometre, before starting a gentle curve towards another straight length which runs south-west, down to the river Avon. The overall length of the Avenue is about 2.75 kilometres (allowing for a slightly dubious short length near the river).

It was suggested by Professor Richard Atkinson (who excavated extensively at Stonehenge in the 1950s), in a book published in 1956,

---

* The evidence for transporting large stones in Neolithic and Bronze Age Europe is now overwhelming, and the recent failed attempt to move a bluestone from Preseli surely says more about the competence of that modern team than about its prehistoric antecedents.

that the Avenue was laid out to transport bluestones from the river Avon, where they had been delivered after a perilous crossing of the Severn estuary following their journey up the Bristol Channel from Wales. This is a satisfying idea, but sadly it won't work, because we now know for a fact that the Avenue was constructed *after* the bluestones had arrived.

The Stonehenge ritual landscape is perhaps slightly less centred than that of Avebury. We have seen that the causewayed enclosure, Robin Hood's Ball, lies at some distance from the stones, and other early components of the ritual landscape are also some way from them. The Stonehenge Cursus is earlier than the stones. Cursuses are currently believed to have been an extreme development from long barrows, which were the principal burial monuments of the Earlier Neolithic period in Wessex and elsewhere. In essence cursuses (the name derives from the Greek word for an athletic race) consist of generally shallow parallel ditches with accompanying banks and closed ends. From the air they resemble long landing-strips (UFO obsessives and Ley Liners have already seized on them). Whatever their original purpose, they served to link different parts of the landscape together. It is not known what the Stonehenge Cursus was linking, but as we now realise that the entire area had been important for a long time, it is entirely possible that it linked wooden shrines or sacred groves of trees – or whatever – that have long since vanished.

The Stonehenge landscape's equivalent of Avebury, the great henge at Durrington Walls, lies almost three kilometres north-east of the stones. The henge itself is very roughly circular or oval, with an approximate diameter of 480 metres. It was marked out by a deep ditch and a bank on the outside. The ditch and bank were broached by two entrances, north-west and south-east. The site was partially excavated by Geoff Wainwright in the 1960s when a road which crossed the site was rerouted across another part of it. In hindsight this seems extraordinarily insensitive, even by the standards of the time. Geoff's excavations were on a large scale and he revealed the entire area under threat in a single huge exposure. There was no good evidence to suggest that people actually lived within the henge, but two large multiple circles of posts were found. In each case the posts seem to have formed a veritable forest. The southern circle was close to the south-east entrance of Durrington Walls, and it too had a clearly defined series of entranceways which faced south-east.

Less than a hundred metres outside the bank of Durrington Walls was another, smaller henge, known as Woodhenge. This too was surrounded by a ditch and bank and its single entranceway faced north-east. The entire area within the ditch was covered by another mass of concentric posts, this time arranged in six circles.

The two circles at Durrington Walls and the posts within Woodhenge have been interpreted as the remains of roofed buildings. I rather doubt that, given what we know about similar sites elsewhere in Britain, and suspect there was more than a small element of 'dig, erect, demolish and rebuild', as Mike Pitts demonstrated at the Sanctuary. That being said, Woodhenge and the southern circle at Durrington exhibit quite a strongly structured sense of order. I see them as timber circles that probably had more of a permanent life – in the sense of a church or a building – than places like the two West Kennet enclosures or indeed the Sanctuary, which were in an intentional state of near-constant upheaval.

The landscape around Stonehenge and the other great monuments on Salisbury Plain is almost carpeted with barrows, in a huge variety of forms and sizes. Frequently they occur in rows along the skyline, the most famous perhaps being those of the King's Barrow Ridge, which dominated, no doubt intentionally, the view east from the stones. Other rows of barrows were placed on the horizon to the north-west and south. The placing of barrows in this carefully structured way proves beyond any doubt that the Neolithic and Bronze Age inhabitants viewed the ritual landscape as a single entity. It was like a living thing, growing and evolving through time. And its individual components – doubtless the burial mounds of families from far and wide – gained significance from being integrated within something altogether larger and more important.

It's impossible to suggest that all this activity both inside and outside the stones was controlled by just one person, as it must have taken pace over many lifetimes. The logical suggestion is that control lay within a powerful ruling elite. By controlling the works, they controlled the workers and indeed the communities that supplied those workers. There is abundant evidence for the existence of such a controlling elite, in the form of the fabulously rich 'Wessex Culture' barrows that are found in groups or cemeteries in the Stonehenge area and further afield in the region. The 'Wessex Culture' is, I still think, a credible entity, although nobody would nowadays accept that it had close links with the eastern Mediterranean and the Aegean, as was believed in pre-radiocarbon days. It was essentially a phenomenon of Atlantic Europe, and the burials which produced the fabulous grave-goods were contemporary with (and slightly later than) the final throes of Stonehenge.

The conditions necessary for rich burials don't just happen over-night. Fortunes have to be accumulated. The beautiful sheet gold work from burials at Clandon, Upton Lovell and Bush Barrow in Dorset and Wiltshire are just three examples of extraordinary opulence that proclaim a clear, if rather chilling, message: our wealth is a symbol of our control, and we intend to take it with us into the next world.

The fabulous richness of the Wessex Early Bronze Age burials takes us naturally to our third example of ritual landscapes, in Brittany. Archaeologists have long acknowledged the links that existed in the early second millennium BC between the two areas, and some of the finer objects placed in Wessex tombs could have been made on the other side of the Channel. Although there is less gold found in Breton graves, a common decorative technique there is the use of tiny gold nails or pins, sometimes less than a millimetre long. These were tapped into a wooden hilt, for example, to give a wonderful patterned and shimmering effect. It's quite possible that the pommel of a bronze dagger from Bush Barrow, near Stonehenge, which was finished with tiny pins, could have been made in Brittany.

At this point I must urge caution. It's very easy to fall into the trap of thinking about the past in modern terms. Today in western Europe we have a market economy, but there is no evidence to suggest that such a system existed in prehistory. It is far more likely that valuable items such as the Bush Barrow dagger were actually given by powerful people to other, equally powerful, people, as part of an elaborate system or network of exchange.

An exchange system works on the principle that one good turn deserves another. Face is lost if a gift cannot be reciprocated. Thus livestock may be exchanged for a wife or husband – the deal being

One of the most extraordinary aerial photographs of British archaeology, taken by J.K. St Joseph in July 1951. It shows cropmarks south of Maxey churh, Cambridgeshire. In the foreground are the marks of the double-ditched Maxey Great Henge and the two parallel ditches of the Maxey Cursus (about 3500 BC) running north.

The immediate effects of de-watering on waterlogged Neolithic wood (3800 BC) at Etton. The piece alongside the scale appears sound when still in place in the ground (left picture). When lifted, its underside is seen to be deeply cracked (right picture).

TOP Evidence for what happened above ground in the Bronze Age is rare. The base of a notched log ladder (1000 BC) was found at the bottom of a large quarry pit at Fengate.

CENTRE The notched log ladder from the Fengate quarry pit. It has been carefully finished and the bark removed. The wood used is alder, a tree which likes growing in extremely wet conditions (the scale is six inches long).

LEFT A notched log ladder in the courtyard of a disused Tibetan Buddhist temple at Namgyaling near Marpha, in the Himalayas north of Kathmandu, Nepal. Ladders similar to this were in common use in Bronze Age Britain. They were replaced by ladders with rungs in Roman times.

The reconstruction of the first Bronze Age roundhouse (*c.* 1500 BC) to be found at Fengate (*see page 30*). The walls are supported by posts and the gaps between the posts are filled by woven hazel rods, known as wattles, which are smeared with a mixture of clay, straw and animal dung (daub). The roof is made from turf laid on a bed of reeds.

Boundaries in the Bronze Age landscape were sometimes marked by isolated burials, such as this skeleton of a young woman (aged twenty to twenty-three) which was found at the bottom of a droveway ditch at Fengate. Her bones have been radiocarbon dated to 3030–2500 BC.

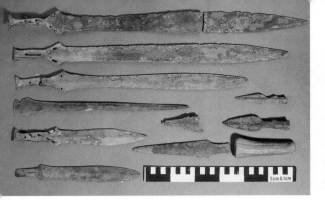

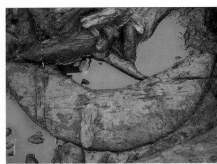

A selection of Bronze Age weapons (1300–900 BC) from Flag Fen. The top three swords, with wide blades, were for slashing; the thin blade at the centre is a rapier, used for thrusting; the lowest three weapons are daggers, one with an antler hilt. To the right are two spearheads and at the centre a chape (the metal tip of a sword scabbard),

Bronze Age wheels were complex constructions using several types of wood. An example dating from about 1300 BC was found at Flag Fen. It is one third of a three-part wheel made from alder wood. On either side were dovetailed oak ties (to the right of the picture), and the three parts were snugly located on close-fitting ash dowels.

ABOVE Middle Bronze Age stone roadway (1200–1300 BC) crossing an ancient stream of the River Thames system at Yarnton, Oxfordshire. Beyond the road can be seen the dark peaty clays of the stream bed. Down the centre of the road is a ridge of fine sand, possibly laid down by the river when the road was abandoned.

RIGHT In the nineteenth and early twentieth centuries, several discoveries of waterlogged Bronze Age oak coffins in Denmark revealed Middle Bronze Age clothes (1400–1200 BC). Mostly these were the garments of older people, but the burial in a barrow at Egtved Farm in southern Jutland was that of a young woman. Her braided mini-skirt and bare midriff caused a sensation in 1921, when the first pictures of the find were published.

closely negotiated by members of the two families concerned. Once these networks had been established, they soon became intricate and sophisticated, operating on many levels and over different spans of time. Thus small exchanges may have been completed rapidly, whereas larger ones, over longer distances, took longer. And, of course, failure eventually to reciprocate in these higher-status exchanges could give rise to serious incidents.

Much long-distance prehistoric 'trade' probably resulted from a series of higher-status exchanges, where the objects in question gained in prestige as the distance from their source of origin increased. Thus Langdale axes were probably esteemed more highly in the Fens than in the beautiful countryside around their quarries in the Lake District of north-west England. There is much evidence for social contact across the Channel in the Early Bronze Age, but this was mainly at a high level in society.

When I first visited the Carnac alignments in 1967, it was still possible to wander freely among the rows of stones. I will never forget the experience. The past was beside and above me. It enveloped me – it almost possessed me. But most extraordinary of all, it generated an internal motion of its own: the lines of stones were arranged by size, with large ones at one end, and smaller ones at the other. This created a feeling of impetus. It was as if one was being drawn along by external forces. Today access is more restricted and it's harder to feel so powerfully at one with the remote past.

The Breton peninsula is itself a huge ritual landscape that dwarfs anything in Britain. The edge of the landscape is defined by the sea, and many of the most important sites can be found close to the water's edge. The sea was certainly a powerful force in the ideological life of prehistoric Brittany, and I imagine that few Bretons would have been surprised by John Lorimer's discovery on Holme beach in 1998.

Not only is Brittany a very large ritual landscape, it's also more ancient than its equivalents in England. This antiquity probably reflects the fact that farming and a more settled style of life reached the area perhaps five hundred years earlier than on the other side of the Channel. In southern Britain the earliest long barrows – the style of communal grave favoured by Earlier Neolithic communities – began to be used in the centuries after 4000 BC; in Brittany, passage graves were first constructed around 4500 BC. The building of religious monuments with large stones – the megalithic tradition – then persisted right through to the Earlier Bronze Age, around 2500 BC. To put that in context, it was a tradition every bit as long-lived as Christianity has been.

I have always been slightly disappointed by the landscape around Stonehenge and Avebury. One is put in mind of Elgar rather than Wagner. Salisbury Plain is just that – a plain. At Avebury the monuments nestle within a gently undulating landscape. Even Silbury Hill makes a quiet statement – unless, that is, one suddenly confronts it as the road rounds the corner, and then the effect is dramatic. But perhaps Silbury is the exception which proves the rule. To my mind, Avebury and Stonehenge are ritual landscapes whose monuments seem to be at one with their low-key, gentle setting.

The same cannot be said for Brittany. If we take, for example, the landscape around the small town of Carnac the picture is very different. Carnac lies close to the Bay of Biscay on the south-west coast of the Breton peninsula. It is protected from north-easterly gales by the Quiberon peninsula, which forms the western arm of the Bay of Quiberon, whose eastern edge is defined by another, shorter peninsula, that of Locmariaquer. On the eastern side of this peninsula is the Gulf of Morbihan in which sits the island of Gavrinnis. It's a rocky, dramatic and varied coastline – quite unlike, one might think, that of north-west Norfolk. But in fact, while the overall landscapes may be contrasting, in matters of detail there are some striking similarities. For a start, both coastlines are sinking – relative, that is, to the sea. This always causes perceptual problems: it's never easy to deny the evidence of one's eyes; this is particularly true when it comes to the sea, whose presence seems to dominate all of one's senses.

Er Lannic is one of those classic sites one learns about as a student, and it sits in one's mind because of its extraordinary setting on the tiny island of Gavrinnis in the Gulf of Morbihan. It is frequently cited in the British literature because it is the only known stone 'circle' on the Continent. We now know that timber circles occur there more frequently than we believed even two decades ago, so a stone circle should cause no surprise. But there are problems. For a start, the stones do not form a true circle. There are in fact two settings, which together form a horseshoe shape whose combined axis is about a hundred metres long. The stones were set in an embankment of stones and earth and secured in the ground with carefully constructed stone packing. Like most of my colleagues I don't see Er Lannic as part of a British pattern at all. Its roots, like the stones themselves, lie firmly within a Breton tradition based around single standing stones, or menhirs. In fact, at the point where the two arcs of stones meet at Er Lannic there was a large, but now broken, menhir, some seven metres long – which is as tall as the biggest sarsen uprights at Stonehenge.

The reason so many visitors to Holme mentioned Er Lannic is its location. One of the two arcs of stones is almost permanently below the sea, whereas the other is partially on dry land. In the 1950s, forty-nine of the stones were re-erected (a move which rightly caused consternation and controversy), but some were left where they lay, as they would have caused a hazard to shipping. Again, it's hard not to see Er Lannic as a site built on the beach – maybe to confront or pacify the beings who controlled the sea. It's an attractive thought; but like many attractive thoughts, it's simply wrong.

In fact the Er Lannic stone 'circles' were built on dry but marshy ground, comparable in many respects to the ancient environment at Holme. To prove this, when the stones were being re-erected, a number of burnt hearths were found in the ground around them. We cannot demonstrate that the hearths were *precisely* contemporary with the stones of the 'circle', as there is abundant evidence for ancient settlement in the area, both before and after the construction of the 'circles' – but there can be no doubt that they were prehistoric. The discovery of evidence for fire beneath the sea has always stayed in my mind. It's a very striking image.

The richness and complexity of the ritual landscape around Carnac is simply breathtaking. All I can do is select a few choice nuggets that are relevant to our story. But I cannot ignore one of the most remarkable, if little-known, prehistoric monuments in Europe: the Grand Menhir Brisé, which lies near the north-east coast of the Locmariaquer peninsula. As a feat of engineering this gigantic stone dwarfs even Stonehenge. Today it lies on the ground, by itself, in four vast fragments. Recent excavations have shown that it originally formed part of a short alignment of nineteen standing menhirs. Like the sarsens at Stonehenge, the rock used for the Grand Menhir was probably quarried a few kilometres away, and the journey itself must have formed an important part of the ceremonies. But here the similarities cease, for not only was the Grand Menhir erected in 4500 BC, some two millennia earlier than the Stonehenge stones, but it weighs a truly awe-inspiring 350 tons. That's roughly eight times the weight of the Stonehenge stones. When erected, it would have stood twenty metres tall – the equivalent of a four- or five-storey building.

The recent excavations have found that the stone-hole was carefully shaped to receive the Grand Menhir. There was another remarkable discovery: the Grand Menhir and the stones next to it were all fashioned from a rock known as orthogneiss; the next few were in another, known as migmatite; and those at the end of the alignment were in granite. This selection was clearly deliberate, just like the choice of bluestone at Stonehenge. What lay behind these choices? Bluestone, for example, has little to recommend it. It isn't very blue, even when freshly chipped, and it isn't particularly easy to work or shape. So presumably it was chosen for other reasons – and I saw a hint of what those might have been in that strange-looking outcrop high in the Preseli Hills. Maybe something similar lay behind the deliberate selection of different rocks for the Grand Menhir's alignment. Put another way, the careful choosing of different types of stone for such an important purpose is a reflection of people's perception of their landscape. It hints at the complexity of those perceptions. People were not just concerned with the quality of land as a resource to be farmed. To the communities who lived in it, the landscape had a life of its own, which had to be acknowledged and respected.

There is one final echo, or rather precursor, of Stonehenge and Avebury in the Grand Menhir Brisé story. That concerns its fall, which was almost certainly a deliberate act which may have taken place around 3500 BC. We know that other large menhirs in the Locmariaquer region were toppled and broken up at this time, to be used as the roof or capstone for chambered tombs, although the Grand Menhir was left where it fell.

Again, we see the process of transport, construction, demolition and re-use that we saw at both Stonehenge and Avebury. This does not mean that the ceremonies on either side of the Channel were closely comparable; apart from other considerations, they did not take place at the same time. What I am suggesting is that we should not become too obsessed with individual points on a map. The ceremonies involved large tracts of countryside, and when seemingly 'finished' the new monuments were promptly altered. As we saw at the Sanctuary, it was activity that mattered. Construction, in other words, was use.

The Carnac area was clearly of special importance. Some of the barrow mounds that were erected over the megalithic tombs are vast: that at Saint-Michel measures 125 by sixty metres and is ten metres high. It's so large that a chapel was later built on it, at one end. Many of the sites were carefully positioned to be visible from the sea. Again, we see here the importance of travel and space. We are dealing with landscapes that have their own internal logic. Lines of sight and travel were clearly key elements in the way the stones at Carnac and elsewhere were organised at any particular time. And doubtless too, these principles and details of organisation changed through time. Ritual landscapes were always dynamic places. Evolution, change and development were always integral parts of what they stood for.

Lines of sight became formalised, like the Ten Commandments, in tablets of stone in that best-known feature of the Carnac area, the great stone alignments. Like other components of the ritual landscape, these were dynamic: they grew in size and were modified through time. It's hard to date them precisely, but they are undoubtedly Neolithic, probably beginning life in the fourth millennium BC, and ending around 2500 BC.

There are about half a dozen known alignments in the Carnac area, of which that at Le Menec is the best-known. It consists of no fewer than 1,050 standing stones, arranged in ten rows, stretching for almost a mile. There are two alignments at Kerlescan whose rows both line up on a central rectangular space, resembling a parade ground. This space is defined on three sides by a 'hedge' of upright stones and by a long mound on the fourth. The stones in the alignments grow steadily larger as they approach this central area, and they also gradually diverge or splay out. This heightens the sight-line perspective and gives a feeling of movement and momentum. Here we have a unique opportunity to appreciate the way these later ritual landscapes worked.

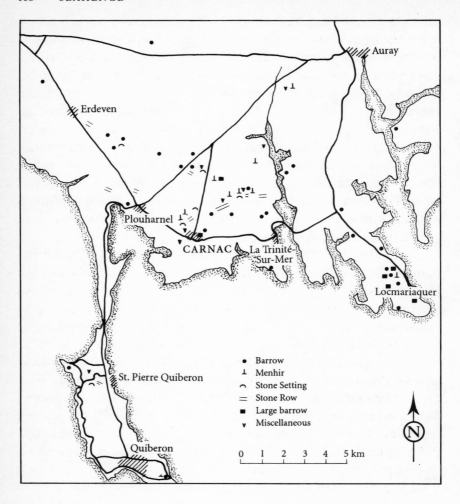

FIG 11   *The ritual landscape around Carnac, Brittany*

They are about sight-lines and stories, deeds of the living and the dead.

Simple analogy is dangerous when applied to something as changing and complex as a prehistoric ritual landscape. I could think of no modern equivalent until recently, when I visited the eighteenth-century landscape garden at Stowe, near Buckingham. As I strolled through it, I was struck by the way its formal structure affected the intensity of one's feelings. Although the great garden park at Stowe is less than three hundred years old, in many respects the people who used it are distant from us. The garden, which is now being carefully restored by the National Trust, is breathtaking. But I have always found it hard to understand how the people who experienced it actually felt, because I cannot enter the mind of a gentleman of the Age of Enlightenment. I am aware, through my reading on the subject, what he is *meant* to have thought, but I cannot imagine him actually thinking and feeling those things. The entire situation is simply too foreign to me: the depth of his Classical knowledge, the class system, his attitudes to women, servants, property, religion and so forth. Although a figure from the comparatively recent past, to me he seems more remote than a man from the Bronze Age.

In many respects Stowe was an intellectual and emotional theme park. It covers rolling acres of the Buckinghamshire countryside, but instead of rides there were bridges, temples, grottoes, lakes, islands and sweeping lawns. Some of the greatest English landscape gardeners – such as Capability Brown – either worked or were trained here. The visitor to Stowe was taken on a series of short walks, each of which ends in a new and carefully arranged view. These vistas often have specific themes, usually drawn from Classical antiquity. Sometimes they are intended to induce an emotion such as awe, sadness or pathos. At other times, as in the case of the well-known Temple of British Worthies, they are intended to make a forceful political point – in this instance a Whig party-political message that would have been immediately understood by all who saw it.

But a visit to Stowe was no casual stroll. When I went, it took three hours to see everything, and there was still much that had yet to be restored. I won't say that it was an ordeal, although it was certainly an effort. But having made that effort, I found that the stories I heard and the views I saw have stayed with me to this day. I don't want to stretch the analogy, but I am sure that those who visited prehistoric ritual landscapes would have made a considerable physical and emotional contribution to the experience. Ask a pilgrim to Mecca and he will tell you it was exhausting, but also life-enhancing. The two are inseparable.

Stowe is a garden whose themes supported the *status quo*, but it was also intended to stimulate discussion and reflection. Like its ancient equivalents, it was constantly being enlarged and modified. Maybe similar general principles lay behind the ever-changing internal articulation of prehistoric ritual landscapes. Put another way, they were organic, with a life and momentum of their own. They were never static, nor concerned with worship alone. They reflected people's view of this world and that of their ancestors. But they were also a forum for debate – and perhaps also an inducement to change.

CHAPTER SEVEN

Etton and the Origins of Ancestral Authority

THIS IS THE APPROPRIATE MOMENT to introduce my wife Maisie Taylor, the second of my long-term collaborators, who joined our team in 1976, at about the same time as Charly French. When Maisie came to us she was completing her degree at the Institute of Archaeology in London, which was also where Charly did his doctoral research. In those days the Institute combined theory and practical research superbly, and it has produced some of the finest archaeologists in Britain. By 1980 our team was beginning to knit together, both socially and intellectually. They were happy years; and I think it shows, not just in the quality of the research, but in the interesting direction it was starting to take.

Maisie's main archaeological interest was in prehistoric woodworking, which she approached from a practical perspective. She has always been interested in the way different woods can be used, and in what they can teach us about the people who used them. But unlike many specialists, she is not obsessive about her study: she sees woodworking as just one of many ways that we can approach the past, and she tries to integrate her discoveries into a broader picture.

Six years before Maisie joined our team at Fengate, when I was reading in the University of Toronto library before setting out for England, I came across another Royal Commission on Historical Monuments volume – to my mind the most important survey they ever produced. It was called *A Matter of Time*, and was published in 1960. This slim book was a survey of the aerial photographs of the lowland river valleys of Britain. By the late 1950s it was known that

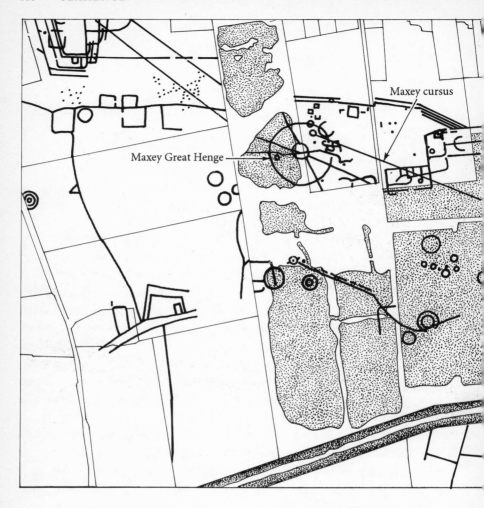

FIG 12   *Cropmarks revealed by air photography near the village of Maxey,*
Cambridgeshire

gravel digging would soon be a major threat to a number of important
archaeological sites, and the report was the Royal Commission's
response to that threat. I was thunderstruck when I first opened it.

At Cambridge I had learned about the wonders of Stonehenge
and the barrows on Salisbury Plain, and the extraordinary prehistoric

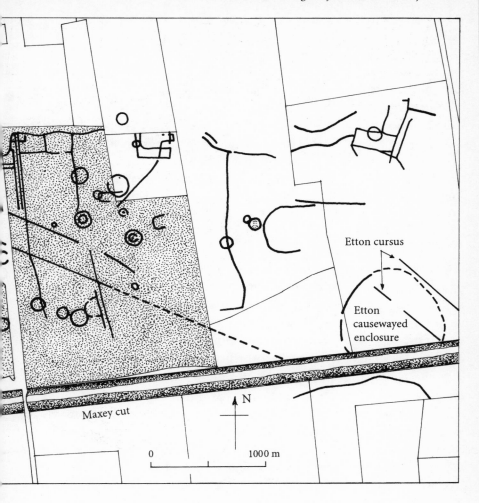

Etton cursus

Etton causewayed enclosure

Maxey cut

N

0   1000 m

landscape around Avebury. But here, staring at me, was a landscape comparable with Salisbury Plain. It was populated by scores of barrows, post circles, mortuary structures and other religious monuments. I knew, with a thrill, that what was in front of me was a prehistoric ritual landscape.

I was looking at a map of the cropmarks in the lower Welland valley, around the little village of Maxey. Like Fengate a few miles to the south, this was a Fen-edge landscape; and as at Fengate, the archaeological sites lay hidden beneath the surface. The ground was flat, and the presence of the ritual landscape was only revealed by cropmarks. When drawn on a map they looked like one of those close-up medical photos of skin infected with measles or some other disease: there were small circles, large circles, circles-within-circles, ovals, pits, circles of pits, pits-within-pits. It was extraordinary. I wish I could have excavated them all before they were quarried away for gravel, but I couldn't. I shall describe some of the sites we did manage to dig in the next chapter. Here I am concerned with the landscape's origins.

The ritual landscape of the lower Welland valley is one of the largest in Britain, but it lacked an obvious point of origin. The ultimate origins of Avebury, for example, lie on Windmill Hill, which is earlier by over half a millennium than the world-famous sites below it. But until 1976 there was no equivalent in the Welland valley. As we have seen, post-war prehistoric archaeology in Europe was turned upside-down by the qualitative changes brought about by radiocarbon dating. The effects of aerial photography were different, and equally transforming. But in this instance the effect was quantitative.

A succession of dry summers, and the availability of light aircraft (and now microlites), have combined to produce hundreds of thousands of new aerial photographs. In 1965, when Isobel Smith published her report on Alexander Keiller's excavations at Windmill Hill and Avebury, there were fifteen known causewayed enclosures in Britain. At the time of writing (early 2000) I am aware of seventy-two, most of the new discoveries being in lowland landscapes. So, not only has the original total almost quintupled, but the main concentration of these extraordinary sites has shifted from the western to the eastern half of the country.

Anyone who had the misfortune to be continuously out of doors during the blazing hot summer of 1976 will remember it. The heat was fearsome, and it made archaeology on the ground extremely difficult. Not only did soil colours bleach out, but after a few days it was no use wetting the ground – perhaps constant re-wetting had a permanent bleaching effect; whatever the reason, watering ceased to work. But while the heat may have made life on the ground hard for diggers, it was an extraordinary bonus for aerial archaeologists.

As the summer sun blazed on, cropmarks formed like never before. They even began to appear in old pasture fields, where usually the thick turf stored enough moisture to allow grass to grow lush and green. Steve Upex, the aerial archaeologist for the Peterborough area, noticed these pasture marks when he was out on one of his regular flights around Peterborough. That set him thinking. If marks were beginning to appear in old pasture, then what about alluvium, the heavy blanketing clay that was deposited across the flat floodplain landscape when rivers were in spate.

A thick surface-layer of alluvium will protect archaeological sites from damage by modern ploughing, it is true, but it also hides them from the aerial photographer. This means that if a threat of some sort arises – say a new road – nobody can do anything to protect the archaeological sites in its path, because nobody knows they even exist. As a general rule, if there is more than about half a metre of alluvium below the topsoil, it will seriously inhibit the formation of cropmarks. If there's more than a metre, forget it.

As usual that summer, it had been a blazing hot day. On this particular early evening I was with Steve in a village pub, and the bar was strewn with his latest photos. He told me that he had decided to focus his attention on the alluviated parts of the Welland valley, where cropmarks were beginning to show up quite clearly. He reckoned that large features such a deep ditches were becoming visible below almost a metre of alluvium. This was unheard of.

Of course, I was astounded. Who couldn't be? At that time the ritual landscape around Maxey was only known from air photos and was entirely confined to the non-alluviated areas around the higher ground of Maxey 'island'. Like many Saxon settlements, Maxey (which means 'Maccus' Island' – Maccus presumably being an eminent man of the region) was built on a natural rise in the ground, and all around the village and its immediate fields were the huge pasture meadows of the river floodplain. This was where the great expanses of alluvium had begun to form, mainly from Roman times. Steve and I were both well aware that entire pre-Roman landscapes must lie buried beneath the alluvium – if only we could somehow see through it. So the extraordinary spread of cropmarks that I'd first seen in *A Matter of Time* – the ritual landscape around Maxey – had edges that were, in effect, false. The sites on the map didn't all stop: many continued below the alluvium, out of the reach of aerial cameras. But not now. Suddenly, I realised, all that had changed.

We were about to leave when Steve reached into his pocket. The photo was already well-thumbed. I asked him where he'd taken it. It was about a quarter of a mile east of the Maxey quarry, just north of Etton. I knew exactly where he meant. Etton is a charming limestone village where some close friends of ours lived. I'd been there often. If anyone had looked over my shoulder, I don't think he would have been as excited as us. The black-and-white photo in my hand looked fuzzy and out of focus, but in fact it wasn't. This impression was caused by a series of dark, swirling cropmarks in a field of ripening wheat. If you looked closely, it was possible to see the lines of individual rows of plants left by the seed-drill and the parallel 'tramlines' used by the sprayers. Like many sprayer tramlines in use then, they were about thirteen metres apart – which gave me an instant rough scale.

The swirling dark cropmarks were plainly made by an old river-course and had nothing to do with the hand of man. They belonged to one of the many streams of the river Welland, before it had been forced into its present-day single course in recent times. Steve's other air photos showed clearly how the stream channels skirted the higher gravel land of Maxey 'island', but the close-up shot I held in my hand showed a series of curving streams, which almost encircled a much smaller 'island', about two hundred metres south of the main 'island' of Maxey.

Close to the streams' edge at the north and west side of the smaller 'island' was a series of faint cropmarks, which looked like a giant necklace. We both immediately recognised these for what they were: the interrupted or discontinuous ditch segments of a causewayed enclosure. There was no doubt about it. The Windmill Hill causewayed enclosure at Avebury was larger and better-known, but this one was here, on the edge of the Fens, and slap bang in the middle of our patch. I can't tell you how excited I felt. Then and there I determined that one day I'd have a good look at it.

I peered closely at the photo and counted the sprayer tramlines. Steve had a go too, and together we reckoned there were about fourteen within the enclosure; but it was hard to be certain, because a hedged field boundary obscured the view. If we were right, the enclosure would be about 182 metres in diameter, which would make it one of the smaller examples in Britain. There was then a theory in circulation to the effect that small causewayed enclosures were late in the series, but Etton was to turn this idea on its head. It was later to produce radiocarbon dates centring on 3800 BC, which made it among the earliest in the country.

The team moved to Maxey from Fengate three years later, in 1979, and we started work on various sites of the ritual landscape that were threatened with destruction by the huge gravel pit on the southern edge of the village. By 1981 the gravel beds in the pit were almost exhausted, and the quarry company decided it would next expand eastwards, towards Etton. At that time planning controls on developments that would involve the destruction of ancient sites were poor – unless, that is, the sites in question were protected by law, which in England means they are given statutory protection under the Ancient Monuments Act. The protection afforded by the Act is pretty good, but the trouble was that in those days it took a long time to have newly discovered sites placed on the protected register, or Schedule. To make matters worse, the hot summer of 1976 had produced an enormous backlog of important sites. So the Etton causewayed enclosure lay there, unprotected. And there was no philanthropic marmalade millionaire like Alexander Keiller waiting in the wings to help us.

By 1981 our team had been working in the Maxey pit for three years, and we had made good friends with the quarry company's regional manager, Bruce Sully. At first Bruce would visit our dig in a desultory fashion, more, I suspect, out of amusement than anything else. But then, quite suddenly, he found himself hooked. Barely a week would go by when I didn't look up from the drawing board to see him striding across the site with yet another senior member of the company whom he was trying to convert to our cause. Thanks largely to Bruce, the company gave us money, the free use of machines and, most important of all, time. They went to enormous lengths to work around us, which sometimes cost them a lot of money.

Bruce told me about the expansion plans, and I told him about the causewayed enclosure. His eyes lit up when I explained what it could contain. The alluvium had protected it from plough damage, so everything would still be there. The land was wet, so the ditches would probably still be waterlogged; that would mean organic finds, such as wood, leather, skin – you name it. By the time I had finished describing the menu of promised archaeological delights, my mouth was positively watering – and Bruce had gone very quiet. I'd never seen him so pensive before.

Three days later, he visited us unexpectedly. He'd been in touch with the farmer who owned the land immediately east of the quarry boundary, and had arranged for us to do some exploratory work, even though the new season's crop had already been sown, and was now quite well advanced. He had also arranged for the quarry's tracked digger and its driver, Eb, to be available on Saturday. Would that be convenient for me? Would it just. I'd have cancelled breakfast at Buckingham Palace to be there.

I arrived at the quarry bright and early on Saturday morning, just as the first slashes of light through clouds to the east were giving way to real daylight. In ten minutes I knew the sun would appear above the long, flat horizon out there in the depths of the open fen, perhaps twenty miles away. The ground was white and puddles were frozen over, but it had not been a hard frost the previous night. Eb was standing high on the machine, watching intently as diesel echoed into its cavernous tank. Neither of us wanted the fuel to overflow, as its distinctive scent always attracted clouds of flies, even on a chill November morning. So I said nothing to break his concentration.

Eb was a large man, but fit and athletic. He still wore his hair long at a time when many of his friends were cutting theirs short. I sympathised – if I was as blond as him, I think I'd have done the same. Like many people from the eastern fringes of England, it was apparent that more than a little Viking blood flowed through Eb's veins.

I heard his shout and immediately threw the valve switch on the diesel tank. We were full up. It was time to head east. I led the way in the Land-Rover, driving for fifty metres, then stopping to wait for Eb and the digger. The engine of the great machine behind me roared like a charging armoured vehicle, but the gearing was so low that it only moved at a slow shuffle. Such a pace was more than my old Land-Rover could cope with, without discharging expensive clutch fumes. Hence the stopping and starting. Travelling in this halting fashion, we slowly snaked our way through the quarry.

The quarry face was about two hundred metres from where we estimated the causewayed enclosure ditch to be, so we climbed the long gravel haul-road out of the quarry. It was dusty and well-travelled. This was where huge dumpers hauled the 'as raised' unwashed gravel. Then they had to bounce their way through clouds of thick dust, half a mile to the west, back to the processing plant at the centre of the quarry. The company had recently had to stop weekend working because the unexcavated reserves were beginning to run low, and they didn't want to have a gap between the current operation and their planned expansion. A break of more than a week or two would mean that men would have to be laid off. Nobody wanted that to happen, least of all me.

At the top of the haul-road I eased the Land-Rover into four-wheel drive. I slowly ground my way across a muddy ditch, up a bank and into a field of young oilseed rape. As I drove slowly forward the rank smell of cabbages from the rape plants beneath my wheels was almost too much. I wished I could have shut the windows, but they'd jammed years ago.

Once Eb and the digger were safely across the muddy ditch, I drove briskly across the field to the spot where the ditch of the causewayed enclosure passed beneath the hedge at the edge of the field. By now sunrise had passed, and the clouds that had looked so threatening in the half-light seemed more fluffy than fearsome. It was going to be a nice day. I took out a copy of Steve's air photo. It clearly showed the short hedge and the trunk of a dead ash tree which I calculated was about thirty metres north of the spot we were looking for.

I walked across to the dead tree and paced out thirty metres. Over the years I've learned how to take an accurate metre step – a useful skill when you've forgotten your tape measure, as I had done. After thirty paces I drove a red-and-white surveyor's ranging pole hard into the ground, and waited for the digger to arrive. Although I knew from the roar of the engine that Eb was travelling as fast as he could, I couldn't believe how long it was taking him to cross that field. He knew full well that I was desperate to get on, so he acted the part of a man suffering the extremes of boredom. He yawned hugely, leaned far back in the cab, his hands behind his head and his feet stretched out through the front window. Inch by inch, the tracks creaked their way towards my pole. Eventually he arrived and I showed him the air photo. Like most of the men at the quarry, he had caught Bruce's infectious enthusiasm and had developed a strong interest in what we were doing. But he always concealed his real feelings behind a veneer of cynical indifference. It seemed to amuse him – and me, come to that.

I showed him where I wanted him to dig, and where he was to put the spoilheaps, with topsoil to the right and sticky alluvium, gravel and subsoil to the left. Then, with a dark puff of smoke, the engine revved into action and we were off.

Whenever I see a really powerful modern digger at work it amazes me. Eb was an excellent driver and he worked the machine with smooth, easy and effortless fluency. It took him just one long, even scrape to remove all the topsoil. By hand, it would have taken two of us a full morning to do what he had just done in twenty seconds. Then he started on the alluvium. It was sticky indeed, and he had to shake the bucket, with a deafening metallic rattle, to release it. Judging by the 'fuzziness' of the cropmarks on the air photos, Steve and I had reckoned there would be at least half a metre of alluvium, but we were wrong. Down and down Eb went, and the alluvium seemed to get thicker and more tacky. We even had to clean out the digger's bucket with spades. Eventually the colour of the ground in the trench far below me changed from yellow clay alluvium to a darker, slightly peaty brown.

Eb held the machine still while I sampled the new brown soil in his bucket with my trowel. I rolled it in my fingers: it did contain clay, but not a great deal. It also crumbled in a way that suggested it had once contained a lot of organic matter, which had quite recently decayed. This, I knew, was potentially bad news. I signalled for Eb to take another scoop and bring it up for me to look at. This time it appeared much more promising. The dry, crumbly feel had gone, and there were also twigs and small pieces of wood. I picked one out and squeezed it between my fingers. Instead of feeling hard and woody, it was soft – almost structureless – and watery. By now my feelings of foreboding had gone, and I was getting excited. I reached into the bucket and found another sample of the organic soil. Eb had turned the engine off, and I sensed his quizzical stare from the cab. I reached into the bucket again, and this time found a larger twig. Again I squeezed it. Clean, clear water oozed from its broken end. I knew that modern, even recently waterlogged wood doesn't behave in this fashion. There's always a woody feel to it, and it's almost impossible to squeeze out clear water, unless you have a truly vice-like grip. No, I mused, this wood *has* to be old. It could even be Neolithic.

I was lost in what I was doing, and looking intently into the bucket, when I felt a tap on my shoulder.

'What's this?'

It was Eb. In his hand was something I hadn't wished to see. It was a large piece of handmade pottery, hard and well-finished, with a fine, almost lustrous outer surface. I snapped a bit off a corner and looked closely at the broken face. The potter had crushed up sea-shells, or fossil sea-shells, and added them to the clay. They had been well mixed in and were evenly spread throughout the fabric of the pot. The hardness, the finish and the thorough mixing together of the clay and the shell temper led me to believe that this sherd was more likely to be Middle Iron Age – I would have guessed around 400 to 200 BC – than Neolithic (4000–2000 BC). Eb was delighted by his find, so I couldn't show my disappointment, but I felt it nonetheless.

The digger took another shallow scoop and Eb held the bucket in front of me, at eye level. My heart fell. There, about three inches from my nose, were two freshly broken pieces of pottery, with their white shell temper shining out like so many smiling teeth. One piece of Iron Age pottery could be discounted, but three . . .

I pulled the larger of the two sherds from the bucket. It came away reluctantly, as its thickened rim was deeply embedded in the organic soil. Thickened rim? That seemed odd. Iron Age pots didn't usually have thickened rims, at least not as heavily thickened as this one. I spat on my hand and carefully cleaned the mud away. And then the truth hit me. The top of the rim had been decorated with a series of shallow diagonal grooves. This decoration and the heavily thickened rim could only belong to one prehistoric style, known as Mildenhall Ware. Mildenhall pottery (named after a site in the southern Fens where it was first recognised) belongs to the Middle Neolithic. It's contemporary with Windmill Hill in the Wessex region. The muddy sherd I was holding in my hands told me we'd hit the jackpot. First time. It *had* to have been made sometime before 3000 B C. It was quite a thought. I also knew we had found the outer, segmented, ditch of the causewayed enclosure. There could be no doubt at all.

I now realise that the reason for my initial confusion about the dating of the sherds was simple. Normally I saw Neolithic pottery that had been exposed to the elements, either within the topsoil or on the surface. This exposure removed the original fine finish; then humic acids in the topsoil dissolved out the shell temper and gave the pottery a less solid look and feel; it usually resembled cork more than ceramics. But the pottery in my hand was from deeply buried, sealed and water-logged contexts. It had never lain around on the surface. Those twigs, too, had found their way into the ground with the pottery. It could not have been a protracted process – maybe it only lasted a few hours, or at most a day or two. So I was holding in my hands the remains of a single event that had taken place over six thousand years ago. It was a strange sensation. For a fleeting moment I felt I was holding time itself, which had stopped dead.

My reverie was rudely interrupted by a shout from across the field. Charly French and two other members of the team had decided to postpone their weekend and had come out to see what I was up to. They carried spades and shovels and were clearly eager to use them. I showed them the rimsherd and the wood and twigs we had found around it. While the other two examined it, Charly was already on his hands and knees at the bottom of the trench, looking intently at the ground. He straightened up.

'Was it the ditch?' I asked him.

He nodded with a big grin. It sure was.

The machine we had borrowed from the quarry was fitted with a toothed bucket, and the bolts which secured the teeth to the cutting edge had been completely smoothed over during its working life, so we couldn't get them off. Teeth can do serious damage to archaeological deposits, so we decided to go no deeper into the ditch filling with the digger. We had no alternative but to dig by hand. I don't think I have ever seen four experienced archaeologists go at a task with greater excitement. The birds sang, the sun shone and we were working, up to our waists, in the most stunning waterlogged Neolithic enclosure ditch. I suppose it's not everyone's idea of Heaven, but it was ours. By the end of the day we had reached the ditch's bottom, and in the process had found yet more Mildenhall pottery, several animal bones, and large quantities of wood which we packed into bags for Maisie to look at that evening.

Before we started work at all, we had had three simple objectives. First, to find and perhaps date the ditch; second, to see whether it was waterlogged; and third, to see what preservation was like within the interior of the enclosure. The first objective was successfully achieved, and we had also established that the ditch was waterlogged; but – and this was worrying – Charly thought he could detect signs of drying out.

The quarry was only two hundred metres away, and, as at all modern pits, the gravel from it was extracted dry. This meant that the entire quarry, where the machines and dumpers were working, had to be pumped dry to a depth of six or seven metres below the surface. Inevitably this tended to pull the level of the groundwater down in the fields around the quarry. One result of the pumping two hundred metres away was that the ditch was beginning to show the first signs of drying out. It was worrying, because the site's real importance – what separated it from all the other known causewayed enclosures in Britain – was its waterlogged ditch.

We also managed that day to achieve our third objective – to investigate preservation within the enclosure. We extended the trench, and below the thick layer of alluvium we found an almost intact buried Neolithic topsoil. I need hardly say that Charly was delighted. It was a soil scientist's dream.

I suppose the downside of having a wife who is an expert in prehistoric woodworking is that often the draining board, sink and scullery floor can be invaded by bags, tubs and buckets of squidgy ancient wood. Quite recently Maisie had the difficult job of examining some nine-thousand-year-old wood from Star Carr, a famous Mesolithic site in Yorkshire. It was amongst the oldest worked wood in Europe, and quite possibly in the world, and it cluttered up our draining board for weeks, making washing up impossible. I used it as an excuse not to wash up – and the effect was miraculous. Within two days it vanished to a university laboratory store somewhere.

This time the wood was from one of our own sites, so I didn't resent its presence in the kitchen. Maisie was washing potatoes when I arrived with the sample bags after that first day at Etton. She finished the spuds and emptied the bags into the sink. Being six thousand years old and completely waterlogged, prehistoric wood doesn't float, so Maisie's hands worked away in the black, peaty water unseen. After a minute or two she pulled a hand out, triumphantly holding a woodchip. It had been detached from an alder tree, and Maisie had no doubt it had been produced by a stone axe. We could clearly see the curved impression left by the axe blade. This was the first time I'd seen a woodchip that had been produced by a stone axe, and it looked remarkably crisp and clear. The woodsman had certainly kept his blade in good condition: it was sharp and only had one small nick – perhaps where he'd chopped into a knot earlier in the day – but when we looked closely at the edge of the chip, where the axe had bitten in, we could see that the wood was slightly blurred or bruised, as if the axe was tearing, rather than cutting cleanly. This is characteristic of a non-metallic axe. If the preservation of the wood had been less than perfect we could easily have been confused, because in other respects, especially its width and size, the cutting edge resembled that of a Late Bronze Age socketed axe – some two thousand years later.

Maisie rummaged around in the soupy water and pulled out another three woodchips, all of them superbly preserved. I told her what Charly had said about the ditch beginning to dry out, and she looked at me in horror. Alder wood is very soft, and as soon as it starts to dry it splits and distorts. If there was any drying out at all in the future, the woodchips would be archaeologically worthless. As Maisie pointed out, this was the first chance we had been given to study in quantity the debris left behind by a Neolithic woodworker. We both knew the archaeological importance of debris and rubbish. You can learn far more from the woodchips and shavings on a cabinet-maker's floor than by studying his finished furniture, from which all the interesting detail has been carefully planed, sanded and polished off.

The following Monday I called a team meeting. It sounds formal, but it wasn't. Our meetings were more like haphazard 'happenings' than structured discussions. But in this particular case we had important matters to sort out, matters that would determine whether or not we had jobs in the year to come. So we took it seriously. It happened at lunchtime in the Maxey pub. As it was an official meeting, I had to buy the beer and sandwiches.

First of all, Charly and Maisie described what they had found when they looked through their samples. I then suggested that if I were to 'sell' the site to a funding body, we'd have to list all the reasons why it was so important. We would also have to think of academic questions that its excavation could answer. Nobody would want to pay for a dig just because we all thought the site was deeply wonderful. Heads nodded in agreement. It was sad, but that was life.

We started by listing the reasons Etton was so special – in the words of Ian Dury's then current hit, the Reasons to be Cheerful. The ditch was waterlogged, and preservation of organic material was excellent. The alluvium covering the interior was thick, and there was a buried soil beneath it. The thick layer of alluvium also meant that any upstanding features, such as banks, mounds, built-up floors or even barrows, would be preserved. At that point brows began to furrow – what else could we add?

Then someone – it could even have been me – pointed out that the site was almost complete. Only a small part – about a quarter of the ditch and a wafer-thin slice of the interior – was not available for excavation, and this would be preserved for posterity beneath the northern bank of the Maxey Cut (the Cut is a modern canalised course of the river Welland, which clips the southern segmented ditch and a sliver of the enclosure's interior). With luck, water seeping from the Cut would keep the buried segments of ditch wet, which would mean there would be something worthwhile to hand on to posterity.

I was about to move the discussion on when Charly made the obvious point, that we all knew already. Etton lay at the heart of the Maxey ritual landscape, which had already been studied, by us and others, in some detail. It would be hard to find a site, with the possible exception of Windmill Hill itself, which had better archaeological contexts. Put another way, if we managed to understand what made Etton tick, we would probably have the key to the later ritual landscape. At this point I had to call a halt. We were moving from facts to speculation.

'No more ifs,' I said. 'Any more factual reasons to be cheerful?'

There was a long pause. Then two people, almost in unison, said:

'But surely, the main reason we want to dig is to find something new?'

They were right, of course, but unfortunately you can't go to a funding body and say, 'Give us £20,000 so we can discover the key which will unlock ritual landscapes, which we're pretty sure lies somewhere under the alluvium at Etton.' The world doesn't work like that – it's never that easy.

I knew that that fundamentally simple question – of what we actually hoped to find on the site – would be lurking behind everything I said to anyone possessing grant money. But I also knew that any archaeologist worth his salt would skate around it. I was sure we wouldn't be asked the question outright; it wouldn't be fair. But at the same time I was painfully aware that I could never be certain.

'Right. Time to move on.' I looked down at my list. 'Second item. The site's as near as dammit complete. That means that whatever we find, it must be a valid sample. Nobody can turn round and say, "That's fine, but what about the rest of the site – the bits you don't plan to dig?"'

Heads nodded. It was too obvious to merit further discussion.

'Good. Next point: waterlogging. Any thoughts?'

As I expected, Maisie had views on this.

'I know what they'll say. All the pot people will want us to find wooden pots that are copies of clay ones, and the wood people will try to prove them wrong . . .'

I interrupted.

'And you?'

'I'll run away to somewhere warm and sunny. I hate that sort of petty academic bickering. I don't think we should dig the waterlogged layers just to find objects, although it would be nice if we do. No, I want to dig the whole thing slowly. We must record the position of every woodchip and piece of bark . . .'

'But Maise,' someone interjected, 'that would take forever and a day. And what on earth would it achieve?'

Maisie was riding her hobby-horse, and she gave it its head.

'What would it achieve? Good grief, what *wouldn't* it achieve?'

The questioner had backed off, but Maisie continued, in full flow.

'I know it would be loads of work, but can you think of another site where anyone has been offered a chance like this? Think what we could discover. Each segment of ditch could have a different tale to tell. Who knows, perhaps they worked tree trunks on one side of a causeway and wove wattle hurdles on the other. We just don't know. And how can you decide what was going on if you haven't recorded it fully? You can't go back and redo it once it's out of the ground. It's too late then. I tell you this: if you dig that ditch like potatoes, I'll be off – and you can sort out the mess you've made when I'm gone.'

Things were warming up, but I wanted light, not heat.

'OK, OK, OK, folks. I'm with Maisie on this. We either go for it properly, or not at all. Let's all agree on that. We've got to stand together.'

There was a pause. All the team were experienced field archaeologists, and we all knew that Maisie was proposing a huge amount of extra work. Someone voiced a doubt, which I know many shared.

'But what if there's not enough cash? What do we do then?'

I did my best to sound reassuring, but I was aware I lacked conviction, as nobody had yet offered us so much as a penny.

'We still go for it. I don't know *how*, but we do. Look, sooner or later we'll find something good. I don't know what it'll be, but then they'll have to take us seriously.'

I wasn't sure who the 'they' were who'd have to take us seriously. But it didn't matter: funds were hard to come by in 1981, and the team's worries were real ones. In fact I shared them, although I couldn't say so. I pressed on regardless.

'Next point: buried soil and preservation. Give us your thoughts, Charly.'

'Well, it's there all right. Can't say much more at this stage. I've taken some blocks for thin section and I'll look at them next week. Then we'll know. But it sure looks good, even now.'

But I needed bullet points for my list.

'D'you reckon we could do phosphate tests on the buried soil of the interior?'

'Yes.'

'And mag. sus.?'

'Yes.'

'Mag. sus.', or magnetic susceptibility enhancement analysis, to give it its full technical name, is a procedure whereby soil is tested for its ability to retain a magnetic charge. High magnetic susceptibility usually means that at some time in the past the ground has been heated, probably by a fire or bonfire. If Etton was indeed a religious site, we might expect to find mag. sus. evidence for funeral pyres. This was an excellent bullet point, and I added it to my list.

'Charly,' Maisie asked, 'do you think you could prove one way or another whether Etton was actually lived in? Was it settlement, or ritual – or both?'

This of course was the big question. Charly was in no doubt.

'Preservation's so good that if we find houses, we'll most probably get their floors, too. Certainly hearths and fires. If there were ploughed areas, or gardens, I should be able to pick them up in the thin sections.'

'So if we don't find houses,' I broke in, 'then it follows there weren't any. Isn't that the main point? On other sites you can blame the absence of house post-holes on ploughing, or hillwash, or whatever. But not here. Am I right, Charly?'

Charly frowned slightly, and replied with his customary scientific caution.

'Yeah, I think you're right. Even if they did build light houses without posts – or had tents – we should still be able to detect floor or midden areas. And the fires, they'd be no problem – I'm sure mag. sus. would work.'

The inhabitants of prehistoric settlements would often store their household and farm refuse in a midden or muck-heap, which would be left to compost for a year or so before being spread over the ground as manure. With the buried soil preserved over the entire interior, we knew we'd have no trouble detecting middens. They'd certainly show up in the phosphate tests.

At the end of the meeting we were all raring to go. Nobody was in any doubt that I'd be able to find money from somewhere: Etton was simply too extraordinary to let slip. It all seemed straightforward. But I was aware I was no longer in Canada. There was no Doug to hold my hand. I was now a smaller fish in a much larger pond.

During the winter of 1981–82 the team turned its attention to the final field at Maxey. This included the two hundred metres that separated the quarry from the causewayed enclosure. One of the discoveries we made was a deep pit which had probably originally been dug as a small gravel quarry at about 1600 BC. It was remarkable, because after it had been dug it had filled with water and seems to have been used for quenching burning wood to produce charcoal. A log would be burnt, perhaps it would be covered with ash and soil to encourage charcoal to form, then it would be plunged into the water. Afterwards it would cool and the charcoal could be axed off. It seemed, and still seems, an odd way to proceed, but it was the only way Maisie could explain why an axe had been used to remove charred wood, and there were several chopped logs that had received this strange treatment.

I can remember looking at the charred Early Bronze Age wood and talking about Maisie's theory to her and Charly, when a nasty thought suddenly struck me. The pit before us was about three metres deep, yet its bottom was bone dry. We hadn't even needed to hire pumps. Nothing was seeping in. I glanced at the hedge and the dead ash tree over to my left. They were only a hundred metres away, maybe a fraction more. Charly and Maisie could see what I was thinking – they were both thinking the same thing: our wet ditch with its precious waterlogged deposits would shortly start to dry out, if it wasn't doing so already. We had to do something, and we had to do it *now*.

In those days English Heritage (the national body responsible for archaeology) was – how can I put it? – *methodical* in the way it funded new projects. First you had to produce a Project Design; this then had to be approved, and the new project would eventually appear in the budget of the following financial year. There was a small emergency fund, known as the Contingency Reserve, but by late 1981 it had already been spent on other projects. It looked as if we were stuck.

I tried pulling various strings, but it was no use: I didn't have sufficient clout. I was also labouring under a perceptual difficulty. If the site was being smashed by maniacs on bulldozers, or unscrupulous property developers, we could have made a fuss simply by telling the press. A word in the right ears, and the whole place would have been crawling with cameramen. But a hidden, insidious threat such as drying-out is far harder to sell. In any case, it was not as if the objects under threat were great works of art. From a journalist's point of view, it's much easier to whip up support for a Turner being exported to America than for a muddy ditch full of desiccating Neolithic wood-chips. But I had to do something.

Shortly before Christmas I decided to take the few pieces of pot-tery, including that decorated rimsherd, to my friend Ian Kinnes in the splendidly named Department of Prehistoric and Romano-British Antiquities at the British Museum. Ian is a highly regarded Neolithic scholar, and I was keen that he should see what we'd found. I'd already spoken to him over the phone, and together we'd decided to write a short note on the site for the journal *Antiquity*. If nothing else, that should help raise our profile within the profession as a whole – but would it do so in time to raise money *fast*? Having seen that deep, bone-dry pit, I now feared the worst. But I had no better suggestions; the museum was the only possibility in sight.

I love going behind the scenes at the British Museum. I left word at Reception that I had a small parcel to show Dr Kinnes, and Maisie and I were ushered to a lift with an operator in a uniform. It was one of those situations where one isn't certain whether a tip is expected or not. But we had no money, so that was that.

Ian was completely bowled over by the pottery. He said he had never seen Mildenhall Ware in such perfect condition. As he was enthusing at full steam there was a knock at his door and Ian Long-worth entered. Ian Longworth was Keeper of the Department, the man in charge. He is also the country's greatest authority on earlier prehistoric pottery – so his opinion mattered. Like the first Ian, when he saw the piece from Etton he was *most* impressed. He asked about the site, and I told him. In fact I laid it on with a trowel. I also stressed the fact that we had good evidence that it was drying out fast. Maisie then told a sorry story of decay and destruction. Both Ians looked suitably appalled. 'Could it be,' I thought, 'that something is going to happen?' And it did.

Ian Longworth picked up the phone to no lesser person than the Director of the British Museum, Sir David Wilson. In five minutes Maisie and I found ourselves walking across the forecourt, beneath the museum's imposing portico, dwarfed by the vast columns. On either side of us were the two Ians, rather like two officers supporting soldiers on their way to face a firing squad. As we walked, they talked about this and that in a cheery, unconcerned sort of way. Deep down inside, I felt I was about to wet myself. I was well beyond nervous. Maisie looked completely calm and collected, which I recognised immediately as a bad sign. Shortly she would pass out cold, I knew it. But strangely she kept upright, and walking.

The Director's Apartments are on the left-hand side as you approach the museum. Inside, the rooms have high ceilings and doors, but although grand, they could not be described as palatial, and one is immediately aware that the building now occupied by the British Museum had once been a private house, albeit a grand one. The Director's Apartments still retained something of this domestic atmosphere.

Sir David can be down-to-earth when he wants to be. And on that occasion he wanted to be. He knew Maisie from her days at the Institute of Archaeology, where he had been Professor and he had wanted her to do his course. Sadly she had decided to opt for prehistory, but Sir David was kind enough to forgive her. Now he was positively inquisitorial, and with good reason: if he were to invest the Trustees' money in our project, then we had better deliver the goods.

Like all busy people, he disliked windbags, so I had to make my case short, sharp and to the point. The two Ians backed me up, and after ten minutes of close interrogation, Ian Kinnes, Maisie and I left the room. Ian Longworth stayed behind with Sir David to do the real talking.

Sir David had to refer our problem to the museum's Trustees, a process that took about three weeks. I'll never forget the day I was given the news. It had poured with rain, and I'd decided to stay at home to catch up on some paperwork. The phone rang. It was Ian Kinnes, and he sounded gloomy. My heart hit the floor. Then I realised he was pulling my leg. His tones were sepulchral, but the news he gave me was good. In fact it was very good. I did my best to sound grief-stricken too, but I fear the effort was not entirely successful, as I'm a poor actor. To cut a long story short, the museum had agreed to support an immediate excavation, but for one season only. I knew that would be enough, as I was sure English Heritage would fund any future work, especially if our initial results were promising – which they were bound to be. The crisis was over.

CHAPTER EIGHT

Rites of Passage in a Private World

MYTHS OF CREATION may justify our place on this planet, but they don't make us feel at home here. To feel at home one must take the word 'home' in its broadest sense. Home is where the family is. This applies today just as it applied in the Neolithic and Bronze Age, and it's the family that unites prehistory with the modern world. I'm aware that today prophets of doom are saying the family is collapsing, but I'm sure this is nonsense. I concede that restrictive social customs, largely inherited from the nineteenth century, may be changing. But the concept of family is not. Indeed, it cannot: blood relationships, what social anthropologists term 'ties of consanguinity', are the basis of all societies. In other words, blood is thicker than water; it's the biological superglue that binds us all together.

It was during the Etton dig that my thoughts on the importance of families, and family ties, first took shape. At the time, archaeological theory was moving in a rather different direction. The emphasis in the mainstream was on power and political interaction. Prehistorians were concerned with social formation processes: the way in which a small band – like the hunter-gatherer communities – grew into a tribe; how tribes combined together to form larger groupings, known as chiefdoms; and finally how chiefdoms formed themselves into alliances, which became the first kingdoms. I remember going to visit sites and being asked anxiously whether I thought a particular settlement belonged within a tribe, chiefdom or kingdom. I generally replied that it didn't matter at this stage. If you don't understand how people lived their daily lives, I still can't see that your thoughts on the way they organised their societies are worth a great deal. Although, of course, it's always fun to speculate.

I suppose my approach to prehistory differs slightly from the mainstream, because I have deliberately chosen to work for my entire professional life in a restricted geographical area. I firmly believe that ancient life is far too complex to understand by whizzing from one place to another. I'm also not particularly interested in examining what happened in a single period over a large geographical area, which is still the accepted way of 'doing' archaeology – so one studies, for example, all Earlier Neolithic causewayed enclosures across Europe. There are plenty of scholars doing those things, and they can sometimes provide useful insights. But I couldn't see then – or indeed now – why I should join them.

For myself, I would prefer to see how people in a given area used their own causewayed enclosure to develop other types of meeting places, and how in turn those physical changes to their surroundings reflected the way people actually lived their lives in the past. In other words, I prefer time-depth to geographical breadth. It seems to me that it makes sense to study, or rather to follow, the lives of a smaller group of people as they lived and died, one generation after another, in one place or region. I think it was George Tait who told me that archaeology was good at revealing the great social changes – the broad brush-strokes of the millennia, rather than the detailed etchings of history.

This way of working requires one to move from the particular to the general if one wants to make sense of one's observations. That's how Sherlock Holmes operated, but it's definitely not how most theoretical archaeologists would like us to work. They regard deduction as mere detective work, broadly comparable with pulp fiction. I would disagree – although I'm not about to rubbish their approach, which can be also be effective.

The accepted mode of archaeological thought is induction. Inductive reasoning was a key part of the New Archaeology (see page 42), and it explicitly mimics the thought-processes of science. In a nutshell, inductive reasoning moves from the general to the particular. So, one conceives the idea of a development from bands to tribes and eventually to kingdoms, then one goes out into the real world and finds evidence to support, modify or reject this view. The eventual aim of the process is to produce a series of general laws or principles. This is fine as far as it goes. But, so far, no general laws of any significance have appeared, and many of the case-studies that were produced to support a given theory have subsequently been shown to be capable of interpretation in a variety of other ways. The problem is that archaeology is not a science. It's a humanity, like social anthropology, sociology or history. In my view we should work in the way that suits our chosen subject-matter best. Sometimes one induces, other times one deduces. By and large I work like Sherlock Holmes, but there are times when I must draw on more general principles. This is particularly true when we come to the difficult topics of religion and ideology.

I wasn't really aware of it, but my way of approaching archaeology was gradually converging with the post-modern approaches that are currently in vogue. Life is a phenomenon experienced by individual *people*. And if we are to give any meaning to lives that were led in the past, we must relate them to the only experience of life that we all know – and that, of course, is our own. To do this, theoretical archaeologists draw widely on the thoughts and experiences of sociologists, historians and social anthropologists. In other words, they are trying – often in a satisfying manner – to relate the past to the present, with the help of experts in the way people live their lives, both in the present and in the recent past. The archaeologists' challenge was to apply these lessons to the remote past.

I have just said that these new approaches are relating the past to the present in a *satisfying* manner. I deliberately didn't say in an *accurate* or *truthful* manner. Remember, archaeology is not a science, and it's extremely difficult to make testable or provable statements, of even a basic sort, that can apply to everything. I have learnt to stay clear of ideas like Truth when it comes to prehistoric life. My quest isn't to understand Truth; it's to experience and illustrate life. I'm not concerned here about whether Truth does or does not exist – I leave that to philosophers. I'm concerned with the experience of life in the past and how it can affect our own lives in the present. This brings me back to where I began: to families and to the living of life within a family. It's one fundamental human experience that we can be sure we share with our Neolithic and Bronze Age forebears. It's a key we can use to unlock the lives we are trying to understand – if only in a small way.

The causewayed enclosure at Etton was positioned at the edge of a low rise of ground within a meander of a stream belonging to the old river Welland system. This specific location was interesting. Why did the local communities choose it? If they wanted somewhere to have frequent social gatherings, surely it would have made more sense to build a site on the higher, better-drained, flood-free ground of Maxey 'island'. But no, they selected a low, flood-prone hump of land that was cut off from the main 'island' by a series of stream channels, which would probably have been impassable in a wet winter without a boat – when the low 'island' they skirted would probably have been flooded.

Why on earth did they choose this remote spot? They weren't stupid. Far from it: they farmed and kept livestock within and at the edge of the Fens, and must have understood how wetlands worked, and how floodwaters behaved. So they must have known perfectly well what they were doing. Which leaves us with only one conclusion: they selected the low, flood-prone and cut-off 'island' because that was the site they wanted. Which of course explains nothing. But it is a start.

I think the key to the mystery does indeed lie in the enclosure's deliberate positioning. It wasn't placed at the centre of the low rise within the meander, where the ground was fractionally higher, and better-drained. No, it was placed at the edge, right up against the stream channel, where the ground was wet, and where the ditch never properly dried out. I have racked my brains, but I simply cannot explain this location in simple, functional terms. There is no evidence, for example, for a landing stage where the enclosure ditch clipped the stream channel. I think the best explanation is actually rather simpler – but it certainly isn't functional (which is not to say that it's irrational).

Many societies, especially mobile societies, hold the landscape in deep respect. They often confer spiritual significance on prominent features, such as hills, mountains or large trees. They might believe, for example, that the spirits of their ancestors resided in a particular place, and protected and watched over them as they passed by. We saw evidence for beliefs of this sort in the mortuary structures of the first landscape at Fengate, which were placed at the point where the dryland trail gave way to the Fens. It is not hard to find examples of similar beliefs in other parts of the world – one thinks immediately of Ayers Rock in Australia.

What I am suggesting is that in a landscape without hills and mountains, rivers become of prime importance. Maybe the hidden meander within the swirling stream channels had been venerated for a long time, before the Earlier Neolithic farmers decided to build their ditched enclosure there in 3800 B C. The people who constructed Etton would have been aware of the low 'island's' significance, and would not have wanted to dominate the already sacred place with what they may have seen as their own puny structure. So it was positioned off-centre, as a mark of respect.

It's difficult to prove this idea, largely because there are problems, once again, of archaeological visibility. The hunter-gatherer communities of the period that preceded the Neolithic, the Mesolithic, lived in small bands. They did not make pottery and they were mobile. As a result, occupation or settlement sites of the period are extremely rare. More frequently you find a few flint tools, but that is all. The chances of finding a thin scatter of such flints below the alluvium at Etton were tiny, and none were found. Other causewayed enclosures have provided circumstantial, and in a few rare instances actual, hard artefactual evidence for pre-Neolithic use.

It is common for causewayed enclosures to be placed within prominent landscape features, but usually they are positioned to one side of them. As we have seen, the Windmill Hill enclosure could have crowned the hill, but it didn't. It was placed deliberately off-centre, and it produced Mesolithic flint implements, which Isobel Smith reckoned had been brought to the site from outside. A recently discovered enclosure at Sawbridgeworth in Hertfordshire was placed directly next to a Mesolithic site. The Stonehenge ritual landscape is famous for not having a causewayed enclosure at its heart; but bear in mind that rather strange segmented ditch that encloses the stones. If it isn't a causewayed enclosure as such, it's certainly closely similar to one – albeit in miniature. And the discovery of those massive post-holes in the car park strongly suggests that the area was revered long before the appearance of the stones.

The point I want to make here is simple: religious *places*, as opposed to single, man-made *sites*, are often ancient indeed. They do not come and go. They reflect something powerful, without which human society might lose its cohesion. In short, they provided a physical expression or realisation of the ideologies that lay behind prehistoric concepts of history. They were a great deal more than important. They were essential – and hence their longevity.

In the modern world we often rely on such physical expressions of history and ideology. Battlefields are a good example. Once the immediate pain associated with a battlefield has gone, one might suppose that the actual place where the bloodshed occurred would lose its significance. But no. When southern England is eventually covered by sprawling estates of identical houses, the last spot to be built on will surely be the site of the Battle of Hastings.

I realised, as we began our first season of excavation at Etton in the spring of 1982, that to excavate a lost world of myth and ideology was the ultimate challenge. Sometimes it felt as if we were trying to dig wisps of smoke. It didn't help, either, that archaeology was then firmly rooted in a functional world. It was not good enough to reveal strange things for their own sake: one had to come up with coherent explanations that made some practical sense. It was rather like having to say that high altars were constructed as internal buttresses to the east fronts of our great cathedrals – which of course would be patently ridiculous.

The dig ended in the autumn of 1987, and I didn't manage to publish the final report until twelve years later. I am aware that this was too long, and I can plead some legitimate excuses. But in truth I was glad of the delay – even if others were not – because it allowed me to take the quest forward in several directions. Slowly my ideas were beginning to reflect the complexities that confronted me. I cannot pretend that our excavations revealed more than a pale reflection of what really happened at Etton five millennia ago, and my interpretation of the site is inevitably flawed and shallow. But I console myself with the thought that any impression is better than none at all.

A ceremonial and religious centre, be it Etton, Stonehenge or Westminster Abbey, only works because everyone in the community recognises it for what it is. Although they are both remarkable buildings, few people would lower their voices in St Pancras or Grand Central Stations. At Etton, and other causewayed enclosures, there is

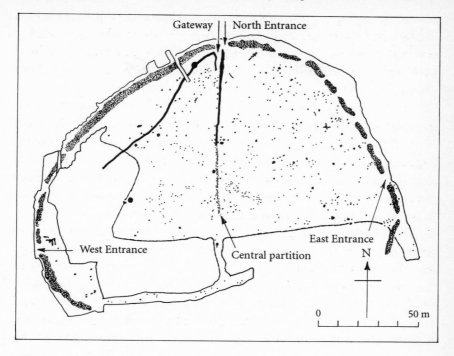

FIG 13   *Ground plan of the causewayed enclosure at Etton, near Maxey,*
Cambridgeshire

evidence to suggest that the initial laying out and construction of the
enclosing ditch, or ditches, was a major event which probably involved
hundreds of people from communities across the region. It was an
important occasion, because it was the moment when a particular
corner of an already venerated place gained new and special significance. Every community that was ever likely to use it was obliged to
recognise that fact.

Viewed from the air, the Etton causewayed enclosure was a
squashed circle, but from the ground it would have appeared circular.
It was entered by three entrance causeways which faced north, east
and west – three of the cardinal points of the compass. The main
entrance faced directly north. It was marked by the widest causeway
and a massive gatehouse constructed from two parallel rows of dressed

oak timbers, about a foot thick. This gatehouse was intended to impress. Opposite the main northern entrance there was probably another, facing south, but unfortunately we couldn't look at this length of ditch, which still lies hidden beneath the bank of the Maxey Cut.

The centre of the enclosure was divided into two halves by a fence-line that ran due south from the main gatehouse. There were also subsidiary, but still important, entrances to east and west. The west entrance was marked by a small structure we named a 'guardhouse', although in fact it resembled one of the Fengate mortuary structures rather more closely than anything else. A mortuary structure, also similar to those found at Fengate, was found just outside a possible entrance causeway at Windmill Hill, and it is tempting to suggest that this too was a 'guardhouse', but of a spiritual rather than a temporal sort.

The key to understanding Etton was the central partition or fence-line. On the east side we found evidence for rites and ceremonies to do with death and the soul's journey to the next world. The west side was different. Here we found evidence for public gatherings and feasting. One way to fix this division in your mind is to associate the eastern half with the rising sun, with a new dawn and a soul's journey to a new world. The western half was the sunset side, where people feasted at the end of a long and busy day – much of which might well have been spent in the eastern half.

We had been digging at Etton for about three years when I remember standing with Charly French in one of the old stream channels that skirted around the outside of the meander. It was a wet and windy day, and the clay in the stream channel built up heavily on our boots to form what Charly used to call 'Moonboots', which made walking hard work. As we leant into the wind and slowly made our way towards the main entranceway of the enclosure, it struck me that this was an odd approach to a major ceremonial centre. It was almost as if it had deliberately been made hard to reach.

At Windmill Hill an entrance causeway faces directly onto a particularly steep slope of the hill – which again suggests that the intention was to make access difficult. At Etton, the fording of a stream channel could have been a form of ritual washing or cleansing that everyone had to undergo before they could enter the sacred area. Given the difficulty of the journey, it is quite possible that young children were excluded until they had passed through the ceremonies of initiation into adulthood – which probably also took place at Etton.

After we had been digging for a couple of years we started to find pieces of broken polished stone axes, in the now familiar distinctive grey-green colour of Langdale stone. I was highly delighted at this, and phoned Mark Edmonds, who was then completing his doctoral research at Cambridge, and knew a great deal about stone axes. Mark is one of those unusual archaeologists who is also good at other things – he had been a furniture-maker before he took up archaeology. He approaches the subject obliquely, as both an archaeologist and a craftsman in his own right. Coming from this perspective, he knew that a craftsman's relationship with his or her materials was never simple, and was certainly never just functional. In some respects it was like a relationship between two people. Just as it is appropriate to be married in a certain place, it was appropriate to perform certain tasks in special places.

When we first found fragments of Langdale stone axes, I was struck by the fact that they seemed to have been deliberately removed from the complete axes. They resembled the flint flakes that were used to make knives or blades, and bore no resemblance at all to the small flakes that might accidentally have flown off the cutting edge when felling a tough tree. Mark had suggested that it may have been appropriate for craftsmen to work stone in the causewayed enclosure ditch, and it would have made it doubly appropriate to work the most valuable stone they possessed, which came in the form of finished Langdale axes. We don't know, but perhaps this type of ceremonial stoneworking took place at a stoneworker's death, or perhaps when he had completed his apprenticeship. Maybe a specialised stoneworker was not involved at all. Maybe valuable axes were destroyed in this deliberate fashion to mark death or some other rite of passage, such as birth, marriage or puberty.

Mark was keen on the concept of rites of passage, and I caught some of his infectious enthusiasm. The more I read about them in the literature of anthropology, the more it seemed to me that these rites often required the removal of the people involved from the main body of society. To move from one state, be it childhood or living, to another state, such as adulthood or death, one needed an intervening or transitional state which was neither one thing nor the other. This transitional state was experienced away from the routine and daily domestic world in a special place – and Etton was just such a place.

So rites of passage ceremonies happened in special places, which were frequently removed from villages and settlements. Julian Thomas, who expressed the idea clearly in an article he wrote sometime before he published *Rethinking the Neolithic*, introduced me to the concept of liminality. The word comes from the Latin *limen*, meaning a boundary or limit. In medicine, the word liminal is used to define the boundary at which something changes. Below a liminal concentration, for example, aspirin has no palliative effect.

Julian and Mark suggested that causewayed enclosures, and certain other special sites, played a liminal role. They were conceived of as being at the edge or boundary of the world we inhabit, and closer to the next world. This liminality was an ideological concept – a myth or a belief – but it was also given physical expression: liminal sites were deliberately placed at the edge of the inhabitable world of the time. So Etton was positioned on a small, frequently flooded 'island' off the main 'island' of Maxey; the enclosure at Windmill Hill was around the summit of the tallest hill for miles around. Water was often associated with the remote places that were selected. As the Neolithic period passed into the Bronze Age, we will see that water was to play an increasingly important symbolic role in the positioning of religious and ceremonial sites.

There's one other point to make before I return to Etton. The anthropological literature makes it quite clear that many rites of passage, especially those to do with the spirit's journey into the next world, were considered to be times of great physical and spiritual danger. The journey might not be completed, in which case the soul was doomed to wander a never-never land, neither alive nor fully dead. It would never rest at home in the land of the ancestors. The journey had to be completed, but even then there were dangers. As a soul passed though the portals of the next world, vengeful ancestors, or those who wished the living no good, could send disease, drought or famine back down the pathway the soul had just taken. It was a matter of sound sense, therefore, to locate the place from whence the soul's journey began at some distance from the settlements where people actually lived.

I have said that the key to Etton lay in its two contrasting halves. I know of only one other British causewayed enclosure that was divided neatly in this way, and it was also found in a wet place. This was at Staines, just a few seconds' flight from the runways at Heathrow. The site at Staines was much more difficult to understand than Etton, because it was less well protected by thick layers of alluvium, which meant that later archaeological features, such as Roman field ditches, had interfered with the Neolithic levels. But the two sites share many points in common.

I'll start my account of Etton where the day starts, in the east. When the eastern segments of the enclosure ditch were first dug, five thousand years ago, I believe that the gravel dug out was heaped around them, as if to exaggerate their size and depth. I say 'I believe' because it's difficult to prove this, as the archaeological evidence was removed when the individual ditch segments were filled in. This happened a short time after their digging. I believe, too, that each segment of ditch was probably surrounded by several dozen people, who stood on the freshly raised gravel banks and observed what was happening in the ditch below them. The newly dug ditch had become, in effect, a tiny amphitheatre in which special ceremonies took place.

As we slowly removed the gravel and soil that filled them, the ditches at Etton revealed a succession of remarkable 'offerings'. With this evidence, aided by a little imagination, we have been able to reconstruct a fairly accurate impression of the sort of ceremonies that took place there.

The clean white gravel of the ditch and bank would have contrasted starkly with the lush grass all around. I can imagine that the people on the raised banks drew back to allow a small funeral procession to walk down into the ditch. At the head of this procession would have been a man carrying a skin bag of ashes and pyre sweepings. Behind him were two men, possibly brothers, who together carried the skull of their father, an antler baton (a sort of short truncheon) and joints of beef to be eaten in the next world. Behind the brothers, to make atonement for the family's sins, were two sisters, one carrying a rock, the other a bowl of honey. The small procession stopped. Each person was standing still, about a metre apart.

Next, the man with the bag of ash and charcoal spread its black contents on the clean white gravel of the ditch bottom, immediately beside the causeway they had just climbed down. Then the brothers placed their father's skull on the ground, with his eye sockets facing along the ditch, staring towards the causeway that separated them from the ceremonies taking place in the next segment. Beside his skull they placed the antler baton he had kept by his bed as a symbol that he was the Master Stag, or head of the Stag family. They then carefully positioned the joints of beef he would need to sustain him on his last journey. Finally, the two sisters placed the pot of honey on the ground, but upside down, so that its sticky contents flowed slowly over the damp gravel and attracted a cloud of wasps, bees and flies – the insects of autumn. As the hum of the insects reached its height, the second sister smashed the pot with the rock.

Regardless of the pain of a score of stings, the two sisters carried the sticky pieces of pottery three slow paces away from the rock and the spilled honey, where they placed them carefully on the bottom of the ditch, fitting the pieces of rim into each other like so many nested pantiles. After five minutes, the pain from the wasp stings became too intense to bear and the girls collapsed, to be carried out of the ditch by other members of the family. Tomorrow they would be the most honoured guests at the family feast.

It was important to complete the next stage of the rites before the insects had finished their sticky treat. While the two sisters were being cared for by their relatives, the people around the ditch took birchbark baskets heaped with gravel and emptied them over the offerings. Suddenly the buzzing ceased. Then the gravel they had dumped was sealed with a thin layer of turf, placed upside down on the ground. When this had been done, the ditch was filled to the top with gravel that had been dug out earlier that morning.

The ditch segment on the other side of the causeway was the scene of another small-scale theatrical ceremony. This group too played a pageant built around the great moments of their family history. At the butt-end of the ditch, close to the causeway which separated their ditch from the Stag family ditch next door, a fox struggled to escape the tether which tied him to the ground. This was the emblem of the family of the Fox. The current master of the family strode forward and severed the fox's head with a single blow of his axe, then held it aloft for a few moments while the warm blood poured down his arms. Next he bowed to the ground, where he placed the creature's head, *upside down*, at the end of the ditch, in pride of place. No farm animal's head – and certainly no human head – was ever treated in this way.

The next morning the ceremonies were to be more private. The main family rites in the ditch segments were completed, and the night's feasting was over. Smaller groups from the various families assembled close to their newly filled-in ditch segments to commemorate those who had died that year and had yet to make the journey to the next world. As dawn broke, fires were lit and the prized possessions, but not the bones, of the dead were burnt. As the flames died down and the embers still glowed hot, joints of meat were thrown into the fire. Soon they hissed and spat into flames as the fat caught fire. Black, acrid-smelling smoke filled the families' lungs. This was a good portent for the final journey.

After midday, the fires were again raked through and warm remnants of bone, pottery and flint tools were scraped together. While one group scraped through the embers of the fire, another excavated a small hole in the ground, just large enough to contain two full baskets of rakings. These were then reverently tipped in, and the turf and gravel that had been dug out was heaped on top of them, as a permanent marker. It would be a serious offence against the departed person's spirit to interfere in any way with that filled pit, which was their symbolic last resting place. All future commemorative pits would have to be located with the greatest care, so as not to violate the space of the individual who had just departed.

One of the most striking aspects of the segmented ditch was that offerings in the ditch butt-ends, on either side of the causeways, never matched. We never found a skull facing a skull, or two complete pots. It was as if the people who made the offerings were asserting their family differences. It could also be that they were deliberately trying to avoid real conflict or disputes between families. Imagine two sets of eyes that eternally stared at each other through the causeway that separated them. It's an image that could have started a long-term family feud. I doubt that full-blown blood feuds were unknown in prehistoric Britain.

I have suggested that the offerings placed in the bottom of the segmented ditch were to do with specific families, and more particularly with family histories. Earlier, I suggested that Neolithic communal and family histories probably reached back to the time of great changes of the fifth millennium BC, when society moved from hunting and gathering to farming, and when the landscape began to be systematically cleared of trees. This view of people's own history might help to explain why wild animals were excluded from social centres such as Etton. Moreover, when they did appear, like the fox's head, they were presented as something almost perverse, something that was at variance with domestic life.

The season of 1986 started with a nasty surprise. We had budgeted to carry out earth-moving on a large scale, and were intending to remove alluvium over about half of the interior of the enclosure. Then, when we had actually started work, we learned that our grant was to be almost halved. In a state of shock Charly and I went to the company who had hired us the heavy earth-moving machines and explained the position, hoping we'd be able to negotiate a lower price. Their offer was much better: they would teach us to drive the diggers, bulldozer and dumpers, then we could operate them at a cheap flat rate. That's what we did, and I still keep in practice as a machine operator. As the machines were hired to us at a flat daily rate, we worked them all daylight hours – something that the Health and Safety Executive would not approve of nowadays. I mention this to explain why one morning I was driving the big Hy-Mac tracked digger.

It was a misty morning and I was feeling drowsy. Suddenly I was jerked awake when the bucket of my machine scraped the top of a large stone. I climbed out of the cab to have a closer look, and saw to my relief that the stone was undamaged. A little bruised, perhaps, but otherwise none the worse for wear. I could also see that the stone was curved. It lay within the buried soil and protruded up through it, a few inches into the alluvium. If this stone was indeed Neolithic, as I suspected, it would have been clearly visible on the surface in that period. Indeed it would have protruded a few inches above the grass. Back in the machine I worked carefully around it, then left it where it was for the team to clear by hand when they arrived later in the morning.

After several days' work we discovered that the curved stone was in fact a complete, but heavily used, corn-grinding stone, known as a saddle quern. Querns were always important objects, but like the axially-perforated cylindrical clay loomweights of Fengate (see Chapter 3), they have not received the attention from archaeologists that they deserve. They are essentially hand mills, and saddle querns are worked by kneeling astride a large bottom stone and rubbing a handful or two of grain with a smaller topstone, which is grasped in both hands. After a few months' use the bottom stone, which began life flat, or slightly dished, soon develops a deep saddle-shaped profile. Saddle querns are highly efficient, and can produce a cupful of flour in a few minutes.

The saddle quern I had revealed with my digger had been placed on edge, near the top of a shallow pit which contained a few pieces of Neolithic Mildenhall pottery, which confirmed its date. But, to our huge surprise, directly *under* the saddle quern, or bottom stone, we found its topstone. Plainly the positioning was a strong symbolic statement. The pit with its two stones was positioned close to the centre of the eastern portion of the enclosure, and directly opposite the eastern entranceway. It was clearly intended that everyone should see it.

When we came to map all the complete and broken pieces of quern we eventually discovered at Etton, we noted that with one exception (which was a pounder rather than a true quern) all were found in the eastern half of the enclosure. This unbalanced distribution was clearly intentional – but what did it mean?

One must be careful not to read too much into symbols, as it's very easy to get things wrong. But I believe that with querns we are on fairly safe ground. They are plainly to do with food preparation, and I think we can also suggest that they were symbols of domestic or family life – mealtimes are when the family comes together. So perhaps the pit with the visible quern was stating to everyone who entered by way of the eastern entrance that the eastern half of the enclosure was the area reserved for ceremonies to do with family life.

The strange arrangement, with the topstone below the bottom stone, which is on edge (and therefore useless), is surely saying that these stones are not for use here, in this life – that is, in the land of the living. In effect, the quern had been ritually killed, or taken out of circulation from amongst human beings. Many of the querns we found in the eastern ditch segments had been deliberately smashed, and in at least one case a large fragment had been placed in the ground with its grinding surface vertical – just like the complete stone in the pit. I suspect that the state of a quernstone, its position in the ground and its contexts all meant different things, depending on how they were combined. In short, we are looking here at a complex 'language' of symbolic expression. The more I worked through the results of the Etton dig, the more frustrated I felt. If *only* I understood what they were trying to tell me.

The western half of the site was different to the eastern half. The outer enclosure ditch showed less evidence for back-filling with clean gravel, so presumably large parts of it stayed open all year round. This may help to explain why so much of it was waterlogged and why we were able to find literally thousands of pieces of wood. Maisie was absolutely in her element, and I don't think I have ever seen her so happy. Despite the earlier misgivings, we had all agreed to excavate the wood in the way that Maisie wanted. And it certainly paid off.

By using a variety of simple statistical techniques, Maisie was not only able to determine that woodworking had taken place in or close to the ditch, she was also able to define the type or style of wood-working that had been carried out there. I will return to prehistoric woodworking in a later chapter, but here I want to show how Maisie's results fitted within our general reconstruction of what had originally happened at Etton. It was not enough simply to show that wood-working had taken place there: we were concerned with why this had happened, and in such a significant location.

There was some slight evidence that large oak timbers had been trimmed up close to the northern entranceway. This was probably to do with the construction of the main gatehouse, which was built from massive squared oak posts set edge to edge. But this comparatively restricted flurry of activity was the only evidence for what today we would call carpentry. Elsewhere, a visitor to the western arc of the ditch would have seen many people working much smaller stems, mainly of willow. These straight rods were taken from bushes that were regularly cut back, eventually to form substantial gnarled stumps, known as coppice stools. We found several of these stools growing in the bottom of the ditch.

You can still see the characteristically long, narrow woodchips that are produced by coppice-work if you visit a hurdle-maker's workshop. Even when using a sharp modern steel axe or bill-hook, springy wood, such as hazel, is best cut with an oblique, glancing blow. Normally this type of woodwork is carried out in the woods, and it is tempting to suggest that the work that took place in the western segments of the enclosure ditch was also partially symbolic. As Mark Edmonds had said about the polished stone axes, it was appropriate to perform certain tasks in certain places

I sometimes think that this wet part of the enclosure was a symbolic representation of the great forests that still covered most of the Neolithic landscape. Indeed, there are slight grounds to believe that the entire causewayed enclosure was a formalised or stylised representation of the contemporary landscape as it was perceived by people living within it. So there was not a clear-cut distinction between the actual, physical components of the landscape – the droveways, hedges, fields, lakes, woods and ponds – and the symbolic roles they played. Wood, for example, would have had a special significance, not just to do with hunting, but also with winter tasks, such as hurdle-making. We can assume, too, that these tasks had their own spirit-world guardians, who were approached through the generosity of the ancestors, at the right time and in the appropriate place. We can only glimpse this world and its complex workings, but I am convinced that it existed, and that it was important to the people living at the time.

Pollen analyses suggested that the bulk of the western half of the enclosure was probably covered by grass and rough grazing. Tests also showed that there was a distinct area of high soil phosphate not far from the western entrance. This may have been where animals were temporarily kept before they were slaughtered for feasts. There was also good evidence that the livestock area could have been enclosed by a trimmed and laid hedge. Several pieces of strange-looking hawthorn twigs that had grown into right-angled or elbow shapes were probably formed by regular hedge-trimming. All of this was in marked contrast to what we had found on the eastern side of the enclosure. The evidence for hedging at Etton is, I think, the earliest discovered in Britain so far. (Incidentally, I personally discovered the two earliest dog-droppings yet found in Britain, at the bottom of a waterlogged Neolithic pit at Etton. We all have our claims to fame.)

The clues that were to unlock what was happening in the western half were first found in the rich organic muds at the bottom of the enclosure ditch. Here we discovered several heaps of bones, mainly comprising the partial skeletons of pigs or sheep. In one case there was a neat bundle of calf spare-ribs, laid at the centre of a butt-end, close to a causeway.

These animal bones were washed as soon as they came out of the ground. I remember walking through the Finds Shed one day and noticing how extraordinarily fresh and clean-cut they seemed as they dried out on their plastic trays. It was almost as if they had come straight from the butcher's. All they lacked was that distinctive meaty, fatty smell. I looked closely at an ox scapula, or shoulderblade, and could clearly see the slight scratches that had been left by the flint knives when they severed the tendons attaching the meat to the bone. It was inconceivable that these bones had lain around on the surface for long, as they would have been gnawed by dogs or foxes.

We interpreted the bone heaps or partial skeletons at the bottom of the ditch as evidence for feasting; but we don't know who precisely was doing that feasting. Was it families together, or on their own? Or was it a larger affair, with people from different families mixing together? My own preference is for the larger gathering. Both human families and livestock farmers must regularly bring in new blood if they are to avoid in-breeding. The big livestock sales of England, such as the horse sales at Appleby in Yorkshire or the eight-hundred-year-old sheep fair at Corby Glen in Lincolnshire, are annual events. In prehistoric times such fairs or gatherings probably took place in the autumn, when the harvest had been safely gathered in. Annual autumn gatherings at Etton would have provided an ideal opportunity for young people to meet new partners, and for farmers to find new breeding stock. So perhaps we can also see the east–west divide within the enclosure as a split between the private (or family) and public (or communal) worlds that we all inhabit, as did our Neolithic ancestors. For me, that link is a direct point of contact with the past. But there is also another.

Returning to the eastern, private or family, side, I was struck by the fact that the small pits never cut into each other. I have already said that I attribute this to the idea of personal space. We all cherish our personal space, and don't like it to be infringed – which is why I dislike travelling on the London Underground in the rush-hour. Sometimes these pits, which I believe represented the lives of individual men and women, were topped off with a valuable object, such as a complete Langdale axe or a beautiful white quartzite axe-polishing stone, known by its French name, *polissoir*.

The pits were grouped around the ditch segments in a way that suggested that the individuals they represented had once belonged to (or had married into) the family whose history was enshrined in the offerings buried deep in the nearest segment of ditch. It put me in mind of family plots around the large central tomb of a dead patriarch in a Victorian cemetery. Although dead, people were proclaiming to the world that they belonged to a family, but were also individuals. At Etton the public/private split was being expressed on the smallest possible scale – that of the individual – within the heart of the 'private', eastern half of the enclosure.

Other things happened at Etton for which there is little direct archaeological evidence. I have mentioned that the animal bones were extremely fresh, and showed no evidence of having been gnawed by dogs. But with the exception of the skulls that were buried in the ditch segments of the eastern half, the human bones were invariably worn and weathered. Frequently they bore the clear circular puncture of a dog's canine teeth.

Is there anything in the state of the human bones to suggest cannibalism? Quite the contrary. Had human flesh been consumed, I would expect the bones to have been respectfully buried, clean and fresh, and complete with knife scratch-marks, like the animal bones. Anthropologically, most cannibalistic consumption of human flesh takes place as an act of respect, usually in a solemn ceremony. It is a way of taking in a dead person's experience or bravery. It's never done just for sustenance. No – I think the weathered bones are evidence for an altogether different rite, known as excarnation.

In many societies it is believed that the soul resides in the soft parts of the body. After death, corpses are exposed on platforms in remote places, or on ledges high in the mountains. Being liminal in many senses, Etton would have been an ideal place for exposing bodies. In order to ensure that they were not eaten by dogs or foxes, corpses would be placed on high wooden platforms, where the flesh would be removed by birds. People believed, as they watched them rise into the sky with the flesh, that the birds were taking the dead person's soul to the next world. Once the process had been completed and the bones were clean, the soul was thought to have departed. Perhaps the skull, with or without the long bones, was then removed to a family tomb somewhere else, but the remainder of the bones were now considered unimportant, and fell to the ground where they were scavenged by foxes and dogs.

Symbolic 'languages', just like spoken languages, change and develop through time. That first great event at Etton, when people from miles around came to acknowledge and mark out the course of the entire causewayed ditch, was probably a one-off. Thereafter communities would return to the site every autumn, perhaps to place more burnt offerings in the small pits, or to solemnify some rite of passage such as the transition from childhood to full adult membership of the tribe. These gatherings would have involved folk from many communities, but I think it highly improbable that the entire ditch would have been dug out and refilled every year. Indeed, the archaeological evidence suggests quite categorically that this did not happen.

It is more probable that individual ditch segments would have been re-excavated when the senior members of the family thought the collective memory was growing dim, or when the family had grown either too large or too small, and new alliances with other families were formed. The shared histories of the new family grouping would be re-enacted before an audience of the adults of the combined new family, and a new set of offerings (representing the new history) would then be placed in the ground and buried, as before. We can only guess at the frequency of these occasions, but maybe they happened every three or four generations.

Because these reworkings of family history took place so infrequently, it's possible to see that a distinct process of evolution, or development, was taking place in the way people expressed their symbolic language. Let's return for a moment to the original ceremony, as I imagined it on the basis of the excavated evidence. We left at the point when the senior member of the Fox family had laid the severed fox head on the bottom of the ditch, upside down. Next to the fox was another head, this time an artificial one. It consisted of a round-bottomed Mildenhall bowl that had also been placed in the ground upside-down. It was precisely the same size and shape as a human skull, and it even fooled us when we first found it. Similar 'fake' pot-skulls are known from other causewayed enclosures in Europe. Next to the upside-down pot was a decorated antler-comb, and beyond that a small flat-based bowl, also complete, but this time the right way up.

I'm not about to attempt another recreation of what myths or family history these offerings might have represented, but they took the form of a series of quite distinct 'statements', arranged in a line straight down the centre of the ditch. So, in symbolic terms they were united by being in a ditch and in a clear line, but there was space between them. This pattern of separate but aligned offerings was frequently found in the first phase of ditch-digging.

In the next phase, perhaps three or four generations later, the gravel was again removed, but only as far as the turf, or some other marker that has long since vanished. The diggers were extremely careful not to disturb the first set of offerings, which were left in the ground, intact. To have done so would have been to infringe not just personal space, but something far more powerful – not so much a symbolic representation of the family's history as the family itself.

The second time the ditch was opened, the recut ditch was smaller. This was not just because the earlier offerings were in the way – the diggers were perfectly capable of enlarging the ditch if they needed to. I am convinced that the reduced recutting of the ditch was because the offerings of the second phase were themselves smaller. For example, instead of a complete skull at the end of a ditch, we found just the frontal (forehead) bone. But the ridges above the orbits, or eye sockets, showed that the eyes had been positioned to stare at the causeway, just as before. There were signs, too, in the recut that families were growing and dividing up. In one instance the line of offerings was carefully divided into three equally-sized portions by two smashed pieces of saddle quern – the symbol of the family unit.

After two episodes of ditch cutting and recutting, the demarcation between the individual offerings began to break down. Sometimes meat bones would be buried between the various placed offerings, creating a more linear feel to the deposit. Again, the offerings in the recut were buried under clean gravel, a marker was probably added, and the whole thing was filled in. Some ditches included a third recut, in which the process of size reduction continued even further. I can think of two instances in which human heads were represented by round stones, one the size of a billiard ball, the other the size of a large marble. In both cases the most distinctive part of a skull, the hole (or *foramen magnum*) where the spinal chord enters the brain, was represented by a carefully pecked-out hole. Presumably the eyes would have been painted in.

The third and final recut was shallow indeed – maybe only two feet deep. This time the offerings formed a continuous narrow band, which looked like a flowing, tumbled stream of bone, pottery and flints. Then, for the last time, the offerings were buried. What are we to make of this gradual evolutionary change in the way people made their offerings? Could it be simply that they were just growing lazy? After all, the process of evolution moved in the direction of less digging and less effort generally. It was a process that we were able to observe in each segment of ditch around the eastern half of the enclosure. I think that's where the clue to the mystery lies – and it's anything but simple.

If the evolutionary process had only happened in, say, one segment, we could attribute it to some 'rogue' factor, perhaps to do with a long-running internal family problem. But it was happening everywhere – and not just at Etton. If one examines older reports of other causewayed enclosure excavations closely, it's possible to detect hints of a similar pattern of change at several other sites in Britain. Etton isn't a one-off in this respect.

Essentially, the process we are witnessing is one of formalisation and specialisation. People were quick to learn the grammar of their symbolic 'language', and they used it to express more, but with greater economy. It is possible, too, that as the 'language' developed, religious specialists began to appear in the larger families or clans. Alternatively, they may have travelled from one family to another. We cannot tell, at this stage, but I do not believe that the complexity and formalisation of these rites was sufficient to justify the use of the word 'priest', although it may well have been appropriate in other parts of Neolithic Britain.

By the time Etton went out of regular use, probably in the two centuries around 3500 BC, family rites had become formal, perhaps even routine. Maybe people felt they were losing control of their own histories. I don't know, but I have a feeling that when the structure and formality arrived, much of the spontaneity vanished, as is happening with institutional religion in Western society today.

Perhaps it was discontent with the way their lives were being organised for them, or maybe it was just a simple desire for independence. But whatever the social cause, Etton was abandoned to the gradually rising waters of the encroaching fen nearby. In the future, family histories would be celebrated on the main 'island' at smaller shrines, where people could gather in family groups to share grief, or to celebrate achievement. We are entering a new world and a new age – the dawn of the Bronze Age.

===

CHAPTER NINE

The Living Dead: Ancestral Spirits in the Landscape

IT WAS A LATE AUTUMN AFTERNOON IN 1972. Down in the dip of Stonehenge Bottom behind me, I could hear the ceaseless rumble of traffic on the A303. I was standing by the side of the smaller road that passes close by the stones, and like many others before me, I was contemplating that most extraordinary of all ancient sites.

My car was parked, illegally, next to me, and in the open boot was a box with the finds from the Fengate Neolithic 'house' – as I then still believed it to be. I had just taken the finds to show Isobel Smith in Avebury, and was both excited and delighted by what she had thought of them. As I sipped a mug of tepid coffee, I noticed that one of the bus drivers from the main car park was wandering towards me. I don't know how – maybe it was the contents of my boot, which included at least one human skull – but he recognised me for an archaeologist.

''Ere, mate,' he asked, nodding towards the stones in all their majestic stillness, 'what's it all about, then?'

Good question. I honestly can't remember what I said, but it was probably something regurgitated from a textbook, perhaps about the calendar, about symbols of power, religious authority and that sort of thing. When I had finished, he pushed his cap back on his head and gave me a look that said, 'So what?' Then, without comment, he rolled a cigarette and wandered back to his bus. My answer had been less than convincing. He knew it and I knew it.

If someone asked me the same question now, I would probably run a mile. But if I couldn't escape, I'd reply that you can't explain places like Stonehenge, but you can perhaps understand them. And that, I suppose, is what my quest is about. If we are to understand individual sites, we must see them as working parts of developing landscapes. And landscapes exist in people's heads just as much as they exist in reality, as hedges, ditches and banks. It's the stories, myths and legends attached to them that really breathe life into land-scapes, both past and present. Take Stonehenge. It makes no sense just to stare at the stones and wonder why they're there, unless you try to understand not the stones, but the *there*. Understand their setting and you understand the stones.

Landscapes are made by people for all kinds of reasons: for practi-cal reasons, to do with farming and settlement; for spiritual reasons, to do with liminality and the afterlife; and for historical reasons, to do with family and communal history. I may be wrong, but I believe that the only way anyone can hope to grasp the meaning of an ancient landscape is to approach it from a historical perspective. It's rather like those evolving deposits in the ditch at Etton: if you view one on its own, it makes some sense, but when you view the lot and the way they all change together, a more general light begins to dawn. Then, archaeology being what it is, you may discover that the new dawn is a false one – but that's another story.

My quest as an archaeologist has become broader in terms of time and place, but has also acquired greater focus – on people and their ideologies. Understand the motives and the thinking of the folk who created a landscape and you begin to understand their history. It's a complex process of detection and induction, and occasionally it can become circular. But I comfort myself with the thought that at least it does justice to the intelligence and sophistication of the communities we are trying to appreciate.

The last chapter closed with the abandonment of Etton to the rising waters of the river Welland and the encroaching fen around it at the dawn of the Bronze Age. That's a suitable cue for a return visit to Fengate, five miles to the south, on the edge of the Fens. We have already seen how the earliest cleared landscape there developed from the seasonal migratory routes of the first farmers, and that these routes were probably based on the journeys of their hunter-gatherer forebears. There was then a gap, of perhaps half a millennium, which we still don't fully understand. Then, around 2200 BC, the first droveway ditches of the main Bronze Age livestock field system were dug. This was the landscape I had investigated in the 1970s.

During my original campaign at Fengate, when I was commuting across the Atlantic, I only had the opportunity to excavate a single barrow, which showed up on air photographs as a dark and distinct ring-ditch. Barrows are, of course, burial mounds, but in the more intensively farmed areas of Britain they usually become worn down by ploughing, so that they barely survive as mounds at all. All that is left is the circular ditch that was dug around them as a quarry to provide material for the central mound. The ditch was very much a part of the monument as a whole, and there were often concentric elaborations, such as an external ditch, then a low bank, then a narrow space, and then, at the centre, the mound. The various ditches, banks – even circles of posts – did not appear at once, but accumulated over time, as the result of many individual ceremonies. Taken step by step, the complexity of the elaborations is rather less daunting than it first appears.

The sad thing about ploughed-out barrows is that most of their history lay hidden in the mound, which is the first thing the plough destroys. We've seen that barrows were rarely single-episode monuments, built for just one person. Often they started in that way, with a primary central burial, but then people repeatedly returned to the same place, just as they had done in the days of causewayed enclosures a few centuries earlier. When they returned they would frequently enlarge or embellish the barrow in some way. Sometimes they would add a ring of posts around the central mound, or add a bank to the ditch. Often they would insert secondary burials into the mound, sometimes bodies, but more often cremations in urns.

I dug my first barrow at Fengate in 1973, and was disappointed to discover that it had been ploughed flat – probably, I now realise, two thousand years ago, in Iron Age and Roman times. I was also disappointed to find no central primary burial, which may originally have been placed high in the mound; I had to content myself with an Early Bronze Age secondary cremation and the skeletons of two children, also probably Early Bronze Age, which had been cut into the partially filled ring-ditch.

John Lorimer holds the bronze axe that started the Seahenge saga. It is many centuries later than the timber circle near which it was found. Recent discoveries suggest it may once have formed part of a small collection of bronze implements, known as a hoard. Hoards were very often votive offerings made at special and sacred places.

A view along the Holme-next-the-Sea peatbeds at low tide, autumn 1998. Today these beds are discontinuous and damaged as a result of fierce storms the following winter. This photograph was taken at the very beginning of the first exploratory excavation; the timber circle is visible by the figure (centre left).

OPPOSITE: TOP The team from the Norfolk Archaeological Unit start work on the accurate surveyed ground-plan of the Seahenge timbers, which had to be completed before the excavation could begin. This view clearly shows how the 'whirlpool' action of the tide flowing past and around the central inverted tree has eroded the beach surface within the circle of posts.

CENTRE A close-up of the post circle shortly after the tide has retreated, showing the eroded and damaged state of the timbers. The posts appear to be separated by gaps, but this is the effect of the sea's erosion: immediately below the surface they touch each other along their entire lengths. Within the circle, the roots of the inverted oak tree have been smoothed and worn down by the waves.

BOTTOM The initial exploratory trench within the circle of fifty-five timbers, autumn 1998. Peat beds are clearly visible in the background, between the beach and the sea. To the right of the inverted oak tree is a spar of timber from a nearby wreck (the ice-ship *Vicuna*, which ran aground after bursting her moorings in March 1883).

ABOVE Part of the inverted oak tree at the centre of Seahenge was exposed by the exploratory trench. This was the first time we became aware that it had been deliberately de-barked. Grey silt is still adhering to the axe-marks left by the de-barking process (scale one foot, or thirty centimetres).

LEFT The excavation and removal of the posts of Seahenge was done entirely by hand. The conditions were apalling, resembling a scene from World War I more than a normal dig. The wood was fragile and the bark detached readily, so great care was required; here a post is being prepared for removal on an ex-army stretcher, held by the excavation director, Mark Brennand (right).

BOTTOM During the excavation of Seahenge samples were taken at regular intervals by the team's soil scientist, Dr Fran Green. Here she is recording the precise position of sample tins which have been placed in the section on either side of a post. Other posts of the circle can be seen in the background (upper left).

The excavation and removal of the Seahenge timbers was controversial. Here a group of Druids occupy the central tree in an atttempt to prevent its removal. In the background the wrecked ice-ship *Vicuna* has just been exposed by the waves.

My main interest that season was in the Bronze Age field system at Fengate, which was then pretty well unique in Britain. I suppose I should have thought more about the barrow than I did – but then, one cannot think of everything all of the time. It was there, nonetheless. The folk who dug the field ditches were aware of it, as the ditches stopped short of it, and avoided it. So it must have been clearly visible to the people who laid out the fields. Anyhow, I wrote my report and thought no more about it.

During the 1980s I was busy in the Welland valley and elsewhere, and Fengate slipped into my subconscious, where it quietly fermented for a long time. In 1990, commercial archaeology was just getting started, and my team won a contract to evaluate the potential of a large plot of land at the edge of the Fengate fen. The field in question was covered with thick alluvium and had been permanent pasture for dozens of years, so absolutely nothing was visible on any air photos.

Part of the plot extended to the edge of one of my old open-area excavations of the 1970s. It was sad to walk across the old dig, which had once been so busy and businesslike, with cleanly-cut sections, string lines, ordered rows of grid pegs – even a viewing platform for the public. Now it was a mess of mud, torn apart by motorbikes, with the remains of our excavated features filled with stagnant water, broken bottles and rusting supermarket trolleys. Tethered gypsy horses grazed the grass-clad spoilheaps.

As I walked across this scene of dereliction, I remembered the earnest look of the City Planning Officer as he asked if I could absolutely and unconditionally guarantee to be off the land by September. Somehow we just made the deadline, but then the developer failed to materialise. That was in 1977.

I had a copy of my final Fengate report with me, and by dint of prodding about near the edge of the old excavation, I managed to find a shallow depression which I recognised as the silted-up remains of an excavated Bronze Age field-boundary ditch. At last I had something to go by. I have long been a believer in the old archaeological adage: always work from the known to the unknown. So that's what we did – we followed the known and once-excavated field-boundary ditch eastwards, down towards the fen.

After about fifty metres I decided to extend the trench to one side, for no reason at all – just on a whim. It paid off. As the alluvium was removed, it slowly revealed the darker outline of a ring-ditch, almost two metres wide. This was far too wide to have been the outer drainage gully of a roundhouse. It took the earth-moving machine a full three hours to fully expose the circle. I went carefully, as I was concerned in case we hit any upstanding features, such as on-edge quernstones. The internal diameter of the ring-ditch was fourteen metres and there was a single, extremely narrow entranceway on the south side. I immediately recognised it as not a barrow ring-ditch, but a henge monument of Class I.

Henge monuments are an archaeological invention that probably had little validity in antiquity. The term derives from the 'henge' or hanging stones of Stonehenge, and it was given its accepted archaeological definition by Professor Richard Atkinson in 1954. He defined henge monuments as having one or more circular ditches, with an external bank and one or more entranceways. Sometimes, but not always, there were settings of posts, stones or both inside the circular ditch. Often there were burials too. Henges with one entranceway belonged to Class I, with two, to Class II. All this is fine, so far as it goes, but I doubt if prehistoric people necessarily made decisions along the lines of, 'Today let's go out and build a Class I henge.' In a roundabout way, this brings me to the significance of circularity.

Henges, as defined by Atkinson, are only found in Britain; but as I have said, it's a narrow definition, which would have meant nothing to the people of the Later Neolithic and Bronze Ages. In fact henges are just one component of a much broader tradition of circular sites and monuments that include timber circles, stake rings and round barrows. Sites of this general type are found throughout Europe, and most particularly in Atlantic Europe: in Britain and Ireland, France and Spain, the Low Countries and Scandinavia.

A circle is a simple, satisfying, all-encompassing shape that is straightforward to lay out on the ground. It's difficult to pin a specific meaning on it. My old friend (now Professor) Richard Bradley, who has provided our teams with numerous bright students, has come as close as anyone. Writing in 1998 about the broad cultural tradition of circular structures along the western margins of Europe, he argues that it reflects something profound, 'a shared perception of the world

– a prehistoric cosmology'. It is worth quoting him at greater length, because he goes on to make an important point that will prove relevant shortly:

> The idea of a circular or spherical cosmos . . . can carry an enormous weight of symbolism, it may originate in the experience of an individual inhabiting an increasingly open landscape. He or she is at the centre of a world which recedes towards the horizon, where the land meets the sky . . . Whatever their ultimate meanings, circular constructions reflect a perception of space that extends outwards from the individual and upwards into the sky. The main fixed points on the land may be natural features like hills, while those in the sky are the sun and the moon, whose positions can be seen to change in relation to such landmarks. This may be why circular constructions are often subdivided according to the cardinal points [of the compass], or why they often stand for a cycle in the human or natural worlds.*

The Fens are, of course, the ultimate flat landscape, where sky and land merge almost imperceptibly. It is no wonder that circular sites were so important here. Now, for a monument, such as a henge, to appear circular from the inside, it doesn't have to be strictly circular. The ditch around Etton appeared circular when we were working on the interior, and I don't think it matters much that it wasn't perfectly circular. It would have been the rounded, circular feel of the place that counted. People only began to worry about strict circularity as their perceptions of religious and ceremonial rites became more formal; and this took time. This is one of the reasons why I find much modern writing about ancient geometry and astronomy so unconvincing. Despite their mathematical sophistication, the authors fail to address the problem of ancient perception; they naïvely assume that Bronze Age folk thought as we do today.

Back in the excavation, I watched while the machine worked its way past the henge ditch. We found nothing of any real note – or so I thought. There was a line of fence post-holes that were heading towards the henge, but not straight at it. Had the line been continued

* R. Bradley, *The Significance of Monuments: On the Shaping of Human Experience in Neolithic and Bronze Age Europe* (Routledge, London, 1998), p.109.

it would just have missed the henge ditch, but would eventually have reached the original field-boundary ditch (the one that we'd followed from the derelict excavation) at right angles. Then a bell rang deep in my subconscious. The presence of the henge was again being respected by elements of the later, Bronze Age, landscape – in this case the line of posts. As I had observed with the 1973 barrow, the Bronze Age farmers hadn't ignored it. And here they hadn't ignored the small henge, either. So both sites must have meant something to them. But for some reason I still failed to make the connection.

There was slight circumstantial evidence to suggest that the small Fengate henge was constructed in the centuries around 2500 BC, at the very end of the Late Neolithic period. But when we came to dig it by hand, we made an extraordinary discovery. Within the area enclosed by the henge ditch were two shallow gullies. One was curved, probably circular, but incomplete; the other was almost circular and had an extremely narrow entranceway: just two hundred millimetres (eight inches), although originally it may have been slightly wider. Even so, most people would have had to breathe in when entering. So it was a Class I henge too, but it was tiny. The internal diameter of its ditch was just 2.7 metres. I believe it's among the smallest henges yet found. Unfortunately it's hard to date the two micro-henges, but I have reasons to believe that they were probably quite a lot later than the main one that enclosed them.

The world of contract archaeology grew ever more cut-throat, and my team failed to win the next big Fengate contract, which was a few hundred metres south of the 1990 henge. The winners were the Cambridge University team and, in fairness, they did an excellent job. In September 1992 they excavated a complex of Bronze and Iron Age field-boundary ditches in the southern part of Fengate. In one corner of the site was a ring-ditch which did actually show up on air photos. The mound of the barrow was severely plough-damaged and barely existed at all. After the Cambridge team had finished their dig, the factory building proposed for the site failed to materialise, and the field lay vacant for seven years. Then, early in 1999, we were invited to re-investigate, and the first thing we found was a body – directly under the barrow. It lay on its side, with legs drawn up. This attitude, which recalls the foetal position, was common in the Bronze Age, and

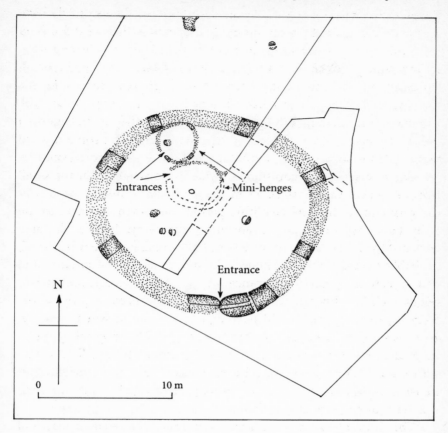

Entrances

Mini-henges

Entrance

N

0

10 m

FIG 14   *Ground plan of the small henge, with two nested 'mini-henges',*
at Fengate

may have expressed a wish that the person would be reborn in the next world.

The body aside, the most interesting aspect of the site was the fact that the ditches of the Bronze Age fields again respected the barrow. In this instance they had to kink their course slightly to get past the mound. It would have been a simple matter to have cut across the base of the mound, but no, they had to divert around it.

The two barrows and the henge appeared to have been arranged along the edge of the fen, at intervals of roughly two hundred metres.

This was also the approximate interval at which the main double-ditched droveways of the subsequent Bronze Age field system occurred. By now the penny was at last beginning to drop. I re-examined all the available air photos, and combed the records in Peterborough Museum, to discover another three barrows, which continued the regular spacing along the fen, further to the north.

Finally the truth dawned. The formal Bronze Age field system that lasted through much of the third millennium and the entire second millennium BC (from before 2500 BC until about 700 BC) was actually based upon an earlier, Neolithic, landscape that was also divided into broad divisions about two hundred metres wide. The big difference seemed to be that the Neolithic folk used barrows to parcel up their landscape, whereas the Bronze Age farmers used ditches and droveways.

But was this apparent big difference real? The more I looked into it, the less real it seemed. For a start, it was clear that the barrows continued to be respected, and indeed to be used, well into the Bronze Age. Recently, with help from Channel 4 television's *Time Team*, we excavated a barrow on the eastern 'shore' of Flag Fen. We found that it was first built around 2000 BC or before, and continued in regular use into the Late Bronze Age – to at least 900 BC. This would suggest that the barrows, which had their origins in the open countryside prior to the construction of the fields, continued to be in use during the almost two-thousand-year life of the fields. But what was their purpose? Were they just obsolete features in a new landscape that were respected simply out of superstition? I think not. No, their role was much more important than that.

Ditches, droveways and hedges are intended to control animals, not humans. When properly laid and maintained, hedges can do this job very effectively. But humans require more powerful means to control them. Slowly it dawned on me that the regularly-spaced barrows were, in effect, spiritual 'electric fences' for the control of people. With the ancestors to guard and watch over the boundaries, nobody would attempt to trespass. This would explain, too, why these sites continued to be venerated for so long.

An interesting independent piece of evidence has recently been found to support this idea. The village of West Deeping lies about two miles north-east of Maxey, in the flat gravel landscape of the Welland valley. The freely-draining gravels are particularly good for air photos, and a recent map of the cropmarks has revealed a remarkable Bronze Age field system. This system is like Fengate, in that it is also based on double-ditched droveways that run down – in this instance to the river floodplain, rather than a fen. The spacing of these droveways is closer to four hundred than two hundred metres, and there is also a series of regularly-spaced-out barrows that more or less coincide with the Later Bronze Age droveways. Again, as at Fengate, we seem to have continuity between the Neolithic and the subsequent Bronze Age landscapes.

But for me the real interest of West Deeping lies in the little ditched livestock-handling yards which are attached to the north-west side of each droveway. Animals would be assembled in these yards to be counted, checked and doubtless sold. Surely they are the Bronze Age equivalents of the small family farmyards that were common in this area until the last war. If the farmyards belonged to the families that farmed the parcels of land between each droveway, could not the earlier barrows have belonged to individual families too? If that were the case, it's quite probable that the Neolithic landscape wasn't, strictly speaking, open and unfenced. It was probably divided up in an informal pattern, marked perhaps by trees and bushes. The barrows served as permanent markers of certain key areas, perhaps where land disputes were likely to occur.

So, at both Fengate and West Deeping we have evidence that the landscape was originally divided into territories (or farms) that were controlled, through the power of their ancestors, by a series of separate families. As the population of livestock grew, and with it the pressure on grazing, a critical point was reached when more formal measures were needed. At that point (at Fengate it was around 2500 BC, at West Deeping probably a millennium later) the landscape was divided into ditched and hedged fields. At the same time the main boundaries were made formal by means of droveways. But the underlying driving force, power, influence – call it what you will – was still the family and, of course, their spiritual allies in the world of the ancestors.

I don't want to give the impression that barrows, henges and other small, mainly circular, sacred sites were used only in this ostensibly

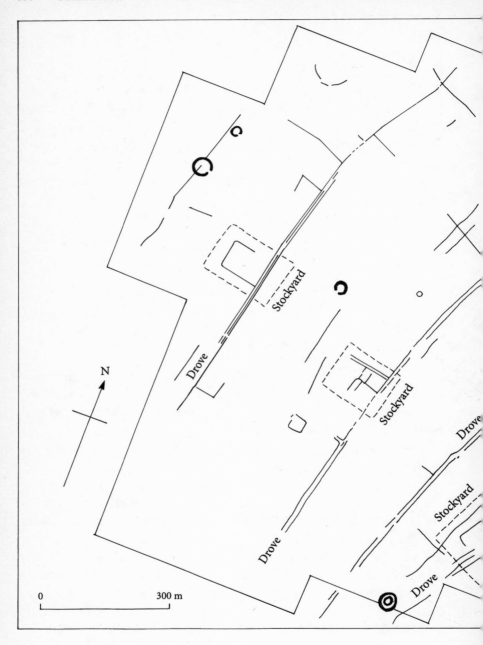

FIG 15   *Plan of Bronze Age fields revealed by air photography at West Deeping, near Maxey. Barrows are shown in bold line*

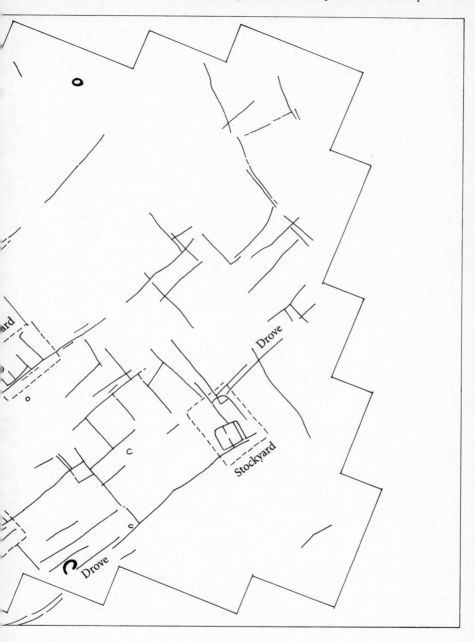

practical way, out in the fields and pastures of the farmed countryside. For a start, the intensively farmed field systems of the Bronze Age are only found in a few places. The vast bulk of the landscape was open grazing, and not necessarily divided up at all. This may apply to the ritual landscape of Maxey 'island', where, despite a most careful search, we have so far failed to detect any evidence of ditched and hedged Bronze Age fields. We know from a number of environmental studies that the Bronze Age landscape here was largely open pasture, and cleared of trees – but so far formal fields appear to have been lacking.

Etton went out of use partly no doubt because water levels around it had begun to rise, but partly too because the enclosure had served its purpose and people wanted to do things differently. In particular, they wanted to take control for themselves of those rites and ceremonies they had performed in the eastern family, or private, side of the enclosure. But how could this be done? The enclosure was universally recognised as the main religious and ceremonial centre – and not just by the living. It was inconceivable to consider abandoning it completely – and we know that this did not happen until very much later – but somehow its special powers had to be conducted across the stream channels and onto the main 'island'.

The means chosen to conduct these special powers was the Maxey Cursus (see page 98 for cursuses). Cursuses, like henges, are unique to Britain. They consist of two parallel ditches with banks on the inner side, and often have closed ends. The longest in Britain, the Dorset Cursus, currently measures ten kilometres in length. I say 'currently' because it regularly becomes extended after a dry summer's aerial photography. Cursuses were constructed in the Middle Neolithic, at about the same time as or slightly later than causewayed enclosures, and are often found within or close by them.

In general the purpose of cursuses remains obscure, but they sometimes contain burials and are usually found within ritual landscapes. Although attempts have been made to understand them as a group, I find such explanations unsatisfactory. It's probably best to treat them on a case-by-case basis, as they appear to differ from one ritual landscape to another. Having said that, they undoubtedly played a non-functional, symbolic role, and often one to do with death. We have seen that in Brittany and elsewhere lines of sight played an important part in the way the various components of a ritual landscape fitted together, or articulated. So a minimalist view of cursuses would be that they identified, and made formal, the sight-lines that mattered, very like the careful way people's thoughts and emotions were channelled five thousand years later at Stowe. With a cursus before him, the visitor to a ritual landscape knew where to look – and probably, too, what to think at that particular point.*

There are two cursuses near the Etton enclosure. The first, known as the Maxey Cursus, has been recognised for some time. It starts near the causewayed enclosure and runs north-west across the stream channel belt and up onto Maxey 'island'. The two ditches are about fifty metres apart and run for at least two kilometres right across Maxey 'island', vanishing under thick layers of alluvium at each end. We know that there was a causewayed enclosure (Etton) at the south-east end, and it's tempting to suggest that another may lurk under the flood clay at the other end. Doubtless time will tell.

The second cursus, known as the Etton Cursus, was found by our team when we were excavating the causewayed enclosure. Most of its course still lies hidden under alluvium, but its north-west end lies partly within the causewayed enclosure. It can be dated to a late period of the enclosure's use – possibly around 3500 BC – and it's slightly wider (about seventy-five metres) than the Maxey Cursus.

The fact that the two cursuses seem to start or finish at the causewayed enclosure leaves me in no doubt that all three sites were closely connected. I have suggested that the Maxey Cursus was perhaps constructed to conduct the special 'magic' of Etton onto, and then across, the 'island' of Maxey. Obviously that's an idea that is hard to prove, but for what it's worth, it does now seem to be widely accepted.

Most British cursuses were constructed in one go, although they may sometimes have been modified later. Maxey, on the other hand, seems rather different. The straightest length is between Etton and the centre of the modern 'island', at which point it kinks northwards. Further along, towards its northern limit, another two ditches appear and begin to diverge, as if the first set had been found to be misaligned.

* Cursuses must not be confused with Ley Lines, which were invented in the twentieth century, and work on the principle that two distant places can be joined on a map with a straight line. They ignore the landscape, its prehistory and all archaeological knowledge.

This would suggest that the cursus was constructed in several quite distinct stages. At the centre of the 'island', close to the kink that might mark the end of the first stage of construction, air photos revealed a large circular ditch with a single entranceway, facing east. Within the gap of the entranceway was a small oval enclosure, and at the centre of the large circular ditch was another. It was concentric with the large outer ditch (diameter 125 metres), and slightly larger in size, but smaller in diameter (forty-two metres) and without an entranceway. We shall call the main outer ditch the Maxey Great Henge, to honour the fact that its diameter is fifteen metres greater than the ditch around Stonehenge itself.

I shall discuss the Maxey Great Henge in a moment, but first I want to mention some of the smaller ring-ditches, barrows and henges of the ritual landscape around it. Air photos show them clustering about the cursus, on the south side of the 'island', between Etton and the Great Henge itself. One of the most famous archaeological air photographs of all was taken by that famous pioneer of aerial photography who found the two West Kennet timber enclosures, Professor 'Holy Joe' St Joseph. Holy Joe's photograph, which formed the frontispiece of the Royal Commission's report *A Matter of Time*, was taken above the Great Henge, looking north-west down the Maxey Cursus, with Maxey church on the left, the cropmarks of the deserted Saxon village around it, and two barrow ring-ditches in the left foreground. As air photos go, it's a masterpiece of composition – and information.

When our team started work at Maxey in 1979 we were aware that we were relative latecomers to the area. The publication of *A Matter of Time* in 1960 had given the archaeological world a kick in the pants. Everyone agreed that something had to be done in the face of so much gravel extraction. So the Council for British Archaeology (of which I am currently President), to its eternal credit, helped set up a local team to investigate the newly revealed ritual landscape at Maxey. It was directed by Gavin Simpson, a keen young archaeologist with new ideas.

In 1964 Gavin's small team discovered an extraordinary pair of miniature henges about 225 metres south-west of the Maxey Cursus, and about the same distance due south of the Great Henge. The two sites were probably constructed and used at about the same time,

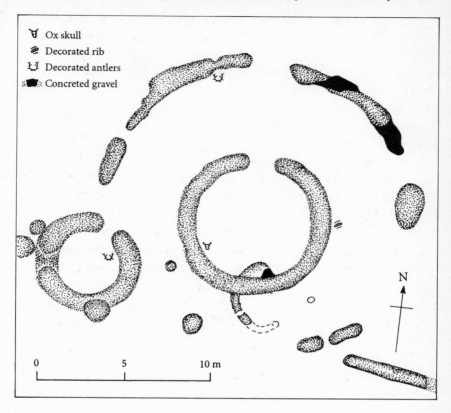

FIG 16   *A group of 'mini-henges' excavated by Gavin Simpson at Maxey,*
1965–66

possibly in the later years of the Middle Neolithic; I would guess
between 3000 and 2500 BC. The external diameter of the smallest
henge was just 6.5 metres, and it had a single narrow entranceway
which faced south-west, in the general direction of the midwinter
sunset. The larger henge consisted of two concentric ditches. The inner
one had a single entranceway facing south, but the outer ditch was
dug in a series of irregular segments, rather reminiscent of Etton, only
tiny by comparison. It too had a southwards-facing entrance.

There were no internal features of any sort in the two henges, but
in the soil and gravel that filled the ditches the team found a complete

ox skull, a decorated red-deer rib and two decorated red-deer antler 'batons'. The decoration consisted of scratched grooves filled with a sticky paint made from red ochre, fat and charcoal. The extraordinary decorated 'batons' are so far unique to Maxey, and Gavin has suggested that they hark back to a series of decorated bone and antler objects made in the Mesolithic period, several thousand years earlier. Whether or not one agrees with that theory, I'm absolutely convinced, with Gavin, that all of these objects were deliberately placed in the ditch, and that it was then promptly back-filled, which of course is highly reminiscent of Etton. The decorated objects can have no possible practical use, and closely resemble some of the special implements used during rites of passage and other ceremonies by shamans in many tribal societies.

Sadly, the tiny Maxey henges have long since been quarried away for gravel, otherwise Charly French might be able to provide scientific proof, using soil micromorphology, that the ditches had indeed been back-filled. But I can't imagine that the objects' painted decoration could possibly have survived if they had lain around on the surface for any length of time.

We were busy during the summer of 1986. By September the excavation at Etton was at full blast and the quarry operators were beginning to breathe down our necks. But there was so much to find that we couldn't have gone any faster. As it was, we worked all daylight hours and most weekends. I remember slumping onto the ground outside the Tea Hut, where Charly was filling in one of our finds forms. He needed to know the date, and I told him. 'Good grief,' he replied, 'whatever happened to August?' If ever I write my autobiography, that would be its title.

To ease the pressure on Etton, the quarry company moved its operations to the north, just across the belt of stream channels that separated us from the main 'island' of Maxey, and we hived off a small group from the main Etton excavation to investigate this newly threatened area. Air photos showed cropmarks of a wide and indistinct – almost blurred – ring-ditch, which lay at the edge of the alluvium. We named the site EL2 (Etton Landscape Site 2). It was 250 metres north-east of the causewayed enclosure and on a low-lying part of the main Maxey 'island'.

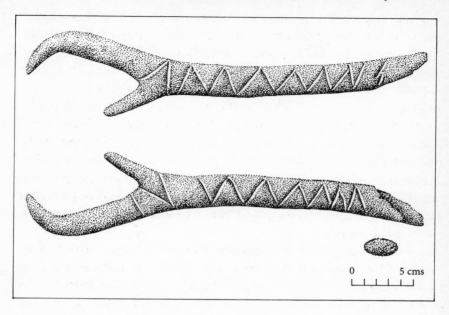

FIG 17   *Decorated shaman's baton from the Maxey 'mini-henges'*

We used a large tracked digger to remove the topsoil and alluvium, which was thicker than we had expected. Directly below the alluvium we found, as expected, the buried prehistoric topsoil, but it was thin across the interior. Charly took samples for micromorph., and announced that it was thin because it had been removed deliberately. Maybe the ring-ditch diggers had cut thick pieces of turf for use elsewhere, perhaps in buildings, but I have to say I don't think such a practical explanation is likely. I was excited at Charly's news, because we had seen precisely the same phenomenon below a barrow mound of turf and topsoil four years previously. We couldn't understand it then, but now we had the confirmation we needed that it was probably deliberate. It was most intriguing, and I shall say more about it shortly.

The reason for the blurred image on the air photograph was apparent as soon as the site was exposed. Instead of a single large outer ditch there were at least three sets of ditches, some complete, others segmented. At the centre was a group of eight round pits. When we dug them we found they had originally contained massive posts, at least the size of large telegraph poles, some even bigger. Three of the posts were arranged in a diagonal row, aligned on the midwinter sunset. The post setting was surrounded by a continuous ditch which probably had an entranceway facing south-west, again towards the midwinter sunset. At some point this entranceway had been deliberately blocked.

During the next phase, which probably happened quite soon after the initial phase, the ditch around the posts was replaced by a segmented ditch. The ditch segments appeared to be doubled up on either side of the south-western entranceway, which was blocked with a particularly large pit. The segmented ditch was back-filled with clean gravel shortly after it was dug. The segments would now be marked by gravel mounds.

The final phase saw the digging of a continuous ditch around the outside of all the other ditches. It was interesting to see that this last ditch never cut into any of the earlier ones, though sometimes it came close. Again, this would suggest that the earlier, filled-in ditches were marked on the surface in some way.

None of the earlier features produced any finds, but the final circular ditch did. It had been dug and then back-filled to half its original depth, then a series of offerings were placed in the ground: smashed pieces of Later Neolithic pottery (dating from around 3000–2500 BC), pieces of red- and roe-deer antler, and a superb flint axe, large and beautifully polished, made from an attractive mottled flint that resembled the marbled endpapers one sometimes finds in old books. This type of flint has little strength because it gets its mottled look from being repeatedly frozen and thawed during Ice Ages; the process creates plains of weakness within the stone, which shatters on impact. So the axe was for show only, and could never have been used. The offerings were then buried, and the ditch was filled to the surface, and above.

How does one describe a site like EL2? At one period it may have been a henge of sorts, but I don't think its precise archaeological definition is relevant. We could find no burials, so it probably wasn't a barrow. I like to think of it as a family shrine, somewhere people went to celebrate significant family events, and perhaps individual achievements too. It was placed on the main 'island', but close to

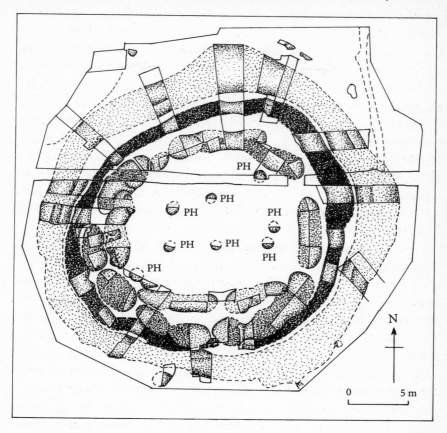

FIG 18   *A complex Later Neolithic henge (Etton Landscape Site 2), showing a succession of ditches, pits and post-holes (PH), from the Etton/Maxey ritual landscape*

Etton, which it resembled in so many respects, such as the offerings, the back-filling and the segmented ditch.

It was sites like this, and the small henges too, that were constructed to replace the segmented ditches on the eastern side of the causewayed enclosure at Etton. There the eastern side was the family side, the private side. But what about the other side, where feasting and other public ceremonies happened? Did people still take part in large communal gatherings? The answer is yes, but the nature of the gatherings continued to change, just as it had done over the lifetime of the causewayed enclosure.

The Great Henge at Maxey has now disappeared into a gravel quarry. When I think of that I feel overwhelmed by the responsibility that archaeology can impose on one. Our report, and the knowledge inside our heads, is all that remains of one of the key sites of British prehistory. Everything else, except a few boxes of finds, has vanished. I sometimes wonder what the original builders of the monument would have thought if they had known that the focus of their ritual landscape would eventually be dug up to provide ballast for concrete bungalow foundations.

The western half of the Great Henge was excavated by Gavin Simpson in 1962–63. We dug the eastern half in 1981, and our results were remarkably similar – which came as a big relief to both of us when we prepared our reports for final publication. The first thing that struck each of us was how little casual debris there was on the sites. We were able to plough the field first, then did a detailed search of the topsoil, and found practically nothing of any importance. This was very different from the time we searched through the buried soil that covered the interior of the Etton enclosure. It was almost as if the air photos had lied, and there was no archaeological site below the surface. I have never dug a site of such importance that produced so little. Cleanliness, or tidiness, was to be a theme of the Great Henge, and to this day I am convinced that it was deliberate. Perhaps it said something about the formality and importance of the place. Whatever the reason, it certainly provided a stark contrast with the situation at Etton, just a generation or two before, where all was hustle and bustle, with rubbish everywhere.

Charly's soil science showed that the cursus ditches had lain open to the elements and been allowed to fill in gradually, through the actions of rain and frost. But they were odd ditches, being both wide and shallow. The Neolithic diggers could have made them deeper, but chose not to. It was as if they had intended to slash two glaring white scars across the otherwise green landscape.

The outer ditch of the Great Henge, and its external bank, cut through the cursus ditch, which had already become partially filled with soil. This filling happened by natural means, such as earthworms, rainwash, frosts, moles and the hooves of grazing farm animals. The cursus ditch was shallow, so this – by its very nature – slow process need only have taken a century or so to complete. But the fact that the outer ditch of the Great Henge cut through it proved beyond any possible doubt that the features of the Great Henge were dug and used later than the cursus, but not much later. The builders of the Great Henge could have seen the two ditches of the cursus as long, shallow ditches in the pasture. More importantly they would have been told about them, and what they meant, from childhood. They would have been an important part of local history.

On the western side of the site were two circles of ten pits each, which could just be seen on the air photos. When Gavin dug them, he found that most had been deliberately filled in, and that none showed any clear signs of having held a post. Gravel from one of them had been cast to one side where it filled part of the southern cursus ditch, which must still have been visible, albeit half filled in, when the pit circle was dug. Unlike the other features associated with the Great Henge, the pit circles produced a few pieces of Neolithic pottery in the Mildenhall style, just like Etton. This is the only dating evidence we have for the Great Henge, and it would suggest that it was constructed sometime around, or just after, 3000 BC.

At the centre of the outer henge ditch, and concentric with it, was a larger ring-ditch of smaller diameter. This ditch had an internal gravel bank, and within that was a substantial mound built up from topsoil, turf and gravel from the ditch. It looked for all the world like a classic round barrow, but neither Gavin nor I found any evidence for burials or cremations.

The Maxey dig was quite stressful. Our site huts were close to the centre of the quarry, which was a noisy, dusty and at times dangerous place, with heavy trucks, dumpers, and large machines thundering around. Tea breaks were never peaceful occasions, and every four minutes the hut would shake violently as a fully-laden dumper truck roared past carrying thirty tonnes of gravel for the washing plant, whose ceaseless splashing and loud grinding sounds still haunt my mind on sleepless nights.

The summer of 1981 was dry and windy. Everywhere in the quarry there was yellow dust. It stuck to your hair, it caked the inside of your nose. By the end of the day my eyes smarted, and rubbing them

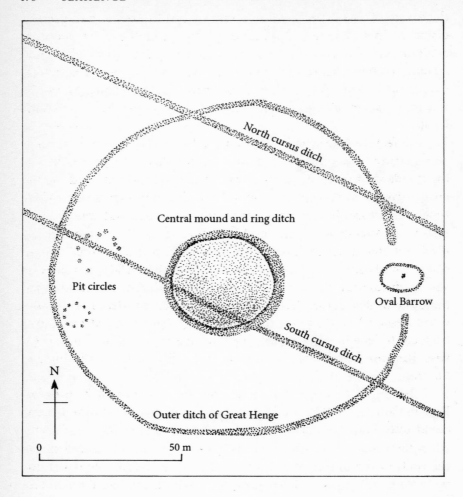

FIG 19   *The Maxey Great Henge complex*

with gritty hands only made things worse. After a few weeks Maisie gave up the unequal struggle and bought us a set of orange-yellow pillow-cases. Not even a good shower seemed to shift the stuff.

Then the heat of the summer gave way to autumn. During the summer we had excavated the outer ditch and the central ring-ditch. As the season grew cooler and darker, we turned our attention to the most intriguing part of the entire site. The mists and melancholy fitted the work – we were peering into a vanished world, but at a respectful distance. There was no jollity, little light-heartedness, which was not at all like us. Somehow the work we were doing seemed to affect our feelings. We were happy – don't get me wrong – but it was a reflective happiness, tinged with another mood, harder to pin down. Maybe it was awe, or something approaching it. I don't know. But it affected us all.

The feature which had this strange effect on us was found in the entranceway through the outer ditch of the Maxey Great Henge. By the standard of most henges this was a wide entranceway, and to our great surprise, at its centre we found the clear soil-marks of an oval timber structure. It measured ten by fifteen metres and was aligned east–west, directly on the core of the inner mound, at the centre of the Great Henge. Once again its builders had used the cardinal points of the compass. By dint of careful scraping of the surface, Maisie was able to distinguish the outlines of the timbers that had been used to build the oval structure. To everyone's surprise they were not round-wood posts. (Roundwood is the name given to timber that may have been cut to length, and had any side branches trimmed off, but other-wise has not been modified by, for example, sawing, splitting or hewing.)

Effective woodworking saws did not exist in Britain before the Roman Conquest of AD 43. Before then the reduction of roundwood could only be achieved by splitting or hewing. Both are best done when the timber is freshly felled, or 'green'. The timbers that formed the walls of the Maxey oval mortuary structure had been squared up by hewing with an axe. Hewing is quite a skilled job, and the timbers of the structure had been reduced to a consistent size (twenty-five centimetres square) and shape. With the exception of the narrow entranceway, we could spot no gaps between individual timbers – which again suggests competent workmanship.

The posts had been set in an evenly dug, vertical-sided bedding trench which was about half a metre deep. Normally you can assume that the height of a post, when standing on its own, will be three to four times its depth below ground. But the squared-up posts of the oval structure would have supported each other even if they had not been fixed or tied together in some way. My guess is that they would

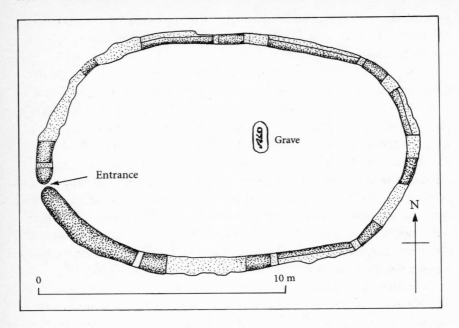

FIG 20   *The oval barrow in the entranceway to the Great Henge at Maxey*

have been taller than a person, but probably no higher than three metres. There is no evidence that the structure was ever roofed. Had it been, I would have expected to find an eaves-drip gully, or gutter, running around the outside of the walls.

The oval structure was aligned east–west, on the centre of the Great Henge, but its narrow (thirty-centimetre) entranceway was placed significantly off-line, towards the south, although not quite far enough to align with the midwinter sunset. Narrow entranceways are as much a feature of mortuary buildings as of megalithic tombs, where two crescent-shaped stones would be placed opposite each other to form a narrow 'porthole'. The idea was to make access difficult, the enclosed space more special – removed, cut-off and remote.

The solid oak wall had burnt down and the posts smouldered into the ground. This may have happened accidentally, but I doubt it. Oak, particularly oak that has had its bark and softer outer sapwood hewn off, is remarkably fire-resistant. No, it seemed to me that some effort was made to fire the walls, and our mag. sus. survey showed that the resulting blaze was uneven and not wholly successful. Whatever the truth was, it happened.

The next stage had been to place a burial near the centre of the structure, in a shallow grave just ten centimetres deep. The body was that of a man aged between thirty-six and fifty-three. The skeleton was buried on its side in a crouching position, the knees drawn up towards the chin. It was aligned due north–south, with the head to the north and the face looking east. The bones were in a poor state, because the body and the interior of the burnt-down structure had been covered with a low barrow-mound that was largely made up of turf and topsoil. This organic soil would have been rich in humic acids, which then corroded the bones. So it's difficult to say much about the man himself, apart from observing that his teeth and gums weren't healthy. He would have been no stranger to toothache.

We were able to work out that the various parts or components of the Great Henge complex shared a common history, which would strongly suggest that they were all in use at the same time. It's an interesting sequence, which echoes Etton and some of the smaller sites in the Maxey ritual landscape. I'm sure that the episodes we were able to follow were in fact acting out or symbolising events in the history of the people concerned. But I wouldn't like to attempt to say what they actually meant. I shall leave that task to posterity.

Charly's micromorph. came into its own at Maxey. He was able to prove that the ground enclosed by the oak wall of the oval mortuary structure was first de-turfed. The turves were quite thick, and in the process of being cut a good proportion of the topsoil was removed. But that was not all. At the same time, thick turves had been cut from the centre of the henge. De-turfing was clearly an important part of prehistoric ceremonial, and turves would also have been useful for the construction of normal, day-to-day buildings. In areas such as the Welland valley, where stone wasn't common, turf would have provided a very acceptable and surprisingly durable building 'stone'. But it would be a mistake to assume that the removal of turf from below a barrow mound was just for practical reasons. Turf stripping is hard work, even with a sharp steel spade. It makes no practical sense to de-turf an area where you intend to build a mound.

I see de-turfing as an act of cleansing or purification that had to happen before certain important rites and ceremonies could take place. Again, we are seeing a profound concern for the ground and for land. The people of Neolithic times did not think solely in terms of what was in the sky or above their heads. The earth had life too.

The next phase was one of construction. The builders dug the bedding-trench and put up the posts around the oval structure. They dug the outer ditch of the Great Henge and erected a bank on its outer edge. They also dug the central ring-ditch and placed banks on its inner edge. While the ditch-digging was going on they also heaped a turf mound over the area they had de-turfed at the centre. I would imagine that this central mound included stored turves cut from the central area, and presumably from the oval structure too.

The third phase was destruction. The timbers of the oval structure were burnt. The banks that accompanied the inner and outer ditches were partially thrown back into the ditches, so that they were half-filled in. In the fourth and final phase the body was placed in what was left of the oval structure and a dumped topsoil barrow was placed over the whole thing. Within the central ring-ditch a large mound, also of dumped topsoil, was placed over the entire central area, covering both the damaged banks and the central turf mound.

We are witnessing here episodes of construction, destruction and reconstruction which echo what was going on in stone-using areas such as Avebury and Salisbury Plain. People are repeatedly returning to a special place to do special things. It is a process that is carried out for its own sake. But it seems to me that the work that went into the construction, destruction and subsequent modification of the Great Henge at Maxey was less daunting than similar processes in stone-using areas. Maisie reckons that the oval mortuary-structure wall contained about 156 square-dressed posts. The oak used had quite thick annual growth-rings (about ten millimetres), which would suggest that the trees came from secondary woodland – woodland that had regrown after a phase of felling perhaps fifty years previously. Trees in this sort of woodland grow rapidly, as there is plenty of light and moisture available. In dense primary, or primeval, forest the width of annual growth-rings is often less than a millimetre.

Younger trees in secondary woodland are much easier to fell and

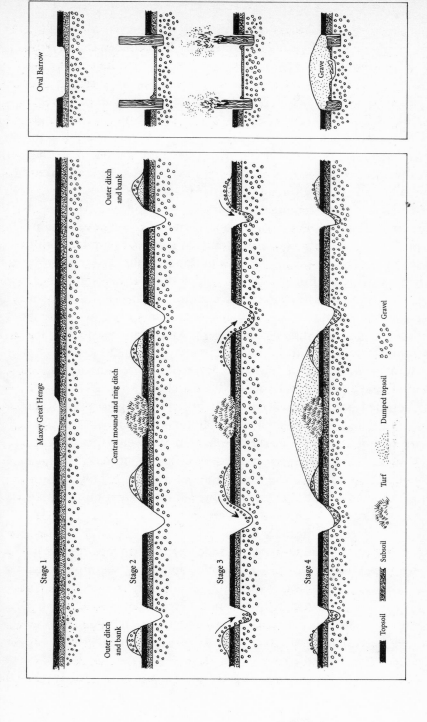

Oval Barrow

Maxey Great Henge

Stage 1

Outer ditch and bank

Central mound and ring ditch

Outer ditch and bank

Stage 2

Stage 3

Stage 4

Grave

Topsoil   Subsoil   Turf   Dumped topsoil   Gravel

FIG 21   Schematic cross-section through features of the Maxey Great Henge, showing phases of construction and destruction (not to scale)

extract than the massive oaks of the primary forest. Even allowing for felling, extraction and hewing, the oval structure could have been built by, say, a dozen skilled men in a week. Likewise, the outer ditch, the central ring-ditch and its various mounds and banks represent weeks, not months or years, of work. Essentially we are looking at manageable tasks that could have been taken on by a group of motivated people without the need for much long-distance organisation or a powerful controlling authority. It's a human-scale operation. If we look further west, towards the massive henges of Wessex, the picture is different. There things were done on an altogether grander scale.

Is there anything remotely comparable with the massive sites of Wessex in our region? The answer, so far, is no. It's the few exceptions that prove the rule, by their rarity. Beautiful goldwork, similar to that in the Wessex graves, was found in a burial at Little Cressingham in southern Norfolk. At first glance this goldwork looks like some of the fine pieces from a classic Wessex grave group, but if you examine the decoration closely it's apparent that the craftsman was very much less skilled than his Wessex counterparts, who were masters of the goldsmith's art. Nearer to home, a primary grave at the centre of a barrow in a gravel pit at Barnack, five miles upstream of Maxey, produced grave goods that included an archer's wrist-guard made from polished greenstone, decorated with eighteen gold press-studs at each end. This is fine material indeed, but it is by no means fabulous, nor are such graves particularly common in the region. Its presence would suggest that there were indeed wealthy and powerful families in the area, just as there are today. But we are not talking about a strong, centralised authority that required the intervention of a full-time priestly caste to keep it in power.

So what does this mean? What lay behind the gatherings that took place at the Maxey Great Henge or indeed at Stonehenge itself? Are we now in a position where we can start answering the Stonehenge bus-driver's question? Just possibly.

The initial gatherings at Etton and other causewayed enclosures were attended by the entire adult populations of the communities who used them. As time passed we have seen how the rites and ceremonies that took place there – and the 'language' in which they were expressed – became increasingly formal and in a sense minimalised. Meanwhile, the population was growing and the landscape continued to be cleared of forest cover. By the time the causewayed enclosures went out of regular use – say around 3500 BC – many, if not all, of the ceremonies would have been attended by representatives or delegates, and not by the entire adult populations of the various families, clans and tribes who had rights of access to them.

These processes of religious formalisation and social delegation continued throughout the Late Neolithic period and into the Bronze Age. By the time the large henge monuments came into existence, the ceremonies that took place within them would have been attended by only a small proportion of the community. It has been suggested that ordinary people watched from the sidelines, outside the outer ditch and bank, but I think this unlikely. If large crowds regularly came to a particular spot, you might expect to find some archaeological evidence for this. I know of none. In fact the area around the Great Henge is spotlessly clear of prehistoric debris.

I would suggest that it was a far more potent symbol of political delegation for a group of elders actually to depart from a village to attend an assembly. I can easily imagine the speeches on departure, promising everyone the world, and the triumphant welcome home, with failure cynically hidden behind honeyed words. Politicians, even prehistoric politicians, are the same everywhere. I doubt whether the delegates would have been elected. Most probably they would have been the senior men and women from the various families and groups of families (i.e. clans or tribes). In terms of modern politics, the gatherings would have been more like the unreformed House of Lords than the Commons. Some archaeologists have suggested that this new representative group of people – I hesitate to use the word 'class' – had more in common with priests than politicians. There may well be some truth in this in Wessex, but in the east of England I believe things were different. There is less evidence here for rapidly increasing social differentiation. In particular, we do not see the emergence of a wealthy political elite that would have required a priestly caste to bolster its political authority.

Does this mean that the east of England was backward in some way? I don't think so for one moment. It all depends on how you choose to measure progress. Spectacular achievements can be used as a smokescreen to cover fundamental weakness. The Sputnik beeping its way through space while the Soviet population below queued for food is a good case in point. Richard Bradley and others have shown that the economic engine of Early Bronze Age Wessex was moving away from the higher ground around Salisbury Plain, down into the lower-lying, flatter and more fertile countryside of the Thames valley. Recent work by one of Richard's students, Dave Yates, has shown that large areas of the Thames valley were being parcelled up into field systems that closely resemble those at Fengate.

These newly-discovered Thames valley field systems came into being after the abandonment of Stonehenge; but, like family wealth, they did not suddenly appear, fully formed. As we saw at Fengate, the Bronze Age fields had their origins in an earlier world. Their appearance, perhaps towards the end of the Early Bronze Age in the Thames valley, suggests to me that the population of people and animals had expanded beyond a key threshold: there was pressure on land and grazing, so the available resources had to be managed more efficiently.

Maybe the extraordinary elaboration of Stonehenge was one attempt, among many, to harness political support to halt, or reverse, a process that was already under way. Who knows, it may have worked for a century or two, but ultimately the economic and social forces opposing it proved too strong.

Recently I was asked what existing building or structure was the modern equivalent of Stonehenge. After much thought I rejected the obvious candidates: cathedrals, or other symbols of power such as the Kremlin, Buckingham Palace or the Pentagon. No: these places are about success in other ways. Stonehenge was rather different, especially in its later phases, when the elaboration of the stone settings became so extraordinary. I believe it had more in common with state-funded schemes that are intended to bring work and a sense of pride to regions that have fallen on hard times. So to me, Antony Gormley's massive steel structure 'The Angel of the North', with its lintel-like wings, harks back to Stonehenge in more ways than one.

I sometimes wonder whether the Stonehenge Avenue, which after all was constructed late in the overall Stonehenge sequence, was a symbolic recognition of the underlying problem. Its course is odd. Why doesn't it continue in a straight line north-east, towards the midsummer sunrise? Instead, it hooks sharply right, and then right again, and runs straight down to the floodplain of the river Avon. Whether it was intentional or not, it seems to me that the Avenue is symbolically tapping into the newly emerging source of economic and social power. It was the flatter land around the fertile river valleys of southern Britain which was to provide the fuel that powered the extraordinary population growth of the Late Bronze and Iron Ages, in the first millennium BC. It was a period which saw the emergence of new identities, such as the Britons and the Celts, which still have a resonance for us today.

I must ask some final questions before our quest moves on. First, does the lack of gold, and the rarity of massive stone or timber monuments, in the east of Bronze Age England indicate either poverty of spirit or failure of imagination? Were the Bronze Age populations of eastern England so intent on earning their living and respecting their neighbours that they allowed insufficient time for higher things? Were their symbolic and ideological lives impoverished? Personally, I never believed this to be the case. Having dug Etton and the other sites of the Maxey ritual landscape, I knew just how rich and subtle their inhabitants' conception of other worlds could be. I also find comfort in the knowledge that their ideological world was in balance with their daily world. To use a Buddhist concept, I believe they had achieved something akin to the Middle Way. Two millennia later, towards the end of the Iron Age, this balance would be mirrored in the region's great wealth and political stability. But even then, by the time of Christ, the roots of that well-being and prosperity were already very ancient.

CHAPTER TEN

The Wetland Revolution

So far our quest has focused on the way people organised their lives within prehistoric society. As part of this we have had to speculate about their religious and ideological worlds. We have been concerned too with the way Bronze Age people shaped and managed their landscapes, and with problems of prehistoric political control, power and authority.

I now want to introduce a significant new theme which has always been central to my research in and around the Fens. It's a theme that has as much to do with archaeological technique as with the reconstruction of the past. This sub-discipline, or species, of archaeology has recently begun to transform our understanding of British and European prehistory. One of its pioneers, Professor John Coles, coined an apt term to describe it: the wetland revolution.

Estimates vary, but most archaeologists would agree that the finds from an average dryland prehistoric site represent perhaps 5 per cent and at the most 10 per cent of the original 'material culture' in use in the past. Here 'material culture' includes everything: houses, farm buildings, fences, troughs, furniture, clothes and fabrics, baskets, vehicles, harnesses and leather, wood or leather handles and hafts, bone and antler objects, pottery, stone tools, metal tools and ornaments. On a 'good' dry site that has not been smashed by modern farming, and where the soil is naturally alkaline, you might expect to recover the final six items on that list. On a very acid 'bad' site, the bone and antler objects would not survive, and even the pottery would be harmed, especially if it had originally been tempered with something calcareous, such as shell.

Wet sites, like dry sites, can be 'good' or 'bad'. A 'bad' site would be in a high-energy environment, such as the seashore, or a scouring riverbed. A 'good' site would be inland, in calmer conditions. But a 'good' inland wet site can rapidly become 'bad', and then almost useless – worse than the average dry site, even – if the water is drained from it.

Water only acts as a preservative for soft organic material such as wood, skin, cloth, leaves, seeds and pollen if it loses oxygen and becomes stagnant. So a fence-post driven into a stream-bed will rot off first at the waterline, where conditions are best for supporting the agents of decay, which are mainly fungi and bacteria. Next it will rot below the water, although some woods, such as alder and elm, can resist wet rot for a very long time. Eventually, after perhaps five or ten years, it will rot to the level of the stream-bed. But below that it will rot very much more slowly. Here there is no fast-flowing water, rich in oxygen to support the main micro-organisms that cause decay. If the stream-bed is made of clay or peat, it is quite possible that the tip of the post could survive for hundreds, even thousands of years. If the bed is more porous and water can flow through it slowly, for example in sand or gravel, the post tip may only last a decade or two.

Acidity affects preservation too, but not in a simple good/bad way. Ancient sites in highly acid environments – for example peaty bogs fed by rainfall – will preserve cloth, leather and hair superbly, but objects made from bone, horn and antler will soon vanish without trace. In certain conditions it's possible to have very localised areas of high acidity, such as the oak coffins found in some Danish burial mounds. Here the naturally acid surroundings of a sandy or clay landscape are massively enhanced by the tannic acid present in oak wood. Accordingly, preservation of cloth and leather is good, but bone rarely survives.

So, waterlogged sites can contain anything up to 90 per cent of a past community's 'material culture'. But there is a downside, of course: by and large people have tended to stay clear of bogs and fens as places in which to live. They are marginal or liminal spots, more suited to religious and other rites. But at the juncture of the wet and the dry you can sometimes run across remains that share the best of both worlds, wetland and dryland. Most of the sites I have discussed so far – Fengate, Maxey, Etton – are like this. They can best be described as 'damp'; they are mainly dry, but deeper ditches, pits and wells are still waterlogged, and provide fascinating glimpses of the missing 70 per cent or so of material culture.

Then there are truly wet sites that can be linked to a dryland landscape. These are important because, isolated from any explanatory context, wetland finds can be very frustrating. You can't ask the obvious questions: how did they get there? Why did they get there? Who put them there? Ancient wooden buckets filled to the brim with butter are quite frequently found in peat bogs. What are they? Are they religious offerings? Was the bog used as some sort of ancient refrigerator, or what? I doubt if we'll ever know the answer to these questions for sure. As my old school teacher would have said, we lack the necessary context. Without it the finds become almost meaningless.

Shortly I will discuss the Holme timber circle and Flag Fen in detail. Both are wetland sites, with superb preservation, but their main interest lies in their dryland connections. In each case we have a pretty good idea of the people who built and used them, where they came from, and why they built them. But the contexts that provided these explanations were dry, not wet. Again, it's a matter of taking a broad view of the problem. It's not sufficient simply to look for wet sites on their own, as these will always prove hard to understand in isolation. First you must come to grips with the contextual landscape and how it worked; how its individual components, wet and dry, articulated with one another. Only then will you be in a position to make use of the extra information a 'good' wet site can provide.

It isn't enough to be amazed at the quality of preservation that wet sites can give us – although I frequently am. A few years ago at Flag Fen we uncovered a prehistoric bronze dagger and its antler hilt that had been roughly torn apart and thrown into the water. I was astonished at the beauty of the smoothed antler and the workmanship of the thin oak wedges which held the hilt and blade together. But I was missing the point. If I had had my wits about me, I should have been wondering *why* the dagger was first wilfully damaged and then thrown into the water. What did it mean? Who did it? I was not aware at the time, although shortly I would have all the information I needed to answer those questions – and many more I had never dreamed of. But I was lazy not to have addressed these questions from the beginning.

Before the 'revolution' of recent years, the Victorians were profoundly fascinated by the phenomenon of 'lake villages' and 'lake dwellings'. The cause of this lay in the particularly severe Alpine winter of 1853–54. A combination of persistent ice and drought cut the flow of water in rivers feeding the lakes, and this caused their levels to fall suddenly and dramatically. People walking along the shores, especially of lakes such as Neuchâtel and Zurich, noticed hundreds, even thousands, of stumpy wooden posts or piles protruding from the mud. Lying among the posts was a profusion of ancient objects; not just axeheads and sherds of pottery, but stone and bronze axes in their wooden hafts, wooden bowls, wooden spoons. Today the great museums of Europe and North America are packed full of Neolithic, Bronze and Iron Age objects from the Alpine Lake Villages.

Of course there had been isolated discoveries of wetland finds before the advent of these Lake Villages, but it was that severe winter which set the ball rolling. By the mid-1850s, public opinion was ready to accommodate the new discoveries. The Three-Age system of Stone, Bronze and Iron was by now fully accepted, and religious authority was rapidly losing its grip on rational thought and observation. By 1859 Darwin was able to publish his *Origin of Species*. So the climate of opinion was right, and the new discoveries were greeted by a large and informed audience, eager to learn about the latest finds. Archaeology had suddenly become a subject of widespread popular interest.

I sometimes think that the late-nineteenth and early-twentieth centuries was a golden age for archaeology. Archaeologists had a clear purpose to their work: the rational explanation of human origins and social development. They had yet to acquire self-doubt. And the finds they made were truly breathtaking. It was no wonder that the educated public were gripped by it all, in a way that could never happen again. Nowadays, archaeology has stiff competition – there are just too many exciting things happening in so many other fields.

The widespread appeal of the subject a century ago was brought home to me when, in my early thirties, I managed to scrape the money together to buy the two reports on the excavation of the Glastonbury Lake Village which were published in 1911 and 1917. As was then often the custom, the volumes were published by public subscription – and there, in the list of subscribers, was my great-grandfather, who wasn't an archaeologist at all. Today, such a thing would be unimaginable. For a start, only a fully qualified professional could understand the technical jargon used in modern site reports; and besides, far too many are written in a tedious, repetitive style that verges on the illiterate. As a consequence, archaeology is offered to the general public pre-digested and second-hand. This a very sad state of affairs, in which both sides are the losers.

As Lake Villages became fashionable, they were discovered all over the place: at Glastonbury and Meare in the Somerset Levels, in Holderness on the Humber and in the bogs and lakes of Scotland and Ireland, where they were known as crannogs. Most of the crannogs were quite small, as man-made islands go. They were usually connected to dryland by a short bridge or causeway and were large enough for a family and its animals. But some, such as Lagore and Balinderry in Ireland, were very much larger, although not as big as the great Alpine prehistoric settlements.

The discovery of ancient Lake Dwellings went hand in hand with the growth of the myth of a Celtic and Aryan Golden Age. I have visited a lavishly recreated Lake Village in Germany that was paid for by Nazi money. And it showed – to the extreme embarrassment of my hosts. You could almost hear the distant call of Wagnerian horns echoing across the steely waters of the great lake. Despite that, it was a memorable experience for purely archaeological reasons too.

The recent revival of interest in wetland archaeology has largely come about as a response to the wholesale draining of wetlands right across Europe. It was a process which began in the later 1950s, gathered pace in the 1960s and hurtled out of control in the 1970s. Slowly some measure of sanity, of control, is being re-established; but it is far too little and too late. Archaeologically speaking the destruction has been cataclysmic. People like John Coles have done everything possible to raise the public's awareness of what has been happening, but their voices are easily lost among the many competing environmental claims for attention. For some reason, we humans seem to be vastly more concerned about what happens to other species than about damage to the history of our own kind.

Vast sums of European, government and private money were poured into land-drainage schemes, to produce fields which would grow mountains of grain, butter and meat that nobody could eat. By now we are all familiar with the story, which has entered the realms of recent history. But its effects on archaeology haven't gone away. You can't replant an ancient site. It's not a hedge. Once you have extracted water and removed the airless conditions that had slowed rot and decay to a virtual standstill, you cannot then stop nature from resuming its course. We learned just how rapid this process could be when we started work on the waterlogged Neolithic enclosure ditch at Etton.

For millennia the woodchips and other debris left by the working of coppiced willow in 3800 BC were resting in stiff muddy clays. From time to time in very dry summers the water level in the ground round about the ditch would fall below it. Normally this would lead fairly rapidly to the destruction of the waterlogged archaeological deposits, but in this case the clay retained moisture long enough to allow the ground water to return to its higher, winter level, so there was no harm done to the preserved Neolithic woodchips.

But then, in late June 1983, the pumps were turned on in the neighbouring gravel quarry. Within a month the water level in the surrounding ground was a metre below the deepest archaeological layers. For a few weeks we could detect no change in the waterlogged wood we were excavating, then Maisie, who was supervising the team of Dutch students from Leiden University working on the wood, started to have intimations. At first it was nothing very definite, more an uneasy suspicion. Then quite suddenly she noticed that the wood was drying out from the bottom up. It was eerie and unnatural, not at all what we would have expected. Normally wood in the ground decays from the top, which is nearest the air and the surface, and then the rot moves down. But not at Etton.

The huge pumps that had been rumbling away day and night in the background for the past eight weeks were still doing their work. I was standing at the edge of the enclosure ditch, staring intently down the lens of a camera mounted on a tripod. The deposit I was photographing looked excellent. Maisie and her team had done a superb job. Nobody would have guessed that the wood was starting to break down. It was cleanly and crisply exposed, and each piece was marked with a short piece of embossed plastic held in place by stainless-steel pins.

I asked two members of the team to move to one side, as their shadows just impinged on the frame I had so carefully composed. Then the sun briefly peeped out from behind a cloud and I pressed the shutter button. There was an audible sigh of relief. I was about to start dismantling my camera when Maisie called me over. She was bending over a large woodchip, about the size and shape of a rat. It looked in good condition, but as I watched she gently gripped it with both hands, lifted it and turned it over. The smooth underside that had lain directly on the gravel of the ditch bottom was a mass of cracks and fissures. I was astonished. The clay in the ditch had held the wood in shape while it dried out from below. At some time in the next few days or weeks, as conditions became drier, that piece of wood would start to part from the clay and would immediately shrink and distort. Instinctively I reached back for my camera and had Maisie replace the piece and then lift it again, as she had just done, while I photographed it. In retrospect, I think they're the most effective photographs in the entire report on Etton. Certainly they say more than a thousand words.

It was hard not to be depressed by what we had just seen. That wood had survived in the ground for nearly six thousand years, but it was now drying out, unseen, below our feet. The same thought must have struck all of us, because the team was unusually quiet and pensive. Then we spotted a 'dust devil' heading towards us across the quarry. 'Dust devils' are what local farmers call sharp miniature cyclones or twisters that appear in late summer on the flat land. They last a minute or two, lifting the straw and dust of harvest from a field, before dying down. This one wasn't very sharp, but it moved quite quickly and we didn't have time to cover the wood in the ditch. We needn't have bothered, as it passed close by the site and all we felt was a light breeze for half a minute or so.

Then one of the students gave a shout of surprise and we all looked across to where she knelt. In front of her lay several of the embossed plastic labels, with their pins still through them. That light wind had been enough to remove them. In other words, the wood had dried out significantly in the few days since the labels had been pinned in place – despite our protective measures, which included wet foam mattresses, wet newspaper, plastic sheeting and repeated watering. There was no alternative: we would have to work much faster.

I helped the student replace the labels, wondering as I did so whether it was worth the effort. In the ground before me were no finished artefacts, no axe hafts, no bowls, no baskets. Just hundreds and thousands of tiny pieces of wood. Carpenters' debris. But in my heart of hearts I knew our task was worthwhile. Besides, we had had a full team meeting and had all agreed to abide by Maisie's plan. So there was to be no backsliding.

I remember a few years ago an agent from MI5 or the CIA, I forget which, was found rummaging through Mrs Thatcher's or President Reagan's household rubbish. Needless to say, there was a public outcry, and the radio news programmes broadcast interviews with an espionage expert who declared – to no listening archaeologist's surprise – that you could understand the way a household worked by looking through its garbage. Early in my career I had acquired an interest in flint implements and the ways in which they were made. I even did a certain amount of flint-working myself, and after much practice I could fashion an acceptable copy of a Bronze Age arrowhead. As I worked, I often cut my fingers, but somehow I managed to retain the sight of both eyes, despite numerous razor-sharp splinters whizzing past my face. I remember cutting myself and looking down at the ground as the drips of blood splattered onto the thousands of tiny waste flakes I had removed in the process of making my arrowheads. As I knew from my courses at Cambridge, this debris of discarded flakes held the clue to the way I had fashioned the arrowhead.

A Dutch archaeologist named Bohmers, in a paper published in 1956, devised a statistical system for identifying flint-working techniques which was based on the dimensions and shapes of the waste flakes that were produced during the process of tool-making. Bohmers's statistics were based on the breadth-to-length ratio of the flakes. This was, in effect, a measurement of shape, which ranged from long and thin at one end of the scale, to short and squat at the other.

For various reasons, the waste flakes of flint-tool manufacture survive well – often better than the finished tools. Indeed, sometimes the flakes themselves are tools – usually known as blades – in their own right. Given the frequency with which they're found, it has long been appreciated that it makes sense to learn as much as we can from them. What the first statistical analyses of waste flakes revealed in the 1950s and early sixties was that the waste flakes produced by the last hunter-gatherer communities of the Mesolithic period and the first Neolithic farmers were broadly similar. They were long, thin and razor sharp. Their tool-making technique involved the careful preparation of a core made from high-quality flint that was then flaked in a very skilful fashion to produce long, elegant blades. I've tried this style of blade production, and I rarely succeed. I simply lack the control and experience to do it properly.

The long, delicate blade-based flint industries lasted from about 9000 BC until roughly 3000 BC, towards the close of the Neolithic period, when there was a shift towards the production of shorter, squatter flakes. By this time there was less call for high-quality cutting tools. Flints were used more for scraping and paring animal hides, butchery and removing bark, so they became shorter and thicker. The quality of flint used was less crucial, so gravel flint was used in place of the more expensive mined flint, which had been the preferred choice of Earlier Neolithic craftsmen.

With the onset of the Bronze Age, flint-working became gradually less important. Bronze replaced it for most cutting purposes, and by the Late Bronze Age flint tools were rather sad reflections of their former glories. There were short, thick arrowheads and pebbles that had been struck in such a way that they broke leaving many sharp points, which were used for piercing and boring bone and leather. Waste flakes from the Late Bronze Age are invariably short and squat, and often show tell-tale signs of a lack of control by the tool-maker. We are witnessing the death of an ancient tradition.

Wood is superficially very unlike flint, but it is manipulated in a fundamentally similar way: both are worked by removing chips or flakes. To use the jargon, both are reductive technologies. Maisie realised this when she was still a student at the Institute of Archaeology in the seventies, but in those days, while there were plenty of flint sites to work with, sites producing wood debris were almost unheard of. As I was then producing the odd fragment from the deepest wells and ditches at Fengate, she joined our team in 1976. Six years passed, and we continued to find just oddments of wood. But as nobody else was finding any at all (with the notable exception of John Coles and his team in the Somerset Levels), she stayed with us. As it transpired, it was as well she did.

The year 1982 was momentous for us. It was our first big season of excavation at Etton, and it was the year I had the good luck to stumble across the extraordinary Bronze Age site at Flag Fen. We'll return to Flag Fen shortly, but in some respects Etton was a greater archaeological challenge. As the wood there was rapidly starting to disintegrate, it was very tempting to take the easy option and simply remove any obviously finished artefact – axe hafts, bowls, planks, etc. – and call it a day. Many people outside the team urged us to take this course; in fact I think we were regarded as rather peculiar for not doing so. But I'm glad our nerves held, for it paid off handsomely.

Maisie wanted to test her idea that woodworking debris could be as informative as flint waste-flakes, and for the first time ever in Britain, the evidence lay spread out before us. It was too good to ignore, whatever the threat of drying out. Recording the length, breadth and thickness of each individual woodchip was painfully slow work, and we were constantly aware that the process of drying out was continuing inexorably. As time progressed we were able to quantify this process, because ancient waterlogged wood, having lost its original resilient woody structure, starts to collapse when the water is withdrawn. Instead of being round, twigs and branches become flattened and oval, rather like Turkish cigarettes. By recording the large and small diameters of the flattened ovals, we were able to map the steady spread of drying out along the segmented enclosure ditch. Later we plotted out the figures, and could clearly see the progress of the process of destruction. I remember well our mixed feelings of horror and fascination.

Somehow we just managed to stay ahead of the drying out, and by the time we had finished we had measured and recorded 4,833 pieces of wood. But what did they reveal? There was little comparative material, so it was difficult to say whether there was much change in woodworking debris through time, although the Etton woodchips, which were produced by a stone or flint axe, are very much longer and thinner than those from Bronze Age Flag Fen, almost two thousand years later. This largely reflects the fact that the woodworking carried out at Etton was what the Victorians would have called 'bodging', being performed on small branches, rather than on the heavy timber which was mainly worked at Flag Fen. But it is also easier to cut into wood at a steeper angle with a sharp metal axe. Working with a stone axe, you tend to cut and split as much as to cut cleanly. In this respect the technique is like using a billhook, the traditional tool of British hedge-laying. A billhook is in effect a very heavy knife – something between a machete and an axe. The angle of strike for a stone axe and a billhook is very much more oblique than for a metal axe – which of course gives rise to longer, thinner woodchips.

Although I described the woodworking at Etton as 'bodging', this is not strictly accurate, as foot-operated pole-lathes were used by bodgers to make chairs, stools and a variety of containers such as trugs, the traditional lightweight gardeners' baskets of southern England. The Etton woodworkers didn't possess lathes. They worked with coppiced rods and poles alone. Instead of pegging and jointing their wood, they twisted and wove it.

We don't know when the practice of coppicing began, but I suspect it could have been at almost any time, as it's based on common-sense observation. When the trunk of a tree snaps off in a winter gale, its stump produces strong, straight growth in the spring. This fast growth is the tree's response to disaster. Somehow it must send out a shoot as high and as fast as it can, or else it will become shaded out by the other trees of the forest, and will inevitably die. Coppicing is the process of stimulating that stress response, by cutting a tree back to the ground. Usually this is done on a regular cycle, the intervals of which are dictated by the size of the wood that's needed. Thin, whippy rods for baskets can be cut after a year or two, thicker rods for wattlework may need five to ten years, and large poles for rafters and suchlike can take ten to twenty years, or even longer, to grow.

The process of coppicing leaves some tell-tale traces, which Maisie has proved very adept at spotting. The stump, which is usually left at ground level, is known as the coppice stool, and is characteristically knobbly, with a swirling, convoluted grain. It's often hard and impossible to split, which was why the inhabitants of Etton used alder stools, which they carved into wooden bowls. They would have looked attractive and wouldn't have cracked after repeated wetting and drying.

The name given to the sharp angle where the shoot emerges from the stool is the 'heel'. Here the wood is dense and thick, but there is a natural weakness, and a well-directed chop with a stone axe, combined with a downwards wrench, can effectively separate a rod from the stool. It's a knack. I can do it with a billhook, but not yet with a stone axe.

As has been noted, coppiced products can be used to make all sorts of things, from baskets to rafters, which are just as useful and important in normal daily life as the more usual objects archaeologists dig up on their excavations, such as pottery, flint and stone. At the heavier end of the coppice scale we find poles. In 1988 I used coppice that the forester told me had previously been cut just before the war, probably in 1938, to build a reconstruction of an Iron Age house. So the poles were half a century old when they were cut, or rather felled. They were ash, dead straight and very strong. The house we were building was quite large, and I don't think anything out of a primary woodland would have done the job properly. As the tall ash-poles were felled, I became aware that they were the Bronze Age equivalent of structural steel. They were used to support the most important part of a building – the part above one's head. And yet this was an element of the 'material culture' of prehistoric people that we had largely ignored, simply because such things rarely survive in the archaeological record.

The thousands of small wood fragments at Etton included many hundreds of rod fragments with the heel still intact. This probably meant that the rod had been intended for use in a woven structure, such as a hurdle, where the heavier, stiffer wood of the heel can be hard to use and is often discarded during the initial trimming-off of side shoots, which normally takes place close by the stool. To our amazement we were able to prove that this actually happened at Etton some six thousand years ago, because along with the discarded heels we found the remains of willow stools which had been growing in the mud on the ditch bottom. It was extraordinary – as if we had accidentally stumbled across a frozen moment of time. I almost expected to find the Neolithic woodsman's sandwiches and flask of warm tea.

Finally, we found a near-complete, but broken, haft for a stone axe lying abandoned amongst the heels and coppice stools at the bottom of the segmented enclosure ditch. Maisie examined it closely and was convinced that the damage had happened when the woodsman struck a blow that was too oblique and caused the haft to twist and shear. Presumably it was a little old, dry and inflexible. I did exactly the same thing to my grandfather's old billhook recently. I was coppicing hazel, not willow, but it was late in the day, the light was failing and my arms were tired. I missed my stroke, caught the wood a glancing blow and the haft split in my hand. Happily the blade didn't fly off, but it was infuriating, and I sympathised with my Neolithic predecessor.

The principle that rubbish reveals the truth was almost taken to extremes at Etton. Maisie's statistics showed a tendency towards shorter, squatter woodchips in the ditch segments nearest the main entranceway, which faced directly onto the old stream channel. Unfortunately water had washed away a large proportion of the evidence, but the tendency was undoubtedly there. But what did it mean? Why were people using their axes at a slightly steeper angle? The answer, as is so often the case in archaeology, was provided by context.

The north entrance to Etton was deliberately made difficult, by forcing people to cross through the old stream-bed, but once across they were faced by a massive timber gatehouse which consisted of two parallel, corridor-like walls constructed of oak-tree trunks. These trunks had been split square and placed in the ground edge-to-edge. Unfortunately they weren't waterlogged, but the post-pipes were quite clear, and I'm in no doubt that it was a very heavily-built construction. Most probably, too, there was an unroofed open deck above the corridor through which everyone had to pass. I can imagine a robed figure standing on the deck and welcoming those about to enter the enclosure with suitably dire warnings. Then, appropriately humbled, they shuffled single-file through the dark and forbidding gatehouse.

The waterlogged muds in the bottom of the ditch near the gatehouse also revealed the only substantial piece of timber to be found at Etton – by timber I mean wood that had been trimmed and prepared for use in a structure. It was a split oak plank, and it still had a clear blade-mark left by a stone axe. This was also the area where we found thick pieces of corky bark. Coppice rods and poles don't have thick bark, as they're too fast-grown and too young. We don't know precisely what type of tree the bark came from, as it was not that well preserved, but it was deeply fissured and could easily have been oak. We now had three pieces of indirect evidence – squatter woodchips, a single plank and pieces of thick bark – to suggest that timber was being worked by carpenters in or near the ditch close by the only heavily-constructed wooden building at Etton.

I find it fascinating that the builders of the Etton gatehouse cleared up their rubbish so carefully. Whenever I have done any experimental reconstruction I am always amazed at the quantities of debris produced. There are off-cuts everywhere: a thick carpet of woodchips, strips of bark and rejects. Usually we end the project with a large bonfire – and we share a few baked potatoes and beers, which is probably what happened in prehistory too. But at Etton the pattern of clearing up within the ditch was at best inconsistent.

The coppice debris was conspicuously not cleared up, whereas the carpenters who had made the gatehouse were scrupulously tidy. This suggests to me that two quite different things were happening. The coppicing was an activity that was taking place as an integral part of a ceremony or ceremonies. Maybe the woods were symbolically celebrated at the very edge of the enclosure – which as I have noted might itself have symbolised the landscape as a whole. Perhaps the people who earned their living amongst the trees were performing their own rites and rituals. Perhaps the ceremonial coppicing and weaving of hurdles was done by young people at a key stage in their lives: at puberty, or marriage, perhaps. Maybe it indicated the end of a period of apprenticeship.

The construction of the main gateway into the enclosure was altogether different. It was a sacred duty, probably carried out by folk from several communities, and special rules of ritual cleanliness would have applied. I suspect that the bonfire at the end would have been a very formal affair. It will be recalled that we found evidence for the cleaning up of the bones left after feasting. Perhaps the clearing of the gatehouse construction debris would have been governed by similar rules. Thus, by looking at debris we can learn not only about the ordinary, mundane aspects of life, but also about custom and practice, thoughts and ideas. Those late-twentieth-century secret-service agents were not as strange as some of us thought at the time.

I have always had a liking for damp sites, but it has taken me a long time to understand why they're so satisfying. It's partly the fact that you can work on two different scales simultaneously. Damp sites require the large-scale open-area excavation appropriate to a dry site, but then you stumble across little windows into the past, where the resolution is very much better. Then detail, not scope, becomes important. It's a question, yet again, of context. Our appreciation of the larger-scale dryland picture gains greatly from the detail and precision that analysis of the wet deposits can provide. Sometimes this new information is environmental. By looking at the pollen, seeds, leaves and twigs preserved in the stagnant mud at the bottom of a wet ditch or abandoned well, we can learn about the trees, shrubs and grasses that were growing at the time. This in turn will allow us to speculate on whether local farmers kept livestock, grew certain crops or maintained hedges. Sometimes we can even gain fascinating insights into that dimension that archaeologists dream about discovering: the world above ground.

The magic of Pompeii is that it survives above ground. I gather from stories in the press that recent excavations carried out before the construction of a new road there have revealed Roman houses buried under four metres of volcanic ash, which means that the upper storeys have survived. I find that quite mind-boggling. I very much doubt whether we will ever find such a thing on a prehistoric site in northern Europe, but occasionally on wet or damp sites we are permitted glimpses of the ancient world upstairs.

I caught my first glimpse of that world in August 1973. We were digging at Fengate and were working near the edge of the ring-ditch that ran around the outside of an Early Bronze Age round barrow. On the air photo the ring-ditch resembled a signet ring; the dark cropmark which made the 'gemstone' was in fact a large, deep pit. By any standards it was a big pit; certainly large enough to have held a car. And it was deep too, with a richly organic muddy layer at the bottom. Most probably it had been dug as a gravel quarry four or five centuries after the barrow had been abandoned. A radiocarbon date from wood at the bottom of the pit gave a range of years between 1750 and 1410 BC – essentially the latter part of the Early Bronze Age.

Most of the wood from the mud at the bottom of the pit was twiggy stuff, pretty scrappy and unexciting. We assumed that it had accumulated within the pit after it had been abandoned as a quarry. But at the time we forgot one thing, which in hindsight was blindingly obvious: people had to get in and out of the pit. We couldn't miss it when we found it, still upright and *in situ*, leaning at an angle that would have clipped the upper edge of the pit. It was of course a ladder. But not a ladder we would recognise today: it had no rungs.

It was a notched log made from alder wood, with the bark removed. The bottom had been chopped flat with a narrow-bladed bronze axe, and the first step was complete. The second was just visible, but the log had rotted away at that point. I couldn't be absolutely certain that this was a notched log ladder, because I wasn't aware that any other had been found at Bronze Age sites elsewhere in Britain, but it seemed a reasonable assumption. Besides, nobody could suggest a better one. Then the story went quiet for a couple of decades.

In the late eighties Maisie was called out to examine waterlogged wood found in two well-like Late Bronze Age pits in the Thames valley near Oxford. One of the sites, in a gravel quarry near the village of Yarnton, produced a superbly preserved oak notched log ladder, with no fewer than five steps surviving. The other, from Radley nearby, was also made from oak, and in this case three steps survived, of which one was complete.

I've often noted how archaeological discoveries come in fits and starts. Progress, it seems, is rarely smooth. At about the same time that the Yarnton and Radley ladders were found, another – again probably Bronze Age – was found in excavations ahead of the construction of a new boating lake for Eton College, in the Thames floodplain near Dorney. Yet another was found further north, at Sutton Common, a waterlogged Iron Age site near Doncaster, in Yorkshire. This find, however, is probably Iron Age – three or four centuries more recent than the others. All the prehistoric British notched ladders we know about were used for getting in and out of wet holes in the ground – presumably to draw water or dig gravel.

At about this time my brother Felix returned from a walking holiday in Nepal. He showed us his photos, as all returning travellers do. Nepal is a spectacular place, so for once I was not bored by holiday snaps. As I was flicking through them, I was suddenly electrified. There, in the courtyard of a disused Tibetan Buddhist temple at Namgyaling near Marpha, in the Himalayas north of Kathmandu, was a most extraordinary ladder. It was made from a single log with steps cut into it in the form of deep notches. Only then did it come to me: if Nepalese ladders could go between the storeys of a building, then why shouldn't our Bronze Age ones? My brother's holiday snap had freed my mind from wet holes in the ground.

It is remarkable how widely accepted, traditional ways of doing things can just vanish, and in a short time. Notched log ladders were replaced by ladders with rungs in the Roman period – i.e. after the Roman Conquest of AD 43. So far as we know, post-Roman Saxon and medieval ladders were invariably made with rungs.

I have already mentioned how I find it impossible to be truly objective, and nowhere is this more apparent than in the matter of judging the past against the present. The issues are simply too big for anyone, other than perhaps a philosopher, to grapple with, and are best approached piecemeal. So far we have looked at religion, and the role of the ancestors in the management of the landscape, and in the next chapter I will discuss daily life in that landscape. I want to finish this chapter with a few thoughts on the living, but non-human, components of the landscape. In this particular field of study, recent wetland research has transformed our view of the past.

I can begin with a simple qualitative statement that nobody can challenge: the modern environment of Britain and northern Europe is a grossly degraded, pale reflection of its Bronze Age predecessor. Over the millennia, the need to feed the rising human population has relentlessly pushed nature back, further and further away from centres of population, to ever more peripheral regions. Taking a particular view, one can approve this process: we now support a world population of billions, and modern science has spared vast numbers of innocent people from the agonies of death through hunger and disease. But the cost to the historic environment has been, and continues to be, appalling. This question of cost is an issue that we cannot resolve now, even if the nations of the world had the will to do so. But it is an issue that will not go away, and in a hundred years' time it will more than haunt us.

I don't want to sound like the prophet Jeremiah, but when I examine the archaeological record, or what's left of it after the depredations of the past forty years, I am forced to conclude that it's the *pace* of modern environmental depletion that scares me. In the past, human beings did indeed push nature towards the periphery; but it was a very slow process – and besides, nature would often return and put matters right.

The Black Death did an effective job in 1348, when the population of Britain was halved in a few years. The prehistoric record, too, is by no means one of continuous 'advancement'. Towards the end of the Neolithic period, for example, there is good evidence for a phase when woodland encroached on cleared land in southern Britain, and scrub took over pasture. In the Fens, the centuries around 1000 BC and into the first millennium BC were times of widespread flooding and abandonment of entire landscapes.

I suspect, but of course cannot prove, that the limit of the world's natural carrying capacity ought to have been reached sometime in the nineteenth or twentieth centuries. Thereafter the population would have remained stable, through a process of ruthless Malthusian checks and balances. If there are too many mouths to feed, starvation redresses the balance. But prior to that, in the seventeenth and eighteenth centuries we discovered how to release the energy hidden within fossil fuel. And unwisely, we have chosen never to look back. It's ironic, but by plundering the resources laid down in the distant past we are ultimately assuring our own demise.

If the rapid pace of modern environmental depletion is the certain sign that the process is reaching a critical point, the effects on the archaeological record are apocalyptic. During the Middle Ages, and in the sixteenth to eighteenth centuries, archaeological sites were destroyed largely through superstition, just as they are today. But it's the sheer scale of destruction that is different now. In the past some of the magnificent stones of Avebury were reduced to stumps in the ground, but even then the stones, as it were, 'hit back'. I'm thinking of the body of a fourteenth-century barber-surgeon that was found crushed beneath one of the massive prehistoric stones which he had been helping to demolish. The unfortunate man's body was found with a pocketful of coins from the reign of Edward I, a short metal probe and a pair of scissors. The destruction wrought by people like the barber-surgeon was considerable, in that a significant number of stones were smashed beyond repair, but it was never total. The prehistoric pits and ramps that were dug to receive the stones have survived, as in many cases have the actual stumps of the stones. The recent excavation of the Beckhampton Avenue revealed six stone sockets of monoliths that were torn down in the Middle Ages and the eighteenth century, so we can quantify with some precision the damage that took place. It was wilful and unnecessary, motivated by fear, ignorance and greed. But it was human, and it happened on a human scale.

Contrast that with what we are doing today to our wetlands, where the archaeological remains are, or rather were, every bit as rich as Avebury, but vastly more diverse and sensitive. The peat bogs of the Irish midlands cover large areas of the country, and whole landscapes have been mechanically planed off to fuel power stations and to fill gardeners' growing-bags. In England, smaller areas of the peats of the Somerset Levels and Thorne Moor, near the Humber, have been given the same treatment. First, mechanical diggers rip out preserved Bronze Age and other prehistoric trees – and also, we suspect, timber circles, coffins and anything else that gets in the way. These are bulldozed into heaps and unceremoniously burned. Then monstrous machines that resemble power saws from Hell mill the exposed peat to a fine, fluffy, cooked-rice-like texture.

In the Fens the damage is not quite so spectacular, but it is far more widespread. Some archaeological material does survive, but usually it's the 5 per cent or so that cannot be destroyed unless the whole site is physically removed. This is because in the Fens most of the destruction has been caused by land drainage. I say 'has been caused' because the worst of the damage was done in the 1960s and seventies, and the finishing touches were added in the last two decades of the twentieth century. I have just learned from the Ministry of Agriculture that as a farmer I can apply for grants to raise the water level on my Fenland farm, *for environmental reasons*. Of course I'll take their money, but would someone please tell those worthy officials – and the politicians who pull their strings – that they are thirty years too late?

The history of Fenland drainage is often told as a story of man's victory over the powers of nature. And it is a heroic tale in many respects – as indeed is that of our neighbours in Holland. But like so many other aspects of the modern world, it has gone too far. It has lost its human scale. It began in the Middle Ages, when the slightly higher ground around the Wash was taken into agriculture a parish at a time, by the inhabitants of the Marshland villages. But the main body of the Fens wasn't successfully drained until the early seventeeth century, when the work was undertaken by an extraordinary Dutch engineer, later knighted by a grateful monarch, Sir Cornelius Vermuyden.

Vermuyden realised that the Fens flooded because the rivers that flowed through them could not reach the sea except by a maze of sinuous channels. So he set about straightening the rivers and the channels, or dykes, that fed them. Once he had established the basic pattern of drainage, generally speaking it worked well. There were problems, of which peat erosion was the most serious, but as a means of preventing the annual and disastrous floods of winter, it worked – and still works. But there is all the difference in the world between flood prevention and wholesale land drainage.

Flood prevention is about removing surplus water safely and efficiently. Land drainage is about lowering the water-table in the ground itself. In Holland they realised that if the water levels in their ditches sank too low, the peats in the fields would shrink, the land surface would drop, and flooding would again be a problem. So they keep the water just a few inches below the surface, and as a result they possess some of the richest, most productive grazing land in Europe. In Britain the story is rather different.

For the first four decades of the twentieth century, otters were a pest in the Fens. The dykes were unpolluted and full of water. Then, in the last four decades of the century, the otters vanished entirely. As I write, in the first year of the twenty-first century, I have heard rumours that a pair have returned to a nature reserve somewhere nearby. But it's all very hush-hush. The reason why the dykes of

Fenland run dry lies in the last war, when the nation's food supply was cut off with the Atlantic convoys, and people were urged to Dig for Victory. The pastures of the Fens were ploughed at this time of national crisis.

After the war, this policy of plant-and-plough continued. Huge sums were sunk in grandiose drainage schemes, and not a penny was spent on monitoring their effects on the natural or historic environment. In 1976 English Heritage launched the Fenland Project, which revealed the extent of the damage, but only in the most general terms – because how could they discover what was being pumped dry, unseen, beneath the ground? My work at Maxey, Etton, Flag Fen and elsewhere took place beneath the umbrella of the Fenland Project. Everyone who worked in the Project has helped transform our knowledge of British prehistory, but it only happened at the very last minute. There's almost nothing wet and worthwhile left now. Just a few boggy spots, like Flag Fen. The rest is dust – and a few scatters of flints lying on the surface of rolling, prairie-like fields of onions or carrots.

'Bog oaks' are a symbol of drainage. They are the trunks and roots of the huge trees that originally grew in the natural depression that forms the floor of the Fenland basin. As the level of the North Sea gradually rose, so water ponded in the rivers that drained into it. Conditions grew wetter and the roots of the great trees of the primeval forest ceased to cope. So the trees died and blew down. Then peat began to grow, and their vast trunks were preserved intact. Nowadays they are removed by mechanical diggers and stacked in great piles near the edges of fields. As I drive around the Fens today I notice that these piles are getting progressively smaller, as the peat itself grows ever thinner. Soon there will be none left. It's hard not to be affected by the sight of a great pile of bog oaks. There's something so inglorious, undignified and tragic about it. Cars flash by on the busy road, but nobody even knows what this strange-looking woodpile is. And if they did, they wouldn't care much. To me, it's a sight every bit as sad as a group of beached whales.

The yawning chasm that separates our impoverished modern environment from the sheer richness and diversity of the ancient wetlands was brought home to me sharply six weeks ago, when I was sitting at my word-processor working on this book. Suddenly my eye was caught by something large and white which flashed by the window. I could see it was a bird, or perhaps two birds, but they resembled no bird I knew. Anyway, my writing was going well and I was loath to break my chain of thought, so I pressed on.

An hour or two later I finished writing and walked up to my main land to inspect the sheep. My dog Jess was with me, in case I spotted any problems and needed to drive animals into a pen. We stood at the gate and I started counting. I had reached fifty or so, when Jess started to growl. I looked down at her. Her ears were pricked and she was staring intently towards a large puddle, or small lake, that had formed in the field the previous day, when we had had torrential rain and the severest north-easterly gales I can ever recall. Then I saw what she was looking at so intently. Standing on the edge of the water was an enormous white bird, rather like a heron, but very much larger, with long reddish legs, black flight feathers and a beak like a carrot.

It looked towards us, then flew off towards the river, where it joined another large white bird. So there was a pair of them. To cut a long story short, they were a pair of white storks that had been blown across the North Sea in the recent gales. By some strange coincidence, they landed at the Holme-next-the-Sea Nature Reserve, where they were officially identified. Then they flew up the coast, and mine was their next official sighting. They stayed with us for two days before flying off. Today they're probably in Poland, where the main European population now resides.

I was warned not to tell anyone about the storks, unless I was confident they could keep a secret. Storks are now rare visitors to the British Isles, and if word had got out, my farm would have been invaded by thousands of 'twitchers' – those people whose dearest wish is to spot a scarce bird and add it to their list of sightings. We knew of people who had suffered an invasion by 'twitchers', and we had absolutely no wish to repeat their experience. But I did manage to get a telephoto view of one of our storks in a flooded field, with some of my Shetland sheep in the background. I was immediately struck by this picture, because I know that storks were common in the Iron Age Fenland, and Shetlands probably resemble later prehistoric breeds of sheep.

We had found well-preserved stork bones in wet Iron Age ditches belonging to the Cat's Water settlement at Fengate. They were not alone: we also discovered the bones of other birds that have become extreme rarities in England: sea eagles, pelicans and cranes. Like our pair of storks, they too are occasionally blown in by exceptionally severe weather. But in the Iron Age they must have been common in the area, or else I don't see how their bones could have come to rest in the muddy ditches of an ordinary farmyard. It appeared that in the past they were not rare visitors, found only on the periphery of the settled landscape.

The Iron Age village at Fengate also revealed the bones of a host of slightly more common birds: greylag geese, mallard ducks, cormorants, herons, swans, barnacle geese, teal, tableduck, goosanders, goshawks, buzzards, coots and crows. Bones of smaller birds, such as sparrows, either didn't find their way into the ditches, or didn't survive when they got there. Domestic animal bones included dogs, horses, pigs and a few goats, but the vast majority were from cattle (no fewer than 2,596 identifiable bones and fragments) and sheep (2,220 bones). Within and around the fields roamed wild animals: fox and otter, red and roe deer; and out in the waters of Flag Fen were numerous colonies of beaver, an animal that has entirely vanished from the British Isles.

In the Bronze Age we know that brown bears and wolves roamed the forest beyond the fields, and they probably did so in the Iron Age, too. But by then the continuing process of pushing back the periphery had removed these more exotic animals from the immediate surroundings of the village. The world was changing even in the Iron Age, but at a human pace. And ultimately it could be reversed.

CHAPTER ELEVEN

The Daily Round

THERE IS A CLEAR DISTINCTION in the Western world between the sacred and the profane. There is also a continuing debate about the role of religion in a secular society. I doubt whether such a debate could have taken pace in prehistory, because in those far-off times the distinction between the daily and the spiritual worlds was far from clear-cut. As we have seen, the domain of the ancestors frequently impinged on daily life, and at several levels. But people did have to lead their ordinary lives and cope with the routines of the farming and domestic year, and that would have been the backdrop against which their spiritual activities took place.

Unfortunately, it's too easy to view the remarkable religious sophistication of Bronze Age communities in isolation, as a phenomenon in its own right. This is highly misleading. I am convinced that such a lack of contextual balance is the main factor behind the growth of the semi-mystical nonsense that is written about the Celts, the Druids, Atlantis and so forth. In reality, the mundane world of the Bronze Age was as rich and complex as its foil, the realm of ideology. Both sides of life contributed equally to what was rapidly becoming an emerging civilisation.

It took three years for us to discover the remains of our first Bronze Age roundhouse at Fengate, back in 1974. I now want to retrace my steps to find out more about the people who lived in that house. We've discussed religion, landscapes and even social organisation at some length, but we haven't said very much about daily life as it would have been led by ordinary folk when they weren't constructing barrows, henges and the rest. I'll use that first Bronze Age house as a peg on which to hang the objects and events of the everyday world three to four thousand years ago. Before I go any further, I must first justify my use of the term round*house* to describe the buildings which are so important to our story.

One often hears people who should know better talking about such houses, and their modern African equivalents, as *huts*. To my mind, a hut is something knocked together in a hurry and without a great deal of care and consideration. Vegetable gardens and allotments are the ideal habitat of the hut. As buildings go, I am sure they have many tales to tell, but they don't contain much information about the way people actually lived. Houses, on the other hand, are places where families of humans dwell. A house says much about the people who use it. It speaks of their pride in themselves, of their wealth, or lack of it, their status within society and their ability to organise their lives. It is far more than just a building.

The Bronze Age houses I have excavated have mostly been round. Rectangular buildings from the period are known in Britain, but they are rare and may well have been communal – perhaps the equivalent of a village hall. On the Continental mainland, on the other hand, rectangular houses were the rule throughout later prehistory, from the Neolithic period right through to Roman times. In Britain and Ireland, Neolithic houses may have been rectangular (they are so rare as to make generalisation difficult), but from the start of the Bronze Age at least, they were almost invariably round, or round-ish.

The size of these prehistoric roundhouses varied, depending on when and where they were built, but most had diameters ranging from about five to ten metres.* There are notable exceptions. Two Early Iron Age roundhouses have been excavated at Cow Down in Wiltshire and Pimperne Down in Dorset. These were truly staggering structures, whose diameter was no less than fifteen metres.

Roundhouses are superb buildings, and I have always been astonished that they were not used more widely on the Continent in prehistory. The shape is inherently stable and sheds the wind well. During the great hurricane that struck southern England in October 1989, I happened to be inside the reconstructed Bronze Age roundhouse that

* It may be worth recording here that the average floor area of Iron Age roundhouses at Fengate compares favourably with terrace accommodation provided by the Great Northern Railway Company for its Peterborough employees in 1850.

we had recently completed building. I remember standing at the door in my shirtsleeves watching while sheets of roofing material and other debris blew across my view. Behind me, the modern factories of Peterborough's Eastern Industrial Area were being seriously damaged by the gales, but, snug inside the roundhouse, all was still and tranquil.

The strongest point in a conical roof is the apex. If the roofing material is lightweight, such as thatch, the entire weight of the roof can be supported on the walls and there is no need for a central post. In the case of very large buildings, such as those at Pimperne or Cow Down, the rafters may either sag or have to be joined, in which case the simplest thing to do is to erect one or more circles of internal roof-support posts, on which rests a continuous circular ring-beam. This ring-beam supports the rafters and helps hold the roof in place. But ideally the house should be about ten metres in diameter, in which case there is no need for posts inside the living area. When you walk into such a building, your immediate impression is of spaciousness. Above you is a high roof into which the light smoke from the central fire swirled. Up there, in the gloom of the roof space, the prehistoric inhabitants would have hung all sorts of good things: smoked hams, dried fish and eels, cheeses, game and other meats.

We built our first Bronze Age roundhouse in the archaeological park we laid out around the Flag Fen excavation in 1987. We also reconstructed the fields and droveway nearby, but not on the original site; instead we placed this reconstructed mini-landscape on land we had available out in Flag Fen, about half a mile to the east. The frame of the house was built of wood and the wall was formed of woven wattle smeared with clay daub. When we constructed the wall, we used thick coppiced hazel rods of about one to two inches diameter. These had to be woven around the wall posts, which were spaced at metre intervals, more or less. The difficult part came when the wattle was rammed or trodden down hard, to make a good tight weave. If the tips of the wall posts aren't adequately buried, the accumulated outward pressure of successive layers of springy hazel rods can force them out of the ground. This accumulated outward pressure is particularly strong at the doorway, whose frame would have been held securely in place by a good stout lintel. The pressure generated by the woven wattle doubtless helps to account for the fact that most door posts were considerably larger than the other posts of the outer wall. After a few months hazel looses its springiness, but by this time the walls have 'set' into an extraordinarily strong and resilient structure.

The excavated archaeological 'footprint' of our first Bronze Age house was slight – just a double circle of post-holes, two slightly larger front-door posts and a continuous shallow ring-gully around the outside. The inner circle of posts supported the centre of the roof rafters. The posts of the outer circle served a dual purpose. They provided pillars, around which the wattle skeleton of the wall was woven, and they also supported the roof rafters.

The ring-gully outside the walls was a very shallow ditch (about thirty centimetres, or one foot, deep) that had been cut into the ground surface about half a metre outside the outer wall. It was positioned directly below the wide eaves that kept the mud-based daub walls dry. Properly made daub, well mixed with plenty of straw and cow dung, will stand up to rain blown onto it in a sharp shower, but it won't tolerate continuous wetness. So the shallow gully below the eaves – known as the eaves-drip gully – was in effect the gutter that took rain from off the roof.

Hundreds of prehistoric eaves-drip gullies have been discovered in Britain, and we found ours worked well. Not only did it prevent splashing when water from the roof hit the ground, it also markedly reduced rising damp around the base of the walls. Normally the gullies stood on their own; they didn't need to drain into a ditch or soak away. But in this instance the original builders must have hit a snag with ground drainage, so the gully was given a short extension, which drained it into a nearby droveway side-ditch. Archaeologically, this was a great stroke of luck for us.

I remember thinking, shortly after we had exposed the slightly darker mark of the ring-gully on the surface of the gravel, how considerate it was of the Bronze Age house-builders to link the gully to the droveway drainage-ditch in this fashion. Without this link, we might have found it difficult to prove beyond all reasonable doubt that the small roundhouse – the diameter of its wall was about eight metres – did indeed belong with the field system. But an actual physical link proved their association beyond any doubt.

Later the following season we found four other roundhouses.

LEFT The raising of the central oak tree at Seahenge was technically very difficult. It weighed approximately 2.5 tons, but its outer surface was extremely soft and covered with fragile axe-marks which could easily have been erased or damaged. Here sheets of foam are being attached to the tree to cushion the straps which will be used to lift it.

BELOW The lifting of the tree was successfully completed on Saturday, 17 July 1999. It required the use of a twenty-tonne tracked excavator fitted with wide, low ground-pressure tracks. To spread the load further the machine worked on a pad of plywood sheeting.

RIGHT The tree trunk was carefully checked when clear of the ground, in case any votive offering or other unexpected find might still be adhering to the wood. This photo shows a short length of twisted honeysuckle rope within one of the two towing ropes which were used to haul the tree to its resting place (centre, midway between the encircling band and the flat base of the tree).

Members of the Norfolk Archaeological Unit preparing to lift the final two timbers of the Seahenge circle in early August 1999. Unusually, these two timbers are not actually touching.

Like a scene from a Christmas crib, the central tree of Seahenge lies in a shallow water-bath in the Hudson Barn Field Centre at Flag Fen, Peterborough. It is midnight and members of the Flag Fen team are putting the finishing touches to the prefabricated tank which is being secured around the tree. By 1 a.m. the sprinkler system would be working and the long process of desalination could begin.

The flat underside of the central oak tree was found to be covered with axe-marks. These had been made with an Early Bronze Age flat axe, of bronze, with a wide (about ninety millimetres) and curved cutting edge, and are believed to be the earliest left by a metal tool yet found in Britain. One of the towing loops, still with honeysuckle rope in place, is also visible (upper foreground, right).

ABOVE The posts of the Seahenge timber circle were taken to a specially constructed series of washing tanks at Flag Fen, where there was adequate space in which to work and a good supply of clean water. Here one of the timbers is being carried to the tanks on the stretcher which was used to raise it from the ground.

RIGHT Wide axe-marks, very similar to those on the central oak tree, were also found on the lower, chopped ends of the oak posts of the timber circle. These examples are on post 60 (the scale is five centimetres).

A full-size replica of Seahenge was reconstructed by Channel 4's *Time Team*. This photo shows the freshly de-barked tree stump with one of the two towing loops and a length of twisted honeysuckle rope ready for attachment. The rope was prepared by Damien Saunders. Strands of freshly cut honeysuckle were soaked and twisted and then plied together. Hitherto unknown to British archaeologists, this rope proved capable of pulling a two-ton oak tree.

The *Time Team* reconstruction reaches a critical stage, with the oak tree poised above the hole dug to receive it. Here the ropes are being re-rigged by Damien Saunders and Maisie Taylor to comply with the pattern found in the ground at Seahenge.

These buildings were on their own, tucked away in the corners of fields or, in one case, within a small ditched yard. Sometimes we found a formless scatter of post-holes, perhaps of an outbuilding of some sort – possibly a dry wood or hay store – but we never found more than one farmhouse together. This would suggest that the people who farmed the fields lived in harmony with one another and did not feel particularly threatened from outside; otherwise we might have found villages, with perhaps a stockade or earthwork around the perimeter, to act as a symbolic and practical defence. Unfortunately, however, I don't think it was quite as simple as that. I don't believe there was much aggression from people outside the region, although I do think there was a good deal of controlled aggression and social competition among the communities living in it. I suspect, too, that this controlled aggression formed an almost routine part of daily life – but only at certain times of the year.

Most acts of aggression can be deflected by providing a symbolic defence, which states in effect that this particular settlement is ours, and that any uninvited outsiders are unwelcome. In some societies the symbolic defence may encourage certain controlled types of small-scale raiding, in which, for example, cattle are rustled. This pattern of raiding only happens at times of the year, such as autumn, when crops and forage are safely gathered in and there is food enough for people to relax – and to think of things other than merely winning a livelihood from the ground.

Rustling is very commonly encountered in traditional societies where livestock are an important part of the local economy. It can be seen as a controlled form of social competition, between individual communities and even individual young men (doubtless to impress certain individuals of the opposite sex). It is most unlikely that older people took part in this rough-and-tumble, but I suggest that they would have tolerated, and even encouraged it. By the same token, prompt action would have been taken if things got out of hand and threatened social stability.

Something as necessarily ephemeral as rustling is difficult to prove archaeologically. Two young warriors gallop across fields and droves, brandishing spears and looking magnificent. Before the gaze of horrified onlookers, they steal a prize bull and ride into the sunset. How can that possibly leave an archaeological trace? I concede that it can't leave a *direct* trace, but we can put together clues from other sources.

Neolithic and Bronze Age people were profoundly concerned with boundaries. They marked them with burial mounds, religious shrines to the ancestors and smaller-scale offerings of all sorts, including isolated burials. Boundaries are crucially important. Not just the big national ones, marked out by customs posts at border crossings; other boundaries are essential to the conduct of normal social life. We require them to 'know where we stand', in all senses of that phrase; without them we're lost, socially, emotionally and possibly physically too.

So boundaries are a key part of our social geography. And they are as important today as they were four thousand years ago. A boundary only gains and retains its significance if it is repeatedly tested, and proved to hold. Prehistoric people couldn't afford the modern luxury of wholesale slaughter, so frequent, smaller-scale, less bloody boundary infringements would keep the position and importance of current boundaries clear in people's minds. Rustling raids would have served this purpose ideally. Doubtless there would be formal, possibly semi-ritualised, apologies between the elders of the various communities involved. These meetings probably took place on a subsequent occasion, after each raid. They may well have happened at the barrows, major droveways and shrines that marked the actual boundaries. I can perhaps put it another way: during a raid, the boundary had been honoured in the breach; in the consequent meeting it was honoured in the observance.

Semi-formalised rustling of this sort was also an opportunity for young men to show off their fighting skills and to brandish their finest weapons, which in turn were a symbol of their owners' status within society. I think it very improbable that a rich Bronze Age father would let his sons go on a rustling raid with second-rate weapons, as things not directly associated with rustling – most notably the family's prestige – would also be at stake.

The bronze weapons of the period are very interesting. Large-bladed thrusting spears were used throughout the Bronze Age, as were daggers and shorter swords, known as dirks. There were no swords in the Early Bronze Age, as the technology of casting them took some time to master. But around 1400 BC we see the appearance of long (up to half a metre), thin and pointed swords; these were thrusting weapons, known as rapiers. As weapons went, they weren't very robust and there were problems in attaching the blade to the hilt. I doubt whether they would have stood up to the rigours of a prolonged campaign, which makes me think their use, in anger, would have been short. More likely than not – and this probably applies to most Bronze Age weaponry – their main use was as an object to brandish fiercely on raids. They would also have been worn in peace, as personal symbols of rank, power and authority.

It's interesting to note that Middle Bronze Age rapiers and their shorter cousins, dirks, are very commonly found in and around the Fens. In recent years my own research in the Fengate/Flag Fen region has revealed three. The Fens in this period were very much given over to livestock-rearing, and it is hard not to see these weapons as having been used on rustling raids.

The widespread introduction of riding, and of horse-borne warriors, was a major change which took place in the Later Bronze Age. I hesitate to use the word 'cavalry', with its suggestion of organised fighting; I think it far more probable that the first horse-borne warriors spent much of their time posing in warlike attitudes, either to encourage their friends or to intimidate their enemies. It's in the Later Bronze Age – in round terms after 1300 BC – that we encounter the first harness fittings and the earliest slashing swords. These are weapons whose weight lies towards the tip of the blade, and which were intended to cut downwards, like the cavalryman's sabre. Sometimes the scabbards of these swords were fitted with so-called winged chapes. The chape is the metal bit at the tip of the scabbard which prevents the sword from cutting its way out when sheaved. Winged chapes were cast with pointed, wing-shaped protrusions which could be held steady beneath the rider's heel, thereby allowing him to draw the sword single-handed across his chest while his other hand controlled the reins.

The first shields also appeared at about this time. They were carried on the forearm, and were very much smaller than the long shields of medieval mounted knights. Most were round, and less than a metre in diameter. The largest ones were made from beaten sheets of bronze and are extremely beautiful objects, decorated with concentric ridges, bosses and rivets. When highly polished and glinting in the sun, they would have looked magnificent. Unfortunately, however, they were useless.

During my final year at Cambridge John Coles, the lecturer involved with wetland archaeology who kept my interest in the subject alive, gave lectures on experimental archaeology. They were superb, and the best of them all was on Bronze Age shields. Using replicas, John showed how the thin beaten shields could be sliced through with a contemporary leaf-shaped slashing sword, like a carving knife passing through tinfoil. I still remember the startled expression on the face of the student holding the useless but beautiful shield.

John then carried out the same experiment, but this time using replica wooden and leather shields, known from peat-bog finds in Ireland. These proved wholly effective – which goes to show that appearances can be deceptive. It also leads us to the inevitable conclusion that the beautiful metal shields were not about actual fighting at all, but were probably made to be carried in processions and ceremonies. If they were about aggression it must have taken a more peaceful form, in which powerful men from great families competed with one another to see who could mount the most magnificent display.

A rapidly growing body of recent research has shown that Bronze Age fields similar to those found at Fengate are known at several locations across East Anglia. Although the fields at Fengate seem to have started somewhat earlier than the others, most came into existence at the close of the Early Bronze Age, around approximately 1500 BC, and continued in use through the Middle and Late Bronze Age, eventually being abandoned in the first half of the first millennium BC. Their demise, in other words, happened gradually during the initial centuries of the Iron Age, or the closing years of the Bronze Age. In nearly every instance that we know about in East Anglia, Bronze Age fields were laid out using the framework of an earlier landscape, which was defined and marked out by barrows, henges and other religious shrines placed at significant boundaries within and around the landscape.

It is sometimes said that the houses and settlements of the livestock farmers who used these fields were unenclosed or undefended; I am not so sure about that. Certainly there were no banks, walls, ditches or stockades surrounding the individual settlements, but that does not necessarily mean they were completely undefended. I am certain they were not open to any passing stranger who might feel inclined to take possession of them.

The boundaries of the land-holdings controlled by the individual farmsteads were very clearly marked out by droveways and large ditches. These in turn were reinforced by the 'spiritual electric fence' provided by barrows and other shrines that were repeatedly visited throughout the Bronze Age. As we have already seen, they *were* defended – or rather, they were watched over by the forces of the ancestors – but at a distance. It's interesting to note that a symbolic, ritualised boundary of this sort only works if the people likely to breach it are familiar with the layout and ownership patterns of a particular landscape. It would be poor sport to trespass into another family's land-holding if you weren't really aware of where it began and ended. Again, this would suggest localised raids rather than long-distance military campaigns.

We only start to find physically defended or clearly delineated settlements within field systems at the very end of the Bronze Age. This suggests to me that the social control which maintained the individual components of the landscape was beginning to break down, for whatever reason. In the new conditions prevailing in the Early Iron Age people began to live together in larger, more nucleated communities. No longer were the spiritual boundaries out in the landscape adequate. Something closer to home and more obviously deterrent was required to keep unwelcome visitors at bay.

We learned a great deal from the reconstruction of that first Bronze Age house at Fengate. We used ash and oak timber cut from a local wood for the wall posts and rafters, cut wattle from ten-year-old stands of coppiced hazel, used reeds placed below a layer of turf for the roof, and plastered the wattle walls with daub. From other experimentally reconstructed prehistoric roundhouses we knew that it would be a great mistake to leave a chimney hole at the centre of the roof, as this had been found to work rather like a blast furnace: the central fire roared away, soon the roof was alight, and the house burned to the ground. We made many mistakes, but were glad we hadn't made that one.

Without a central chimney, smoke filters out through the thatch and coats it with a thin layer of ash and carbon. This coating not only preserves the reed, it also helps to prevent water from being absorbed. But, of course, there is a down-side. If you burn wet, or even damp or freshly-felled wood, the smoke given off is far too dense to filter out through the roof. Soon everyone in the building has streaming eyes and the sound of coughing can be heard miles away. We also found that certain woods burn with less smoke than others. Dry, well-seasoned willow, for example, is a smokeless fuel. It's inconceivable that they didn't know these things in the Bronze Age – which is why I'm sure each household must have had a special building as a dry-wood store, where wood could be kept for at least a full year before being thrown on the fire.

We don't know what medicines were routinely used, but many folk remedies are highly effective and have roots of unknown age. Willow bark contains high levels of aspirin, and can be chewed to ease the pain of toothache; it can also be heated up to make a very effective analgesic tea to cure headaches or hangovers. I suspect that the former would have been more common than the latter in the Bronze Age, because it is possible that the consumption of alcohol, perhaps in the form of mead or ale (beer made without hops), only took place during religious ceremonies. In many tribal societies the recreational use of alcohol is not allowed. It is seen as something special, to be appreciated in a special way and on special occasions. By the Iron Age, drinking had become a feature of life in high society, and by the dawn of the Roman period wealthy Iron Age Britons were importing wine from the Mediterranean in amphorae.

The Bronze Age saw the introduction of many things that we now take for granted. The wheel is perhaps the most obvious example. We don't know when the very first wheel was introduced to Britain, but it was probably some time in the Early Bronze Age. The earliest wheel yet found in Britain is somewhat later, although still well within the Bronze Age, and I had the good fortune to be closely involved in its discovery.

It was found in 1994 at Flag Fen, where it seems to have been used simply as a short, flat piece of wood, thrown onto a damp piece of ground along with other wooden bits and pieces, to raise a pathway above the surrounding water. This probably happened between 1200 and 1300 BC, in the Middle Bronze Age. The piece of wood was crescentic and made from alder, a wet-loving tree that is fine-grained and naturally resistant to rot. The central plank and the other crescentic piece were missing, but wheels of this type, made in three parts, are not uncommon in Holland and Germany, and our wheel was almost identical to other tripartite wheels found on the Continent and in Britain and Ireland. In fact they are so similar, it's tempting to suggest that the design had been got right. Clearly the wheels worked well, as they were made to the same pattern for centuries.

When we came to look at it more closely, we were struck by the wheel's sophisticated construction. You might imagine that the simplest way to make a wheel is to saw a thin slice through a round log, Flintstones fashion. Unfortunately such a wheel might last for an hour or two, but soon it would split from the centre when it wobbled on its axle – wood splits very readily from the centre to the outside. Also, the outer sapwood which would have formed the wearing surface of this Flintstones-style wheel becomes brittle when it dries out. Besides, saws that could cut through large logs were not available until Roman times. All in all, such a wheel would not have been possible, let alone a success.

The Flag Fen wheel was cut from three hewn planks of alder which were held firmly together by two oak braces in dovetail slots, one on each face. The three planks would have flexed against themselves as the wheel revolved had they not been pinned in place by two snug-fitting ash dowels. Each type of wood used was the right one for the job, with the right properties of strength, workability and resilience. In its way the wheel was a miniature masterpiece. But there were two aspects of it that we found particularly remarkable and exciting.

The first, and perhaps least unexpected, was the discovery of two gravel pebbles that had been forced into the wheel by normal pressure on the road. At first glance there's nothing remarkable about that – except that the wheel was found in soft, peaty alluvium which was entirely stoneless. During its life it must have run on a fairly hard road, probably surfaced with gravel. So, on the one hand we have – admittedly rather tenuous – evidence for made-up or surfaced roads, and on the other a firm indication that the wheel was a real one, as used in daily life. It was not something that was made to be thrown into a bog as a religious offering.

Strange as it may seem, offerings in bogs, ponds, lakes and rivers were a very common feature of the Bronze Age across most of Europe, from Italy to Scandinavia. Most finds of Bronze Age metalwork, for example, come from wet places, and it has been suggested, quite reasonably in my view, that these objects were not necessarily as strong or as well made as those that were in actual daily use. That cannot be said of our wheel. Two years previously at Flag Fen we had found half an oak axle that probably went with another wheel. It had been quite heavily worn; again, this suggests that it had seen regular use and was not a specially made religious offering.

I mentioned that the three original parts of the wheel were held in place by two dovetail-shaped oak braces, one on each side. These braces were cut from the outer part of a young oak tree, and a thin layer of bark still adhered to the surface in a few places. This is fascinating. The outer wood of a tree carries the sap, which, as lovers of maple syrup know, contains the sugars and other nutrients the tree requires in order to grow. As wood, it is almost as strong as heartwood, but it's more flexible. This flexibility comes at a price, however. The sap soon dries out, and then the sapwood becomes brittle and prone to cracking. Being full of nutrients, it is also very prone to rot.

Do these weaknesses suggest ignorance on the part of the Bronze Age wheelwrights? I think not. In all other respects the design of the wheel is exemplary. They selected oak sapwood deliberately, knowing full well that it had a short use-life, but that it didn't matter. Nowadays we'd say that this particular component of the wheel was expendable. It was, perhaps, the ancient equivalent of a modern shear bolt – a component designed to shear off and bring the machine to a sharp halt in order to prevent damage to other, more expensive parts. I would suggest that the sapwood laths were replaced every time the wheel was overhauled. The wheelwrights would not have been aware of it, but a new age, that of routine mechanical maintenance, had begun.

I don't know why, but whenever I talk to people about the Flag Fen wheel they immediately assume that it was off a cart or farm wagon, as if the earliest wheels had to be large and crude. But those ultra-crude Flintstone wheels were part of their cartoon Stone Age car. Possibly without knowing it, the television animators had got it right. The diameter of the Flag Fen wheel is about nine hundred millimetres. That's smaller than most bicycle wheels – hardly a farm cart. Examples of stouter wheels are known from the Continent, but this one was slender and lightly built. Maisie reckoned it was more likely to have been part of a Bronze Age governess cart, light trap, or even a wheelbarrow, than a farm wagon.

In 1997, three years after finding the wheel, we made another quite unexpected but altogether remarkable discovery. I was directing excavations in a gravel quarry on the edge of the Fens about five miles north of Peterborough. The site was in the Welland valley at the point where it opens out into the great Fen basin. As valleys go, it appeared almost identical to the lower Nene valley immediately to the south. It was flat, low-lying and richly strewn with prehistoric fields, farms and settlements. The quarry itself was actually below the water level of the modern river Welland, which flowed behind its high bank, well above our heads. Hence the name of the quarry, Welland Bank Quarry.

Like Fengate, Welland Bank was only a metre or two above sea level, and like Etton, four miles upstream, it was buried beneath thick layers of river-borne flood-clay alluvium. Like Flag Fen, the date of the site was Middle and Late Bronze Age. Beneath the alluvium was the preserved prehistoric topsoil, which was carefully removed with large machines under the close supervision of an archaeologist. I forget precisely who it was who spotted them first, but I remember the Site Supervisor, Mark Dymond, calling me across to have a look. And they were very odd indeed.

At first glance they looked like the marks left by a sledge dragged through deep mud. They had first appeared directly below the buried prehistoric topsoil when it had been stripped off by the digger, and consisted of two parallel grooves, filled with buried topsoil, that had been cut or squashed into the underlying gravel. They were quite distinct, but very shallow – no more than an inch or two deep, and about the same in width. They could be traced for about fifty metres, and at one point another, identical set of ruts crossed them.

When their full extent had been revealed, it was quite clear that they couldn't possibly have been made by a sledge. They had to be wheel-ruts. In one place we could see where the vehicle had see-sawed to and fro, either when stuck or when turning around. The way the marks curved so smoothly, and never made awkward or jerky patterns, also suggested wheels rather than runners.

The width of the ruts matched the Flag Fen wheel precisely, but what interested us more than anything else was the distance between them, which was always precisely the same: just 1.10 metres. That's hardly the width of a farm cart. Besides, the ruts were definitely made by a two- and not a four-wheeled vehicle. To my mind that clinched it: this very early wheeled vehicle was built for people. I'm sure there must have been larger goods vehicles at the time, but the fact remains that the Welland Bank ruts and the wheel and axle at Flag Fen were from a very much smaller carriage.

This is very important, because it's not as if people couldn't get around before. After all, we know there were plenty of boats and waterways, and besides, riding was becoming increasingly common-place at about this time. No, I think that here we have yet more evidence for our human obsession with display and prestige. The man or woman with a wheeled vehicle was greatly superior to anyone without one. I would imagine the vehicle itself would have been made to impress, with fancy fittings and suchlike. In modern terms the light carriage was a status symbol, having more in common with a Rolls-Royce than a Mini.

The wheel ruts at Welland Bank seem to have been made off-road, probably in a wet field. I've no idea why somebody should take a narrow-wheeled vehicle out into a muddy field on a wet day, but people have always done strange, inexplicable things. Even in the Bronze Age wheels performed best on harder surfaces; which brings us to the much-neglected topic of prehistoric roads.

In English schools the National Curriculum starts the historical record with the coming of the Romans. As a prehistorian, this myopic decision makes me angry, and I shall continue to lobby to have it changed. The Romans were in England for less than four centuries, and although they undoubtedly left a big mark on the place and the society of its people, they were, at best, an episode. They did not form our culture; they merely influenced it. They gave us *a* road system, it

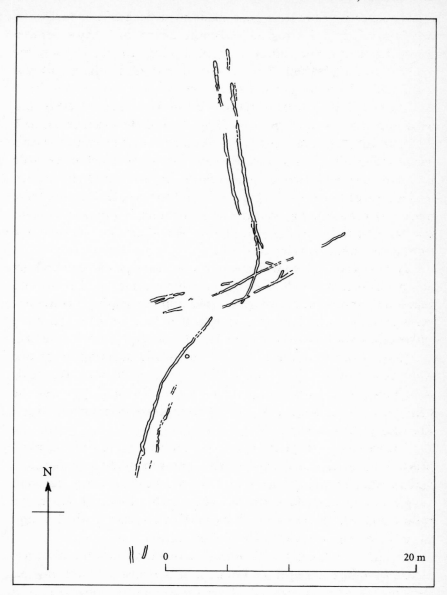

FIG 22   *Later Bronze Age wheel-ruts at Welland Bank Quarry, south Lincolnshire*

is true, but I am convinced that there must have been an effective network of roads for at least two millennia before the Romans arrived in A D 43. What is my evidence?

The modern, Roman-based, system of roads uses London as a hub from which most major trunk routes radiate. We have become so used to this that we take it for granted; it even affected the way the Victorians laid out their railway system, and I believe it has had profound adverse effects, such as the general attitude of central government to the regions. The ultimate blame lies with the military-minded and control-obsessed Roman conquerors of almost two thousand years ago. Surely a more sensible way to get around the country would be based on a network of roads that tied individual communities together without any thought for the capital.

A net-like road system, without any major trunk routes, will inevitably leave a very slight archaeological trace, except in places where civil engineering is required to get across obstacles. Local roads will follow traditional routes, which in turn will tend to keep to freely-draining terrain, whilst avoiding cliffs, bogs and other natural hazards. But roads also exist to avoid human hazards. Today we think of a road as something which links point A with point B. But that is a linear way of thinking, which goes with our linear approach to other things, such as time.

Imagine a road between A and B, two settlements in a flat, featureless plain. Common sense would suggest it should follow a straight line. But it doesn't. Instead it takes a broad, sweeping curve which respects and marks the traditional boundary between tribes C and D, who occupy the land between our two settlements. Thus the road serves more than one function: it links A and B, but it also provides C and D with a boundary which is respected by everyone. If it hadn't followed that sweeping curve, it simply wouldn't have worked, and A and B would remain isolated from one another.

It is often supposed that traditional boundaries were all over the place, twisting and winding their way across the landscape. In fact this was not always the case. Certainly the traditional roads would have been more sinuous than the Roman system, which was often (although not always) imposed on the landscape by unsympathetic military engineers. But it also depends on what one means by sinuous.

We have seen that Bronze Age field systems were carefully laid out to divide the landscape into family holdings of roughly equal size. From the air, the overall effect appears almost regimented, with long, straight droveways and fields set out in an orderly manner. Yet we know that these landscapes have roots extending back for millennia. So they are deeply traditional, yet at the same time their fields and droves are generally straight, or very slightly sinuous.

I believe that the droves and trackways found everywhere that field systems occur *are* the road system of prehistoric Britain. Over time, doubtless some became more important than others, and by the Iron Age there is increasing evidence that some traditional routes, such as the Icknield Way in Hertfordshire, were simply adopted by the Roman authorities, more or less as going concerns.

The more we discover about the organisation of Bronze Age Britain, the more apparent it is that people in widely separated parts of the country were in regular contact. There is evidence – those polished Langdale stone axes for example – of long-distance exchange, but I'm less interested in that than in the way many aspects of material culture seem to have evolved at much the same pace in different places. It's a synchronised dance to the music of time: henges come and go; long barrows give way to round barrows; pottery styles spring up, develop and go out of fashion; roundhouses become ubiquitous; weapons grow ever more deadly; and so on. I could cite dozens of other examples, but it's most striking how small, portable items such as pottery and metalwork change synchronously across the country throughout prehistory. It's as if regional character developed in the form of the landscape and in the way different societies organised themselves, but despite this, the ordinary items of daily life evolved in much the same way all over the country. I'm in no doubt that people were in regular contact, often over long distances. This would have been impossible without an effective network of roads.

I've mentioned the Icknield Way, and there are others – Peddars Way in Norfolk and the most famous of them all, the Ridgeway which ran from Dorset up towards Avebury. In many cases these routes were also boundaries, and boundaries need regularly to be tested and reinforced. That's why John Coles and his team have found votive offerings placed in the water alongside Neolithic trackways across the Somerset Levels: a bundle of arrows, complete pots and, most extraordinary of all, a beautiful polished stone axe made from Alpine jadeite, which is, and must always have been, a treasured item of great value. Offering it to the waters alongside the prehistoric trackway was no empty gesture.

Two summers ago I had the good fortune to visit Gill Hey's excavation in a gravel quarry at Yarnton, in the Thames valley outside Oxford – the site that produced the notched log ladder. Gravel quarries are the same everywhere: thundering trucks, clouds of dust and weather-beaten, gravel-coloured archaeologists down on their hands and knees. This particular part of the quarry was deep within the Thames floodplain and the land was traversed by numerous relict stream channels that together comprised the braided courses of the river Thames.

We have grown used to living with tamed rivers, and the Thames is a very tamed river. The process has taken place gradually, from medieval times. It was paid for by the Church, landowners or local communities, and the engineering works mainly involved embanking and dredging. The end result was what we have today: tidy rivers that obediently flow along their allocated courses. For most of the time, that is. Like tamed tigers, they can still sometimes turn nasty.

In prehistoric times the rivers were lords of all the valleys they flowed through. If the valley was wide – as many Ice Age, glacier-widened valleys are in southern Britain – the river would spread to fit. Instead of just one course, its component streams would meander their way through the countryside; until the rains came, and then the streams would unite to form one massive sheet of water. But for most of the year the lowland river was like a partially unravelled rope – a series of roughly parallel braided streams, all flowing in broadly the same direction. This, then, was the situation Gill was confronted with at Yarnton.

We walked across several small relict streams which were now dry. You could spot them easily. The gravel was churned up and stained a dark brown colour; there were also patches of peaty mud and thick accumulations of alluvium. Gill tells me that some of the relict stream channels still flood in very wet seasons, and for a few days you can glimpse traces of the ancient river-system in the modern fields of corn.

We arrived at a large relict stream-course about thirty metres wide, where Maisie was going to take some wood samples. Gill's team had found a beautifully-constructed stone-built ford or causeway. It ran directly across the stream-bed and was five metres wide, roughly the width of a modern country road. Its size and scale and the evident engineering skill of its constructors at first led Gill to suppose that it was medieval or Roman. Such carefully-built fords from those periods are not uncommon in the area.

When Gill's team started to raise the stonework to examine what lay below, they discovered that the rocks rested on lattice-like timber foundations which had been shaped by narrow-bladed axes that resembled Bronze Age tools. Then, a few weeks after our visit, they found Middle Bronze Age metal objects lying at the same level as the foundation timbers beneath the stones, including a very distinctive spearhead known as a socket-looped type. Spearheads of this sort don't occur after the Middle Bronze Age. Presumably it and the other objects were sacrificed during the causeway's construction, around 1200 or 1300 BC. The implications of this discovery are considerable.

The Yarnton causeway might suggest that road traffic was sufficiently heavy to require such elaborate engineering works. This in turn might imply that traffic had to be two-way – a single track with passing places would not have been adequate. But we must be careful: the spearhead, and also what we know about the way Bronze Age people treated boundaries and crossing places, should make us suspicious. It would be a mistake to think too functionally. My feeling is that the Yarnton ford was over-elaborated for all sorts of symbolic reasons. I don't believe there were sufficient people and vehicles around at the time to necessitate two-way traffic. It's a nice thought, and in many respects I hope I'm proved wrong, but given our knowledge of the Middle Bronze Age, I believe that in this instance, as in so many others, we're seeing ideology and the world of the ancestors extending into daily life.

I've often been asked what the population of Bronze Age Britain was. It's a good question, if impossible to answer now, but I think we may be in a position to make an informed estimate in twenty to fifty years. At present we lack any information from huge areas of the country, but that is changing. Today there is a proliferation of random transects through previously unexplored landscapes, brought about by archaeological research along the routes of new roads, pipelines and the like. These are throwing up unexpected evidence for settlement and land-use in areas that were previously thought to have been uninhabited in prehistory.

This new information will certainly transform the picture, but it will take time. All I can offer now is a rough-and-ready guess at the prehistoric population: say 250,000 (the population of modern Leicester) at the beginning of the Early Bronze Age, shortly before 2000 BC, and 500,000 at the end, just over a millennium later. Although these are guesses, I would be surprised and disappointed if, in fifty years' time, archaeological demographers came up with reliable figures that were double or half that size. But then again, guesses are just that. They shouldn't be relied on too heavily.

We can be rather better-informed at the local level. My own and others' work around Peterborough and in nearby parts of the Fens indicates that quite large areas of the low-lying gravel plain around the Fen basin were still covered with trees at the onset of the Bronze Age. So far as I know, the hilly hinterland was not permanently settled, and the clay landscapes between Peterborough and Huntingdon to the south were almost certainly still primeval forest. Maybe we're looking at a population in this area at that time of a few thousand. By the end of the Bronze Age large areas were cleared of trees, and there were organised field systems and substantial settlements. To my mind, this suggests a regional population of at least ten thousand, and quite possibly more. By national standards this was quite a heavily populated part of the country, so these figures cannot be extrapolated to Britain as a whole.

Professor Barry Cunliffe has suggested that the gravel floor of the Nene valley, which runs almost the entire length of Northamptonshire and drains into the Fen basin at Peterborough, was settled and farmed at the start of the Iron Age. By the third and fourth centuries BC this was not enough land to support the growing population, and more had to be cleared along the higher flanks of the valley. I can't see this type of pressure being generated by populations of hundreds or a few thousand. We must surely be talking in terms of tens of thousands.

Another commonly asked question is, what did Bronze Age people look like? The short answer is that you can see them walking around in any north European country. They were appreciably smaller than the modern population of Britain, but this was simply a question of nutrition. Today we take it for granted that we can eat well throughout the winter, but in prehistoric times winter protein was hard to come by – and a regular supply of protein is vital for growth.

Personal appearance is about more than skin, eye or hair colour. These are just the basic ingredients, and in many respects they are not very important. We know that personal adornment was important from the very outset of the Bronze Age. Elaborate, multi-stranded necklaces, with single beads and larger spacer beads incorporating two or more threads, were made from black shale, amber or shiny black jet. Highly polished toggle-like conical buttons were made from jet and shale. These buttons were large and fancy, and I know of no evidence for buttonholes as such, so they may have simply been sewn onto fabric, rather like large sequins. Alternatively, as they mainly occur early in the Bronze Age, perhaps before the widespread adoption of loom weaving, they could have been used to secure hide or leather garments, or belts. The usual way of securing fabric was with a tie or sash band, and there were also bone, antler and metal stick-pins, rather similar to the long hatpins used by Victorian and Edwardian ladies.

The Bronze Age is famous for its goldwork, which in Britain mainly came from natural sources in Ireland and Wales. In the Early Bronze Age it was usually worked down or beaten thin, and the best-known adornments made of this thin sheet-gold are known as lunulae. As their name suggests, they were shaped like the crescent moon, and being flat they were probably worn low on the neck. Often they were decorated with slightly stiff, complex geometric designs which lack the fluidity and movement of Iron Age Celtic art almost two millennia later. Subsequently in the Bronze Age we find the first appearance of twisted, bar-like true neck ornaments, known as torcs. And there were all shapes and sizes of gold and bronze bracelets, armlets, earrings and sundry other bangles. One extraordinary example of Bronze Age beaten goldwork was found at Mold in north Wales. It is no more and no less than a short cape, highly decorated and fully large enough to cover a man's shoulders.

Many of these finds come from burials within barrows, and it has been suggested that the day-to-day appearance of ordinary Bronze Age folk was very much more plain and simple. I'm not convinced. If elaborate personal adornment was a feature of people's passing from this world to the next, I can't see why their daily, routine appearance needs necessarily to have been different. I accept that one wouldn't wear the Mold gold cape when fixing a hole in the roof, but even so, it seems to me that adornment was part of Bronze Age culture. It permeated it through and through, like music in some cultures today.

It's a very great shame that fabric is so fragile. Clothes are, after all, the main component of our appearance, and in prehistory, just as today, they would have said much about individuals' social status. There are also far subtler messages concealed in clothes, accessories and the way they are worn. In the Bronze Age, just as today, these would only have been understood by one's immediate contemporaries. Sadly all of this is lost beyond recall.

Knotted or netted fabrics may well have been in use in Britain before the Bronze Age, and there is certainly evidence for the production of quite fine fibres from flax (a length of twisted flax twine was found at Etton, dating from around 3800 BC). We know that Neolithic sheep, of which the Soay breed is a survival into modern times, produce fine wool, but there isn't hard archaeological evidence for spinning in the Neolithic. This does not mean it didn't happen, of course. Simple spindles can be made entirely from wood, and they work well – modern craft spindles are almost always made of wood. Perfectly good fabrics can also be made by other techniques – for example felting, which involves a combination of soaking and beating wool.

Quite suddenly, towards the latter part of the Early Bronze Age, we are confronted by a wealth of evidence for the production of fabrics. Perforated disks in stone or fired clay were used as spindle whorls for drop-spinning. This is a simple technique, where a spinning-top-like spindle is tied to a length of fleece, spun between the fingers and dropped. As its weight pulls it slowly downwards it spins, and the wool is carefully teased out with both hands; this transfers the spin into the fibres. The spinning is the hardest part, but I managed to spin a passable thread after about an hour's practice. The individually spun threads have no real strength of themselves, but by spinning two together, in the opposite direction to the way they were originally spun – a technique known as plying – they are made more than twice as strong.

Then there are the first of those axially-perforated cylindrical clay loomweights which were such an important feature of our early excavations at Fengate. These suggest the production of cloth in some quantity; they also produced cloth of much higher quality than had been possible before.

But what did the clothes look like? Weaving allows you to create patterns of texture and colour. If Bronze Age sheep did indeed resemble Soays, then they had brown fleeces. I have kept Soays for some time, and there are two quite distinct colour strains, a rich, dark chestnut brown and a paler, honey colour. There are also patches of paler wool around the rump and sometimes on the belly. It is possible too that sheep began deliberately to be bred for different-coloured fleeces at some time during the Bronze Age. Other primitive breeds, such as Shetland sheep, which may well hark back to the Iron Age breeds of northern Europe, come in a huge variety of colours: white, cream, honey, mid-brown, dark brown and near-black. By judicious selection of fleeces and parts of fleeces it would have been possible to weave colour-fast patterned cloth, without recourse to less stable dyes such as red ochre or plant extracts, for example rose madder, elderberries, blackberries, alder bark (brown/black) or alder leaves (yellow).

What did these patterns signify? Again, we can only guess, but there is some very indirect evidence to suggest that the patterning on Neolithic and Bronze Age pottery was not mere idle whimsy – abstract art, if you like. Instead it now seems probable that the decoration on pottery had something to do with the families of the people who made and used it. It wasn't just decoration; it was more important than that. In this respect it was somewhat akin to the pattern of Scottish clan tartans. To the initiated it would have told a complex story involving family history, myth and legend. Recent examples of knitted fishermen's sweaters in Britain are not only traditional to specific regions, but also to separate families and indeed to individuals. I wonder whether Bronze Age fabrics served a similar purpose. The patterns, the quality of the wool and the weave would have proclaimed the wearer's social status and family background.

Most examples of Bronze Age fabric in Britain survive as slight impressions in the rust-like corrosion products of bronze, where it has been in contact with textile fibres, usually underground, after burial. I remember the first time I saw one of these imprints. It was of a woven linen fabric in the corrosion products on a bronze axe from a barrow close to the Ridgeway in Dorset, and was far finer than the picture I had had in my mind's eye, which was of something resembling sackcloth. The textile could easily have been tailored into a pair of trousers that would not have invited unwelcome stares in Savile Row.

Complete garments, even large pieces, are unknown in Britain. So it is most fortunate that a series of remarkable discoveries have been made in Danish barrows.* As with so much Bronze Age material, these finds were in graves, so we cannot be certain that the clothes were indeed those worn during daily life. That said, they are sufficiently varied to suggest that they probably were. Woollen fabrics will be best preserved in either extremely dry or waterlogged conditions; the Danish barrows in question contained stout oak coffins, hollowed from tree trunks, which were sunk into, or enclosed within, sticky, damp clay. The combination of airless, stagnant, acid wetness and tannin from the oak is ideal for preservation, and the woollen fabrics inside the coffins were in excellent condition. In broad terms they date to the latter part of the Middle Bronze (1400–1200 BC).

The earliest fabric from within a wet oak coffin under a Danish barrow was found in 1827 by tomb robbers who chopped their way into the coffin and smashed most of the fragile contents in their search for valuable metal objects. The local priest learned about the find and managed to recover a cap and a cloak made of woven woollen fabric. This find stimulated more orderly research, which was conducted by some of the earliest pioneering scientific archaeologists in Europe, under the supervision of no less a person than the King of Denmark himself, Frederick VII. One of these barrows investigated, at Borum Eshøj, was very large, and revealed three oak coffins in which lay the remains of an elderly man and woman and a younger man. This may have been a family tomb.

* These Danish finds are so remarkable that they deserve a book to themselves, not just a few lines. Happily that book has been written, by the Danish archaeologist P.V. Glob: *The Mound People: Danish Bronze Age Man Preserved* (London, 1974). I recommend it highly.

The elderly woman's coffin was revealed by workmen who didn't realise its significance at first, so the precise arrangement of things inside it wasn't recorded. But they included an openwork hairnet which tied below the chin. It was finely made in a knotless netting technique known as 'sprang'. We found a charred, thumbnail-sized piece of sprang fabric in the charcoal-filled Early Bronze Age pit just outside the Etton causewayed enclosure, so it was probably a technique in widespread use at the time. It doesn't require much equipment, and I can imagine women making sprang hairnets in the evening while sitting around the fire, or when keeping an eye on young children. It would have been the Bronze Age equivalent of knitting.

The woman also wore a short, sweater-like tunic with three-quarter-length sleeves and a wide crew-neck. Her full skirt was ankle-length, secured at the waist by a woven belt which passed around the body twice. The ends of the belt were finished as tassels. Among the items placed in the grave with her was a torc neck-ornament, a bone comb, two bracelets, three decorated bronze discs (which were probably worn at the midriff), a dagger and a finely decorated safety-pin-style brooch. To judge by this array of fine things, she was obviously a person of some standing.

Her husband's coffin was excavated by archaeologists from Denmark's Museum of Northern Antiquities. Its bark had been removed on the spot, and debris from this process lay around it. This might suggest that the ritual removal of bark was part of a purificatory process that took place during the funeral. When the massive lid was opened it revealed a man lying on his back, with his arms at his sides. He wore a thick woollen cap, his face was clean-shaven and his fingernails had been looked after with some care. He was aged fifty to sixty and was 5 feet 7½ inches tall. He suffered from rheumatism, and would have walked stiffly or with a limp. He wore only a woven knee-length, skirt-like loincloth, but he lay on a cow hide and a woven cape had been placed over him. At his feet were two woollen foot-wraps.

The body of the young man, who may or may not have been their son, was superbly preserved within its coffin, which had also had its bark removed. He wore a long, shirt-like tunic, held at the waist by a leather belt secured with a wooden toggle. At his right shoulder were the remains of a broad baldric (a sword-belt that passed from one shoulder to the opposite hip). Like his father's, his body had been draped in a voluminous cloak, and at his feet were traces of leather sandals.

But the discovery that brought the past to life most vividly was made in an oak coffin inside a barrow at Egtved Farm in southern Jutland (the mainland part of Denmark) in 1921. Like the coffins at Borum Eshøj, this one too had had the bark removed. The body was that of a young woman, and, as many archaeological commentators have noted, she was wearing 'summer clothes'. Certainly the way she dressed would not have been appropriate to the rigours of a Danish winter, but in the sixties I can recall students wearing mini-skirts on winter evenings. Besides, there's always such a thing as a good, long, thick cloak if it's needed. I suspect her clothing isn't in itself conclusive evidence that she died during the summer, but simply that she was wearing a young person's clothes, and wouldn't have been seen dead wearing the older women's long skirts. Sadly, as it happened, she had her wish fulfilled.

Her coffin too was remarkably well preserved. It consisted of an oak tree trunk which had been split in half and the centre hollowed out. No attempt had been made to smoothe off the join between the split halves, which was left unfinished and consequently fitted together snugly, as if the people who made the coffin wanted the join between the halves to be seamless. Invisible. As if she had been enclosed within a de-barked tree trunk.

She lay beneath a cow hide, which in turn covered a large piece of woollen cloth that enveloped her body from head to toe. She had been buried during the summer, as the coffin contained the flowers of the medicinal herb yarrow, which grew round about, and was barely twenty years old at death. She wore a thigh-length skirt made simply of braided woollen cords joined at the waistband and hem. The cords themselves were loose and had not been interwoven. The effect, when she moved, would have been sensational. Archaeologists at the time of her discovery were lost for words to describe it. Was it, they wondered, an underskirt? Moreover, she wore no pants beneath it. I will pass on rapidly. Her midriff was bare except for a woven belt which held in place a decorated bronze disc in front of the navel. On her top she wore a short tunic with three-quarter-length sleeves and a high crew-type neck, similar to the one worn by the older woman from Borum Eshøj. As an outfit it was young, attractive and bursting with life. Certainly it was sexy and provocative, too. But then, that's what a normal youth in any culture has always been about. Without that *joie de vivre* and drive, the species would soon die out. I still find that young woman's grave almost unbearably poignant.

There were other finds of clothed bodies, but one in particular is relevant to our story. The mound of Muldbjerg is in hilly country in north-west Jutland, and was dug by a team of archaeologists from the Museum of Northern Antiquities in 1883. In this instance I don't want to concentrate on what was found inside the coffin so much as on the coffin itself and the way it had been positioned in the ground. Having said that, the dead man, described by P.V. Glob as the 'Muldbjerg Chieftain', was out of the ordinary. He was clean-shaven, his clothes were well-made, he wore leather shoes and was accompanied by a fine sword in its scabbard.

His oak coffin had had the bark carefully removed and had then been placed on a bed of large rounded cobbles. But in this instance the coffin was not alone. It lay beneath half the trunk of a much larger oak tree, which had been hollowed out and fitted over it, like a close-fitting protective vault. Although it could easily have been removed, the bark still survived intact in many places on this outer container. It was clearly an arrangement that was rich in symbolism, and involved much painstaking labour. It must have taken many men several days to complete work on the coffin and its wooden 'vault'. In the end, the effect they achieved was of a trunk within a tree. It was a theme that a different team of archaeologists would encounter on the other side of the North Sea, 116 years later.

CHAPTER TWELVE

═══════

Between the Tides

IT WAS MY TURN to do the washing up. I had just plunged my hands into the suds when the phone rang. I paused, waiting for Maisie to answer, but then I remembered she had just popped into the garden to pick parsley. Dammit, I thought, as I wiped off the suds and picked up the receiver. I did my best not to sound too irritable as I answered.

The man at the other end was gritty and American – definitely not Canadian. He asked to speak to Maisie, and I was about to say she was out when I saw her walk past the kitchen window. I jumped up and down like a mad clown waving a dishcloth, and managed to catch her attention.

'Could I ask who wants to speak to her?'

'Sure,' came the reply, 'but she won't know me. Tell her it's Bill Boismier' – pronounced Boys-mire – 'from the Norfolk Unit.'

Which is what I did. I handed Maisie the phone and returned to the pots and pans. I had no idea what he wanted to talk about. Probably they'd found wood down the bottom of a Roman well, or something like that. It wasn't the sort of work that would set the archaeological world on fire, but the Norfolk Unit paid promptly, and at the time we were running a bit short of cash. Both of us being freelance, sometimes the cash-flow can slow to a trickle. In lean times we tend to eat a lot of spaghetti – and these had been spaghetti weeks, so the work would be welcome. I resumed washing up with added vigour.

After ten minutes or so, Maisie hung up.

'That was interesting. He said a local chap has found something unusual on the beach near Hunstanton, at Holme-next-the-Sea.'

It was an area I knew quite well.

'What, near those peat beds?'

'Yes. They say it's below them. Or at least that's the impression I got.'

'What, part of the drowned forest?'

Maisie looked uncertain.

'I suppose so. Or . . . no, *that's* right. They don't think it's part of the forest beds, but they do want me to see the wood.' Then she added, as if as an afterthought: 'They said you could come along too, if you wanted.'

I decided to ignore the wind-up. But I had to admit, it sounded intriguing. I was, as they say, all agog.

'Why don't they think it's part of the forest bed?'

'He wouldn't let on. He said he'd rather not say any more, as he didn't want me to pre-judge anything. He was obviously pretty excited, though.'

Much to my annoyance I had to see a client about a commercial job on 16 October 1998, the day Maisie went to Holme for the first time. She returned full of it all. She described a circle of oak timbers around something very odd indeed, but wouldn't let on what it was. I probed as subtly as I could; I even tried veiled threats, but she would have none of it. She looked straight through me and changed the subject. It was plain she wanted me to see it for myself. Like Bill Boismier, she seemed intent on getting an unbiased opinion.

The following Wednesday Maisie and I found ourselves driving towards King's Lynn along the road from Wisbech. It had been a few years since I had last travelled this road. In the interim it had been improved. Villages had been bypassed and there were two lanes of traffic – and in the process, the route had become detached from the countryside through which it passed. Like so many modern improvements to life, the upgrading of the A47 had removed its historical links. I could have been driving through any flat landscape. Or watching a film of a man driving through the countryside. I felt uncomfortably disengaged.

Sadly the route now bypassed the beautiful town of King's Lynn, and it was not until we had almost reached the royal estate at Sandringham, about five miles east of Lynn, that the road began to look familiar. Instead of brutally slicing its way through woods and fields, we now followed the lie of the land. Corners became unpredictable and fun

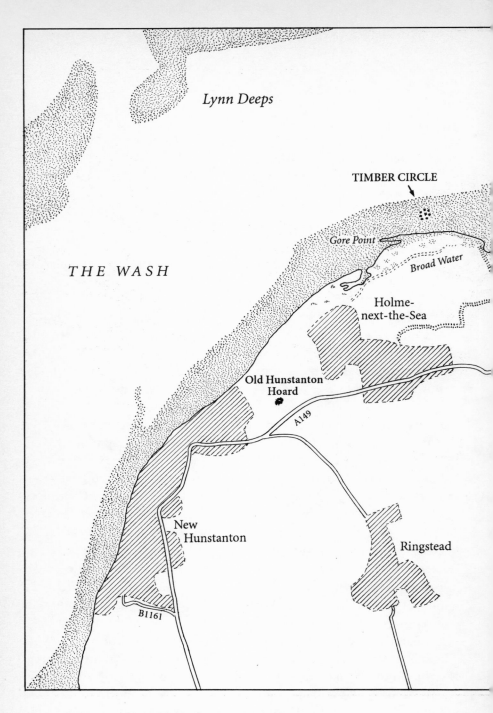

Lynn Deeps

TIMBER CIRCLE

Gore Point

Broad Water

THE WASH

Holme-
next-the-Sea

Old Hunstanton
Hoard

A149

New
Hunstanton

Ringstead

B1161

FIG 23   Holme-next-the-Sea and the surrounding area

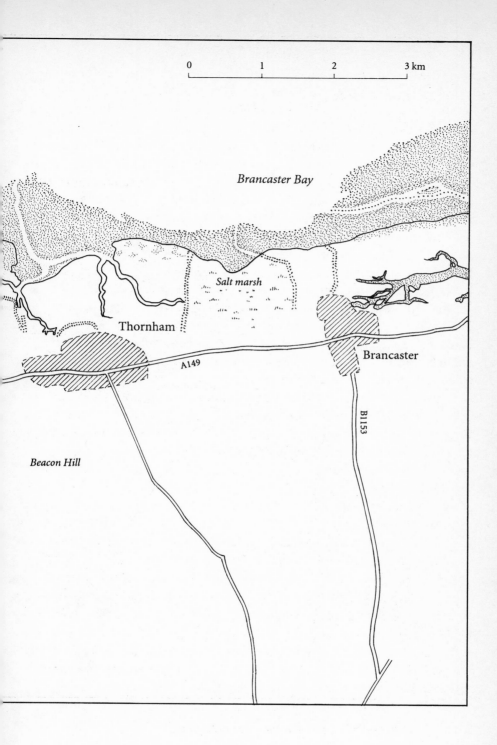

to drive around. Odd things happened in unexpected places – like a group of six peacocks strolling around a small roundabout, as if they owned the place. Soon we were skirting the seaside town of Hunstanton, and there was the sea spread out below, grey, brooding and gorgeous. I couldn't resist a childhood habit, and shouted out excitedly, 'I saw it first!' Maisie gave me an old-fashioned look of some disdain.

After driving for ten minutes beyond Hunstanton, we turned sharp left into the narrow leafy tunnel that leads down to Holme beach. It takes about fifteen minutes to reach the nature reserve from the main road, and we drew up in The Firs car park, close to the spot where John Lorimer and Gary had parked on that spring day when they took their shrimping net for its first outing. There was a breeze blowing off the sand dunes as we walked towards the beach through the belt of Corsican pines. On our way we passed twitchers draped with binoculars and cameras with immense telephoto lenses. They were cheery enough, and told us where some unpronounceable bird was currently to be found. We thanked them profusely.

We walked for hours – or so it seemed – across tracts of sand, blasted from time to time by penetrating winds. At last we reached the circle. Three archaeologists from the Norfolk County Unit were clearing washed-in sand and debris from the gales of the previous day. As we arrived the sun came up, and I rapidly clicked off half a roll of film. The site was much smaller than I had imagined, but extraordinary nonetheless. I was struck by its simplicity. It consisted of a rough circle or oval of oak posts, with what looked like an upside-down oak in the middle. I can only guess at what this inverted tree meant, but I felt it had something special to tell. Maybe, I thought, corpses were placed in its root 'fingers' to await the arrival of tidal waters, which would then carry the body away to another world. But then I recalled that Bill Boismier had told me the environmental evidence clearly suggested the circle was built on dry land. So that idea was out. The sea and the circle seemed so inextricably linked that I have to admit I still find it hard to make my brain accept what my intellect tells me: it was indeed a dryland site.

I have rarely experienced anything so moving as the first time I saw the Holme circle. It simply had to be Bronze Age or Neolithic,

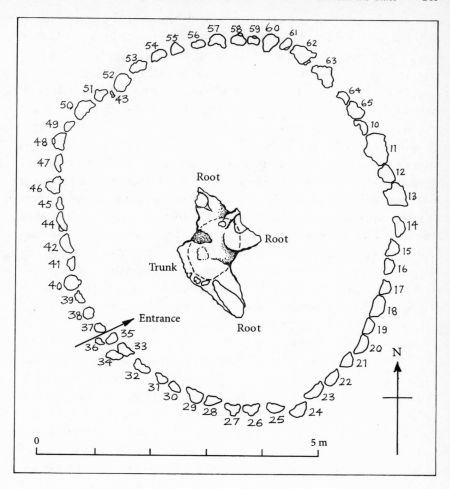

FIG 24   *Plan of Holme timber circle (Source: Norfolk Archaeological Unit)*

but I knew that tree-ring dating should be able to sort out the dates
one way or another. The central tree was certainly large enough to
give a good run of rings – in fact we were shortly to learn that it was
167 years old when it was felled.

Tree-ring dating, or dendrochronology, works on the simple principle that a tree lays down a growth-ring each year. In wet years the
tree will tend to grow more, and faster, than in dry years, when it

lays down a narrow growth-ring. Some trees, like alders, lay down two rings in one year, but at random. Some, such as willow, grow too fast to provide a reliable indication of local growing conditions. Trees like oak, ash and pine are ideal for growth-ring dating, as they tend to reflect the weather in their pattern of growth. And oak is the best of the lot.

Starting with modern trees and working back in time via medieval beams in churches, timbers from Roman wells, prehistoric sites like Flag Fen and even great bog oaks, dendrochronologists have been able to construct a long graph which shows the wiggling fluctuations of wet and dry seasons in northern Europe over seven thousand years. It's not uncommon to find a solitary waterlogged oak timber on a site, and if it has about a hundred growth-rings it's possible to produce a short graph of seasonal 'wiggles'. The trick is then to fit that short graph to the main one, a process known as 'wiggle matching'. This is best done with the aid of high-precision radiocarbon dates taken at fixed intervals – say every ten years – through the ring sequence.

Once a wiggle match has been achieved (and this can be tested using quite simple statistics), a date can be given to the year of felling. But it gets better. If the dendro sample is complete, careful examination of the pore size of the sapwood directly beneath the bark will allow the dendrochronologist to determine the actual season – spring, summer, autumn or winter – when the tree was felled.

On her first visit to the site Maisie had spotted that the central tree was upside down, but she hadn't told me. She wanted to see whether I agreed with her when I saw it too. Which, of course, I did. It couldn't possibly have been anything else. But at least one visiting expert firmly held the view that we were wrong, and that it was a stunted tree which had grown in that strange shape because of the harsh coastal conditions. I thought he was highly plausible, and his doubts made me more than a bit worried at the time. Maisie thought he was mad.

There were fifty-five timbers in the 'circle', which wasn't actually a precise circle at all. I paced across it, and found that its diameter was about six and a half metres. Each timber in the circle appeared to have been split in half, with the split surface facing inwards, to present a flat wall, and the bark facing outwards. It was difficult to be certain, however, if all the posts had been halved, because their tops had been worn away by the waves and were encrusted with mussels and small barnacles. When I looked at it closely, I saw that the wood had been pitted by hundreds of small, boring molluscs, known as piddocks, with razor-sharp toothed shells. These left deep holes, rather like giant woodworm (the diameter of the holes was between five and ten millimetres – say an eighth to a quarter of an inch).

Lying within the circle was a spar of timber that had become detached from the nearby wreck. Presumably it had been carried over the top of the posts during a storm, as there was no sign of an entranceway through the timbers at any point. This lack of any apparent entranceway puzzled us. I remember asking Mark Brennand, the leader of the team of archaeologists who were clearing the site, whether they'd done a metal-detector 'sweep' following John Lorimer's discovery of the axe. They told me that detectors were banned because the beach had been used as a gunnery range during the last war, and unexploded shells were still found there from time to time – often, he said, in shrimp nets. That made me wince, although I suspect John's new net was solid enough to be bomb-proof. Mark pointed to a lump of barnacle-encrusted metal lying near the peat beds. It was part of a German bomber brought down in the war – a Heinkel or a Dornier, I forget which. I imagine it had a sad tale to tell.

In the short time since the site's recognition by the archaeological world, Bill Boismier and the Norfolk Archaeological Unit had organised funds from English Heritage to carry out an exploratory excavation. This would involve the cutting of two trial trenches (the universal name in archaeology for exploratory holes). At this exploratory stage none of the timbers would be moved. The first trial trench would extend from the central tree to the ring of posts. The second would be cut outside the posts to discover whether there was any evidence for an external ring-ditch, which you would normally expect to find around the outside of a barrow. Somewhat to our surprise, no such ring-ditch was revealed.

Already the project had taken on its own form and structure. The Project Manager was Bill and his site director was Mark Brennand. I got to know them both well in the months that followed.

Bill Boismier is American. I wouldn't like to guess his age, but he has plainly seen much of life, and some of it – Vietnam in particular – has been hard on him. He did his doctoral research in England and is a highly experienced field archaeologist. He didn't know it then, but he would shortly have to draw heavily on all his experience – archaeological and military. He knew how to handle a crisis and he never lost his cool, although sometimes the cigarettes took a bashing. His job was to see that the project ran smoothly; that everyone, including specialists such as Maisie and Charly, got paid; and that English Heritage, who actually funded the work, received all the paperwork – accounts and reports – they required.

Some of Bill's time was inevitably spent in the unit's office at Norwich. But he, and his battered old Land-Rover, were always to be seen on the beach when something important or unusual was about to happen. I was impressed by the way Bill supported Mark when the going got tough – which was quite often. They made an excellent team.

Mark is younger than Bill. But unlike some younger field archaeologists working in the world of contract and commercial excavation, he retains his interest in academic research, and still keeps an active involvement in Sheffield University's research excavation at Dun Vulan, an Iron Age site on the island of South Uist, in the Outer Hebrides. And thereby hangs a strange tale.

Speaking from bitter experience, I can confidently say that the process of digging prehistoric waterlogged wood can be difficult. This is because the wood may look like wood, but it is no longer wood. Most of the cellulose which gives wood its flexibility and 'woodiness' has been replaced by water. Sometimes you can break ancient waterlogged logs the size of large drainpipes across your knee. Oak tends to retain its strength quite well, but even so its exposed outer surfaces can become extremely soft – soft enough to gouge holes in with your fingernails.

Maisie, who was well aware of the difficulties of digging old wet wood, was delighted by Mark's wood-digging. He was fast, but delicate too. He never scratched the wood or left a mark. One day, about a year later, towards the end of the main dig at Holme, Mark and Maisie were chatting together, and Mark said he planned to return to the university research dig in Scotland to help with the supervision there. Maisie mentioned that she was the wood consultant to the project, then remembered a remarkable discovery she had made two years previously.

One waterlogged Iron Age layer, dating to about 100 BC, had produced lots of wood, and some of it was superbly excavated. One piece in particular caught her eye. It was a spear-like object, and lying in the ground around it was the debris of its manufacture. These woodchips were pitted by the distinctive holes of the ship worm, a wood-boring insect found only in warm seas. Bearing in mind that the site was located in the Outer Hebrides, this struck Maisie as odd. But it was to get odder. She examined the spear-shaped piece and the woodchips closely under a microscope and discovered that the wood used was *Larix laricina* (Tamarack, or American Larch), a native of north-east America.

Eventually she pieced together the story. The tree had grown in north-eastern Canada, had fallen into a river and been carried to the sea at Labrador, thence to the warm waters of the Caribbean, where it was attacked by ship worm. Then it floated into the Gulf Stream and eventually arrived at Dun Vulan, where timber was in very short supply, and every piece of driftwood was gratefully received.

This story could never have been revealed if the spear-shaped object and the woodchips around it hadn't been superbly and delicately excavated in the first place. And the person who did it? You've probably already guessed, but it was Mark Brennand.

Everything to do with the excavation of the Holme circle was difficult, or hazardous, or both. Things that we take for granted on inland sites, such as maps, were non existent. Fortunately the Norfolk Unit could draw on modern technology, and were able to pinpoint the site with extraordinary precision. Having positioned it accurately, one of the first jobs of the assessment, before the trial trenches could be started, was to survey-in the posts accurately, using modern laser-based technology. This survey showed that the circle was in fact an ellipse (with a maximum diameter of 6.6 metres, or twenty-two feet), whose axis ran north-west to south-east.

The trial excavation was about a metre deep, and every time the tide came in it was filled to the brim with loose, runny sands and silts. These then had to be baled and shovelled out – a process which took upwards of an hour – before work could be resumed at the point where it had been abandoned the day before. It was very much a case of two steps forward and one step back. Sometimes the tides came in slowly; other times they tore their way landward at breakneck pace. These fast tides were known as rip tides, and a member of the team was always deputed to keep an eye on the sea as soon as the tide turned. It simply wasn't worth taking any risks.

The initial trial trench ran between the central tree and the posts to the west. It was wide enough to accommodate a person's shoulders and to allow a little movement – but not much. As it had to be re-excavated every day, it made practical sense to keep it as narrow as possible. There was also a good possibility that if two or more posts were fully exposed down to their tips, they might well become loosened by the waves and fall into the trench, even if reinforced with sandbags. So the trench was carefully positioned to expose just one post, and a few inches of the posts on either side of it.

The chosen post (number 41) was selected because it seemed, on the surface, to be fairly typical of the posts in the circle as a whole. It was oak, like all the others, and was split neatly in half. Although the posts on the surface looked almost like distinct 'teeth', with spaces between them, this was a false effect produced by tidal wear and tear, which had removed the outer, softer sapwood and bark, leaving only a harder core of heartwood. This in turn was honeycombed with the holes left by piddocks.

The surface appearance – of a ring of separate posts around an inverted tree – was striking, but it was entirely false. The photographs that appeared in the press did indeed look like a post-built henge, similar to (but simpler than) Woodhenge, near Stonehenge. But in fact the ring of posts was a wall of wood, more reminiscent of the solid wooden-walled oval structure at Maxey, or the oak-walled main gateway at Etton. Below the surface the posts were butted-up to each other, and in almost every instance they touched along their entire lengths. This would undoubtedly have given the wall a great deal of extra strength. For what it's worth, true henges never have internal post settings forming solid walls; invariably the timbers form rings or nested concentric circles, where the posts can be seen to stand on their own.

It was hard to be absolutely certain, because it had to be left in the ground, but the trial trench suggested that post 41 was half a fast-grown young oak tree-trunk, of perhaps fifty years' growth. It was the sort of timber that might have been felled in woodland which had regenerated after a major episode of felling, where all the tall, old trees had been removed. With the shading canopy of leaves above them gone, the young trees and the shoots from the stumps of the felled giants would grow fast and straight – just like post 41. Rejuvenated woodland of this sort can be made to form in primeval or secondary woodland, and is an important source of good straight timber. This was what Maisie and I had expected to find, and we were both pleased by it. But, sadly for our theories, we were later to learn that post 41 was by no means typical of the rest. We were also delighted to see that the tip of post 41 appeared to have been sharpened to an off-centre V-shape. We knew this wasn't sharpening at all, but good evidence that the split timber came from a felled tree trunk.

Now, when you set out to fell a tree, it's desirable to ensure that you don't squash your friends and relatives in the process. Usually bystanders get killed or injured either when the tree hits them directly or when it's deflected sideways. Put another way, it's important to be able to fell a tree accurately, so that it lands either where you want it to land, or where you can predict it will land – which are by no means always the same thing.

The simplest way to achieve this is to cut the tree from opposite sides, with a deeper cut on the side where you want the tree to topple. The wood between the two cuts is known as the hinge, and it plays an important part in controlling the tree's fall. I have been known, when feeling frustrated with a stubborn tree on a windless day, to cut away at the sides of the hinge. The resultant lack of control was spectacular – and very dangerous. If, having felled your tree, you then split the trunk in half at right-angles to the direction in which you worked when you felled it, the unequal-sized felling cuts appear in profile on the lower end of the two split surfaces. This outline is V-shaped and off-centre – like the tip of post 41.

The other end of the trial trench exposed part of the central tree trunk, and to everyone's amazement it was evident that the bark had been deliberately removed. Maisie was in no doubt that this de-barking had been done in the Bronze Age, because clear axe-marks were visible on the surface of the tree. Although it was hard to be certain at this early stage, Maisie was fairly convinced that the width and curvature of the blades suggested the axes used were more like Early Bronze Age than later types. That certainly fitted the other archaeological evidence.

By dint of getting extremely muddy, Mark Brennand was just able to feel what he thought was the bottom of the inverted tree. Later we were to discover that it wasn't the bottom at all, and that the stump was about half a metre longer than we'd thought at first. But Mark's exploring fingers were able to feel the distinct shape of clear and sharp axe-marks. That was encouraging. If axe-marks survived on the chopped end of the tree we would be able to learn a great deal about Bronze Age tree-felling techniques.

But then, there was something not altogether right about that felled end, too. It was too – what's the word – *flat*. It was at about this point that Maisie began to doubt whether it had been felled at all; and I had to agree. Of course we didn't know then that our doubts were based on the shape of a false felled end, but they stayed with us all the same – and even much later, when we realised our mistake. In fact they then became even stronger.

I couldn't help thinking about what the timber circle at Holme would have looked like had it been located on a conventional dryland site. For a start, none of the wood would have survived – unless, like the Maxey oval mortuary structure, it had been burnt down. So we would have been confronted with an irregular, roughly circular trench with closely set post-pipes, surrounding a large pit in which we probably would have recognised the pipe of an enormous post. But we would have had no idea that the post was, in fact, an inverted tree. As sites go, it would have been relatively run-of-the-mill, nothing to get particularly excited about. By comparison with what we had, it would have been like looking at an empty picture-frame after thieves had cut out the painting.

The sight of the timbers was so extraordinary that I had trouble trying to get my brain to cope with them. I was used to working in a two-dimensional world of flat plans and flat sections, but here I was confronted not just with sodden wood, but with something far more slippery: I was confronted with human intention. Why, I kept asking myself, did they invert the central tree? Why did they arrange the ring of posts with their split surfaces facing inwards and the bark outwards? Why did they remove the bark from the tree trunk? And then why did they hide the carefully de-barked trunk deep in the ground? I knew that it was no good to deny these questions. They would not go away. And they were important, because all of these things were done intentionally. Being deliberate actions, they demanded explanation.

I found the de-barking of the central tree particularly fascinating. It was so completely senseless and pointless. Removing the bark wouldn't have made the tree any easier to transport, or to tip into a hole. So why do it? At first I approached the problem head-on. I thought about bark – all the bark I had come across in my archaeological life, which wasn't a lot.

A segment of the waterlogged enclosure ditch at Etton produced a large, complete sheet of birch bark, cut square at each end. We can't be sure, but this sheet was probably in the process of being soaked to make it pliable, to be used for waterproof containers, or even a type of cloth. I couldn't help thinking of Mark Edmonds's idea that certain jobs were performed at sacred sites *for their own sake*. Was this the explanation here? Possibly, but I was not entirely convinced.

I recalled that we had also found large pieces of oak bark in the Etton enclosure ditch, close to the main northern gateway. The evidence suggests that the gateway timbers were stripped of their bark before they were squared-up. Again, this seems odd. Why remove the bark if you are going to square-up a timber? Surely the squaring-up process automatically involves the removal of bark with the removal of wood? It was frustrating. Enlightenment was proving elusive.

Shortly before the discovery of the timber circle I was researching a book I was writing about prehistoric farming, and found myself reading through some of my old work. As I was working my way through the Maxey volumes I came across Charly's report on the oval barrow, where he proved that the ground beneath the turf and topsoil mound had been de-turfed before the mound was thrown up. I remember thinking that to de-turf was no more pointless than to de-bark a tree, and then plunge the de-barked trunk deep into the ground.

Then it came to me. Both de-barking and de-turfing were essentially rites to do with purification and cleansing. The outer, soiled, layer was being removed to expose the purity beneath. I knew that rites of this sort are often associated with death and the spirit's journey to the next world. Was this the explanation? We'll never know for certain, of course, but I think it makes good sense.

In later autumn the tides along Holme beach don't retreat so far, and the 'windows' when the timber circle was accessible enough both to record and excavate became ever smaller. Onshore breezes also helped prevent the tide from retreating, so the trial trench was completed and the site was abandoned for the winter. At the last minute English Heritage decided to take some dating samples from the central tree and four of the posts in the circle. For reasons that are still not entirely clear, these samples were taken with a chainsaw. The damage to the posts could have been worse, as the cuts were made directly below the weathered stumps that protruded above the sands. But the wound to the central oak was frankly shocking. I remember feeling, when I saw the deep gash some months later, that the tree had been desecrated.

Everything went quiet over Christmas, as it does these days. I can't remember how long the holiday period actually was, but it seemed interminable. In the new year I was contacted by Simon Denison, the journalist employed by the Council for British Archaeology to edit its excellent journal, *British Archaeology*. He had got wind of the Holme timber-circle story, and had obtained an excellent photo. He wanted a good quote from me, not just as a specialist in the area and period, but also as President of the CBA. So I gave him one. The piece was published, and to my amazement the media failed to pick it up. But then, quite suddenly and unexpectedly, all hell broke loose. To say that the media picked up the story would be a gross understatement. They picked it up, ran with it, tossed it around in the air, and devoured it. Archaeological websites were jammed with people demanding that something be done to save the timbers from the sea. At some time during this spate of news coverage an enterprising journalist coined the name 'Seahenge', which I'm afraid has stuck.

The storm of media interest abated by the end of January 1999, and it was then time to assess what we really knew about the timber circle and its setting, bearing in mind what we had already discovered about religious sites and the landscapes in which they were built.

Peter Murphy is an old friend of Maisie, from the time in the

1970s when they were the only two people to attend a graduate course on ancient wood given in London by the English Heritage Ancient Monuments Laboratory. Peter is now the English Heritage Environmental Archaeologist for eastern England. Over the years he has accumulated a vast store of knowledge, and he's one of those people who are more than happy to share what they know. He prepared a short report on the prehistoric environment of Holme beach and its hinterland as part of the overall evaluation process. It's technical, as such reports tend to be, but it came to one striking conclusion. As I have already suggested, 'Seahenge' was never at sea. The timbers were constructed on dry land. Of that there could be no possible doubt.

Peter showed that the sticky grey mud in which the timbers were embedded had formed after 9000 BC in a post-Ice Age environment of mudflats, protected from the sea by sand and gravel barriers. The mudflats were dissected by numerous creeks and ponds filled with fresh or slightly salty water. We still don't know how far out in the current North Sea these barriers were, but the evidence would suggest some distance – perhaps a kilometre or more. Over the years the barriers have been pushed back to their present position by the steady rise of post-Ice Age sea levels. This happened in a series of events, in which the barrier would be breached, the sea would pass through and another barrier would reform a little further inland. This process has never stopped, which is the main reason why the timbers were at such grave risk of destruction.

Peter's environmental reconstruction has been very useful. Not only has it allowed us to recreate a mental picture of the area in the Bronze Age, but it has helped dispel a persistent image which many prehistorians must have had – I know I did. It's the image of Brittany, where individual monuments were located within sight of the sea, and where the sea itself seems to have been the major focus of interest and attention. Those stone 'circles' on the beach at Er Lannic, for example, are hard to get out of your mind. But you should make the effort, as the evidence would suggest that Er Lannic was built on marshland, and Holme was naturally hidden from the sea by a natural coastal barrier of sand. Certainly anyone in the backswamp would be only too aware of the sea's powerful presence nearby. Even today, on a windy day at high tide, you can hear the crash of breakers and feel the sting of salt spray behind the dunes. It's the lurking, ominous presence of the sea which helps give the place such a special atmosphere – and I'm sure the same would have applied in the remote past.

A long-term study of Holme beach and dunes by a team from Newcastle University's Department of Marine Science and Coastal Management has shown that the beach is actively eroding, and that its shape, or profile, is progressively altering. Essentially it's becoming steeper. Both of these processes are bad news for the timber circle.

The peat beds along the beach formed in shallow freshwater in a wet woodland composed largely of alder trees. Alder roots are particularly well adapted to permanently waterlogged conditions, and the peat that started to accumulate around them would have been formed from reeds and rushes, and of course the leaves and wood of the alder trees themselves. This alder peat is the forest bed that I immediately thought of when Bill Boismier made his initial phone call. Radiocarbon dates have been taken from peats about four kilometres to the east along the beach, near the village of Titchwell. These suggest that peat was growing in the centuries around 1500 BC, some time later than the timber circle, which had just been provisionally dated by radiocarbon to the years 2310–1740 BC.

To sum up, the circle was built in quite a wide 'backswamp' behind a coastal barrier. The ground was firm underfoot, but the groundwater table was high. This would suggest that when the posts were placed in the ground they were in fact lowered into water, which would explain why they were preserved so superbly. Although technically dryland, this was nevertheless always a very wet landscape, as is demonstrated by the growth of peat at the end of the Early Bronze Age. At best it would have been barely habitable, and certainly unsuited to any permanent settlement.

Does this sound familiar? It ought to: although the sea was not directly involved, wet conditions were deliberately selected by the people who constructed the enclosure at Etton. I'm sure the same applied at Holme. The place was always remote, marginal and, to use that word again, *liminal*. It was in every respect an ideal spot at which to undergo a rite of passage, whether one was living or dead.

There is one pressing archaeological problem that needs to be sorted out. Dry sites such as Maxey usually allow you to make a pretty accurate 'guesstimate' of the level of the ancient ground surface. It is essential to know with more or less precision at what level people would have stood at the time under examination. The Old Land Surface, or 'OLS', is a key component of context. Without it, life becomes very difficult for the archaeologist. At Holme the sea has eroded the surface, and it's difficult to estimate how much ground has been removed. The level of the base of the later peat is some guide, but we still don't know the extent to which the OLS might have been worn down before the peat formed. This is precisely the sort of problem that Charly's soil micromorphology is good at sorting out.

Charly drove up from Cambridge, and when I met him on the beach he looked distinctly unenthusiastic. Admittedly a cold onshore breeze didn't help us feel cheery, but he wasn't happy about the conditions generally. Apparently the constant wetting and drying at every tide has a damaging effect on the soil structure, and he didn't hold out great hopes for micromorph. We'll have to wait and see what he discovers.

In January 1999 we received the preliminary results of the tree-ring dates. The dendrochronologists from Sheffield University were able to state that the central oak and the four circle posts that were sampled (numbers 23, 42, 60 and 63) were probably felled in the same year. The central tree had lived for 167 years, and the ages of the four sampled posts ranged between eighty-nine and 128 years when they were cut down. At that stage the measured sequence of tree-rings had not been pinned down to a particular range of years BC. This wiggle-matching was to happen soon, but in the meantime it was sufficient to know that four of the posts from around the circle were felled at the same time, but that they did not share the same number of growth-rings. This would suggest that the structure was built during one event, and was not subsequently enlarged or altered. At last, it would seem, a coherent picture was beginning to emerge.

On 16 March Geoff Wainwright phoned me. I was slightly surprised to hear from him, as I knew he was serving his last few days as English Heritage Chief Archaeologist before retiring. He told me that English Heritage intended to excavate and remove the timbers from Holme-next-the-Sea. The work would be carried out by the team from the Norfolk Unit. If Fenland Archaeological Trust* agreed, the timbers would then be transported to our Field Centre at Flag Fen. At FAT we routinely process timber from sites all over Britain, so Geoff's suggestion came as no surprise. Little did I realise at the time that it would shortly give rise to howls of protest from a small but vociferous proportion of the inhabitants of north-west Norfolk. These protests were encouraged by the local press – presumably to keep a good story running.

At the Flag Fen Field Centre we would build holding tanks for the timbers and a viewing platform for visitors. Maisie would be able to record all the tool-marks and anything else she wanted to examine. When the process of recording was finished, a decision could be made about what to do next. Ideally, Geoff said, this would happen in close consultation with people in Norfolk. While the timbers were being recorded, conservators and other specialists could make the decision about how and where to conserve them – if, that is, conservation was physically possible. We were all greatly relieved: at last something positive was being done. It was the best news I had heard for a long time.

The following day I learned that the whole process was to be filmed for Channel 4 television as a *Time Team* special, which I knew would be great fun, as I'd worked with them on three previous occasions. Executive Producer Tim Taylor was most excited, and had just heard that Channel 4 had given him the go-ahead. Because of tide problems, it would be best if the timbers were removed sometime between mid-April and mid-May. That at least was the theory – in the event it took until early August.

Mark Brennand, as before, was in charge of the field team, and he made a brave and wise decision at the outset: to excavate and lift all the posts in the circle by hand. He would use a machine only to raise the central tree, because no amount of manpower could lift over two tonnes, given the relatively short dry 'window' between tides.

Everyone involved in the project was acutely aware that this was the archaeological opportunity of a lifetime, and that it simply had to be done to the highest possible standards. We were also aware that

* Maisie and I set up FAT, an archaeological charity, in 1987, as an umbrella organisation for our work in the Peterborough area.

the eyes of the world were upon us. Mark and Bill were determined that it wouldn't just be a lifting exercise, but a proper, no-holds-barred archaeological excavation. Again, given what they knew about the conditions out there on the beach, it was a brave decision; but I am quite convinced it was the right one.

Most archaeological sites don't get flooded every three hours and then have to be pumped out and re-excavated before work can resume. Mark decided on using a variant of a technique that had been successfully employed in Holland before the war, known as a continuous or creeping section. Essentially what happened was that a trench was dug on the opposite side of the circle to the original trial trench. It was slightly wider than the trial trench, and allowed two posts to be exposed. The long section between the central tree and the posts was then carefully drawn and sampled before the two posts were removed.

The next stage was to enlarge the trench to include the next two posts. Again, the section was drawn, but this time a far more extensive series of samples was taken to be sent off to Charly, Peter Murphy and other specialists. In effect this meant that the circle was recorded in a series of radiating sections, rather like the spokes of a wheel. Whenever posts had to be left unsupported for any length of time they would be shored up with sandbags. The area around the circle was also ringed with a wall of sandbags which acted like a coffer dam. This arrangement allowed the team to pump out as soon as the sea had retreated. Without the sandbags, that would have been impossible.

The actual process of lifting the posts was much harder than expected. The inner surface was exposed, but the outer surface remained in contact with the sticky grey clay mud into which the posts had been sunk. As it was the outer surface which still had bark on, it required a great deal of careful manipulation to break the vacuum without detaching the bark. But it could be done, provided the task was carried out slowly and gently.

Once the vacuum holding the post against the wall of grey clay had been broken, an ex-military wood-and-canvas stretcher was placed up against it, and together they were lowered gently to the ground. Four, or sometimes six, members of the team then removed the post on its stretcher to the trailer for transport to Flag Fen behind our Jeep. Usually we took two posts and two stretchers on each trip.

Most of the prehistoric timbers I've come across – and I must have seen several thousand – are relatively straight and clean-grained, but the ones from the circle were completely different; and they bore precious little resemblance to post 41, the half-split timber exposed by that first trial trench. For a start, they were far from straight. Most had had side branches trimmed off, and splitting them must have been extremely difficult, as they were full of knots. When laid out side by side in the tanks of the Flag Fen Field Centre they looked most peculiar – more like misshapen modern sculpture than timbers that had been used to build a structure.

Why was this? One could conjecture that all the good-quality straight timber had been used for farm buildings and houses, and that the knotty, bendy, branchy wood from the tops of the trees was kept aside for use in non-functional structures, such as our timber circle. But that fails to convince, for the simple reason that people usually think the other way around. Take Ely. The cathedral used the finest oak available, and the poorer townspeople's houses had to make do with second quality timber. Likewise, I am convinced that no self-respecting Early Bronze Age person would consider for one moment palming his ancestors off with anything other than the best.

That leads one to the conclusion that the bendy, branchy wood was the best that was available locally. I think the key point is availability. The circle was constructed in a barely dry 'backswamp', which is not an ideal environment for the growing of sturdy oaks, so it's quite possible that the central oak and other oaks growing in the vicinity never had long, straight trunks in the first place. Maybe the trees were always short, with branches that began low down on the trunk – rather more like hedgerow trees than stately giants of a wood or forest.

The team had recorded and raised well over half the timbers in the circle by the end of the third week in July, so there was now space for a large tracked excavator to trundle close to the central tree and lift it without disturbing any posts of the circle. Mark and Bill consulted their tide tables and came to the conclusion that Friday and Saturday, 16 and 17 July would be the best days to attempt the big lift. We all kept our fingers crossed that there wouldn't be an onshore breeze on those days that would prevent the tide from retreating fully.

That would be the only reason, we naïvely thought, that we might have to call things off. Sadly, we were wrong.

The lifting of the timbers, while welcomed – indeed called for – by most people, had upset two groups. The first were the Pagan, Druid and New Age communities. We were able to communicate with the Pagans and Druids, and although they sometimes disagreed with what we were doing, they recognised why we were doing it, and were invariably polite and courteous. They often held small ceremonies at the site, which the team accommodated by stopping work if necessary. The New Age people were far harder to communicate with for simple, practical reasons, as many of them were travellers; but they could also be abusive and unpleasant. They had an extraordinary knack of turning up whenever television news cameras were present – indeed, it was almost as if somebody was tipping them off, as they rarely appeared when the media weren't there. I had the impression that their interest in archaeology was slight.

The second group consisted of local people, who either didn't believe that the circle was under threat from the sea, or who objected to the timbers being moved to Flag Fen, which was seen as being a long way away (about fifty kilometres). The threat from the sea is now so apparent that even the most diehard sceptic must surely have come round to a more rational view. As to the people who objected to the circle being removed, I can only say that I can't understand how the rumour that Flag Fen was going to keep the timbers permanently started. But it did; I've even seen it repeated in the press, although it was always completely unfounded, and it persisted for several months. Sadly, rumours have a life of their own which must be lived out, come what may; they can never be scotched. For what it's worth, ancient timber from sites all over Britain is routinely processed at Flag Fen, and if it wasn't regularly returned to its owners the place would soon grind to a halt. In this regard, Holme was not a special case.

The press were informed on Thursday, 15 July 1999 that Mark and his team would lift the central tree the following day. True to form, the New Age group picked up this information and occupied the site – and wouldn't budge. They basked in the publicity, and one of them struck rather childish heroic poses while standing on top of the central oak. The television cameras loved it, although we all found his posing more than slightly offensive. He was standing at the very heart of the shrine, at a spot which would have meant a great deal to people in the past. It was rather like prancing around on an altar. Having said that, we were also very aware that the central tree had been chain-sawed in the name of archaeology, so we had to hold our tongues. It was annoying and frustrating. Still, being stuck on a beach on a sunny English summer's day is not exactly a hardship; it could have been a lot worse.

The following day the team arrived early, and a police escort ensured that the lifting operation went ahead. Halfway through, a young woman made a rush for the tree, but was stopped by members of the team and two police officers. Had she managed to reach it, she could have been seriously hurt. That temporary panic aside, the lifting went remarkably smoothly. The machine driver, Bryn Williams, did a superb job, and when we eventually got the tree back to Flag Fen, it hadn't been marked at all. Not even a scratch.

This is how I wrote up the day in my diary:

> We grabbed a quick bite about 10.00 and then set off for Holme in the Jeep, which we took down to the site. The sand was still wet and we needed four-wheel drive and low-ratio gears. We were almost the first to arrive and were greeted by Bill Boismier who was not in the sunniest of moods over yesterday's fiasco. I told him I had good vibes for today, and he shot me the American equivalent of an Old Fashioned Look. The steel stakes we use for hanging ropes on were protruding above the water, but there was no sign of the central tree roots. It was sunny, there was a light offshore breeze and little crabs scuttled everywhere as the tide slowly retreated. After about ten minutes the Unit's red hired Land-Rover arrived (the other one had broken down the day before), and people asked if my Jeep could be used as a general dumping ground for coats, lunchboxes, cameras etc. Soon it resembled a used-clothes stall in a madman's jumble sale.
>
> So far so good. Some of the team were roping off the dig and the central tree's roots were now fully above the water. Almost every-one present was on our side, or else were interested holiday-makers, who invariably saw things from a common-sense perspective. After we had been on site for about half an hour, we could see Bryn Williams' machines, a dumper with shoring and ropes etc. and a

twenty-ton tracked excavator, which Bryn was driving. They were in the distance, slowly trundling towards us along the beach, as if coming from Hunstanton. As they crawled towards us, I got talking to a local man who was much on our side. He said he'd heard rumours that further disruptions were planned for today. He didn't know what precisely was planned, but he warned us to stay alert. As if we needed telling.

David Miles [Geoff Wainwright's replacement as English Heritage Chief Archaeologist] couldn't be on site, as he had to be on an interview panel to select the person to run the newly-created English Heritage Archaeological Centre in Portsmouth, so I was briefed to handle archaeological questions from the press. I wandered off to think things through in peace, and when I looked back after a moment or two of solitary pacing about I noticed a sudden change in the way people had organised themselves. All at once there was a clear division: hard hats and reflective jackets were inside the ropes, and everyone else was outside. It was almost as if this were the Wild West and the settlers' covered wagons had formed a defensive circle at the approach of Red Indian braves. Happily I was wearing my hard hat and reflective jacket. Pointless bravado has never been a strong point with me, so I rapidly retreated into the safety of the roped-off circle.

By this time, three New Agers had arrived: two women and a young man. We had met the young man before and he was mentally disturbed. In point of fact, he was a genuinely sad case. The two women were, however, different. One had two young children with her.

Mark Brennand and Bryn spent about twenty minutes securing padding, ropes and ratchet straps to the tree. Then Bryn gently started to lift with the machine. For what seemed like an eternity nothing happened, then I noticed a thin crack develop at the base, between the wood and the mud, and I knew that the vacuum had been broken. It was a tense moment indeed. Then, while all eyes were on the tree, the policewoman on our side called across and I looked up to see one of the team stop the young woman (the one who came with the two children), who was making a dash towards the tree. He brought her to the ground. Immediately the policewoman took over, while the intruder screamed blue murder, and the young man with the intellectual impairment screamed wildly, adding to the general cacophony.

To be honest, I watched this out of the corner of my eye. It was much a sideshow to the main event. Afterwards I got to speak to the young woman and she treated me to a rambling diatribe about the irrelevance of knowledge and how we didn't need to excavate sites, as all we had to do was feel their vibrations and spirit transmissions. That was enough. I replied as mildly as I could that I had never experienced those forces. Then I made my exit and left her addressing a group of archaeologists, whose looks made it plain that they found the dishevelled young woman and her rambling words a source of acute embarrassment. But I'd escaped.

When the tree was safely out of the ground I took a good look underneath it, and to my surprise it wasn't hollow. Nor was there an offering in the hole left behind it. I then had to explain this to the press without using words like 'anticlimax' or 'disappointment' – which was quite a tall order.

The digger and the suspended tree then slowly retreated and started the long journey back along the beach. Then my mobile phone rang and I was summoned to do a live interview for Sky News, which I had arranged previously but had completely forgotten about. I had to dash across the beach then struggle up the soft sand of the dunes. Arrived hot and breathless to have a tiny earpiece shoved in me. Then I had to greet the nation in cheery fashion.

It took a couple of hours to load the tree onto two pallets on Bryn's lorry. It was a slow and tense process, but eventually it was completed. Then we drove for an hour and a bit to get it to Flag Fen. I remember feeling slightly anxious as we crossed the county line – somehow the blue sign 'CAMBRIDGESHIRE' seemed to have been written too large and too loud. I was waiting for an ambush from the youth wing of the Norfolk Liberation Front as we drove up to it, but nothing happened. We arrived around 9.30 at Flag Fen, just as it was getting dark, but they had assembled powerful floodlights in the Field Centre. There was also a business-like three-ton forklift which we scrounged from our neighbour Tony Darlow, the potato merchant. Tony also provided the services of Kevin, his nephew, who drove the thing as if it was an extension of his arm. By 10.45 we had completed unloading and had rigged up a temporary water-supply which would suffice until Monday, when we could do something a bit better. We had expected the tree to arrive vertical, not on its side, so the arrangement we had prepared wouldn't work too well. It was a case of make-do and mend (which archaeologists are extremely good at). At 10.30 Malcolm Gibb [Manager at Flag Fen] produced two bottles of pink champagne, with which we toasted the tree, Bryn and Mark, who also supped a glass each before speeding off into the night.

We then had problems with the circulation pump and temporary sprinklers, otherwise we'd have followed them. Exhausted, and by now ready for bed, we pressed on, and managed to soak ourselves thoroughly, many times. Eventually, by using penknives and bits of string, we rigged up a sprinkling system that worked quite well – certainly well enough to keep everything nice and wet until Monday morning, when we would have the time, light and patience to do a better, more permanent job. By 1.00 a.m. we were driving out of the Flag Fen car park, and by 1.30 we were in bed. Then we slept. And how we slept.

After the tree had been lifted clear, Maisie and Pete Murphy examined the hole left behind. It was devoid of anything resembling archaeology, except for a short length of honeysuckle rope which had been pressed into the grey mud when the tree had originally been toppled into its huge post-hole. We had first come across this rope in the trial trench dug the previous autumn. It appeared to have been wrapped around the trunk close to its tip, at the bottom of the trial trench. Maisie looked at it under the microscope as soon as we got home and confirmed it was honeysuckle, but the cell structure had been damaged, as if the long stems had been deliberately twisted and then plied back against themselves, just like rope, or indeed spun woollen yarn. I should add here that Maisie loves wool and textiles. She hand-spins our own fleeces and can knit the most complicated patterns imaginable. So she understands knots, fibres and twine at quite a profound level.

When the 'rope' was originally found, someone suggested it could have been a natural occurrence – three strands of intertwining honeysuckle that had been growing up the tree in the forest. But given the fact that the tree's bark had been deliberately removed, it seemed highly improbable that a length of creeper would have been left *in situ*. The discovery that the strands had been twisted and then plied proved beyond any doubt that the rope had been deliberately created.

Maisie started to excavate the rope exposed in the side of the tree-hole with her bare fingers, as it was extremely delicate. After she had been working for about ten minutes she became aware that the strands had been twisted in a peculiar way. Suddenly she realised that this strange twisting was a knot. In fact it was a loose variant of a half-hitch, which only locked if the rope was pulled from above. In other words, bearing in mind that the tree was upside down, for the knot to have worked properly the rope would have to have been held in tension from above – from the direction of the roots. We thought long and hard about this strange configuration, but its significance was not to become clear until much later, when we reconstructed the timber circle for television.

The final two weeks of the dig, after the removal of the central tree, were less fraught and a good deal more pleasant for everyone. The New Agers left us in peace, and with them went the atmosphere of fear and loathing. We had visits from various Druids and Pagans, and on their behalf Maisie presented offerings of oak leaves, flowers and tomatoes to the hole where the tree had been. The last two timbers of the circle were lifted on Monday, 2 August 1999.

One final thing, before we move from the beach to the Field Centre. Mark always used to examine his change carefully, when in the pub or buying his lunchtime sandwiches. He was looking for coppers minted in 1999. In the nineteenth century, archaeologists would sometimes have little bronze plaques specially cast for them. When an excavation was finished, the plaques would be left in the completed trenches before the workmen arrived to fill them in. Their presence would inform some unfortunate future archaeologist that he or she had just thrown away a hard-won research grant, because the site in question had already been fully excavated by Colt Hoare (or whoever) in, say, 1815.

It was the least Mark could do. As the grey mud was shovelled back into the trenches, he distributed his coins. I even added one of my own. I suspect they'll survive rather longer than the tomatoes.

=====

CHAPTER THIRTEEN

The World Turned Upside Down

I'm a practical person, and I prefer practical solutions wherever possible. So I was delighted when Tim Taylor, Executive Producer of *Time Team*, told me that he was planning to make an accurate reconstruction of the Holme timber structure as part of the documentary film. By this point Maisie and I already knew what the actual timbers were like, and when I was talking to Tim I must have said something which implied that strict authenticity would be impossible. His reply was terse and to the point: it would be as authentic as we could possibly make it. End of discussion. I was impressed.

The most challenging part of the reconstruction was undoubtedly the felling and grubbing-up of the central oak tree. For a start, it was important to find a tree which was going to be felled anyhow, as part of a woodland management plan. We knew that we'd receive complaints whatever we did, but at least this way our consciences would be clear. The same applied to the smaller trees that would be split to make the circle of posts.

An important archaeological discovery was made at the outset of the reconstruction project. Key members of the team who were to carry it out came to Flag Fen to view the inverted tree in our Field Centre. The timbers were held in four plastic-lined wooden tanks which resembled large paddling pools. They were just deep enough to immerse the timbers, which were laid in them horizontally. The central tree was also in a large bath, with water constantly being pumped over it. For the opening scene of the reconstruction sequence the film-maker, Graham Johnston, wanted a general shot of us standing around the tree, talking and looking interested – in a lively, intellectually-aware sort of fashion. So we gave him animated conversation and nodding heads. It seemed to go well.

The next scene featured Maisie and two of her students from Flag Fen, who were cleaning mud from near the end of the central tree that had been tipped into the ground. As she worked her way gingerly towards a thick patch of mud that had been left in place to protect the surface beneath, her fingers suddenly met the familiar fibrous feel of honeysuckle rope. She felt again and removed a larger piece of mud. There could be no doubt at all, it was the same honeysuckle rope we had encountered before.

She worked away, with Graham filming reels and reels of film. Sometimes he asked her questions, but only received brief, monosyllabic replies for his pains, as Maisie was concentrating hard on the work at hand. After twenty minutes she could see form and pattern below the mud. The original outline of the mud patch was a hollow that had been chopped through the sapwood on the outside of the tree. Within the hollow, but now using the harder heartwood within it, was a thick, axed-out loop, through which the rope passed.

Realising at once what she'd found, Maisie waded round to the other side of the tree. And there, directly opposite, was another, identical patch of mud, complete with a stub of rope protruding from it. The two patches of mud were both filled hollows in which were strong loops, through which the rope was passed. These were undoubtedly the towing loops that had been used to drag the tree to the timber circle. It was a unique, an absolutely astonishing find. But what about the ropes? Nobody knew anything about honeysuckle as a material for ropes. Would it be strong enough? Only one man could answer that question.

Damien Saunders has had a lifelong interest in ropes, fibres and cordage. He loves the subject and is vastly knowledgeable, being equally at home with a tarred rope from the *Mary Rose* as with a piece of Early Bronze Age honeysuckle. He tried to reproduce Maisie's find in various ways without success, until he hit upon the idea of soaking the honeysuckle for several days, then twisting it. Treated this way it was strong indeed, but only for a quite limited period – about three weeks. If it was kept any longer, it became brittle.

The next step towards an accurate reconstruction of the creation of the site was rather unexpected. Some time before, Maisie had told me that several of the posts in the circle had actually been placed in the ground upside down, as if echoing the central tree. I'd forgotten that she had said that – the way one does – when I arrived at the Field Centre to take some routine photographs. I looked at the timbers arranged in a great circle in the tanks, and was suddenly struck by the fact that several of them were upside down. To my surprise, when I enthusiastically told Maisie of my discovery, she failed to greet this announcement as the revelation I believed it to be. Indeed, I recall she looked skywards briefly, and resumed compiling her record cards without further comment.

Slightly crestfallen, I returned to my cameras. I had photographed about three timbers when David and Michael, my two assistants, brought in a most unusual one lying on its stretcher. It looked particularly odd – as if an insanely courageous soldier had been detecting mines with the tip of his nose, then one had exploded and removed the entire upper part of his body, so that all that remained were his hips and legs in their trousers.

I asked Maisie what the number of this forked post was, and she told me it had two: 35 and 37. I pondered for a moment. That meant it had appeared on the surface as two close, but distinct and separate posts. The join, the crutch, was below the ground. That could only mean one thing: the 'trousers' were in fact a narrow entranceway. The posts were about twenty centimetres (eight inches) apart when excavated, and they could possibly have diverged further above ground – but not much. As I looked at them in the tank, they appeared pretty straight, and I knew that oak isn't the easiest of woods to bend. So the gap between them must have been the approximate width of the entranceway. It was a case of turn sideways and breathe in sharply to enter. There could be no doubt that this was a deliberately restricted entranceway – just like the oval structure at Maxey or the small henge at Fengate.

As we munched our lunchtime sandwiches sitting on the edge of a tank, I asked about the 'trousers'. Maisie said that the gap between them had been blocked with a small, thin piece of wood, driven into the ground less than half the depth of the fifty-five main posts, on the outside of the timber circle. 'Ah,' I thought, 'so it wasn't blocked on the inside.' That was important.

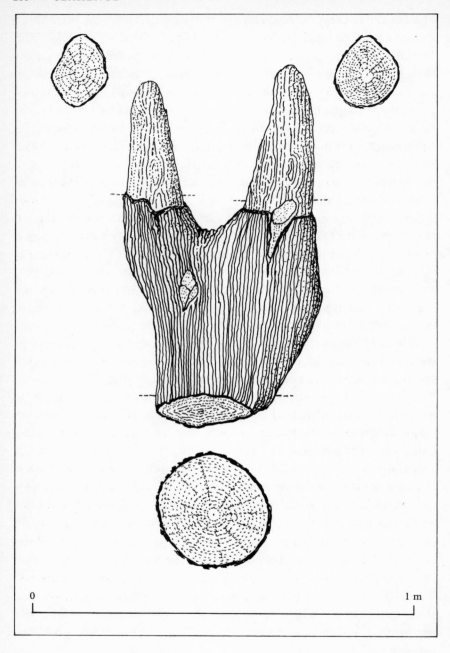

0   1 m

FIG 25   *The forked double posts (posts 35, left, and 37, right) that together formed the narrow entrance to the Seahenge circle*

The archaeological world had been fascinated by the Holme timber circle ever since its discovery was announced in that short piece in *British Archaeology* in January, and I found it impossible to go to any sort of archaeological gathering without hearing people's views about it. I won't say that the subject had begun to bore me, but it had certainly begun to lose some of its initial excitement. Without exception, all were agreed that it wasn't a henge, in the sense defined by Professor Atkinson in the 1950s (see page 158). But it wasn't a *timber circle* in the strict archaeological sense, either.

Timber circles, as defined by prehistorians, consist of perfect or near-perfect circles of posts. They are often found within a henge, either occupying the whole area or as discrete circles within a much larger enclosure. Woodhenge and the two circles within Durrington Walls, near Stonehenge, and the Sanctuary at Avebury are four of the best-known timber circles, *sensu stricto*. The recently discovered post settings below the well-known stone circle at Stanton Drew in Somerset are another exciting example. Here there are nine concentric rings of posts, ranging in diameter from eighteen to ninety-five metres. Some people have suggested that timber circles were originally roofed, but I have always found their arguments unconvincing. Two examples should illustrate why I have doubts.

It was common for timber circles to be replaced by stone circles towards the end of their lives – the Sanctuary and Stanton Drew are classic examples. If the timber circles were roofed, the roofs would have had a short life if wind could get beneath them. Thatch is particularly vulnerable in this respect. One good storm and they would have been blown to pieces. So the outer setting of posts ought to have incorporated a windbreak of sorts: perhaps plain woven wattle, or a full wattle-and-daub wall. When the sites were later set in stone, you might expect the outer setting to be a drystone wall; but this is never the case. Posts are 'remembered' by individual stone monoliths, but not by a wall. Mike Pitts's recent excavations at the Sanctuary have comprehensively knocked the roofed hypothesis on the head. It seems quite inconceivable to me that a structure subject to such regular – and seemingly haphazard – episodes of construction and destruction could ever have been roofed.

So if the Holme circle was neither a henge nor a timber circle, what was it? There are only two possible alternatives left to us. The first is a barrow. We've come across several barrows in our quest, and in the east of England they are almost invariably sites of many periods of use. Typically there would be one or more settings of posts, a small central mound, a primary burial, a ditch and bank or banks, and a much larger final mound, into which would be set a whole variety of secondary cremations. But Holme seems much simpler. In part I suspect this apparent simplicity may reflect our old friend archaeological visibility. Put simply, the complexity has been washed out to sea. But has it? Mark Brennand's team cut a hand-dug trench four metres out from the circle of posts and failed to find any evidence at all for a ring-ditch. A ditch, or a substantial hole of some sort, would have been needed to provide material for a mound. When the *Time Team* reconstruction was built, the spoil dug from the bedding trench of the timber circle and the pit for the central tree would have provided enough material for a low mound (perhaps a foot or so high) around the tree, but there wasn't enough material remotely to cover the tree.

Then there is the problem of the high groundwater table. To judge from the report produced by Peter Murphy and his colleagues, if the builders of the circle had dug down a spade's depth, water would probably have seeped into the hole. Go down any further, and water would become a distinct problem. At Maxey the water table was also high, although by no means as high as at Holme, and there the body at the centre of the oval structure was buried in a shallow scoop grave. It would seem that Neolithic and Bronze Age people had a horror of placing the bodies of their loved ones into water-filled graves. This is not an unusual feeling – just look at the raised graves in the cemeteries of the Mississippi delta swamplands, around New Orleans. They are built up above the ground, to keep the bodies of the departed dry. But abhorrence of a wet grave is not the same as abhorrence of water.

In many societies, such as the Vikings, burial at sea was a preferred way to make one's final journey. But, ideologically speaking, that isn't the same thing as burial within a waterlogged grave. Of course, we cannot be certain that Neolithic and Bronze Age communities in Britain had this horror of wet graves, but it is remarkable how rarely waterlogged burials are found. There is no evidence to suggest that even the Danish oak coffins were interred in wet ground. The waterlogging happened slightly later, certainly after the funeral.

While the dig at Holme was in progress John Lorimer made several visits to the site, and on one occasion found pieces of Late Bronze Age pottery about a metre outside the post circle. The team investigated the findspot, and I was able to examine it closely myself. So far as I could see the pottery had come from a thin layer of settlement refuse – in other words, domestic rubbish – at the base of the peat. To my mind this suggested that there had never been a substantial barrow, or else it would have collapsed outside the timber circle when the posts retaining it in place had rotted. This would have either buried the pottery or raised the ground on which it was found.

It seems to me that the presence of John's pottery can be explained rather more simply. The timber circle was placed on a natural low hummock in the landscape. It only had to be a few inches above the land round about it to stay significantly drier. Even in the Late Bronze Age – a millennium or more after the construction of the circle – this low hummock would have provided a dry spot for a family to rest, perhaps on their way to visit an ancestral shrine.

If the circle of timbers had been a wall around a vertical-sided, drum-shaped barrow, as some still believe, it makes no sense for it to have an entranceway. And it makes even less sense to block the entrance with a small piece of wood on the outside. Surely it would have been better to use a larger timber, and to place it on the inside, so that it could better resist the outward pressure of earth in the mound? No, if there was a barrow mound at Holme, I think it would have been a small one – more a final gesture than a major part of the structure. Again, we found something similar when we dug the low turf-and-topsoil oval barrow and the central ring-ditch of the Great Henge at Maxey, where the final mounds sealed everything in place.

I've said what I *don't* think the timber circle was (a henge, a timber circle or a barrow). So what was it? Here I have a rabbit to pull from my hat, in the fair form of English Heritage's dating specialist Alex Bayliss. I've worked with Alex on a number of projects, and she understands the language of mathematics in a most extraordinary way.

Alex is an applied mathematician, and much of her work is involved with Bayesian statistics. The Reverend Thomas Bayes, an eighteenth-century mathematician, realised that numbers rarely exist on their own, and that when you have a group of numbers you can do interesting things with them if you know in what order they ought to appear. As with archaeology, so with numbers: it's the context that matters. Sadly for the Reverend Bayes, his formulae were too many and too complex for people at the time to apply, so his idea had to wait a couple of hundred years before it could be put into effect, with the use of high-powered computers. Today Bayesian statistics are mainly used by actuaries when making calculations to be used by life-assurance companies. But Alex has turned the principle in a more unusual direction.

Using a combination of high-precision radiocarbon dates and tree-ring dating, Alex and the team of dendrochronologists at Queen's University, Belfast were able to demonstrate that the central oak tree at Holme was felled in the year 2050 BC, between April and June. The four sampled posts from the circle were felled the following year, 2049 BC, again between April and June. We cannot therefore state that the tree was placed in position a year before the posts, but it would certainly make practical or constructional sense if it were placed in the ground first, with the posts around it being added later.

The season of felling – if indeed the central tree was felled – is interesting. In spring and early summer it's much easier to remove bark; but I'm sure that wasn't the reason that time of year was selected – if indeed it was selected. It could equally have been chosen because of external events, such as somebody's death. But whatever the reason, April to June is the time of year when everything is bursting into new life. That, I suspect, is the real reason behind the selection of the season.

Next we come to the debate about the height the timbers reached above ground. Again, had it been a drum-shaped barrow, the height of the timbers around the outside would be much constrained by the pressure of the earth they enclosed. The normal rule of thumb is that a post usually protrudes three to four times the depth it is buried. Thus a fence-post driven in one metre will safely extend three metres above ground, or even four metres if it is part of a supporting structure, such as a building. The Holme posts were sunk about a metre into the existing ground. We still don't know precisely what the level of the original land surface was, but it is unlikely to have been lower than it is today. So we can conservatively estimate that the posts *could* have extended three to four metres into the air. Given the twisted, bendy, gnarled and knotty wood used, I would suggest that three metres is a great deal more probable than four.

So, we have a structure built in a damp backswamp. It was probably built in one, or at most two, distinct episodes. It has a single narrow entranceway facing south-west, which is also the direction of the midwinter sunset. On a dryland site I wouldn't hesitate to identify the ring at Holme as a mortuary structure, built in the tradition established in the oval structure at Maxey, which it so closely resembles. But what about the body? Given what we know about wet graves, I would argue that the body would have been placed in the 'arms' of the inverted tree's roots. Of course, I cannot prove this. There are numerous examples from sites all over Britain for the rite of excarnation, or the defleshing of bones. Etton provided abundant evidence for it. During the excarnation process the body has to be exposed or visible long enough for people to *see* that the flesh is being removed and the soul is ascending into the next world, otherwise it has no point. The tree could have provided a superb excarnation platform, but I cannot prove it.

It is entirely possible that Seahenge belongs to an entirely new category of site that has not yet been classified. I don't want to give the impression that all Bronze Age religious shrines can be slotted into neat classificatory boxes. They can't. Very often it's hard to decide whether a particular site is a henge, a ring-ditch, a barrow or a timber circle. And opinions will always differ. Several strange sites are known from this period, and one, which was dug between 1984 and 1986, was even given an appropriately baffled name by its excavator, Blaise Vyner – the Wossit. The site was placed on top of a hill near the village of Street House, north of Whitby in East Yorkshire. In size it was slightly larger than Seahenge (about ten metres across), and it was roughly circular in shape.

The Wossit consisted of four arcs of post-holes set in bedding trenches. Between each length of palisade were narrow entrances, partially blocked by posts. One of the entrances through the outer palisade had been blocked by a saddle quern placed on edge. At the centre was a large pit rather reminiscent of our oak tree's hole. This

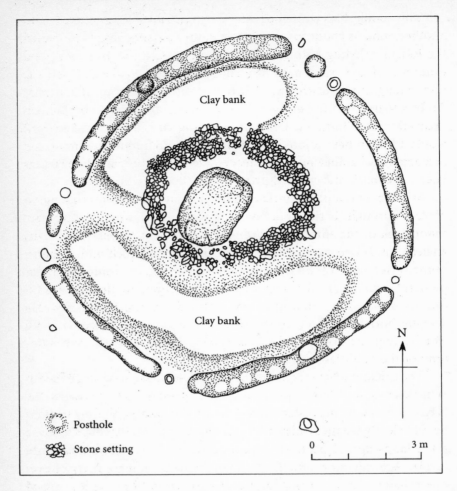

FIG 26   *The enigmatic Street House 'Wossit', Yorkshire*

strange site is known to be contemporary with Seahenge, and there are obvious similarities between the two. But whatever their precise role, the roots of both Seahenge and the Wossit lie firmly within the Neolithic, and they belong to a long-established tradition of circular and near-circular sacred sites. I suspect, but again I cannot prove, that both were family shrines, built and used by a relatively small number of folk.

This book has contained some remarkable coincidences, and another one was about to take place. On the very morning I completed the foregoing paragraph, I was about to trawl the literature for good examples of sites similar to Seahenge in eastern England. Then the phone rang. It was Chris Evans, Director of the Cambridge University Archaeological Unit, one of whose teams was doing a commercial excavation at Whittlesey. Chris said the dig was nearly finished, and would I like to have a look? I had already heard about the site on the archaeological grapevine, and I needed no further bidding. Four hours later I was back at my word-processor.

Whittlesey is a pleasant market town about three miles south-east of Peterborough. It sits on a low hill of clay that was laid down in a muddy sea in the Jurassic period, some sixty million years ago. This ancient mud, known as the Oxford Clay, is very thick and contains numerous fossils of marine dinosaurs. But more importantly for modern industry, it also contains much carbon. In the nineteenth century it was discovered that, when heated up sufficiently, this clay actually burns. In effect, bricks made from it are self-fired. It is no wonder that the brick industry has long been important to the economy of the Whittlesey area.

The brickpit where the Cambridge team were working was between Whittlesey and Peterborough, on rising ground that overlooks the Flag Fen basin. In the distance, perhaps a mile away or slightly further, I could clearly see the fields and factories of Fengate. Between stretched a flat landscape of peat. The excavations had revealed a small Late Bronze Age village or settlement and the remains of three Early Bronze Age religious sites: a henge and two barrows, which were arranged in a row. The henge had two entranceways, facing north-west and south-east, and was marked out by a circular ditch. Twelve large posts were set at regular intervals in a circle (diameter thirty metres) around the inner lip of the ditch, and the two entranceways were elaborated with porch-like structures made up from four posts.

The two barrows were unusual in that the ring-ditch which surrounded each of them was broached by a single narrow entranceway – a pattern reminiscent of a henge. The larger of the two barrows, which was twenty-eight metres in diameter, had a deep central grave, containing a single burial in the remains of a log coffin. The skeleton

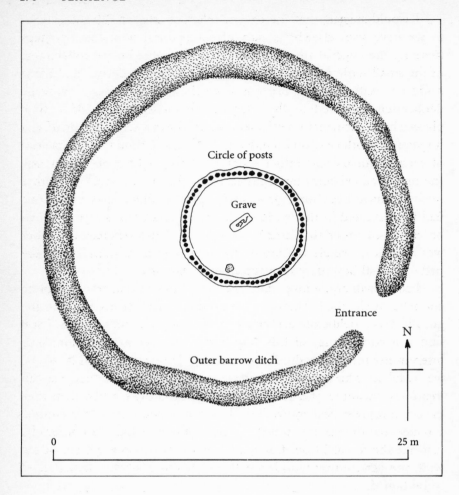

Circle of posts

Grave

Entrance

N

Outer barrow ditch

0   25 m

FIG 27   *Ground plan of a barrow at Whittlesey, near Peterborough (courtesy of Cambridge University Archaeological Unit)*

was accompanied by a small polished flint knife. The grave was encircled by a ring of posts, which were set closely together, but not actually touching, as at Seahenge. There was also an elaborate Early Bronze Age cremation and several Late Bronze Age cremations, both within and outside the barrows. These later cremations were probably placed near the barrows by the inhabitants of the small village nearby.

I would suggest that the row of religious sites at Whittlesey was, as we have seen elsewhere, part of a territorial boundary, perhaps marking the edge of the land that was controlled by the inhabitants of the small settlement and its Early Bronze Age predecessors. In that respect it differed from Seahenge, which was in a ritual landscape deliberately removed to the edge of the inhabitable world – to a place where permanent settlement would have been difficult, if not impossible. Both were on boundaries, but the scale and the significance of each boundary was rather different. This might explain why one site produced evidence for repeated use and re-use, whereas the other seems to have been built in a single episode. Put another way, one had been located in the world of the living and needed repeatedly to be visited in order to reaffirm what it stood for, whereas the other was built for a single ceremony that may well have transcended the petty internal boundary disputes of everyday life.

People will argue long and hard about the central tree at Holme and what it signified. There can be no doubt that its inversion in the ground was a deliberate act, and one of strong symbolic power. I still find it a compelling, slightly frightening and eerie image, and it is often in my mind. But does it have a specific meaning? And if so, can we 'read' it? The answer is that we cannot, any more than we can 'read' the meaning of a religious service. Symbols are like that: they proclaim a great deal more than their face value alone. It is entirely possible that the oak tree was the symbol of a particular clan or family, just like the fox at Etton. But again, the fox was also a symbol of the wild, pre-agricultural world 'out there'. It was a symbol that needed to be tamed.

I am convinced that the oak tree also had a deeper symbolic meaning, as did its strange inversion – the world turned upside down. We have already seen that sites like Etton have shown that the prehistoric view of the cosmos didn't extend up into the sky alone; it also reached down into the ground. And the Holme tree also provides strong evidence for this.

Possibly the safest form of analogy that might help us understand the deeper meanings behind the Holme circle can be found in archaeology itself. We do not necessarily need to search the literature of more recent tribal societies to seek enlightenment. Take, for example, the time of year when the tree was felled. For practical purposes the period April to June is perhaps the worst possible time to fell a tree. The tree itself and everything around it is in full growth. No self-respecting forester would dream of felling timber at that time of the year. But if the tree was seen as a symbol of life itself, then surely this would be the time to gather it in. It could be believed that its life forces were most vigorous in the spring and early summer.

By inverting the tree in the ground, those life forces are being returned to the earth, the source of all life. The removal of the bark was the purification process that was needed before the tree could release its energies back into the ground. But these powerful forces required constraint. They were dangerous and mysterious. Life must be contained by a living thing, so the purified tree, perhaps with its human cargo, was contained within a far larger symbolic tree, represented by the solid circular wall of posts. Remember the Danish Muldbjerg Chieftain in his de-barked oak coffin beneath the half-tree-trunk vault (see page 235)? Surely we are here seeing the same powerful symbolic forces in action, just a few centuries later.

There is a real danger of circular argument when you apply folk-lore, history and modern anthropological observations of tribal societies to the remote past. Put simply, the circular argument is this: if it hasn't been done by people that we know about, it could never have been done. The archaeologist would reply that no existing or recent society has ever closely resembled the world of Early Bronze Age Britain. It's possible to find people who worked great stones – Easter Island is a good example – but other aspects of their society are completely different. It's possible to find people who use Neolithic-style tombs – on the island of Madagascar, for example. But again, their societies differ from those in prehistoric Britain. You can gain general insights into ancient Britain by looking at these more recent communities, but you mustn't attempt to draw specific parallels. Let me give an example.

Mike Parker-Pearson is a British prehistorian who has lived with the communities on Madagascar I've just mentioned, and his work has provided us with some unusual insights. The people he has worked with regard wood, for example, as the material of the living. So ceremonial sites built in wood make reference to the here and now.

ABOVE The roots of the central oak are levered upwards, using poles, and the two-ton tree drops into position. The rope throws up a cloud of dust at the moment of impact.

RIGHT The tree is manhandled upright. Note the position and rigging of the honeysuckle rope, which precisely echoes what was found at Seahenge itself. The tree used here is very similar in shape to its Bronze Age counterpart, but is perhaps 20 per cent smaller.

Aerial view taken during the final stages of the reconstruction. This photograph emphasises the small scale of the timber circle.

The interior of Seahenge during the *Time Team* reconstruction. Diagonal wood props were needed to support some of the posts until the final forked posts of the entranceway were secured in position. When completed, the structure was remarkably stable.

ABOVE The Bronze Age religious site at Flag Fen, Peterborough, consisted of five parallel rows of posts which ran across an area of flooded ground about a kilometre wide. The posts, which were driven into the ground between 1300 and 924 BC, formed the framework for layers of horizontal timbers on which people could walk. In this view the excavators are working on the highest level of horizontal timber.

RIGHT It took four years to excavate and record the thousands of horizontal timbers at Flag Fen. As the excavations progressed, numerous additional posts were found, and some of these were re-used. In this view the archaeologist has just revealed part of a wooden axle from a light cart or wagon which had been jammed between two large posts.

LEFT The oak axle from Flag Fen (1200–1300 BC), the oldest known axle found in Britain. It had been cut in half (left of picture) and used as a peg within the rows of posts at Flag Fen. Wear-marks left by the wheel hubs are clearly visible; the neatly cut square mortice hole is for the wooden linchpin which held the wheel in place.

CENTRE Many valuable objects were thrown into the waters around the Flag Fen posts as offerings to the gods and ancestors. Most were deliberately damaged before being placed in the water. This picture shows three typical Late Bronze Age (about 1000 BC) items: a damaged sword scabbard tip, or chape (top), a bent spearhead (centre) and a bent and broken ornamental stick-pin (bottom).

BELOW During the Iron Age, which followed the bronze Age, patterns of life changed. People ceased to live in isolated farmsteads and came together in larger groups which resembled modern villages. This view is of a later Iron Age village at Cat's Water, Fengate, dating to the final three centuries BC.In all, it consisted of about fifty buildings, most of which were roundhouses.

Stone, however, was the material used for the dead and for the world of the ancestors. As an idea this has much to offer. It might, for example, help to explain the relationship between Stonehenge and Woodhenge, nearby. But it doesn't explain why stone sites are almost unknown around the Wash. That has mainly to be put down to geology – there aren't any suitable sources of stone to hand.

Mike's observations on Madagascar have greatly influenced the way all prehistorians think about death, burial and religion. He has shown that the process of physically removing a body from the world of the living is both extended and complex, and plays an important part in cementing family and other ties. Such aspects of death as the odours of putrefaction, regarded as repulsive in the modern world, have altogether different meanings in more traditional societies. But his work has to be taken at a general level – it is more theoretical than practical, in a case-by-case sense. It explains how prehistoric people in Britain might have regarded death and the next world, but it does not set out to say how they regarded these things. His great contribution to prehistory has been to broaden our minds.

I mention these things because I have often been asked why the tree at Holme was inverted, and what it meant. Again, I find myself in much the same dilemma as when the bus driver came up to me at Stonehenge. Only this time I'm older and wiser, and I no longer spout trite phrases from textbooks. Our quest has uncovered many clues to the mystery, but in forensic terms these clues are still circumstantial. I doubt very much whether we'll ever find any direct clues. And if we did, we'd most probably misinterpret them.

The strange world-turned-upside-down burial of the quernstones at Etton is making a broadly similar symbolic statement to the Holme inverted oak. The partial burial of these things suggests symbolic links between the air and the ground, between the living world and another world below the ground. The quernstones symbolised domestic or family life. The mighty oak perhaps symbolises life itself – the Tree of Life of medieval mythology. So a living organism of this world is being offered to the world below the ground, which was possibly seen as the source of all life. It's about propitiation and renewal. It's also about the cycle of life and indeed the cycle of the seasons.

Prehistoric people did not share our view of the world as a resource to be exploited. I think that the modern concept of rubbish – something dead, useless and to be disposed of quickly – would have been entirely foreign to them. Food, once consumed, would be returned to the cycle of birth, growth and renewal. That is why, for example, we find the heaps of animal bones deliberately buried in the ditches at Etton. That is why the small pits there commemorate a dead individual. He, or she, is being returned to the earth from whence he came. The same surely applies to the inverted tree and the posts around it. Their life forces are being returned to the source of all life.

It is entirely possible that the Holme circle was never about human life and death at all. It could have been a shrine – possibly built by a family that identified with oak trees – to the trees themselves. After grazing, wood was possibly the most important resource available to prehistoric people. It provided them with shelter and fuel. It was essential to their survival. So it would not be surprising to find that such a shrine was placed in the most sacred landscape known to them: the landscape on the edge of existence. If this is indeed the case, then it would seem that the forces controlled by the ancestors applied to all living things.

Bearing in mind the dangers of drawing parallels that are too specific, and bearing in mind, too, the huge length of time that separates the Early Bronze Age from today, inverted trees are not as unusual as you might otherwise expect. I remember discussing these things with Richard Bradley shortly after his return from a study visit to Norway in 1999. When he got there he had excitedly told his Norwegian hosts about Seahenge. They in their turn were very interested, but not as surprised as he expected them to be. Such things, it would appear, were only to be expected. They gave him numerous instances in which inverted trees played prominent roles.

In the mythology of northern Europe, the Lapps, for example, have a perception of the world as a three-part cosmos. There are the worlds above us, around us and below us. They see the underworld as if it were this world, but folded over. In their perception, an inverted tree would have roots in our world, but it would exist – it would be growing – in the underworld. In other words, the tree would be seen as the means of drawing different worlds together, a way of communicating between our world and the world below the ground.

We cannot simply infer from what the Lapps believed that Early Bronze Age Britons believed the same things. But it would not be unreasonable to suggest that something akin to a three-world cosmos may also have applied in British prehistory. The point I want to make is that there are certain fundamental ideas that can be taken as linking these various beliefs together. We do not need to take such complex concepts as parallel ideologies at face value. We are looking for indications, for pointers. We do not seek absolutes. If we search for explanations – or worse, simple explanations – we won't find them.

I've already mentioned that the 'backswamp' behind the coastal barrier at Holme-next-the-Sea would have been a damp, marginal spot, not the sort of place you would choose to build a house. I've come across the remains of prehistoric houses in some remote places – like above the tree-line in the mountains of Wales – but I don't think there were settlements close by at Holme. And why not? Quite simply because there were liminal – and therefore in a sense hostile – places, such as Seahenge, in the immediate vicinity. By and large, ritual landscapes are not places where you expect to find major or long-term prehistoric settlements that are contemporary with the barrows and henges. But where is the evidence that Seahenge was part of a ritual landscape? One site doesn't make a landscape.

No, it doesn't. But most ritual landscapes are not being eroded by the sea, either. There are stories of other possible circles of posts on Holme beach that have been seen by walkers or windsurfers, although to my knowledge none of these have been confirmed. But I would be surprised indeed if the Holme timber circle was ever on its own.* Small sites like it are almost invariably found within larger ritual landscapes. And as we've already seen, the coastal 'backswamp' is an ideal marginal world-within-a-world, rather like the fringes of Maxey 'island', or the low-lying watery knoll on which the causewayed enclosure at Etton was sited.

An indirect argument in favour of a wider ritual landscape on the

---

* My suspicions that Seahenge was part of a larger ritual landscape were recently confirmed when John Lorimer discovered the remains of a probable barrow close by. It is below the high-tide mark and includes a mound and at least one circle of small timbers. John has also found two additional Bronze Age metal objects at the same spot where he found the original axe. This suggests that the axe was part of a hoard, or votive offering.

low-lying coastal plain east of Hunstanton as far as Holme is provided by John Lorimer's original discovery of the axe, and some other Later Bronze Age metalwork finds. John's axe was probably made about a millennium after the post circle was built, and I cannot imagine that the two are directly connected, other than by the fact that they were both located on a low natural rise in the ground surface. At least one other bronze axe is known to have been found on Holme beach.

Strange as it may seem, to judge by the many hundreds of finds of their axes, Bronze Age carpenters were not careless or slapdash people. I can think of few axe finds which could reliably be considered as losses during work, although I can think of several wooden axe hafts – usually split or damaged in some way – that have been cast aside during work. So why do we have so many Bronze Age axes in our museums?

If you closely examine the records that accompany each axe find it is usually the case that they came from ponds, rivers, lakes, fens or streams. These are not places where carpenters or foresters are likely ever to have worked. Often the axes are found in hoards, with several other Bronze Age objects or just half a dozen other axeheads. Some hoards may have been the scrap metal that a working smith would carry around as the raw material for making new tools, but in most instances they were offerings of some sort. In Neolithic times the equivalent would be the smashed Langdale stone axes we found at Etton, or indeed hoards of unused stone or flint axes which have been found elsewhere in Britain. By the onset of the Bronze Age there was already a long tradition of treating axes in a special way.

Less than three kilometres west along the beach from the timber circle, a drainage ditch (or dyke) ran across the remnants of the originally much larger 'backswamp' behind the coastal barrier dunes at Old Hunstanton. In prehistoric times, this would have been the self-same landscape as the one in which the circle was built. These 'backswamp' fields at the foot of the higher ground were poorly drained, and the landowner, Mr Hamon le Strange, had had the dyke which ran through them enlarged and improved, more than doubling its depth from a metre to over two metres. Mr le Strange was a keen amateur archaeologist, and was particularly interested in field-walking. It's a wonderfully therapeutic form of taking a structured walk, which

I greatly prefer to pointless walks. I'd much rather be out on my own, head down into the wind, staring at the surface of a ploughed field and stopping every so often to pick up a flint tool or a broken piece of pottery. That's what field-walking involves, and Mr le Strange was good at it.

It was 23 January 1974, and Mr le Strange was field-walking along the northern bank of his recently enlarged dyke. Suddenly something unusual caught his eye on the opposite bank, about a metre below the surface of the field. He hurried round and discovered it was a type of Middle Bronze Age axe known as a palstave. He then looked carefully at the bank and found parts of a twisted bronze torc, or neck ornament, about a metre away. Shortly after, he found a large bronze pin, resembling a Victorian hatpin, and a plain, untwisted torc. It had been a good day's work.

Five days later he took the finds to King's Lynn Museum, and in an act of extraordinary generosity donated them on the spot. The next month, on 25 February, the museum organised a local club of metal-detector enthusiasts to do a 'sweep' across the field near where Mr le Strange had found the four bronzes. They revealed a single find, about ten centimetres below the surface. But it was a good one: a solid cast-bronze bracelet delicately decorated with lightly incised geometric patterns. It had been broken when the dyke was machined out, and was found in three separate pieces.

Hoards of ornaments such as this one have been dated around 1400 to 1250 BC, in the Middle Bronze Age. They're more frequently found in the south-west, in Devon and Somerset, but some are known in eastern England. What I found intriguing about Mr le Strange's hoard was its composition: an axehead, a dress pin, two neck-rings and a bracelet. Now, an axehead with, say, a chisel and an adze I could understand. Some poor carpenter had lost his tools. But an axe and *ornaments*? The only answer must be that this little group of valuable objects had been placed in the ground deliberately, as an offering to the ancestors.

It wasn't long into my quest for Bronze Age religion that I realised the importance of time and place. In prehistory the two were, I suspect, inseparable. We have seen how those huge post-holes were likely precursors of Stonehenge, followed the transmission of Etton's 'magic' onto the higher ground of Maxey 'island' by way of the cursus, and seen how the Fengate and West Deeping Bronze Age fields were laid out along long-accepted land divisions marked out by earlier barrows. All of those processes took time and space. Prehistory was never in a hurry – which is why ritual landscapes were so long-lived. They were sacred places for century after century.

We have no idea when the Holme ritual landscape began, but I would guess that its Neolithic origins now lie well beneath the waves, and probably date to the years around 4000 BC. By 2050 BC it would have been well-established, and by the thirteenth century BC, when the Hunstanton hoard was buried, it was approaching its twilight years.

These vast expanses of time are difficult to grasp, especially for modern people, who live from hour to hour and whose ideas of the distant past might be the time of their great-grandparents. But I think it was ever thus. In prehistory people had a different concept of time, but their personal histories were measured by the passing of successive generations. The lives of real people merged gradually into myth and legend. Today we have a linear concept of time. We see the past in terms almost of Darwinian evolution – I always think of those drawings of human development which start with something ape-like, small and hunched and progress towards ourselves, marching proudly forward, chin out and head held high.

In prehistory the concept was different. People weren't concerned with evolution, development or progress: they thought in terms of cycles. As we have seen at Etton and Holme, everything, even time, told a story. Like all narrative it had a beginning, a middle and an end; and the end was rooted in the beginning. This is why it's such a mistake to believe that Stonehenge was a calendar of some sort. It wasn't: calendars measure linear time – which was of no concern to the builders of Stonehenge. Rather it was about the passing of the seasons, and the endless procession of the months. Stonehenge didn't measure so much as mark, or celebrate, the passing of time.

The *Time Team* reconstruction of the Holme circle, which took place on the edge of the modern village, was a most remarkable achievement. The central tree and the smaller ones for the posts were selected from trees that had been earmarked for felling as part of a woodland management scheme which aimed to return a piece of ancient woodland in the outer fringes of south-east London to its original, medieval state. The medieval woods provided poles and wattle from coppiced trees that were cut down to the ground on a regular cycle. As a response to this cutting-back the tree would send up straight stems of rapid growth. Regularly spaced around the woods were large mature trees whose presence helped to draw the coppice stems up towards the light and which provided medieval builders with their main, heavy-duty, structural timber.

The wood had been neglected for decades before the management plan was adopted some fifteen years ago. Contrary to ill-informed opinion, a neglected wood does not thrive. It will become choked with sycamore and other seedlings, and soon the trees grow thin, spindly and weak. Proper woodland management has always involved the felling of trees, because ancient woods were a productive, renewable resource. To neglect them through misplaced 'green' concern is to do them no favours at all. In fact, it's killing them with kindness.

We learned many archaeological lessons from the reconstruction. First, it now seems most unlikely that the central tree was felled and then toppled over. More probably a rope was fixed high up in the branches of the crown and the tree was gradually rocked. This loosened the earth from around the roots, allowing them to be cut, one by one. As the roots were cut, the rocking became more vigorous, until the tree toppled over. It is also possible, of course, that the tree simply blew down in a gale and was cut up on the ground. The reason we don't believe that the stump was grubbed up after felling is quite simply that this proved almost impossible to achieve, even with a large team of fit young men and modern hand-tools. Eventually a tractor had to be brought in to help. There's no doubt that rocking the tree would have been far easier.

The honeysuckle ropes worked superbly, and were quite strong enough, provided that even pressure was maintained – sudden jerks were bad news. The tree was slid into its hole along a series of greased rollers, but this didn't work well. In the past I've moved two-ton tree trunks with just two men, using two parallel rails laid on the ground like railway tracks. Rollers are then placed on the rails and the tree rests on the rollers. Once started, it can be moved just by pushing, but levers are useful to get it going.

In the televised reconstruction there was a ramp which led into the hole for the central tree to be manoeuvred down. After we finished the job, many of us felt we would have preferred a clean drop into the hole. Had that been the method chosen, the re-rigging of the honeysuckle rope which Maisie had observed in the hole on the beach would have served to steer the tree as it began its descent into the ground.

The narrow entranceway formed by the forked 'pair of trousers' timber worked very well indeed. If we had simply left a gap in the timbers there would have been nothing to prevent them from sliding sideways. As it was, the three-metre-high wall remained remarkably stable. We had the strong impression that the builders of Seahenge had done this sort of thing many times before.

Finally there came one of the most important questions we hoped would be answered by the reconstruction: what did it feel like inside the circle? I can only say that it was profoundly moving and peaceful. Somehow the thick timbers excluded nearly all sound from outside. I was also strongly affected by the strong smell of freshly split oak wood. You could almost cut the tannin in the air. The cleft-oak interior harmonised with the de-barked tree trunk in an extraordinary way. It was as if this special enclosed space had truly been cleansed and purified, in a fashion which simply didn't apply on the outside. The outside of the circle was remarkable for the fact that it didn't stand out. It blended with the world around, as if it were camouflaged.

At the end of the reconstruction we stood around outside the circle, chatting and drinking mugs of tea; but inside, people talked less, and tended to walk around on their own. Perhaps the split between the public and private worlds we all inhabit applied here in a particularly strong sense. Whether or not the roots of the inverted tree ever held a corpse, I don't know. But something did seem to be missing. The tree was the focal point of the entire monument, yet it was empty. Maybe that was the effect the builders of the monument intended. We can't tell.

We now know that the site was constructed in a short time. I would go so far as to suggest that it represents a single event, and I am also confident that once the event was over, the circle ceased to retain its special 'magic'. I don't think this site was revisited subsequently. A final important point: I don't believe that the *particular* spot on what is today Holme beach was especially important in the Bronze Age. I suspect it was chosen because the group who built the circle controlled or had access to that area within the larger ritual landscape, and the precise spot was selected because it may have been slightly higher than the ground round about. Maybe there was some other reason – perhaps the presence of an oak seedling, or a gull's nest. We can only guess.

After filming the reconstruction, we were all tired and emotionally drained. It had been hard work. Graham Johnston and the film crew had asked some tricky questions and posed some difficult practical problems, but it had been well worth the effort. After the last day of filming, Graham dropped me off at Flag Fen. I felt I had to take another look at the great tree before I drove home in the drizzle that was starting to blow in from off the Wash.

The tree lay in its bath, the sprinkler jets playing gently on its surface. Finally I turned around and walked out of the Field Centre. The drizzle had turned to rain, and mist was forming in the dyke before me. I remember thinking about Hamon le Strange and his remarkable find as I looked across the much larger dyke that ran through the centre of Flag Fen. I found my gaze had focused on the clean orangey-yellow gravel foundations of the Fen Causeway Roman road at the point where it was cut through by the later dyke. That was the precise spot where in the late autumn of 1982 I had discovered a prehistoric religious site every bit as remarkable as John Lorimer's circle. And now the two had come together. Was it fate? I honestly don't know, but there are times when I think it was.

CHAPTER FOURTEEN

The Passage of Arms

THE LECTURE was not going well. I was tired after a long day's digging, and now the ancient extractor fan was making a persistent racket behind me. I knew that soon I'd lose my audience. I could hear the first dry coughs, and someone's shoes scratched noisily against the wooden floor. These were bad signs. In a few minutes everyone would be clearing their throats and the scratching of shoes would sound like a platoon of soldiers on parade. Suddenly the light went on. I breathed a sigh of relief. It was half-time.

Over a cup of tea I told the Society Secretary about how I had found the site. She was an attractive young woman, so it was not entirely impossible that I may have been showing off just a tiny bit. In any case, her eyes positively gleamed as I spoke. Then I had a brainwave: 'Why not repeat the story now, in the second half of the talk?' After all, she had enjoyed it and something fresh was urgently needed. Either that, or I'd lose my audience entirely. But first I had to look out a few extra slides from my reserves. I glanced across at the clock above the door. Five minutes to go. I'd better get a move on. As I held each slide up to the light, I could feel the adrenalin beginning to flow.

Soon it was time for me to resume the lecture. 'We've only a short time left, and you've been such a good audience,' I heard myself saying, 'that I thought I should take you into my confidence. Would any of you care to hear what it was like actually to find the site?'

There was a distinct, but restrained, murmur of approval, and one or two muffled calls of 'Yes, please.' One lady, her head starkly silhouetted against the glare of the projector's beam, stood up and loudly declared that she was 'all ears' – which in fact she was, or rather appeared to be. The meeting had at last come alive.

I started my story: 'It was a late November day in 1982. Some of you may remember that autumn. There were freezing fogs and all-day frosts . . .'

I sensed that the audience were now with me 100 per cent. I waited until the last murmurs had died down, and continued: 'We were following the draglines as they cleaned out the dykes. That morning it had been foggier than usual, and my ancient Land-Rover had refused to start. Damp in the distributor. Eventually I got it going and I drove the back way from Parson Drove, through Thorney, staying clear of the A47. Too many lunatic drivers for my taste.'

Draglines are pre-hydraulic mechanical excavators. In principle they work like cranes, with a bucket suspended on wires which is pulled towards the digger by a powerful winch. My audience, which included many fen farmers, knew these machines, and the places I mentioned, well.

'Anyhow, we felt our way gingerly from Dog-in-a-Doublet sluice and fetched up at the Padholme pumping station. It had rained hard that night, and the pumps were going flat out. My companion that day, Dave, was waiting for me there. Poor chap, he was soaked. He'd stood in the rain and drizzle for the best part of an hour waiting for my arrival, and he was not best pleased. He'd been kept waiting by my old Land-Rover several times before.

'In the distance, through the murk, we could occasionally hear the low throb of the dragline's engine. Every so often a chain clanked against the sides of the bucket as the machine swung across the dyke for another scoop of mud, reeds and slub. There was a strong stink of stagnant mire and rotting plants.

'In October 1981 I took our team to Holland and spent time walking along their dykes, trying to spot ancient remains that lay deeply buried beneath the thick layers of muck and peat. The more we learned about the way Dutch archaeologists made discoveries along their dykes, the more I became convinced that we could do the same here. So that's what we did. For five years we followed the big machines that cleaned out the dykes. When we looked carefully at the freshly-scraped dykesides we could spot the changes in colour that told us there was archaeology there.

'Now, I had always suspected that there must be something out there in the wet peats of Flag Fen. Three thousand years ago the area was a shallow marshy lake, especially in wet winters, but in summertime it would have been dry enough for grass to grow, and you must imagine the countryside covered with hundreds of cattle and small brown sheep. Around the edges of Flag Fen, at Fengate, the land rose gently. In the Bronze Age this was flood-free pasture, divided up into hedged and ditched trackways and paddocks, with round farmhouses dotted amongst the fields.'

My next slide showed a freshly-cleaned-out dyke, with the dragline in the distance. The different layers on the dykesides were clear in the low sunlight of late autumn. I pointed to a band of bright-orange gravel that lay directly above the dark, motionless water at the bottom of the dyke.

'This gravel was laid down in the Ice Age, perhaps a hundred thousand years ago. Above it there's a pale grey line about nine inches thick. That's the topsoil which started to form after the Ice Age, some ten thousand years ago. Then above the old soil you can see a thick band of black peat which continues right up to the surface. That peat formed in the Bronze Age, three to four thousand years ago, when Flag Fen was first flooded.'

I sensed I should now quicken the pace. The next slide showed a view of the dyke taken from the air a year after the previous one. The plane was about five hundred feet up and was banking steeply when the shot was taken. You could clearly see the paler dryland at either side of Flag Fen where the black peaty fields formed a dark, brooding mass that obscured everything below the surface. A large drainage dyke cut a diagonal swathe through the peat. My cane pointer whacked the screen rather too firmly: 'There's the dyke, and there – that spot there is where we made our big discovery.'

I took a sip of water and changed the slide to another view of the dyke, but taken from the field surface and looking slightly down and along it. With the eye of faith you could just discern the dragline in the distance. In the foreground the lip of the dyke was thickly spattered with a mess of mud and reeds, dumped there by the dragline.

'The surface of the brink' – I used the Fenland term – 'was horrible, a mess of slub and muck; but there was nowhere else to walk, so we had to wade through it. Several times it came over the tops of our boots. As I picked my way through the muck along the brink I thought I must be mad to be there at all. I nearly turned back, but I knew that in another hundred yards or so we'd find the spot where a Roman road, known as the Fen Causeway, had been cut through by the drainage dyke when it was first dug in the early Middle Ages.'

The next slide was a close-up of the road where it was cut by the dyke. It was a typical archaeological record photograph, and largely devoid of human interest. It showed a great dump of orange gravel in the dykeside, a tape measure for scale, and little else.

'The road was built in the years AD 60 and 61. Roman army engineers simply dumped thousands of tons of gravel onto the peat. Sometimes they laid down bundles of brushwood as a firm bed, but not here – presumably because the peat was already pretty hard. Most of the actual work would have been done by local people, unpaid. Slavery, in other words.

'We spent a couple of hours measuring and drawing the exposed cross-section through the road, and we also took a series of photos for our project archives, such as this one. Then it began to get colder and the fog started to thicken. I looked at my watch; it was dinnertime. We'd both had enough, and Dave was beginning to look pinched and cold. So we repacked the mass of kit we have to carry with us on these jobs – cameras, surveying equipment, a spade, trowels, sample bags, notebooks and a small drawing-board – and started to trudge back the way we had come.

'Dave was walking in front, and I can remember laughing as once or twice he nearly lost his foothold in the deep muck. Then I almost tripped over myself, which of course was less amusing. In fact I nearly fell flat. My left foot had caught against something hard, but rounded, and deep in the mud. I prodded it gingerly with the toe of my boot. It felt like a log. Then I did something I still can't explain. I laid my various cameras and things to one side, hung my coat on a surveyor's pole, rolled up my sleeves and plunged both hands into the cold, clammy mud at my feet. My fingers soon confirmed that my guess had been correct. It was indeed a log. I could distinctly feel pieces of bark along one edge. Then I pulled it from the mud.'

At that the slide changed to show a log of about six inches diameter, split cleanly along one side.

'I held it at arm's length, as it was wet and dripping with mud. At first glance it appeared to be an ordinary log, but it was much heavier than normal, and it felt slightly spongy to the touch. I slithered down the dykeside and washed it as best I could in the water, which in the sunless air at the bottom of the dyke was starting to freeze. Long, pointed ice crystals were forming on the surface. I don't remember having cold hands, although they must have been perishing. But I was too fascinated by what I was doing to care. Once the wood was cleaned, I looked at it closely. I saw that it had been split across the grain in a unusual way.

'Now, you can tell a lot from a bit of wood. Technically speaking, this type of parallel-sided split is known as tangential, and I recognised it at once. I've split a few trees, and I can tell you that tangentials are difficult to do, and require large, slow-grown trees and good-quality wood, with few if any knots. These were the sort of trees that gradually disappeared as the primeval forests were cleared. That's why tangentially split timbers are often pre-Roman.

'I clambered back to the top of the dyke, where I could stand without danger of slipping back into the water. I then carefully broke a piece off one end of the log, and was amazed at how soft it was. It had none of the strength of "real" wood. This meant it had been lying waterlogged for a very long time indeed. The structure of the wood on the freshly-broken face was clear. I could see every growth ring, and there could be no doubt: it was oak, and slow-grown oak at that. I looked around me. There wasn't a tree in sight, let alone an oak tree – and besides, oak trees won't grow in wet ground. Wherever that piece of split oak had grown, it wasn't Flag Fen. And it certainly hadn't been dropped there recently, either.

'I looked back into the dyke. This length of it had been cut through the deepest part of Flag Fen, which is why it's so big. It's also why the upper eight feet of the dykeside hadn't been touched by the machine, which only cleared out the bottom. As I looked down, my footmarks in the tufty grass were clear, but I also thought I saw small lumps of dark brown wood, where my boots had cut into the wet turf. That was odd. I clambered back in to have a closer look. I was right. They were indeed small bits of wood, but they were very decayed.

'I was examining one of these fragments closely when the tuft of grass I was using as a foothold suddenly broke away and I fell flat on my face against the side of the ditch. I frantically stabbed my trowel into the bank to stop my rapid slide, but it was no use. I flailed about, but could only find soft peat. It was like slipping down a playground slide. I could do nothing to stop my fall. Just as I was about to slide into the freezing water, which I knew to be at least six feet deep, my foot caught against something hard. The sliding stopped, and I breathed a huge sigh of relief. I was saved. I shouted out to Dave, but there was no response. He was far ahead by now, intent on reaching shelter and a flask of warm tea. I couldn't blame him.

'At first I didn't look at what it was that had stopped my fall. That could wait. Instead, I chopped away at the dykeside with my trowel for all I was worth. Soon I had cut a secure ledge in a layer of clay which capped the gravel just above the waterline. I moved both my feet to the new step, and was able to relax for a moment. Then, almost as an afterthought, I crouched down and groped below me for the thing which had saved me from a cold soaking. It felt like the stump of a post, but it was soft and round, not at all like the sawn posts the drainage boards use to shore up unstable dykesides. I felt around to loosen it, and after a few sharp tugs it came free.'

The screen showed the tip of an oak post, of about four inches diameter. The wood was dark brown and the pencil-like tip had been sharpened with an axe.

'It wasn't as clean as this when I pulled it from the ground, so I dipped it in the water and rubbed it gently with my fingers. One or two of the axe-marks were almost complete, and I could see that the axe used had been narrow, with a blade width of perhaps two inches. The blade was also curved, as the marks on the wood felt slightly hollow or spoon-shaped – quite unlike the straight, flat marks left by a modern axe.

'Standing on my secure new shelf, I started to clean away the muck and mud from the dykeside. If the post was indeed pre-Roman, as I was beginning to suspect, then I should find evidence for horizontal wood as well. Only horizontal wood – in other words wood laid down to make a path or trackway of some sort – would be able to provide me with a reliable level for the structure. I had to have a level if I was to guess at its age. After all, the tip of the post could have been driven down to any depth.

'I'd only been working from my ledge for about ten minutes when my trowel struck some horizontal twigs, and then some larger roundwood, about the diameter of my arm. It was dried-out from having been exposed to the air on the dykeside for several years, but it was quite recognisable as wood. I crouched down so that my eye was level with it, and sighted back along the dyke to the Roman road, which clearly stood out as an orange streak against the peat. I'll never forget that instant. Every nerve tingled as I realised that the twigs and roundwood I had just found lay at a level of about three feet *below the bottom* of the Roman road. That meant the twigs had to be *much* earlier than the road, which was built around AD 60. I leant back against the dykeside and tried to remain calm. After all, one post and some horizontal wood isn't exactly the *Mary Rose*. But even so . . .

'The next thing I knew was that my trowel had struck another post. I could see immediately it was oak. That was it. I was convinced I had found an ancient site – but little did I realise how important it would turn out to be. I'd been so intent on my work that I hadn't noticed how the fog had built up, and I knew it wouldn't be long before darkness fell. But I also knew I had to have a record, so I took this slide.'

A stranger walking in from the street would have found it difficult to understand the scene before him. A packed roomful of people were sitting in total silence, staring at the strangest of images with rapt attention. On the screen was a muddy dykeside complete with rank, tufty grass and rotting vegetation. At the bottom of the picture was the short stub of a post, with traces of another alongside it. In the centre of the frame there were some dried-up sticks which protruded horizontally, straight at the camera. At the top was the dirty red-and-white surveyor's ranging pole on which hung my grubby ex-NATO army coat. It could have been a view of a trench somewhere in Flanders, 1916.

My original intention as I took the photo had been to include the

Roman road in the background, but the descending fog had not left me sufficient light for the depth of field needed. Instead, the picture acquired a surreal, still-life quality. A frozen moment in time. Whenever I showed that particular slide I was transported back to that extraordinary moment in my life. Now, even with an audience waiting for my next words, I reflected on the way a still image can capture the sprit of a time and place so clearly. Then the rattle and hum of the accursed extractor fan brought me back to reality. The slide required explanation. In all the many lectures I've given, I have never enjoyed talking about this slide – perhaps it's *too* personal to me – so I was brief: 'There's the horizontal wood, at the centre. Down there are the two posts. I left the ranging pole in place as a marker when I eventually went home.'* The next slide was of Flag Fen in the winter. Actually it was taken a year before the discovery of the site, but nobody needed to know that. I pressed on: 'That evening and the following day it snowed long and hard, and we were unable to return to the dykeside for two or three days. I was bursting to get back, but had to cool my heels in the office. You can imagine how I felt. People kept well out of my way. When the weather improved I returned, this time with the rest of the team. In all, there were six of us, and we'd decided in advance that the only way to proceed was to take drastic action – which is precisely what we did. When we arrived back at that surveyor's pole I'd left as a marker, we fanned out along the dykeside on either side of it. We left about five paces between us – to give us room – and then we set to with a will. The first thing we did was to extend the small step I had cut just above the water-line.'

In the next slide, shrouded figures could be seen crouched along a two-foot-wide step immediately above the water, prodding the dykeside with trowels.

'Soon, despite the chill of the day, coats came off and sleeves were rolled to the elbow. We had hardly started actually looking for wood when I heard a muffled curse from someone about twenty yards from the spot where I'd made the first discovery. One of my team members, Charly French, was standing on the newly-cut step shaking his hand.

---

* On my birthday in January 2000 we had a devastating fire at Flag Fen, and I lost thousands of slides – including this one.

He'd jarred his wrist. I hurried along the step to where he was digging. The hard thing he'd hit with his spade was a large horizontal oak plank. It had a dense, black centre but the outside was soft. I knew at once that it was ancient. Then I looked at the twenty yards between where I was now standing with Charly and where I had made the initial discovery. It was a long way. Far too wide for a trackway – but was it necessarily part of the same site? Maybe there were two?

'As if to answer my question, our animal-bones specialist, Miranda, who had insisted she be liberated from her laboratory to do some digging for a change, suddenly let out a joyful whoop. Although we knew we shouldn't, we all ran across to see what she'd found. She was working about ten yards from my original findspot, midway between it and where I now stood. Like everyone else, I was soon by her side.'

The next slide was taken two days later, and though I say so myself, it was a good one. The step along the waterline had been enlarged by trampled-in peat removed from around the ancient timbers above it. In the middle of the screen was a large oak plank with a square hole cut through. A wooden peg could just be seen passing through the hole, securely fastening the plank to the ground. There was wood everywhere, much of it finely split oak. I pointed to the peg in the mortice hole.

'That peg is very important, because it proves beyond doubt that the plank through which it has been driven is in its original position. In other words, it hasn't fallen into the peat from a higher level – from the superstructure of a raised trestle walkway, for example. If people were indeed walking along those timbers, then that' – my cane prodded the screen – 'is where their feet would have been.'

One particular oak log dominated the slide. It had been partially dressed square and lay about two yards away from the pegged plank. This was the timber our bones specialist had found. I continued:

'Miranda was kneeling beside a large piece of oak and was gently removing peat with her bare fingers. She had already revealed two half-inch-long, slightly curved cuts in the surface of the log. We all watched as she deftly removed more peat. Soon we could see that the cuts were the marks left by two chisels that had been driven hard and vertically into the wood. Alongside were more chisel marks, in line with the first two. Close to the end of the log she revealed four much larger marks, undoubtedly left by axes.

'It was now obvious what we were looking at. This oak log had been used by a Bronze Age carpenter as a temporary workbench on which he had securely "parked" his expensive metal tools to prevent them slipping into the muddy water. To my knowledge this was the first direct evidence anywhere in Europe for the size and composition of a working prehistoric carpenter's tool-kit.

'On that first day we concentrated on the central twenty yards of dykeside. After lunch we set our heavy tools to one side and knelt on the step with trowels. As we worked we could see the outlines of numerous timbers slowly beginning to appear. At first they were indistinct, almost ghost-like, as they were still partially shrouded in reed roots, grass and decaying vegetation. It was difficult to avoid damage as we gingerly pulled wiry living roots from off or out of the much softer ancient wood. Only the largest oak timbers were hard. All the others were much softer, and broke off if we pulled on a root too hard.'

The final slide was a more distant view of the dyke. Figures could be seen on the step just above the water, and a small fibreglass boat was tethered to a spade driven deep into the dykeside. Someone was carrying a large bundle of shiny plastic bags, each containing a piece of ancient wood, towards the boat, which was already partly filled.

'I don't suppose I will ever live through another three weeks like that again. Everywhere we looked we found wood, but the posts I had first stumbled across were confined within a narrow band, about ten yards wide. When I returned home in the evenings I found it almost impossible to sleep. All I could think about – all I could dream about when I did manage to nod off – was prehistoric wood. By the time we'd finished, we had exposed some five hundred timbers, and the step we worked from was almost a hundred yards long. The site was truly *massive*, but what on earth was it for?

'We knew its approximate age, which was soon confirmed by a radiocarbon date that the British Museum rushed through for us. This told us that the timbers were at least three thousand years old – but that was all we could say. We had hundreds and hundreds of timbers, although we hadn't the faintest idea why they had been floated or carried out into Flag Fen in the Late Bronze Age. But we did know from the single small peg holding that plank in position that the timbers were still in place. It also meant that, whatever its purpose, the timber structure had been built deliberately. It wasn't just a haphazard pile of driftwood that had been washed there from somewhere upstream.'

I turned on the main lights in the room and switched off the projector. I was dazzled for a moment, as was my audience, and people were rubbing their eyes. I wrapped the evening up: 'So we're back to where we started, and you know the rest of the story. Well, that was how we found the site – and I hope it made sense. Thank you all very much for inviting me along. Good night.'

The summer and early autumn after the original discovery we returned to the dykeside, and in the drier, less frantic conditions we observed a thin layer of sand and gravel lying amongst the timbers. We thought this sandy layer had been spread on the wet wood to prevent people slipping over. In other words, the wood was a floor. This idea was soon confirmed when we also found fragments of Bronze Age pottery and animal bones. We assumed, as one would on a dry site, that these sherds and bones were rubbish that had accumulated on a kitchen floor. So the posts were the walls of a large, but otherwise straightforward, house or dwelling.

That theory didn't last long. It was comprehensively refuted when Dr Mark Robinson from Oxford University Museum produced the results of his study of the Flag Fen beetles. We had sent Mark samples taken from the sandy 'floor' layer, and had expected him to find evidence (i.e. small fragments of dead insects) for the species of beetles that are known to have lived in the roofs of wooden houses. Woodworm – a beetle despite its name – was the obvious candidate. But there was nothing. In fact Mark was convinced that the 'floor' was not a house floor at all.

The next blow to the house theory came from another scientist who examined samples taken from the sandy 'floor'. This time it was a specialist whose subject was rather less savoury. Dr Andrew, or 'Bone', Jones, of the York Archaeological Trust, specialises in the microscopic analysis of dung, or faeces. The floors of Viking-period houses at York contained, among other things, large numbers of human parasite eggs, which derived from faeces. We expected to find something similar at Flag Fen – but again, there were none. Bone too was convinced that the 'floor' was not the scene of domestic life.

What was going on? We began to get hints at the truth about three years after the site's discovery, when we found that the fragments of pottery we were slowly accumulating from the sandy layer could actually be mended together to form near-complete vessels. This was strange, as pottery from house floors only rarely mends together, because most of it either gets cleared up and thrown out with the rubbish or is ground to powder by people's feet.

The year we mended the pottery, 1985, was also the year we discovered several large fragments of beautifully-made shale bracelets. These too came from the sandy 'floor'. Shale looks like shiny coal when polished, and in the Bronze Age was mainly traded around southern England from quarries on the south Dorset coast. It must always have been an expensive, luxury item, and it was unusual, to say the least, to find fragments of shale bracelets lying on the 'floor'. Then we found part of a bronze dagger. Now that really would have been out of place on a household floor. We were forced to abandon the domestic idea, but we had no credible alternative to put in its place. Subsequent years revealed further non-domestic objects.

In 1988 we found more bronze weapons and an almost complete shale bracelet in two halves. It appeared to have been deliberately smashed. Slowly it dawned on me – and I have to admit I was not the quickest to make this intuitive leap – that we were digging up the remains of ancient ceremonies. The pots had first been smashed and then dropped in the water, as had the shale bracelets and most of the bronzes.

The next unexpected discovery was made by Paul Halstead, a bone specialist at Sheffield University. Some of the animal bones we had found on the 'floor' and amongst the timbers were from cuts of beef, mutton and lamb. These bones were probably the residue of meals or feasts, but for every meat bone, many more were from dogs – and these quite clearly had not been eaten. It looked as if man's best friend was being sacrificed or offered to the waters. The Flag Fen dogs, Paul Halstead told us, were larger than the Bronze Age norm, which was collie-sized. Ours were a bit smaller than a labrador, but not much. I have held a dog jawbone from Flag Fen up to my black labrador Major's great white teeth, and can vouch that Paul Halstead was quite right.

Then, in 1989, all the pieces fell into place. Almost half a mile west of the spot in the middle of Flag Fen where I had first tripped on the piece of wood in 1982, the New Town authorities had decided to construct a brand-new power station. It would be huge, and built on the edge of the fen in Fengate, in an area I hadn't been able to examine in the 1970s. We carried out an excavation ahead of its construction and revealed that the place where it was to be built was the site of some two thousand Bronze Age oak posts. They were laid out in a narrow band or row, about seven metres wide, and ran out into Flag Fen and straight towards the spot on the dyke where I had made the initial discovery.

We now know that the posts form both a wall and a wide pathway, which was liberally dusted with sand and gravel. It ran across Flag Fen to dry ground on either side, and was over a kilometre long. We have been able to date it precisely, using tree-ring dates, and know that it was built and maintained in use between 1300 and 924 BC.

The tree-ring dates showed that the timbers at Flag Fen lasted for some four centuries – roughly the span of time between us and Shakespeare. Given such longevity, it stands to reason that there must have been more to Flag Fen than just a pathway or maybe a wall across the wetland. After all, how does one explain the complete pots, the dog bones, the shale bracelets and the bronze weapons? There was far more to Flag Fen than mere objects, but ironically it was these objects – and there were some fine things among them – which were to lead me to that conclusion.

My second breakthrough was not a discovery at all. I had asked the members of the local metal-detecting club to come and run their machines around the newly exposed posts on the power-station site. At the time this invitation caused a few raised eyebrows in the archaeological world, where metal-detectorists were extremely unpopular. The dozen or so club members arrived on a Sunday morning in early summer. The birds were singing, and it was a gorgeous day. I showed them around the site, then introduced them to the student archaeologists who would be listing, bagging up and mapping any finds they might make.

Being English, we didn't start work immediately. Instead, we had mugs of tea and biscuits. While we sipped I chatted to the club members. I already knew Terry, a keen local amateur archaeologist and regular visitor to the Flag Fen dig. Sadly, Terry is no longer with us, and he was actually in the early stages of his terminal illness then, although he did not know it. He had moved to Peterborough from south London, and at the time of the club visit he worked at the big Perkins diesel engines factory, whose vast rumbling and brooding presence still dominates eastern Peterborough. Terry was always joking, and I rarely saw him down in the mouth, even when shortly afterwards he learned the truth about his health. He was one of those people who could drink a scalding-hot mug of tea as if it were orange juice. That morning he set his mug down a full five minutes before anyone else. He was raring to go, and had already assembled his detector.

He plucked the permanent cigarette from his lips and ground it under his heel. 'Mustn't contaminate the radiocarbon,' he said, knowing full well that it takes more than a bit of cigarette ash to do any damage – but no smoking on site was a rule with me, nonetheless.

I stood well back while he adjusted the controls of his machine. Like an idiot, and without thinking, I had put on my usual steel-toecapped safety boots that morning, although I knew the effect they had on machines as sensitive as Terry's. Everyone was watching. Terry was a bit of a performer, and he made the most of his moment.

'Well, Francis,' he called, as he finished tuning his instrument, 'what d'you want?'

I paused to think. He made a few suggestions: 'King John's treasure, the Crown Jewels – what d'you want?'

For reasons I still can't fathom, I replied: 'A sword, Terry. A large, leaf-shaped Late Bronze Age sword.'

With a grin and a huge thumbs-up, Terry set to work. He walked away from us, his body upright and his right arm, which held the detector, swinging evenly from side to side. His head was turned slightly to one side as he concentrated on the faint sounds from his headphones. I knew he was good at it, and that I was useless at it, as

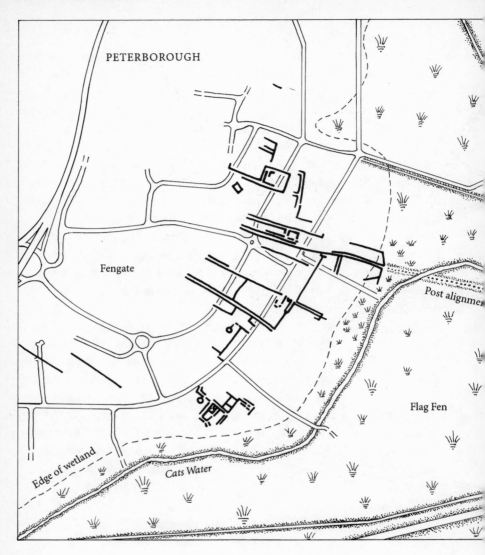

FIG 28   *Fengate and Flag Fen basin, showing the course of the Bronze Age post alignment and timber platform*

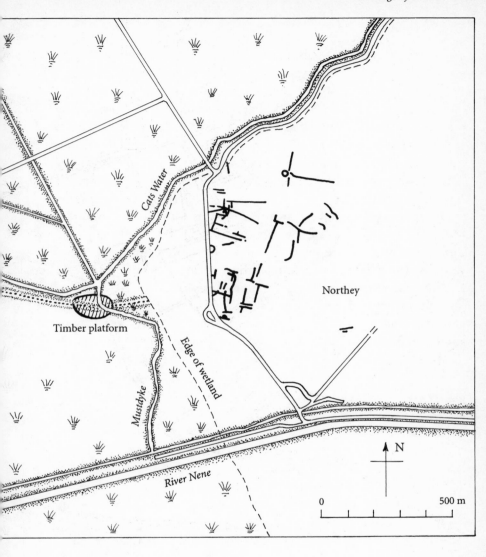

Cats Water

Timber platform

Mustdyke

Edge of wetland

Northey

River Nene

N

0   500 m

were most of my crew. Detecting is a skill which comes naturally to some people, and Terry was one of the best.

I wandered back to rejoin the main group, who were now beginning to assemble their detectors. I made sure the students had everything they needed – clipboards, paper, pens, tapes, etc. – then started to assemble the surveyor's level that we would use to record the precise height and location of each find. At this point came the second moment of discovery in the Flag Fen story.

I was fiddling with the level's fine adjustment, and was having trouble getting the bubble in the spirit-level to centre-up properly, when there was a yell from Terry. To my surprise his shout came from quite far away. I looked up, and there was a brief bleary moment as my eyes changed focus from the instrument in front of me to the small gesticulating figure in the distance. Terry was jumping up and down; he had plainly found something exciting. I was desperate to join him, but my professional discipline was just strong enough to ensure that I finished setting up the level. That done, I could contain myself no longer, and I hared across the site to Terry, a few steps behind everyone else. The small crowd parted and let me through. In his excitement Terry had re-lit the back-up cigarette that lived behind his ear, and there was a strong, sweet smell of his favourite tobacco, Old Holborn. I knelt down on the ground beside him. His right hand grasped the detector by the shaft a few inches above the detector-head, while his left gently sifted a loose patch of soil. Every so often he would stop stroking the soil and pass the detector over the spot a few times, listening intently to his headset as he did so. Through his headphones, we could all hear the strong signal he was receiving.

'Sounds good, Tel,' another south London voice said from the back of the crowd.

Terry just nodded, and his fingers continued their delicate work. For such a large man he was very gentle. There was definitely something there. And then I saw it: the slightest hint of a green stain in the earth below his fingers.

I grasped his arm.

'Steady, Terry.'

He needed no urging from me. His hand now parted the soil as if he were wielding a feather duster. As I watched, I can remember being aware that I was holding my breath, thinking as I did so that I was being ridiculous. A few breaths more or less would hardly affect Terry's work.

Slowly the green stain turned into something flat and pointed. My mind raced through a catalogue of possible artefacts: could it be a razor? Or a knife? A spearhead? No, it lacked the median rib. Could it be a dagger? No, it was too long . . .

Terry's hand worked gradually back towards where I was kneeling, and then the speculation was over. Only one thing could be that long, flat and weighted towards the tip. It was now obvious: Terry had found a Late Bronze Age leaf-shaped sword. After about an hour we had it out of the ground. It was superb: almost a metre long. We were exultant. No angler had ever landed so prized a fish.

Leaf-shaped swords were intended for slashing, like a cutlass or scimitar, and as has been noted, it is generally believed that they arrived in Britain with the advent of riding. This one was so well-preserved that I was able to place it within a specific group of such swords, named after the Fenland village of Wilburton and made shortly after 1000 BC. The date was important, because it meant that the sword and the posts were in use at precisely the same time.

I cannot remember what else we found that day, but the score was about fifty items, including at least one more sword. After another four or five weekends we had found well over three hundred bronzes. This splendid collection included four complete swords, three rapiers and two daggers, not to mention part of a bronze shield and several spearheads, scabbard tips and ornamental pins. I believe it's still the largest collection of prehistoric metalwork from a British Bronze Age excavation.

The bronzes were found amongst the posts and to one side of them only, on the southern or landward side. Beyond the posts, in other words towards the open fen, we found nothing other than several dogs' bodies and a badly decayed human skeleton. This one-sided distribution suggested to us that the posts had formed a barrier – perhaps even a defensive barrier – across the only access into Flag Fen from the open watery landscape to the east. So the metalwork had been placed on the defended side of the posts, on the 'safe' side, as it were.

Many of the bronzes had been deliberately smashed before being dropped in the shallow waters, and some of the weapons had broken along flaws or planes of weakness in the original castings. Put another way, they had failed quality control, and could not possibly have been used in battle. But why were they not simply melted down and reused as scrap metal? Why throw them away in such an extravagant fashion?

These are the questions which automatically occur to a rational, modern-day Westerner who sees bronze as a valuable commodity to be preserved at all costs. Perhaps attitudes in the Bronze Age were different. Perhaps the sword found by Terry was cast for a particular warrior, and had been given a name and acquired a personality – like the famous Arthurian sword, Excalibur. A weapon of such importance could not just be discarded and treated as scrap. No, it had to be given a send-off appropriate to a living, named person. Perhaps it was thrown into a lake by a Bronze Age Bedevere. But was it then caught by a slender hand as it entered the water? If you believe in magic, then perhaps.

But I believe this image to be misleading, so far as Flag Fen is concerned. The Arthurian gestures are grand. In my mind's eye I see Excalibur flashing high into the sky before describing a graceful arc into the welcoming waters and the hand of the Lady of the Lake. Such a magnificent gesture could have been seen by hundreds of cheering – or alternatively, awe-inspired – people. But the archaeological evidence suggests that the scale at Flag Fen was altogether different.

There were many examples to indicate this, but one sticks in my mind. At one point the detectors picked up the signal of something dagger-sized, and I decided to excavate it myself. About three inches below the surface of the grey prehistoric soil into which the Bronze Age posts had been driven, I came across a Late Bronze Age dagger with a distinctive tongue, or tang, which fitted within the hilt. After a couple of hours' work I gingerly removed it from the ground and set it to one side. As I looked into the small hole left by the blade, the grey soil seemed rather peculiar – in retrospect I can't say why, but it did. I gently worked at it with my bare fingers, and found it hard, smooth and strangely knobbly. It took a moment or two before I realised that the 'soil' wasn't soil at all, but a large piece of antler. A few moments later it was in my hand, and I found myself holding the hilt of the dagger. Inside the socket for the tang of the dagger were two slender wooden wedges, which had once secured the blade to the hilt.

Everything about this find suggested that the rites conducted on the site were small-scale, even intimate. To pull the hilt off a dagger so gently that the wedges remain in place is one thing. But then to place both in the same small scoop in the ground is such a modest gesture that it could only have been intended to be seen by a handful of people. In some instances the 'offerings' placed in the waters around the Flag Fen posts were so intimate that I wonder whether the act was ever seen by an audience at all. They were gestures made by individual people, for themselves.

We have seen evidence of such rites in the small, filled-in individual pits at Etton, the tiny micro-henges at Fengate or the beautiful polished flint axe from the complex henge-like site at Maxey. All of these were spots where private or family-centred rites took place. And that is what I believe was happening out there in the watery world of Flag Fen. Again, it was remote, secluded, cut-off; and in every respect it was *liminal*.

In archaeology it's often difficult to prove precisely when events, such as regular communal gatherings, took place. This was well illustrated at Silbury Hill, where the presence of flying ants was an unreliable indicator that the great mound was necessarily erected in the summer. At Seahenge, which I believe was probably a short-lived shrine, the evidence of the tree-rings is quite convincing: it was built, and the ceremonies probably took place, in the late spring or early summer. At Flag Fen, some of the timbers were felled in the late autumn, but the site was by no means a one-off – it was physically maintained for at least four centuries. So there is no reason to suppose that the building and repair of the structure took place at the same time as the meetings and ceremonies. We have, therefore, to determine a possible time of year by using more indirect arguments. My own view, being a livestock farmer myself, is that the farmers at Flag Fen, who depended on sheep and cattle for their livelihoods, must have had fixed annual meetings. New bloodlines would have to be introduced to their flocks and herds at regular intervals. The best time for such an event is in the autumn, before any pre-winter cull takes place and when grazing is still plentiful and animals are looking at their best. At this time of year crops would have been harvested and water levels in fen and river would be low – making travel to and from the gatherings simpler. As we have seen, in many tribal societies autumn was the favoured time of year for rustling, because people had the time and leisure to do it.

At Etton I suggested that the private, family and personal rites took place when communities came together for larger public cere- monies which involved feasting, meeting people, exchanging livestock and generally having a good time. Did this happen at Flag Fen, too? I think it did, but by now the public and private aspects of the regular communal meetings took place in separate spots. Yet at the same time they were physically connected. I think this paradox was deliberate. It may have been a symbolic expression of tension; for there is always tension between the public and the private sides of our lives.

I was forcibly struck by this tension in September 1997, as I watched the television pictures of the progress of Diana, Princess of Wales's hearse through the Northamptonshire countryside towards her burial- place at Althorp. I knew the roads well, but found it hard to identify with them when they were emptied of all traffic. The hearse and the police outriders looked like visitors from another world – which of course they were. They were from the capital, the centre of things, the world of influence, power and authority, and they looked out of place in the county of spires and squires. Finally they drew up at the iron gates of Althorp, which swung open and closed behind them. And we, the billions who viewed these events through the eyes of television, were excluded. The royal princess had become a private person – Diana Spencer, a Northamptonshire lady. I felt the tension expressed by the iron gates and the flowers laid in the road outside by the mourners. The feeling of exclusion was extraordinary, but it was also personal. I became acutely aware that one could have seen something similar acted out, albeit on a much smaller stage, at Etton, Maxey, Seahenge or Flag Fen.

I mentioned that the private and public worlds at Flag Fen were physically connected. This connection was made by a double-ditched droveway – one of our earliest discoveries at Fengate. It ran 'inland' from the point where the great rows of posts reached dry land. After about three hundred metres it entered an area of elaborate ditched stockyards and subsidiary droveways, which I have interpreted as 'community stockyards' – the modern equivalent would be a livestock market. It was here that the large autumnal meetings might have taken place. I can imagine small groups of people detaching themselves from the milling crowds to walk out along the timber walkway, deep into the mists of Flag Fen, where some recently deceased relative would be commemorated by members of his or her family in a simple private ceremony.

One of the most striking aspects of Flag Fen is its longevity. It was first constructed just two centuries after the death of King Tutankhamun, during the latter part of the Middle Bronze Age, and the last 'offering' was made to the waters during the lifetime of Christ. That's a span of thirteen hundred years. As we have seen, certain fundamental ritualistic themes persisted over a very long time indeed: a couple of examples are the use of querns to symbolise family life, and the breaking of valuable items such as polished stone axes or bronze daggers. French anthropologists have termed this the *longue durée*, and a feature of it is transformation and change. The basic idea may remain essentially the same, but it finds expression in a variety of different guises. It is persistent because it serves a social purpose that people cannot do without. Of course, archaeologists have to be careful. It is one thing to suggest that querns stand for family life, but it is quite another to suggest that the legends behind King Arthur originate in the Bronze Age. Having said that, I believe they do. I'll give one example that some might think outrageous.

The drawing of the sword from the stone is one of the most evocative images in the Arthurian legend. Iron Age, Roman and medieval swords were beaten out from bars or rods by a swordsmith. Bronze swords, on the other hand, are cast in a two-piece clay mould which is fired to the consistency of pottery and then broken open when cold. In effect, a sword within a stone.

The actual timber structure at Flag Fen only lasted until 924 BC, when the builders gave up the unequal struggle against the gradual but inexorable rise of Fen water-levels. But that didn't mean that people then turned their attentions elsewhere. Far from it. As at many religious sites, the tradition of sanctity lingered on. I was also struck by the persistence of certain rites, century after century. This ritual consistency argues a degree of conservatism, and I would imagine that the dress and the language deemed appropriate for the rites may deliberately have harked back to earlier times, as we still find, for example, in the Church of England.

I have mentioned that the rites at Flag Fen generally appear to have been small in scale, and this continued throughout the life of the site. There was also an emphasis on particular types of objects as offerings to the waters: weapons, such as swords, daggers and spears were frequently used, as were ornaments. Tools were rarely parted with – with the exception of metal-workers' implements, which occurred quite regularly.

Technologically, the weapons changed through time. In the Middle Bronze Age we find light thrusting weapons, such as dirks and rapiers. During the Late Bronze Age slashing leaf-shaped swords appear, and in the Iron Age swords become longer and more versatile – and, of course, are made from iron. But ritually they were all treated in much the same way. When found, the blades are usually bent or broken. The rivets that attached the hilts to the blades are often bent or missing, and close examination of the cutting edges of the slashing swords of the Late Bronze Age shows them to have been smashed against stones or rocks. Ornaments were mistreated too. One fine Iron Age brooch we found, for example, had its securing safety-pin-style clip twisted round several times. Stick pins – the nearest modern equivalent are Victorian hatpins – are invariably found bent or broken.

One could explain this deliberate destruction in simple, practical terms. Breaking a sword or defacing an ornament would prevent someone else from coming along later and stealing it for themselves. But I'm not at all convinced by this. For a start, the objects themselves were not as valuable as the metal they were made from. Bronze was a rare and valuable commodity in the second millennium BC, and it's a metal that can be melted down relatively easily. So a few snapped blades or twisted pins would not have deterred scrap-metal thieves.

It seems to me that the deliberate destruction at Flag Fen is similar to that of the polished stone axes and saddle querns at Etton, two thousand years previously. Essentially these things were being taken out of circulation in this world, thereby being transformed into functioning objects in the world of the ancestors. It would have been viewed as a process of transformation, rather than destruction. And anyone who dared risk the wrath of the ancestors by removing the objects from Flag Fen or Etton would know what was coming to them, which is why nothing was taken.

The respect with which society seems to have treated these valuable objects offered to the waters is informative. It contrasts, for example, with the elaborate measures ancient Egyptian kings and queens were forced to adopt in their vain attempts to baffle the tomb-robbers of the time, and suggests that the religious views of the rich and powerful in Bronze Age Britain – the sort of people who possessed swords and elaborate brooches – were also held by the population at large. If this were not the case, I doubt whether the waters of Flag Fen would have yielded such a plentiful harvest of ancient metalwork.

But why did people continue to place their offerings in the waters around the posts long, long after the posts themselves had become mere rotted stumps? I think the answer lies in the deliberate conservatism of the rites. The transition from the second millennium to the first millennium BC – in other words, the centuries around the end of the Bronze Age and the beginnings of the Iron Age – was a time of great social and environmental change. I believe that generally speaking the social changes were more important than the environmental ones, but in the Fens rising water levels were a force that simply could not be discounted.

The main effect of wetter conditions underfoot was to undermine the basis of the local livestock-based economy. Animals could no longer be driven out into the lush fen pastures every summer. Speaking as a sheep farmer myself, I think that as soon as the summer pastures became *unreliably* available, alarm bells would have sounded. I can imagine what the livestock farmers of the time must have thought as the dry fen-edge pastures were grazed flat by hundreds of rapidly growing lambs, while the nearby Fens remained obstinately flooded. They would have been appalled. Wetter conditions would also have caused animal health problems such as foot rot and liver fluke. So how did they respond?

Like their modern counterparts, they were forced to diversify. They switched from a largely livestock-based system to a mixed system involving sheep, cattle, pigs and cereals (wheat, barley and oats). By the Late Bronze Age we also see the introduction of a much-improved new species of wheat known as spelt, or *Triticum spelta*. This new style of farming required new field systems and a new pattern of settlement in which people grouped together in small hamlets and villages – perhaps, among other things, to provide continuous protection for stored crops. The new pattern of living was just one of the factors which led to the growth of a distinctive style of Iron Age life, which Roman authors labelled Celtic.

It has been suggested that the Celts were a separate culture with a distinctive, lively style of art who came to Britain and Atlantic Europe from Central Europe. This idea has recently been challenged by a number of archaeologists on various grounds, including art-historical and linguistic. Looking at the question from a lifetime's study of one small region, I can also find no evidence to suggest that the Celts moved to Britain from Continental Europe. I am quite convinced that ethnically they were the same people who had always lived in Britain and northern Europe.

The strongest argument for continuity is provided by Flag Fen itself. That extraordinarily persistent religious conservatism has to be explained somehow. I find it hard to accept that at some point the rites were seamlessly taken over by an incoming culture. Surely one would expect to uncover *some* evidence for such a dislocation?

The religious conservatism can also tell us another tale. The first five hundred years of the first millennium BC were, I think, centuries of some turmoil. The old system of farming was collapsing, the new one was proving hard to establish, and the population was beginning to grow rapidly. The change in the way people settled in the landscape must also have been accompanied by major social changes.

In times of change and upheaval, people require a core of stability to hang onto. We can see this process at work in the Near East and elsewhere today, with the rise of religious fundamentalism coinciding with major economic and social changes in the world as a whole. The certainty and truth that religion can provide gives people something solid and reliable at the centre of their changing lives. I think something similar was happening three millennia ago. The religious conservatism at Flag Fen was deliberate; and it was needed.

Flag Fen is a very visual site, with beautiful objects and hundreds of massive ancient timbers. Almost as soon as I'd found it, I knew it would make an ideal place for people to visit. But I couldn't persuade anyone locally to take it seriously. Most of the site was owned by the then Anglian Water Authority, which was shortly to be privatised by Mrs Thatcher. I tried as hard as I could to make my voice heard, but I couldn't penetrate a brick wall somewhere in the middle management of that large organisation. It was extremely frustrating.

Then one day I found myself reading Clement Freud's splendid *Book of Hangovers*, which I had been given the previous Christmas by my brother Felix. I was laughing at one of Bill Tidy's cartoons when a thought struck me. Clement Freud was my Member of Parliament; why not write to him? So I did. I explained about the site and why it was so important, and I got a letter back saying that Freud was having lunch with the Chairman of Anglian Water the following week, and would raise the matter with him. Eight days later I found myself able to reach the most rarefied heights of corporate power and influence.

With a lot of help from Anglian Water and other corporations and local businesses, Maisie and I set up the Fenland Archaeological Trust, or FAT (we very nearly called it Fenland Archaeological Research Trust) as a charitable trust and leased or bought twenty-five acres of Flag Fen, including a large part of the great row of posts. We built a visitor centre and museum in which our finds are displayed. I am glad that they are permanently housed at the centre of Flag Fen, where their original owners had placed them.

Most of our early efforts went towards visitors and tourism, because that was the way we were to generate the money we would need to do archaeological work when our grants from English Heritage ceased in 1995. More recently we have built a large timber barn-style Field Centre, in which we process waterlogged wood from Flag Fen and many other ancient sites all over Britain. This wood laboratory is Maisie's domain – and she rules it with a rod of iron. But little did either of us suspect that one day it would temporarily house a massive oak tree and fifty-five strange-looking wooden posts.

CHAPTER FIFTEEN

Retrospect and Prospect

MOST OF THIS BOOK has moved through the last five thousand years, concentrating on just four sites within a small geographical area: Fengate, Etton/Maxey, Holme and Flag Fen. So in one respect this has been a tale set around the parish pump. It's the passing of time which gives the story another, transcending dimension.

Past times are just that – times that have past. Any mystery and magic inherent in them are mystery and magic that were there when they were in the present. The passage of time in itself adds nothing. But neither does it remove anything. That's one reason why we must be careful not to patronise the lives and achievements of people who, after all, cannot speak for themselves. Anthropologists warn against ethnocentricity, the placing of one's own culture first and at the centre of one's arguments. It's also possible to patronise past communities and cultures in a similar manner – I call it chronocentrism. The cruellest thing one can do to a past culture is to use it for one's own ends, whether to legitimise spurious political history or to give false roots to a modern ideology. Chronocentrism is a form of intellectual and spiritual imperialism.

Certain threads have helped to pull the various strands of our quest together: families and family structure; life, death and the ancestors; symbols of all sorts. Sometimes old symbols turned up in the most unexpected places, such as querns in the middle of a waterlogged fen.

There were other remarkable discoveries out in the depths of Flag Fen, at the point where the great row of posts crossed the wettest peats. A bronze flesh-hook, for example. These have been found elsewhere in Europe alongside huge bronze cauldrons, and were probably used for fishing pieces of meat out of an enormous, bubbling stew. We also found a deliberately broken sheet of bronze that once adorned the outside of a short sword's scabbard, and was superbly decorated with a pair of stylised dragons. Again, we are seeing the same themes re-emerging: liminality (the fen all around), domestic life (the querns), deliberate destruction, feasting (the flesh-hook) and symbols of personal power (the sword scabbard-plate). But this time the context in which the rites took place has changed. The great enclosure at Etton gave way to the isolated family shrines of the Neolithic and Early Bronze Age, which in turn were replaced by a central, unified sacred place at Flag Fen. We see the same themes intertwining and changing through the ages.

The final prehistoric change, that from isolated family shrines to a central sacred place, happened in the Middle Bronze Age. In our area it took place around 1300 BC, at Flag Fen. Few earlier sites of this type are known, but later ones are abundant in Britain and across Europe. Perhaps the most famous of all was excavated a hundred years ago in a marshy inlet of Lake Neuchâtel, in Switzerland. It was called La Tène, and produced vast numbers of broken Iron Age swords. For years La Tène has been regarded by archaeologists as the finest Celtic site.

Why was it that these latter changes happened at all? It would be rash to suggest that there was a single, simple reason. Religious change is often slow, because of the innate conservatism of most people and the natural reluctance of those in power to disturb the geese that lay the golden eggs. Religion plays an important part in holding society together and in allowing people to adapt to changes. As I have said, it provides a central core of stability. This is doubtless why the new style of religion retained so many fundamental features of the old ways of worship, with special importance being given to the family and to family ties.

Offerings of weapons, especially swords, are found with greater frequency after the Middle Bronze Age. Does this mean that society was becoming more warlike, and less stable? I think not. On the contrary, I believe these swords were not about battle, but about personal power. The same goes for the proliferation of hill forts in Iron Age Britain and Europe which was taking place at about the same time. These spectacular fortifications were placed atop the most visible hills and mountains, and were clearly designed to impress, besides being difficult to attack successfully. The process we are looking at is one of population growth and a far more structured partition of the landscape than previously. There is a greater need for social control. Everyone must know their place, and the hill forts provided people with a constant reminder both of who they were and why they differed from their neighbours. In short, they were about identity.

It was believed for a long time that hill forts were placed at the centre of tribal territories. I have always held, on the other hand, that they were placed at the boundaries, because it was there that identity most needed to be asserted. Later on, in the Middle Ages, the largest and fiercest-looking castles are to be found at disputed borders – in the Welsh Marches, for example. Boundaries are a theme which has occurred regularly throughout our story, marked at different scales by skulls, querns, lines of posts or, as now, hill forts. They are important because they express a fundamental human and animal motivation, what Desmond Morris called the Territorial Imperative.

Towards the latter part of the Bronze Age, around say 1000 to 900 BC, we see a more formally structured pattern of settlement appearing. Before this period, settlements were generally small, and many people lived in isolated farmsteads dotted across the countryside. After it, there were subtle changes. Larger settlements came into existence. Farmsteads would come together to form hamlets of two of three houses. By 500 BC we see large settlements in Continental Europe, and in Britain hill forts like Danebury in Hampshire almost resemble small towns, with clearly defined streets. These new sites were often surrounded by a defensive stockade or multiple banked ramparts of earth.

I would not for a moment suggest that the defences around these great hill forts were never used, but the evidence for large-scale pitched battles is hard to pin down. Most warfare probably amounted to little more than glorified cattle-rustling which, as we have seen, would have occurred in the autumn when the crops had safely been gathered in. If serious warfare did take place, it probably initially took the form of display and bravado. David and Goliath is a fine and probably accurate Bronze Age story. The two armies were lined up opposite each other, and there was much sabre-rattling and taunting, but the actual fighting was confined to the two principal protagonists. At the end of the 'battle' there was just one casualty. Would that the Great War had been handled in such an uncivilised prehistoric fashion.

I would suggest that the religious changes at the end of the Bronze Age are a response to, and a reflection of, the social changes of the times. They reflect the way that society was coming together, and also served to express the importance of the emerging social structures; hence the emphasis on power and authority. But the roots of the emerging new styles of religion were set firmly in the past.

A number of Later Bronze Age and Iron Age religious sites have now come to light in Britain and Europe. Many are in wet, liminal, places, and nearly all have produced broken weapons and ornaments. But that is not to say they are all identical. Indeed, far from it. Their size, form and contexts suggest that they, like Flag Fen, arose as local responses to widespread social and ideological changes. That is why I find it difficult to accept the idea of a universal priesthood, called the Druids.

We owe our accounts of the Druids to Roman authors. They were ethnocentric in the extreme, and viewed 'barbarian' Europe with the greatest suspicion. It was in their internal political interest to maintain that the opposition they faced was as organised and cohesive as their own empire. But it wasn't. There may well have been priests in the lands occupied by the Romans, but the archaeological evidence, taken as a whole, suggests that they reflected local traditions rather than a universally acknowledged ideology. Organised religion, in the sense that we know it today, simply did not exist in 'barbarian' Europe.

How does this affect modern attitudes to the past? For a start, I believe that each case should be taken on its own merits. It seems absurd to judge something like the removal of the Holme timbers by the same criteria you would apply to a nineteenth-century native North American cemetery. One of the things that disturbed me profoundly about the New Age attitudes to Seahenge was the explicit condemnation of knowledge. Along with this was an implicit statement of exclusivity. The New Agers saw themselves as the 'rightful' guardians of the timbers, and believed that archaeologists 'knew nothing' (a phrase I heard repeatedly), and therefore had no rights. I believe that the people who held this view were in a minority. They were extremists, fundamentalists within the broad Neo-Pagan community. Many Neo-Pagans and modern Druids had a different, more reasonable, attitude. Several said to me that they regarded archaeologists as important because we could provide them with new information about the Old Religion – or religions, as I personally believe them to have been.

There is plainly a need for greater understanding and communication on all sides. Having said that, it seems to me deeply misguided to believe that archaeological and scientific research is unnecessary because the Truth is already known, by means of mystical memory and emotional osmosis. To me that is a rerun of the battle between the Church and Galileo. I would hate to see empirical knowledge suffer at the hands of superstition, dogma and received wisdom. Ancient religious places are important to all of us. Nobody has exclusive rights to them. This, of course, applies to archaeologists too.

Let me finish with a true parable. It's about inclusion, not exclusion. It's painful for me to tell, but like the parables in the Bible, it contains a vital lesson.

We take many school parties at Flag Fen. About five years ago, the head teacher of a local primary school phoned to book in a party of fifteen youngsters. Three weeks later they arrived in a mini-bus. As the teacher paid for their admission I heard her say that there were only fourteen children, because one was ill and couldn't make the trip. I thought no more about it.

Shortly after the visit, we received a phone call from a local funeral director. He said he had a most unusual request, and would quite understand if we couldn't oblige him. A young girl from a Hindu family in town had missed her school's visit to Flag Fen because of her terminal illness. As she lay dying, growing weaker by the day, she repeatedly asked her parents if they could take her to Flag Fen when she got better. Of course they promised they would, knowing in their heart of hearts that it was unlikely. Eventually her nine-year-old frame could take no more, and she died. The funeral director's request was simple: would we allow the youngster to have her longed-for and promised visit? What could we say but yes?

I remember the day well. It wasn't raining, but neither was the sun shining. The air was still. As it was out of season, there were no other visitors. The hearse drove up to the shore of the lake, below whose waters rest the Bronze Age timbers and the offerings around them. It stopped, turned and reversed right up to the edge of the water. The driver opened the rear door, which slowly rose to reveal the small coffin within. Then the parents got out and walked to the back of the hearse, where they stood, close to each other, beside their daughter. For five minutes they looked across the peaceful scene. Then they resumed their seats, the rear door was closed, and slowly the hearse pulled away.

FURTHER READING

This list does not pretend to be exhaustive. Wherever possible I have cited work published since 1945. The textbooks I have mentioned all contain full references.

CHAPTER ONE

Most of the topics covered in this chapter are considered at greater length in the standard textbook:
> C. Renfrew and P. Bahn, *Archaeology: Theories, Methods and Practice* (3rd edition, Thames and Hudson, London, 2000)

The environment and climate of Britain in later prehistory are discussed in:
> A. Harding (ed.), *Climatic Change in Later Prehistory* (Edinburgh University Press, 1982)
> I. Simmons and M. Tooley (eds), *The Environment in British Prehistory* (Duckworth, London, 1981)

CHAPTER TWO

The book which delivered the *coup de grâce* to old concepts of diffusion from the eastern Mediterranean was:
> C. Renfrew, *Before Civilization* (Jonathan Cape, London, 1973)

The Anglo-Saxon village at North Elmham, Norfolk is fully published:
> P. Wade-Martins, *Excavations in North Elmham Park 1967–1972*, 2 vols (*East Anglian Archaeology* no. 80, Gressenhall, Norfolk, 1980)

The employment of earth-moving machinery is now commonplace:
> F.M.M. Pryor, *Earthmoving on Open Archaeological Sites* (Institute of Field Archaeologists, Technical Paper no. 4, Birmingham, 1986)

For a general scene setting of the Fens:
> H. Godwin, *Fenland: Its Ancient Past and Uncertain Future* (Cambridge University Press, 1978)

For a more recent account of the work of the English Heritage Fenland Survey:
> D. Hall and J.M. Coles, *Fenland Survey: An Essay in Landscape and*

Persistence (English Heritage Archaeological Report no. 1, London, 1994)

The report that drew my attention to the Peterborough area, and which contains all the references to earlier work in the area:

Royal Commission on Historical Monuments, England, *Peterborough New Town: A Survey of the Antiquities in the Areas of Development* (Her Majesty's Stationery Office, London, 1969)

CHAPTERS THREE TO FIVE

These chapters cover the excavations at Fengate, which have been fully published in four detailed academic reports:

F.M.M. Pryor, *Excavation at Fengate, Peterborough, England: The First Report* (Royal Ontario Museum Archaeological Monograph 3, Toronto, 1974)

F.M.M. Pryor, *Excavation at Fengate, Peterborough, England: The Second Report* (Royal Ontario Museum Archaeological Monograph 5, Toronto, 1978)

F.M.M. Pryor, *Excavation at Fengate, Peterborough, England: The Third Report* (joint Northamptonshire Archaeological Society Archaeological Monograph 1 and Royal Ontario Museum Archaeological Monograph 6, Toronto and Leicester, 1980)

F.M.M. Pryor, *Excavation at Fengate, Peterborough, England: The Fourth Report* (joint Northamptonshire Archaeological Society Archaeological Monograph 2 and Royal Ontario Museum Archaeological Monograph 7, Toronto and Leicester, 1984)

I have also written a shorter, more user-friendly version (now out of print):

F.M.M. Pryor, *Fengate* (Shire Books, Princes Risborough, 1982)

CHAPTER THREE

Much has been written about aerial photography and it is well covered in the textbook by Renfrew and Bahn, listed under Chapter 1, above. My own personal choice, although now rather old, is:

D.R. Wilson (ed.), *Aerial Reconnaissance for Archaeology* (Council for British Archaeology Research Report no. 12, London, 1975)

For a landscape approach – and the work of a very talented individual:

D.N. Riley, *Early Landscape from the Air: Studies of Crop Marks in South Yorkshire and North Nottinghamshire* (Department of Prehistory and Archaeology, Sheffield University, 1980)

The standard work on Roman roads is still:

I.D. Margary, *Roman Roads in Britain* (John Baker, London, 1973)
For more on the Roman British countryside:

R. Hingley, *Rural Settlement in Roman Britain* (Seaby, London, 1989)
A good review of Roman towns and their countryside:

J.S. Wacher, *The Towns of Roman Britain* (Batsford Books, London, 1995)
Roman pottery made clear and simple:

P. Tyers, *Pottery in Roman Britain* (Batsford Books, London, 1996)
The seminal book for the New Archaeology in a revised and comprehensible edition:

D.V. Clarke (revised by Bob Chapman), *Analytical Archaeology* (2nd edition, Methuen, London, 1978)

CHAPTER FOUR

Two books by Richard Bradley which pioneered new approaches to the prehistoric landscape:

R. Bradley, *The Prehistoric Settlement of Britain* (Routledge, London, 1978)

R. Bradley, *The Social Foundations of Prehistoric Britain* (Longmans, London, 1984)
A good layman's introduction to the British Bronze Age:

M. Parker Pearson, *Bronze Age Britain* (joint publication by Batsford Books and English Heritage, London, 1994)
For more on the Fengate Neolithic 'house' which became a mortuary structure:

F.M.M. Pryor, 'Earlier Neolithic Organised Landscapes and Ceremonial in Lowland Britain', in I.A. Kinnes and J. Barrett (eds), *The Archaeology of Context in the Neolithic and Bronze Age: Recent Trends* (Sheffield University Department of Prehistory and Archaeology, 1988), pp.63–72

CHAPTER FIVE

It's hard to find a layman's account of Neolithic Britain. Colin Renfrew's excellent discussion of the origins of Indo-European languages paints with a broad brush and sets the scene well:

C. Renfrew, *Archaeology and Language: The Puzzle of Indo-European Origins* (Penguin Books, London, 1987)
A widely available textbook, with a clear, well referenced and up-to-date account of the Neolithic (by Alasdair Whittle):

J. Hunter and I. Ralston (eds), *The Archaeology of Britain* (Routledge, London, 1999)

A stimulating reworking of his definitive work *Rethinking the Neolithic*:

J. Thomas, *Understanding the Neolithic* (Routledge, London, 2000)

For a review of the techniques of archaeological science, see Renfrew and Bahn, listed under Chapter 1, above.

For more on alluvium and the archaeology it conceals:

S. Needham and M.C. Macklin (eds), *Alluvial Archaeology in Britain* (Oxbow Monograph no. 27, Oxford, 1992)

Prehistoric farming has been reviewed a number of times recently. My own book purports to be about Britain, but is in fact mainly about the Fens:

F.M.M. Pryor, *Farmers in Prehistoric Britain* (Tempus Books, Stroud, 1998)

Other reviews of prehistoric fields and farming in Britain and Europe include:

B. Bender, *Farming in Prehistory: From Hunter-Gatherer to Food-Producer* (John Baker, London, 1975)

H.C. Bowen, *Ancient Fields* (S.R. Publishers, Wakefield, 1961)

A. Fleming, *The Dartmoor Reaves* (Batsford Books, London, 1988)

P.J. Fowler, *The Farming of Prehistoric Britain* (Cambridge University Press, 1983)

R. Mercer (ed.), *Farming Practice in British Prehistory* (Edinburgh University Press, 1984)

C.C. Taylor, *Fields in the English Landscape* (Dent, London, 1975)

CHAPTER SIX

A stimulating introduction to the archaeology of death:

M. Parker Pearson, *The Archaeology of Death and Burial* (Sutton Publishing, Stroud, 1999)

On the archaeology of power and elites:

D.V. Clarke, T.G. Cowie and A. Foxon, *Symbols of Power at the Time of Stonehenge* (National Museum of Antiquities of Scotland, Edinburgh, 1985)

For stone circles in general:

A. Burl, *The Stone Circles of the British Isles* (Yale University Press, 1976)

A few popular references on the Avebury ritual landscape:

A. Burl, *Prehistoric Avebury* (Yale University Press, 1979)

M. Gillings, J. Pollard and D. Wheatley, 'Avebury and the Beckhampton Avenue', in *Current Archaeology*, 167 (2000), pp.428–33

C. Malone, *Avebury* (Batsford Books and English Heritage, London, 1989)

M. Pitts, 'Return to the Sanctuary', in *British Archaeology* (Council for British Archaeology, York, 2000)

M. Pitts, *Hengeworld* (Century Books, London, 2000)

More technical papers on sites in the Avebury area:

I.F. Smith, *Windmill Hill and Avebury: Excavations by Alexander Keiller 1925–1939* (Oxford University Press, 1965)

P.J. Ucko, M. Hunter, A.J. Clark and A. David, *Avebury Reconsidered: From the 1660s to the 1990s* (Institute of Archaeology, University College, London, 1991)

A. Whittle, *Sacred Mound Holy Rings – Silbury Hill and the West Kennet Palisade Enclosures: A Later Neolithic Complex in North Wiltshire* (Oxbow Monograph 74, Oxford, 1997)

A. Whittle, J. Pollard and C. Grigson, *The Harmony of Symbols: The Windmill Hill Causewayed Enclosure* (Oxbow Books, Oxford, 1999)

A selection of popular references on the Stonehenge ritual landscape:

R.J.C. Atkinson, *Stonehenge: Archaeology and Interpretation* (Penguin Books, Harmondsworth, 1979)

C. Chippindale, *Stonehenge Complete: Everything Important, Interesting or Odd that has been Written or Painted, Discovered or Imagined, about the Most Extraordinary Ancient Building in the World* (Thames and Hudson, London, 1983)

G.S. Hawkins, *Stonehenge Decoded* (Delta Books, New York, 1965)

J. Richards, *Stonehenge* (joint publication by Batsford Books and English Heritage, London, 1991)

More technical papers on Stonehenge and sites around it:

J. Richards, *The Stonehenge Environs Project* (English Heritage Archaeological Report no. 16, London, 1990)

G.J. Wainwright, *The Henge Monuments: Ceremony and Society in Prehistoric Britain* (Thames and Hudson, London, 1989)

G.J. Wainwright and I.H. Longworth, *Durrington Walls: Excavations 1966–1968* (Report of the Research Committee of the Society of Antiquaries of London no. 29, London, 1971)

The definitive and exhaustive modern statement on Stonehenge:

R.M.J. Cleal, K.E. Walker and R. Montague, *Stonehenge in its Landscape: Twentieth Century Excavations* (English Heritage Archaeological Report no. 10, London, 1995)

A good textbook on European prehistory:

T. Champion, C. Gamble, S. Shennan and A. Whittle, *Prehistoric Europe* (Academic Press, London, 1984)

An old, but amusing account of Carnac, written with great flare:

    G.E. Daniel, *Lascaux and Carnac* (Lutterworth Press, London, 1955)

Another older account of Brittany, comprehensive in its scope:

    P.R. Giot, *Brittany* (Thames and Hudson, London, 1960)

A more recent review of French Neolithic and Bronze Age archaeology:

    C. Scarre (ed.), *Ancient France* (Edinburgh University Press, 1983)

An excellent account of several key prehistoric sites in Britain and Europe, including Carnac:

    C. Scarre, *Exploring Prehistoric Europe* (Oxford University Press, New York, 1998)

A thoughtful look at Stowe and other eighteenth-century parks and gardens:

    T. Williamson, *Polite Landscapes: Gardens and Society in Eighteenth Century England* (Johns Hopkins University Press, Baltimore, 1995)

CHAPTER SEVEN

Maisie Taylor's introduction to ancient wood (now out of print):

    M. Taylor, *Wood in Archaeology* (Shire Books, Princes Risborough, 1981)

The survey of sites facing potential destruction in gravel pits:

    Royal Commission on Historical Monuments (England), *A Matter of Time: An Archaeological Survey of the River Gravels of England* (Her Majesty's Stationery Office, London, 1960)

A good, succinct introduction to causewayed enclosures:

    R. Mercer, *Causewayed Enclosures* (Shire Books, Princes Risborough, 1990)

The paper that showed how widespread causewayed enclosures were in Britain:

    R. Palmer, 'Interrupted Ditch Enclosures in Britain, the Use of Aerial Photography for Comparative Studies', in *Proceedings of the Prehistoric Society* vol. 42 (1976), pp.161–86

For causewayed and other Neolithic enclosures in Britain and Europe:

    N.H. Andersen, *The Sarup Enclosures* (Jutland Archaeological Society, Moesgaard, Denmark, 1997)

A collection of essays on causewayed enclosures in Britain and Europe:

    C. Burgess, P. Topping, C. Mordant and M. Maddison (eds), *Enclosures and Defences in the Neolithic of Western Europe*, 2 vols (British Archaeological Reports, International Series no. S403, Oxford, 1988)

The latest work on the Mesolithic site at Star Carr:

P. Mellars and P. Dark, *Star Carr in Context: New Archaeological and Palaeoecological Investigations at the Early Mesolithic Site of Star Carr, North Yorkshire* (McDonald Institute for Archaeological Research, Cambridge University, 1998)

CHAPTER EIGHT

An accessible book on Neolithic religion and beliefs, with many fresh ideas:
  M. Edmonds, *Ancestral Geographies of the Neolithic: Landscapes, Monuments and Memory* (Routledge, London, 1999)
A fine collection of papers, but written from a more traditional perspective:
  A. Gibson and D.D.A. Simpson (eds), *Prehistoric Ritual and Religion* (Sutton Publishing, Stroud, 1998)
Proceedings of an important conference:
  P. Garwood, D. Jennings, R. Skeates and J. Toms (eds), *Sacred and Profane: Proceedings of a Conference on Archaeology, Ritual and Religion, Oxford, 1989* (Oxford University Committee for Archaeology Monograph no. 32, 1991)
The academic report on Etton (with references to other sites):
  F.M.M. Pryor, *Etton: Excavations at a Neolithic Causewayed Enclosure Near Maxey Cambridgeshire, 1982–7* (English Heritage Archaeological Report no. 18, London, 1998)
For more on the Neolithic stone axe 'trade':
  T.H. McK. Clough and W.A. Cummins, *Stone Axe Studies* (Council for British Archaeology Research Report no. 23, London, 1979)
  T.H. McK. Clough and W.A. Cummins, *Stone Axe Studies Volume 2* (Council for British Archaeology Research Report no. 67, London, 1988)

CHAPTER NINE

A concise, well-illustrated summary of henges:
  A. Burl, *Prehistoric Henges* (Shire Books, Princes Risborough, 1991)
An important book about prehistoric thought and religion:
  R. Bradley, *The Significance of Monuments: On the Shaping of Human Experience in Neolithic and Bronze Age Europe* (Routledge, London, 1998)
The small henge, and other work at Fengate since 1984, is described in the Flag Fen report:
  F.M.M. Pryor, *The Flag Fen Basin: Archaeology and Environment of a Fenland Landscape* (English Heritage Archaeological Report, London, 2000)

For the West Deeping fields see Chapter 8 of:

> F.M.M. Pryor, *Farmers in Prehistoric Britain* (Tempus Books, Stroud, 1998)

For cursuses:

> A. Barclay and J. Harding (eds), *Pathways and Ceremonies: The Cursus Monuments of Britain and Ireland* (Oxbow Books, Oxford, 1999)

The academic report on Maxey:

> F.M.M. Pryor and C.A.I. French, *Archaeology and Environment in the Lower Welland Valley* (*East Anglian Archaeology* vol. 27, Cambridge, 1985)

For Bronze Age fields in the Thames valley:

> D.T. Yates, 'Bronze Age Field Systems in the Thames Valley', in *Oxford Journal of Archaeology* vol. 18 (1999), pp.157–70

CHAPTER TEN

An excellent account of the Wetland Revolution, with good historical chapters:

> B. and J.M. Coles, *People of the Wetlands: Bogs, Bodies and Lake-Dwellers* (Thames and Hudson, London, 1989)

An early collection of recent wetland research:

> J.M. Coles and A.J. Lawson (eds), *European Wetlands in Prehistory* (Oxford University Press, 1987)

A well-illustrated summary of recent work in the Somerset Levels:

> B. and J.M. Coles, *Sweet Track to Glastonbury: The Somerset Levels in Prehistory* (Thames and Hudson, London, 1986)

The Glastonbury Lake Village re-examined:

> J.M. Coles and S. Minnitt, *Industrious and Fairly Civilized: The Glastonbury Lake Village* (Somerset Levels Project and Somerset County Council Museums Service, Exeter, 1995)

A varied collection of wetland papers:

> B. and J.M. Coles and M.S. Jørgensen (eds), *Bog Bodies, Sacred Sites and Wetland Archaeology* (Wetland Archaeology Research Project, Occasional Paper no. 12, Exeter, 1999)

Another collection of wetland papers, also of worldwide scope:

> B. Coles (ed.), *The Wetland Revolution in Prehistory* (Wetland Archaeology Research Project, Occasional Paper no. 6, Exeter, 1992)

Two popular but authoritative books on Danish wetland archaeology:

> P.V. Glob, *The Bog People: Iron Age Man Preserved* (Faber and Faber, London, 1969)

P.V. Glob, *The Mound People: Danish Bronze Age Man Preserved* (Faber and Faber, London, 1970)

A recent comprehensive round-up of Bog Body research:

R.C. Turner and R.G. Scaife, *Bog Bodies: New Discoveries and New Perspectives* (British Museum Press, London, 1995)

CHAPTER ELEVEN

Daily domestic life in later prehistory is well illustrated in an excellent book:

R. Bewley, *Prehistoric Settlements* (joint publication by Batsford Books and English Heritage, London, 1994)

A popular book by a pioneer of experimental archaeology:

P.J. Reynolds, *Iron Age Farm: The Butser Experiment* (British Museum Publications, London, 1979)

More on experimental archaeology:

J.M. Coles, *Archaeology by Experiment* (Hutchinson, London, 1973)

D.E. Robinson (ed.), *Experimentation and Reconstruction in Environmental Archaeology* (Oxbow Books, Oxford, 1990)

CHAPTER TWELVE

Coastal erosion is a very serious problem. For a good review of the archaeological implications see:

M. Fulford, T. Champion and A. Long, *England's Coastal Heritage* (English Heritage Archaeological Report no. 15, London, 1997)

The first account of the Holme-next-the-Sea timber circle:

M. Brennand and M. Taylor, 'Seahenge', in *Current Archaeology* no. 167 (2000), pp.417–24

For Dun Vulan:

M. Parker Pearson and N. Sharples, *Between Land and Sea: Excavations at Dun Vulan, South Uist* (Sheffield Academic Press, 1999)

For more on tree-ring dating:

M.G.L. Baillie, *A Slice Through Time: Dendrochronology and Precision Dating* (Batsford Books, London, 1995)

For Hamon le Strange's discovery at Old Hunstanton:

A.J. Lawson, 'A Late Middle Bronze Age Hoard from Hunstanton, Norfolk', in C. Burgess and D.G. Coombs (eds), *Bronze Age Hoards* (British Archaeological Reports, British Series no. 67, Oxford, 1979), pp.42–92

CHAPTER THIRTEEN

A review of timber circles in Britain:
>A. Gibson, *Stonehenge and Timber Circles* (Tempus Books, Stroud, 1998)

For the hidden timber circle at Stanton Drew, Somerset:
>A.C.H. Olivier, 'Archaeological Activities Undertaken by English Heritage', in *Stanton Drew, English Heritage Archaeology Review 1997–98* (London, 1999), pp.50–2

For more on inverted trees in Lapland:
>R. Bradley, *An Archaeology of Natural Places* (Routledge, London, 2000)

For more on the mysterious Wossit:
>B. Vyner, 'The Street House Wossit', in *Current Archaeology* no. 111 (1988), pp.124–7

The Whittlesey dig is still hot news:
>M. Knight, 'Henge to House – Post-Circles in a Neolithic and Bronze Age Landscape at King's Dyke West, Whittlesey, Cambridgeshire', *Past* (Newsletter of the Prehistoric Society) 34 (April 2000), pp.3–4

CHAPTER FOURTEEN

A popular, if slightly out-of-date, account of Flag Fen:
>F.M.M. Pryor, *Flag Fen: Prehistoric Fenland Centre* (joint publication by Batsford Books and English Heritage, London, 1991)

The academic report on Flag Fen and its landscape:
>F.M.M. Pryor, *The Flag Fen Basin: Archaeology and Environment of a Fenland Landscape* (English Heritage Archaeological Report, London, 2000)

For Iron Age and Roman shrines:
>A. Woodward, *Shrines and Sacrifice* (joint publication by Batsford Books and English Heritage, London, 1992)

The all-encompassing, standard work on the British Iron Age is still:
>B.W. Cunliffe, *Iron Age Communities in Britain* (3rd edition, Routledge, London, 1991)

For a refreshing post-modernist perspective on the Iron Age:
>A. Gwilt and C. Haselgrove (eds), *Reconstructing Iron Age Societies* (Oxbow Monograph no. 71, Oxford, 1997)

For other sites, wet and dry, in Iron Age Europe:
>V. Kruta, O.H. Frey, B. Raftery and M. Szabo (eds), *The Celts* (Thames and Hudson, London, 1991)

For a modern, minimalist view of the Celts:

S. James, *The Celts: Ancient People or Modern Invention?* (British Museum Press, London, 1999)

For the origin and history of the ancient Druids and the modern Neo-Druids:

S. Piggott, *The Druids* (Thames and Hudson, London, 1968)

INDEX

Page numbers in *italic* refer to illustrations.